The Family in Political Thought

THE FAMILY
IN POLITICAL THOUGHT

❀ *Edited by Jean Bethke Elshtain*

The University of Massachusetts Press
Amherst

Second paperback printing, 1987

Acknowledgment is herewith made for permission to reprint several portions of this book which have appeared previously in the following journals.

Susan Moller Okin, "Philosopher Queens and Private Wives: Plato on Women and the Family," *Philosophy and Public Affairs* 6 (Summer 1977): 345–69 (Princeton University Press); Jean Bethke Elshtain, "Aristotle, the Public-Private Split, and the Case of the Suffragists" is a revision of "Moral Woman/Immoral Man: The Public/Private Split and Its Political Ramifications," *Politics and Society* 4 (1974): 453–73; Mary Lyndon Shanley, "Marriage Contract and Social Contract in Seventeenth-Century English Political Thought" is a revision of an essay of the same title in *Western Political Quarterly* 32 (March 1979): 79–91 (University of Utah, copyright holder); Joan Landes, "Hegel's Conception of the Family," *Polity* 14 (Fall 1981); Tony Tanner, "Julie and 'La Maison Paternelle': Another Look at Rousseau's *La Nouvelle Héloïse*," *Daedalus* (Journal of the American Academy of Arts and Sciences), Winter 1976; Tracy Strong, "Oedipus as Hero: Family and Family Metaphors in Nietzsche" is a revised version of an essay in *Boundary 2* 8 (Winter 1981), Special Nietzsche Issue, ed. Dan O'Hara; Jean Bethke Elshtain, " 'Thank Heaven for Little Girls': The Dialectics of Development," is a revision of an article in *Politics* 10 (November 1974): 139–48.

To the memory of William K. Lind and to Mary Frank Lind
dear Grandma and Grandpa in the country

Contents

Acknowledgments

I wish, first, to acknowledge the major contribution of Bradley Klein to this volume. Mr. Klein, a graduate student in political theory at the University of Massachusetts, spent many hours discussing with me the structure of the volume and he read and offered critical commentary on nearly all the essays. His involvement in *The Family in Political Thought* has been vital, intelligent, and energetic, and I appreciate it very much.

Over the years when this project was in the process of becoming a reality rather than simply a "good idea," many colleagues and friends offered encouragement and advice. But the contribution of Richard Martin, editor at the University of Massachusetts Press, has been particularly important. Mr. Martin knew that I was at work preparing a collection of essays on the family. He offered his support in ways direct and indirect well before I chose to submit the volume to the University of Massachusetts Press. As an editor he has been tops: thorough, informative, perspicuous.

My husband, Errol L. Elshtain, engaged in a variety of tasks in connection with this work including occasional typing, Xeroxing, mailing, checking out and returning books, and reminding me that I had "better work on the family book now." This is my public acknowledgment of a contribution for which I have already proffered my private gratitude.

Jean Bethke Elshtain
Amherst, Massachusetts

The Family in Political Thought

Preface:
Political Theory Rediscovers the Family

❁ *Jean Bethke Elshtain*

Political thinkers in the contemporary age have not, until recently, been much enamored with what Freud called "the family romance." The task of taking the family seriously for purposes of scholarly inquiry was assigned first to sociology, the discipline deemed most appropriate to familial concerns. If families in primitive or non-Western societies were the topic, then anthropology was considered the appropriate arena for research and debate. Political scientists focused on the big questions: sovereignty, relations between nation-states, institutions (Congress, the presidency, the judiciary), or political processes (voting, lobbying). Few treated terms of political discourse—power, justice, equality, rights, interests—and fewer still found continuing vitality in the tradition of Western political thought. The family remained invisible or was seen as part of that vast consensus-making machinery necessary to a stable, well-run political society.

If political analysts turned to a theory or model of the relationship between the family and the larger society, with politics construed as part of the social world, the most likely choice—from the 1950s until critiques of pluralism and positivist methodologies were mounted in the 1960s—was the functionalist sociology of Talcott Parsons. The implicit acceptance of the functionalist model by political scientists precluded taking either an interpretive or a critical approach to the family and its relation to politics. The functionalist perspective cannot incorporate the self-understanding of social participants into its account and it mutes social and political critique because the model presupposes a stable congruity or fit between the modern industrialized economy and the nuclear family. Family functions are given: male and female roles are predetermined and asymmetrical. Because the fundamental division between what Parsons called the instrumentive, adaptive male role and a nurturant, expressive female role was seen as necessary to the ends of system-adaptivity, goal gratification, integration, and pattern maintenance, it went, for a time, without serious challenge.[1] The family becomes, in functionalist terms, one substructural buttress in the pattern of systems maintenance. In other words, the family is viewed solely in instrumental terms.

These were the assumptions that underlay much of the socialization literature in political science, the effort to determine how it is the family goes about socializing the young who will one day be voters, law abiding citizens, purveyors of public opinion, and overall supporters of the system. The family became a problem only if it botched the job of providing for systems maintenance, for consensus and stability. It failed to perform its functions smoothly, if it spawned individual "deviants," to borrow the sociological term or, more ominously, if an identifiable class or group within the society consistently socialized children in a manner deemed incompatible with the requirements of an upwardly mobile, democratic society. For example, Seymour Martin Lipset, in his classic study, *Political Man: The Social Bases of Politics*, characterized working-class modes of child rearing as more authoritarian than those of the middle class; hence, working-class children grew up with a lower commitment to democratic forms.[2] Lipset, however, downplayed his discovery of pervasive working-class authoritarianism as a potential threat to systems stability by making the concomitant happy discovery that far greater numbers of working-class people, as adult citizens, stayed away from the polls and eschewed political participation than did their middle-class counterparts who were committed to progress and democracy.

Political scientists who took up political socialization most often began their research with a set of fixed presumptions shared broadly with Parsons and Lipset. That is, they were preeminently concerned with order and conformity, with how children could be most effectively induced into relatively nonproblematic acceptance of established political authority, a hierarchical social structure, and wide disparities in power and privilege between races, classes, and men and women. Because the status quo was deemed good, the socialization process was seen as a major force in instilling acceptance of it. This meant that certain questions were not asked or were posed rarely.

For example: one didn't find, in the socialization literature that began to flourish in the 1950s, this question: Is the current political status quo one children *ought* to be uncritically socialized into?[3] What if the status quo is a corrupt or inegalitarian one? These questions lay dormant until the political and social changes of the 1960s, together with scholarly innovation in other disciplines, forced the hands of political thinkers.

The interest in the family for the past fifteen years has been marked by the flourishing of serious scholarly treatments, particularly historical ones, with the publication of such important works as Edwin Shorter, *The Making of the Modern Family* (New York: Basic Books, 1975); Lawrence Stone, *The Family, Sex and Marriage in England 1550–1800* (New York: Harper and Row, 1977); Herbert G. Gutman, *The Black Family in Slavery and Freedom 1750–1925* (New York: Vintage Books, 1976); Randolph Trumbach, *The Rise of the Egalitarian Family: Aristocratic Kinship and Domestic Relations in Eighteenth Century England,* and Carl Degler, *At Odds: Women and the Family in America, from the Revolution to the Present* (New York: Oxford University Press, 1980). In sociology, the functionalist model was challenged and its ideological functions explored; indeed, Christopher Lasch, in *Haven in a Heartless World: The Family Besieged* (New York: Basic Books, 1979), indicted nearly all established approaches to family life as having implicitly conformist political implications. Anthropologists, who had never stopped describing and analyzing alternative family systems, renewed their efforts with an eye to issues raised by feminists concerning the mutability or universality of male-female relations along a range of possibilities. One major anthropological reconstruction along feminist lines was Michelle Zimbalist Rosaldo and Louise Lamphere's collection, *Women, Culture and Society* (Stanford: Stanford University Press, 1974). Economists, too, got into the act. Those informed by Marxist theory questioned the hypothetical construct presumed by neoclassical market economics, that rational calculator of marginal utility who goes by the name *homo economicus,* and began to locate him and previously invisible women within families as units of production, reproduction, and consumption. Outside the halls of academe we have seen a creative outpouring by American novelists on the themes of family and domestic life, an intense, rich focus on family relations as an arena of "limitless possibility."[4]

All this ferment stirred a response by political theorists, for it is a truism that political theory tends to flourish when disintegration, chaos, eruption, and decay threaten the thinker's own political society. In Norman Jacobsen's words: "Political theory begins precisely at the moment when things become, so to speak, unglued."[5] We live in unsettled and unsettling times, an epoch in which the markers of once secure identities, public and private, are being displaced, shifted, overturned. That so many thinkers independently began to concentrate upon a topic at roughly the same time is powerful evidence of perceived changes, breakdowns, and new possibilities in a commonly shared social location. The essays that appear in this volume represent not only a startling reversal of the previous silence within academic political science on questions of marriage, the family, and politics, but serve also as a potent sign of a time of troubles. None of the authors in this volume would accept without question the thesis most recently enunciated by Jacques Donzelot in his work, *The Policing of Families* (New York: Pantheon, 1980), which holds that the family has been thoroughly colonized and penetrated by social forces and is under continuous surveillance by ceaseless technocratic interventionists. (If true, this theory renders moot, if not altogether anachronistic, explorations of the relationship *between* the family and the wider order.) But each contributor has a sense, nonetheless, of social transformation whose outcome remains in doubt—though some are optimistic and others not at all sanguine about the future.

Those involved in rediscovering the family as a legitimate concern and focus for political theory are not, it turns out, so much engaged in a totally radical departure from the tradition of Western political thought as they are in an imaginative and critical reordering of that tradition as a way of informing and instructing the present. Those thinkers whose work comprises the canon of the Western political tradition found it necessary to situate the family within their overall vision of political society. Some placed the family into a private sphere deemed nonpolitical by definition and design. Others linked the family to the political community as one of its necessary conditions if not its integral parts. The family analogy, a theoretical argument based upon the presumption that familial and political authority, governance, and order were analogous one to another, dominated political discourse for centuries. Indeed, the family didn't disappear from view until the vocation of the political theorist itself went into decline. Interest in the family and a renaissance of political theory have gone hand in hand. Both are surely linked, in turn, to the deterioration of that image of cozy consensus that stifled creativity and controversy, or simply couldn't call it into being, in the 1950s. With the resurgence of radical social critique in general, and feminism in particular in the 1960s, a rethinking became possible—some might say inescapable.

Today the family—its fate, its future, its demise, or its possible rebirth—is a ubiquitous topic which leaps at us from the pages of newspapers and popular magazines, forms the subject of endless workshops, symposia, clinics, retreats, and conferences, and has become a veritable research industry. The federal government and various foundations have poured hundreds of thousands of dollars into research projects on such matters as child abuse, spouse abuse, effects on the family of dual-career parents, the family and the newborn, the family and the elderly, the family and mental illness, the family and the developmentally disabled, the family and teenage sexuality, the family and divorce, remarriage, cohabitation, child-free marriages, postponed pregnancy, role reversal and the family, effects on the family of changing demographic patterns, inflationary pressures, and chronic illness: there is no end in sight.

Given this smorgasbord of concerns, this focusing of microscopic attention on every nuance and aspect of family life, those concerned with the family find themselves overwhelmed with an indigestible flood of data, hypotheses, prophecies, and panaceas. What is frequently missing is conceptual clarity and something approaching coherence in most thinking on the contemporary family and its relationship to a larger social and political framework. The essays in this volume aim to fill this gap. The first eight essays following the introduction reexamine the terms under which selected thinkers from Plato through Nietzsche treated the family. The list of thinkers is not all inclusive, but those considered serve to demonstrate the richness and diversity of alternative approaches to the family in the great tradition. The five essays that follow this rethinking of the past focus on contemporary approaches to the family in political thought from a variety of perspectives. To prevent, or attempt to prevent, any new orthodoxy from emerging on the question of the family and politics, multiple interpretations of every complex theoretical argument are required and are here represented. One central purpose of *The Family in Political Thought* is to spark debate and to inspire future research and thinking. It follows that no essay has been treated as final and authoritative. The volume will have succeeded if it inspires reflective discourse on how political theorists in our time can continue to rediscover the vitality of the family as a concept, a living reality, a troubled social institution, a metaphor, a nightmare of repressive constraint, and a dream of infinite possibility.

Introduction: Toward a Theory of the Family and Politics

⚙ *Jean Bethke Elshtain*

The question of the family and its relation to the broader social and political order has bedeviled Western political discourse from its inception. Was the family to be seen, as Aristotle saw it, as a "necessary condition" for the *polis*—for the creation of a space within which the activities of free citizens occurred—but not as one of its integral parts? Were the social relations of the family, with their competing loyalties and standards of human conduct, a threat to political order and authority or a constituent feature of that order, as many current radical critics of the family claim? Opting for the former position, Plato aimed to eradicate or devalue private homes and sexual attachments, at least for his guardian class, as these militated against single-minded, total devotion to the ideal city. He cries: "Have we any greater evil for a city than what splits it and makes it many instead of one? Or a greater good than what binds it together and makes it one?"[1] For Plato authority must be single, but for Aristotle diverse forms of authority were possible and might coexist as long as the end of the greater and more inclusive association was served. Variants of these Platonic and Aristotelian themes on the family and politics echo throughout Western political thought and reverberate within contemporary debates on the family.

There is one position not to be found in the tradition of Western political thought until the late nineteenth century and the work of Nietzsche, and that is the radical view that the family, together with other traditional social forms, including politics, must be radically deconstructed—that we can either have done with them or transform them so dramatically that they will bear little resemblance to what went before. Twentieth-century variants on this theme reached their apogee with certain modes of cultural radicalism and schizophrenic politics of the 1960s.

The essays in this volume, taken as a whole, provide sharp evidence of the internal debates within political theory that any serious treatment of the family inspires. But the essays suggest more. Together with the critical debate and interpretation that is their source and that they in turn inspire, they provide intimations of a theory of the family and politics for our time. In this introductory essay I will move toward such a theory by offering an immanent critique of *The Family in Political Thought* construed as a kind of theoretical collage. A collage is a work of art within a single frame that brings structure to its diverse parts. In order to probe and illumine the meaning of a collage, interpretation of each element and of the work as a whole is necessary. As one views the collage, one moves from particular to general and back again, for abstraction and concreteness require one another if light is ever to dawn over the whole. My interpretations of each essay in this discursive collage on *The Family in Political Thought* represent a commitment of my own and a challenge to others who would engage in the task of thinking politically within our era, an era that is frequently inhospitable to the theory enterprise and surprisingly hostile to politics and families both.

I shall begin at the beginning with Plato's dramatic proposals for the inclusion of women in the ruling elite of his ideal state. Susan Okin's essay, "Philosopher Queens and Private Wives: Plato on Women and the Family," is a sympathetic reading of Plato's treatment of the relationship between the family and the political community, especially his "radical proposals" for equality between the sexes for that minority of men and women of his guardian class. These are proposals that startle the first-time reader of *The Republic* even as they shocked Plato's contemporaries. In her explication of Plato's argument for *unity* above all, Okin accepts Plato's characterization of "private wives" as a potentially subversive element within the city. The particularity of private life and the devotion of wives to their families are at odds with Plato's ideal of the "unified city." Plato's most radical proposal for dealing with this female threat to political order is a thorough-going deprivatization of the terms of male-female relations. Okin follows Plato's reasoning and shares his conclusion as she argues that the fact that women are "private wives curtails their participation in public life." The immediate question, then, must be, Are we to be thoroughly deprivatized, along the lines of Plato's familyless guardians, in order to provide for the full participation of women in the public sphere? Although Okin does not address this question directly she suggests, at least with reference to the world of fourth-century Greece, that women had little to "give up anyway so Plato's terms for equality would have been acceptable." This is an issue that must be posed to contemporary feminist theorists, whether feminist thinkers pose it directly or not. The troubling questions suggested by Okin's treatment of Plato emerge later in the volume in the essays by Jane Humphries, Jane Flax, and me.

Doubts concerning Plato's solution linger. Although Okin is surely correct to suggest that the aghast attitude of some male scholars at Plato's arguments for guardian class sex equality derives from questionable motives and antiegalitarian impulses, reasons for concern and room for debate remain. As Abigail Rosenthal argues in her provocative essay, "Feminism Without Contradictions," there is little evidence that people *desire* Plato's solution, one that would require the thorough subjection of all human life to rationalistic standards. "People do not merely fear its abuses," Rosenthal writes of Plato's *Republic,* "They do not desire its success."[2] Why? Rosenthal locates her own answer in Plato's severance of reason from our historical, embodied selves whose passions and particular identities he seeks to control and submit to abstract standards. Rosenthal has hit on an important theme that Okin, whose argument is framed from within Plato's variant on the Greek male point of view, omits.

Okin's defense of Plato's elimination of the family from his vision of the ideal city turns on her acceptance of the claim of the historian, M. I. Finley, that the family did not loom very large in the Greek way of life in any case; that it was not, in Okin's words, "the locus for the expression of the deepest human emotions." If this is true, it seems likely it was so only for that class of males of which Plato was a member, a class whose erotic ties and most vital intimate relations were homoerotic and did take place, as Okin argues, outside the home. This being the case, Plato's elite class of males was not required to give up much in the realm of Eros in order to become a guardian. Women, however, would be compelled by Plato's argument to relinquish that sphere within which they exerted great psychological and social power despite all the constraints of law and the repressive force of custom and sexual mores. In accepting Plato's argument, buttressed by Finley's downplaying of the centrality of families in Greek life, Okin is forced by the logic of her argument to gloss over a rich body of counterevidence and to adopt, implicitly, the notion that, because women's sexual activity was constrained and hedged about with sexist custom, women's central role in reproduction and the rearing of the young can safely be slighted as well.

I shall take up this last point for further explication first. The claims of Eros involve far more than freedom for adult genital contact: ties between mother and child are powerfully libidinized as well. This is one potent theme. The home was an arena of Eros from which men were excluded and within which women were enormously powerful. Think of Clytemnestra's rage at Agamemnon's usurpation of her control of the activities of her housewife's domain. He calls her and their daughter, Iphigenia, to Aulis with the lie that the girl will marry Achilles when, in truth, she is to be a human sacrifice to bring wind to Greek ships of war. After Iphigenia is sacrificed Clytemnestra plots and takes dreadful revenge on Agamemnon— hardly the activities of a passive, thoroughly subordinated woman who was not particularly involved in family life. Anyone familiar with the cycles of Greek tragedies will question Finley's insistence, repeated by Okin, that the family didn't figure importantly in Greek life.

In his fascinating study, *The Glory of Hera*, Philip E. Slater observes the paradox he discovered when he turned his attention to the role of women in Athens. Slater states: "On the one hand, one is usually told that the status of women in fifth- and fourth-century Athens achieved some kind of nadir. They were legal nonentities, excluded from political and intellectual life, uneducated, virtually imprisoned in the home, and appeared to be regarded with disdain by the principal male spokesmen whose comments have survived. . . . On the other hand, as Gomme points out: 'There is, in fact, no literature, no art of any country, in which women are more prominent, more important, more carefully studied and with more interest, than in the tragedy, sculpture, and painting of fifth-century Athens.' " Slater goes on to trace the official powerlessness of women, which Okin stresses, but he refuses to stop with this "generally accepted view of the status of women. . . ." He finds much evidence to point to women's importance, particularly in the home. Slater suggests that the proliferation of rules and customs aimed at curbing, checking, inhibiting, and constraining women was motivated by the need of Athenian males to reject and to derogate domesticity, the home and family life, the sphere in which women prevailed. Why? Because "the Athenian male child grew up in a female-dominated environment. As an adult he may have learned that women were of no account, but in the most important years of his psychological development he knew the reverse was true." This theme is suggested as relevant to our own time by the psychoanalytic feminists discussed by Jane Humphries in her essay on feminist theory and the family. Slater concludes that the "social position of women and the psychological influence of women are thus quite separate matters. The Greek male's contempt for women was not only compatible with, but also indissolubly bound to, an intense fear of them. . . ."[3]

If Slater is correct—he is certainly suggestive—Plato's abstractly couched recommendations for equality between the sexes of the ruling elite required very little sacrifice on the part of homoerotic males but demanded that women relinquish altogether the psychological and social power they wielded in the nursery and the household, the *oikos*. Plato's arguments take on a very different hue seen in this light. The psychological meaning of his radical proposals rises closer to the surface and one is forced to ask in whose behalf Plato's dream of unity and perfect order was being dreamt? Plato's "bold suggestion," in Okin's words, that there is no difference between the sexes "apart from their roles in procreation" can, within this diverse frame of reference, be seen as yet another repudiation of a sexed identity in general and of female sexual identity in particular, for "roles in procreation" are important rather than superficial differences. To require women to surrender an activity that offers them vital human meaning as embodied and sexed beings seems to demand an inordinate sacrifice for the "boundless" possibilities of the guardian class.

Although this was not one of Aristotle's explicit critiques of Plato's theory, such criticism of Plato's quest for unity and forced sexual egalitarianism for a ruling class is implied in Aristotle's very different treatment of the family and politics. I offer some harsh criticisms of a mode of reflection on the public and private inaugurated with Aristotle's arguments in Book 1 of *The Politics* on the distinction between the household and the *polis* in my essay, "Aristotle, the Public-Private Split, and the Case of the Suffragists." Aristotle presumed that the life of the *polis* with its activity for a citizen was the vastly superior life and one from which women were excluded categorically because their lesser capacities for reason and goodness consigned them to the limited sphere of the household. I argue that Aristotle's influence became infused within a particular perspective that promoted, in the hands of later thinkers, a functionalist treatment of the household in its relation to the *polis*; that is, the existence of the household or private sphere was conceived as a necessary condition for, but not as an integral part of, the *polis*. This view—colored by the history of politics as the exercise of force and violence, and political theory as the expression of that exercise—is at work in the background to the thought of the nineteenth-century American suffragists.

But the influence of Aristotle on debates over the family and politics cannot end there, nor has it been entirely baneful. One could, for example, rethink Aristotle's insistence on the relationship between diverse social forms in a reconstructive light. That is, one need not accept his views of males and females and their absorption into spheres appropriate to each to adopt his insistence that there are diverse ends and purposes of the *polis* and the household respectively; that neither should be subsumed within the other; and that the art of household management, as he called it, was a moral art. The political thinker who was able to make use of the Aristotle who opposed Plato's attempt to make One out of the many would see human society as an attempt to create a meaningful sense of commonality out of diversity with certain principles shared, though not totally and uncritically, by all or most. Individuals in this Aristotelian image are pictured as located simultaneously in a number of overlapping social spheres that exist less to meet an overarching single end than to enhance and promote the emergence of authentic, diverse human purposes. This Aristotle doesn't figure in my essay, but he should not be forgotten in the construction of a theory of the family and politics. My essay intends to force us to explore how we go about distinguishing between that which is politics and that which is not. If a particular definition is seen as arbitrary, what would be a nonarbitrary way of distinguishing between public and private activities, ends, and spheres? How are the values of politics *and* private lives and loyalties to be preserved, cherished, and strengthened?

According to Mary Shanley and Peter Stillman's essay, "Political and Marital Despotism: Montesquieu's *Persian Letters*," Montesquieu, from his vantage point in late seventeenth- and early eighteenth-century French society, proffers a negative answer to that question by showing us how we can structure familial and political life so that we *guarantee* the debasement and degradation of each.

In the *Persian Letters*, Montesquieu (1689–1755) turns the family analogy in on itself in order to expose a despotism characterized by jealousy, hypocrisy, fear, and hatred. His tale was meant to instruct his French contemporaries by pointing out the corrupting dimensions of certain ways of ordering male-female relations and by asserting that the familial and political realms, if not precisely analogous to one another had, nonetheless, important links. This meant that the corrupting effects of relations of dominance and submission on either or both levels permeated one another. No one remained untainted, including the oppressed wives and eunuchs in the despot's harem.

The seraglio or harem, argue Shanley and Stillman, was a hothouse of duplicity and vice. The master's rule was by definition unstable and arbitrary for it was based on fear and he could reward and punish as he desired. This led Montesquieu to suggest that all forms of arbitrary rule must be curbed lest citizens be at the whim of an authoritarian leader or despot. Montesquieu strongly intimates that in the arena of intimate relations the despotism of the harem precludes the attainment of genuine love and affection, which must be freely given and received. Montesquieu's insights into sexual politics lead Shanley and Stillman to declare him a forerunner of those twentieth-century feminists concerned with manipulation and coercion, dominance and submission, in intimate life.

A question not addressed by Shanley and Stillman but one suggested by their essay and necessary to any complete theory of the family and politics is to what extent it is coherent for feminist thinkers, or anyone else, to deploy their own arguments from analogy in their treatment of the family and politics. That is, in insisting that contemporary conditions are identical in kind and in intent to those of the master class of Montesquieu's seraglio or Filmer's *Patriarcha* (which I discuss briefly below), and that, by analogy, these private relations extend into and define all life including politics, are we not guilty of a distortion of social reality? Is the middle-class American wife really "nothing but" one of the master's hapless and helpless slaves? As Shanley so meticulously documents in her second essay, "Marriage Contract and Social Contract in Seventeenth-Century English Political Thought," arguments from analogy must be drawn with care for they can be easily undermined, particularly if they fail to provide a realistic characterization of an ongoing social life. The history of political thought contains a powerful object lesson for contemporary theorists as to how (and whether) to draw their arguments from analogy.

Shanley picks up debates on the "family analogy" in an epoch— seventeenth-century England—in which patriarchalism, absolute male rule, as a dominant ideology and way of life was on the wane. The thinker responsible for articulating a full-blown paradigm of patriarchalism was Sir Robert Filmer (1588–1653). For Filmer, the earthly authority of all fathers and of the king was identical in kind, not simply analogous to one another. His *Patriarcha* is the most uncompromising and bold statement of political patriarchalism. In Filmer's world all individuals, male and female, are privatized and silenced except the king, the Supreme Father, whose words are cast by and for him in the mold of the Father of all.[4] In Filmer's world there is no split between, or even drawing of, public-private lines; indeed, there is no private sphere—in the sense of a realm demarcated from politics—nor political sphere—in the sense of a realm divergent from the private—at all. Filmer politicizes the family and "familializes" the commonwealth to such an extent that individuals can conceive of themselves only as subjects, with absolute power and authority over them, or as lords (if they are men), exerting absolute power in turn over their wives and children.

The contractarian, constitutional, and voluntarist theories of politics that superseded Filmer's—including Thomas Hobbes's (1588– 1679) *Leviathan* which fused absolutism with consent[5]—recast distinctions between the public and the private, in part to take the family out of politics and politics out of the family. But the theorists found that the remnants of patriarchalism were not so easily expunged, perhaps because they, too, wished to cling to aspects of patriarchal privilege, as Shanley argues. At the point Shanley picks up the debate between the patriarchalists and their contractarian opponents, Filmer's uncompromising articulation of the patriarchalist hard line had already been transcended. Defenders of royalism now pressed for an analogy between familial and political government rather than for a total meshing of the two.

Shanley demonstrates that marriage and the family could not remain untouched by the changes signaled with the shift from "status" to "contract" notions, including the presumption that human beings were born free and equal in the state of nature. If consent became the only legitimate basis for the rule of one man over another in political society, what about marriage which had been conceived traditionally as consent to what then became an unchanging status? The newly hatched contract theories implied that the marriage contract, like all other contracts, could be altered. It fell to John Locke (1632–1704) to attempt to resolve the various dilemmas posed by contractarian arguments. He did so by accepting the premise that all family members were naturally "free and equal." He went on to reject the family analogy, arguing instead that familial and civic authority were not analogues of one another but qualitatively different from one another. This led Locke to insist that the family was a private association that predated the formation of civil society; it was not the creature of civil society. Because it was an association with its own values and purposes, "the state had no right to intrude upon or into it": thus Shanley summarizes Locke.

A problem suggests itself immediately. It is a bind that confronts liberal thinkers from Locke to the present and it is hinted at in Shanley's essay. The bind goes something like this: under liberal principles we create a zone of privacy in which the state's writ does not run, a sphere that is not politically defined, controlled, or conceived as analogous to political rule. So far so good. But, as Shanley notes without explicating fully, Locke anticipated "important reforms in marriage law and practice," reforms, paradoxically, that presuppose and rely upon civil authority and political power to bring them into existence and to enforce them. In the twentieth century, marriage and family law reforms have served as the impetus to create a swollen bureaucratic edifice of medical, legal, and psychiatric ancillaries to state power. Originally created for the best of humanitarian reasons, they now allow for increased surveillance and control of familial relations by the state. Should families organize to resist these intrusions or does the modern family, buffeted by social, technological, economic, and political forces of great strength and daunting complexity, require, even demand, such intervention in its affairs? No theory of the family and politics can ignore these questions.

Finally, Shanley's essay suggests a vexing conceptual and political problem for contemporary feminist theory, particularly those feminist accounts that continue to define all aspects of the political and social world as 'patriarchal.' Shanley demonstrates convincingly that patriarchalism as a historic formation was already a lost cause by the seventeenth century. The Royalists lost the conceptual war to the liberal contractarians. The economic base that had sustained patriarchal social relations was eroding rapidly and disappeared altogether by the twentieth century in the industrialized West. Primogeniture, entail, and status were replaced by contract. If patriarchalism as a way of life and a political paradigm were long ago discredited, to be replaced by the social forms and notions attendant upon and internal to capitalist society, why have so many feminist thinkers insisted that contemporary women continue to live within, and daily confront, implacable patriarchal authority in all spheres, public and private? What is the base of this patriarchalism? How is it sustained? Is the label "patriarchal" theoretically compelling or only an ideological and rhetorical device? These questions and challenges to a theory of the family and politics are posed by contemporary feminist theory, particularly that branch of it known as radical feminism and examined by Jane Flax in her essay and discussed later in this introduction.

If the liberal-contractarian tradition and the uneven shift from patriarchalism pose daunting problems for a theory of the family and politics, Jean-Jacques Rousseau (1712–1778) adds another set of paradoxes and conceptual entanglements. In the matter of women and the family, as with so much else, Rouseau is one of the most controversial political thinkers. His work is so rich and unsystematic that he alternately enrages and disarms the reader. Over the past few years, as feminist political thinkers looked at the Western tradition of political thought, Rousseau was frequently singled out for special attack because of what were seen as his misogynist views. Perhaps because his name is linked with revolution, with liberty, equality, fraternity, and because, more than his predecessors or contemporaries, he took up questions of male and female, "nature and nurture," human sexuality, love, passion, and speech, Rousseau is an obvious and apt target. He is a thinker whose voluble self-indulgent excesses invite attack and whose felicitous turns of phrase inspire admiration.

Out of Rousseau's life as a perpetual alienate, a role at least in part self-chosen, there emerged a sensibility unusually attuned to the strains and undercurrents of his epoch. Rousseau notes, or, as Tony Tanner suggests in his essay, "Julie and 'La Maison Paternelle': Another Look at Rousseau's *La Nouvelle Heloise*," feels in his bones, the conflicts between the authority of the fathers and an egalitarian political ideology: between the "chaste idealized virtue of mothers" and the demands of uncontrolled sexual desire. As Tanner demonstrates eloquently, the harder Rousseau strives for some happy resolution to the tensions and binds in his novel, the more the familial world of *la maison paternelle* collapses about him. Through the subtle use of structuralist psychoanalytic thought and semantics Tanner has captured, as more narrowly political treatments of Rousseau's thought have not, the nuances and ambiguities at work in Rousseau's thinking on matters of paternal authority and the sexual politics of his age. The sense of an emotional hothouse of domesticity, forced in upon itself by external pressures and internal temptations is conveyed first by Rousseau, then within Tanner's essay, with great power. This sense of impending doom is recaptured for our own time in James Glass's treatment of Kafka, Laing, and the family.

Tanner does not treat explicitly Rousseau's discussions of the family and its relation to politics and civil society in his best known political treatises, *The Social Contract*, *The Discourse on Inequality*, and *The Discourse on Political Economy*.[6] I shall take up briefly the links Rousseau forges between familial and political authority, drawing upon his political writings. If Rousseau's version of the state of nature puts pressure on the contractarian visions of Locke and Hobbes, his arguments concerning the nature and purpose of, and relation between paternal authority and political authority distance him from Sir Robert Filmer and from contemporary patriarchal feminists. Filmer saw political power as the absolute and unquestioned authority of the ruler, a direct outgrowth of God's grant of dominion to Adam, which was passed on to all subsequent fatherly lords and lordly fathers. Patriarchal authority was thoroughly political and political authority thoroughly patriarchal on all levels. Rousseau rejects this and goes about knocking at least some of the conceptual props out from under patriarchal political theory.

In contrast to Filmer, Rousseau argues that paternal authority acquires its principal force *from* civil society; that political authority is neither deducible from, nor an outgrowth or mirror reflection of, paternal authority. Although Rousseau claims in *The Social Contract* that the family is the "most ancient of all societies and the only natural one," this passage does not place him in a hard-line patriarchalist posture. Rather, Rousseau is being quite careful to posit an analogy—here we go again—rather than an identity between familial and political society. The ruler, he argues, corresponds "in some sense" to a father, and citizens, to children. But an identity between each is inappropriate and ultimately destructive because "in the family the father's love for his children rewards him for the care he provides, whereas in the State, the pleasure of commanding substitutes for this love, which the leader does not have for his people."[7] In the state love gives way to pleasure in domination.

For Rousseau, the authority of the body politic is grounded in a social compact that brings it into being and grants it power over its members through means of the general will. Legitimate power alone is sovereign and right and *only* this sort of power is properly political. The illegitimate use of force is mere physical power without moral effect. "Yielding to force," Rousseau observes, "is an act of necessity, not of will. . . . In what sense would it be a duty?" No man has *natural political authority* over his fellows, as in patriarchal theory. Yet the basis of family authority lies in large measure, Rousseau argues, in the superior strength of the father who deploys it to protect his children and to command their obedience. This paternal authority "may be reasonably said to be established by nature." No legislature has, can, or should decree it. It predates the creation of civil society, going back to an earlier stage in human evolutionary history, one in which there was a closer assimilation of social man to natural man. The father's duties are dictated to him by no external authority but are prompted by "natural feelings and in such a manner that he can rarely disobey."[8] "Natural" is deployed here as roughly synonymous with an imperative anchored in biological and evolutionary history; it has a basis in biology but serves a desirable and necessary end in human social existence.

Is there any hypocrisy on Rousseau's part in granting no moral imperative or legitimacy to the use of force within political society, yet lodging the right of the father "in very nature" to command in familial society partly in his physical advantages? If Rousseau's intent were a simple misogynist one, he wouldn't have placed himself in so many difficulties in his exploration of these matters. He could, for example, have postulated a state of nature in which male domination exists by definition and allowed this patriarchal dominion to go unchanged and unchallenged in civil society. By insisting upon a reexploration of male-female relationships and positing an ambivalent relationship between the family and the polity, Rousseau opens up a whole range of questions others failed to treat.

Yet Rousseau emerges with a surprisingly tedious conclusion: the man is physically superior; the man should have the final say. Actually his position is not quite so simple, for the father's right "from the nature of things" to command is further justified on the grounds that parental authority "should not be equal."[9] Rousseau, like Plato, Hobbes, and a host of others, feared divided households—families in which endless dissension, discord, and debate were the daily bill of fare. Rousseau would put a finger in the dike of familial disruption by retreating behind a notion of the indivisibility of familial authority. In this sense he is consistent in tracing lines of influence from state to family and in demanding unity from them both. But, as Tanner strikingly shows, in tracing out his mode of thought Rousseau ultimately defeats it—and himself.

It was left to G. W. F. Hegel (1770–1831) to take up Rousseauian themes with the aim of absorbing and transcending Rousseau's paradoxes and conceptual binds and forging them into a higher unity purified of the contradictions that defeated Rousseau. Hegel's political thought has most often been analyzed at its pinnacle—his concept of the State. Or Hegel's dialectical method has served as the focus of discursive practice. Perhaps his forbidding complexity and his distinctive language help to account for the relative lack of attention thus far given Hegel by thinkers concerned with the family and politics, particularly feminist theorists.[10] Then, too, Marx's claim that he had upended Hegel and salvaged whatever was worthwhile is perhaps more widely accepted than it should be.

Joan Landes's essay, "Hegel's Conception of the Family," stands out as a serious attempt to situate Hegel within his own frame of reference even as she demonstrates the manner in which his work anticipates that of "many contemporary feminist thinkers." The strength of Hegel's account of the family in its relation to civil society and the State, in Landes's view, is his stress on ethical life and his insistence that one cannot understand the family unless one grasps and appreciates its ethical root and its centrality as an expression of a concrete morality. Acknowledging the "immense appeal" of this view, Landes nonetheless finds Hegel's argument flawed in several important ways that bear on theories of the family and politics in general.

Hegel, she argues, is dramatically at odds with the "abstract person" featured in liberal contract theory and with the reduction of human social relationships to the terms of contract. Hegel's account of the family is rich in part because he recognizes the impoverishment of the contract view of the person and of social life and, in addition, because he recognizes that familial life has taken alternative forms historically. To many contemporary feminists, particularly those who call themselves radical, the familial form is universal, unchanging, and patriarchal. Like the liberal contract theorists, they posit an abstract, ahistorical truth, where Hegel, with the weight of historical evidence on his side, presents a concrete historical account. Hegel links changes in modes of production and political organization with shifts in familial forms in the direction, in his own era, of a "sentimental family." This family remains grounded in the father's control over family resources, property, and membership in the public sphere.

Hegel's women are accorded a "spiritual reverence" whose pitfalls I probe in my essay on "Aristotle, the Public-Private Split and the Case of the Suffragists." Despite this nod in the direction of celebrating female spiritual superiority—a superiority that has always gone hand-in-hand with women's subjection—Hegel's account is prevented from being tendentious by his adoption of a classical ethical standpoint, that of Antigone, as his ruling image of the woman and her vital role in ethical life. With his embrace of this image, Landes contends, Hegel provides the intimation of a "more humane form of social life," one that can help to create individuals without falling into rapacious individualism. Hegel and Landes both suggest, and thereby criticize implicitly, one major mode of contemporary feminist political thinking, that such individualism erodes and finally destroys the foundation necessary if intimate social relations are to be sustained and authentic individuals are to emerge. Hegel's account, then, has both a radical and a conservative edge. But may it not be the case that in our era, when the fruits of predatory individualism have begun to sour and social relations are increasingly fragmented, that what is most conservative about Hegel—his insistence on male-female mutuality and on the growth of the self only in and through intimate involvement with others—is also what is most radical—his dramatic opposition to the prevailing terms of market society? If the answer to that question is "yes," the only conclusion to be drawn is that much of the so-called liberationist philosophy of our time represents a new form of bondage, not so much an advance as a capitulation to the terms of ongoing market-oriented, consumerist reality. For a theory of the family and politics to be rich and complete, the theorist cannot opt for one side or the other of the Hegelian ledger. He or she must explore the deep inner relationship between the self, the "little commonwealth" of the family, and the broader social and political world without losing sight of the concrete individual at any point along the way.

Richard Krouse goes on to illumine the sad dilemmas posed by liberal contract theory in his essay, "Patriarchal Liberalism and Beyond: From John Stuart Mill to Harriet Taylor." Krouse picks up the trail of liberal views on individuals, individualism, families, and politics with Mill, the greatest nineteenth-century philosopher of liberalism. Krouse notes, as others have, the "fundamental tension" in the liberal tradition "between an abstract philosophical commitment to formal equality of civil and political right, on the one hand, and continuing acceptance of concrete inequalities in the distribution of economic and social power, on the other." Given this simultaneous commitment to formal equality and actual social inequality (lodged in inegalitarian political *and* familial relations), Krouse calls the form of thought he examines at its nineteenth-century apogee in the work of John Stuart Mill (1806–1873) "patriarchal liberalism." Mill's most important, influential, and avowedly feminist work, *The Subjection of Women*, is finally defeated by Mill's commitments to formal equality between the sexes and to "a traditional division of labor within the family." The conceptual resources needed to resolve Mill's dilemma were available to him, Krouse argues, in the "more radical position" of his wife, Harriet Taylor. In Taylor's work, and in certain conceptual categories of Marxism, Krouse finds a proposed solution to the liberal dilemma. Yet, he concludes, the Marxist position as articulated by Frederick Engels in *The Origin of the Family, Private Property and the State*, and Taylor's position as set forth in several essays, present serious shortcomings of their own. Jane Humphries, in her examination of the working-class family, probes the same set of problems from within an economic framework.

The concluding section of Krouse's essay is rich with implications for contemporary feminist thought and for a theory of the family and politics. To oversimplify his argument, he suggests that the Taylor/Engels solutions to the problem of the traditional division of labor within the family create a number of undesirable consequences, including the erosion of what might be called the family's "ethical Hegelian moment." Krouse forces the theorist on the family and politics to consider what limits are acceptable for overturning contemporary social arrangements and relations.

In the history of Western thought, the work of Friedrich Nietzsche

(1844–1900), together with that of Sigmund Freud, represents a bold theoretical rupture that changed the way people looked at the world and themselves. In this volume Tracy Strong brings the family-polity analogy dramatically into the twentieth century in his essay, "Oedipus as Hero: Family and Family Metaphors in Nietzsche." Strong situates Nietzsche as one of a handful of late nineteenth- early twentieth-century thinkers who, without precisely playing out the family analogy, deploy metaphors drawn from family life in order to explain and to understand social life. Although Nietzsche and his illustrious contemporary, Freud, were not political thinkers in the traditional sense, their work bears important, indeed inescapable, implications for twentieth-century political and social thought.

For Nietzsche the family served as concept and symbol and signified as well that past (both personal history and collective history) from which he would sever himself altogether. By contrast, Freud's approach to the individual and collective past was more redemptive. The choice of familial imagery and metaphor in itself serves as one indication that a thinker's thought moves along a vector that reaches into the past, even if his ultimate aim is to escape it. Through Strong's account we are made aware of the poignancy of Nietzsche's struggle lodged in his conviction that one *is* oneself only because of one's past; yet to achieve a personal rebirth, true *self* identity, one must isolate oneself from one's past, one must achieve a radical break. Although Strong doesn't presume to pose with this essay a theory of twentieth-century culture, his analysis of Nietzsche's triumph and tragedy suggests one, or presents a necessary feature of one. What engages the twentieth-century mind is the nature of the self, of personal and social identity. The inescapable question is: "Who am I?" This question assumes the centrality that the nature of the political community did for thinkers in the classical mold of Western political thought. For an Aristotle or a Hegel, for example, the answer to "Who am I?" flowed from the individual's situatedness within a wider, given social network. The question of the "self" could neither be posed nor answered outside the markers of the community as a whole. With Nietzsche and Freud, however, the "I," Freud's *das Ich*, is the prior question, for the self has become increasingly problematic as the traditional moorings of social life erode under the combined assault from the forces of industrialization, bureaucratization, modernization, nationalism. Finally, one's social locus is reduced to an intimate few—hence Kafka's tragic Gregor

Samsa, interpreted by James Glass in his essay—to the family or, in more radical cases, to the self alone.

The finally tragic dimensions of Nietzsche's personal resolution to the problem of the self is inseparable from his thought and forms part of his troubling importance for the modern political imagination. To consider the man in assaying his thought is inescapable, as Strong points out, in Nietzsche's case; indeed, he would be the first to insist upon it. What then, can we learn from Nietzsche's tragic and heroic Oedipus, and how does it bear on the family and politics? First, according to Strong, we can learn much about "the power and strength and effect of the family structure" in general as we witness Nietzsche's particular struggle with and against that power. Second, from the drama of Nietzsche's solution to the question of identity we learn the awful perils that come from giving birth to one's self, for such a claimed or chosen self-identity means one "never encounters what the child with parents, with a past, must do to achieve a resolution of the psychological situation in which he finds himself." He or she must annihilate the entire Oedipal situation. If Nietzsche's life instructs us, it is that self-annihilation lurks within that process.

As one confronts today the claims of various liberationists that the past, including the family, is dead or that one must kill it, Nietzsche's ghost hovers nearby shouting a silent warning that this is the route to madness, not political transformation or secure self-identity. One is free to take it, if one must, but one must not be deluded about what is going on. Where does this leave us heirs of Nietzsche and Freud? According to Strong, the Freudian resolution remains—we should pay the price for civilization and that includes a measure of human self-control, of setting limits on untrammeled desires.[11] To this Strong adds the Arendtian political ideal,[12] the notion that we pay the price for politics by reciprocating with others and not living for ourselves alone. Jane Humphries, in "The Working-Class Family: A Marxist Perspective," presents us with actual case histories of people who have always lived, or tried to live within the frame of communitarian social relations.

Humphries's essay presents a challenge to contemporary Marxist views on the family that require that the analyst see the family exclusively in those functionalist terms I criticized in my Preface. Marxist functionalists share with others of the genre a tendency to analyze the family, including that working-class family that is the focus of Humphries's discussion, in terms of the "needs" of the "macro-order," the "functional prerequisites of capitalism." Concerns of consciousness, intimacy, and culture are washed out in such Marxist approaches, including those of Marxist feminists. Humphries attempts to right the balance by looking at the continuing vitality of working-class family life, particularly insofar as that family life serves as the base for working-class political and economic struggle. Humphries's interests are both analytical and avowedly political for, as she correctly observes, the perspective one adopts toward the family has ramifications for one's views on women and their oppression. She not only throws down the conceptual gauntlet to the Marxist feminists (which is taken up in the essay that follows it, by Flax), she reminds us that *any* theory of the family and politics, even one that is not openly and militantly political, nevertheless secretes political implications. The responsible theorist acknowledges these implications and goes on to examine their possible impact.

One vital area that Humphries covers and that no theory of the family and politics can ignore is the historic evidence that shows the corrosive and repressive effects of formalized relations of dependency of families on the state in the form of what was called "poor relief" and is now called "welfare." Political conservatives, to their own ends, have spent decades denouncing welfare-state liberalism, in part because they claim it saps welfare recipients of their initiative. Humphries's essay suggests that there is a grain of truth to the conservative lament. Seen from a Marxist perspective, however, the solution lies not in allowing the market free reign but in moving toward an economic system than can provide a living "family wage" to its members. Finally, the concrete examples provided by Humphries of nineteenth-century working-class families as loci of "radicalization and the nurturance of unconventional idealism" does much to undercut stereotypic views of the family solely in terms of its role as an agent of social conformism and repression. (James Glass, in "Kafka and Laing on the Trapped Consciousness: The Family as Political Life," makes a powerful case for seeing the family in just such stark terms.)

The final four essays in this volume cluster together as variations on a number of contested contemporary themes concerning the family and politics. Each, implicitly or explicitly, is concerned with methodology and the construction of theoretical perspectives. Each addresses some facet of ongoing debates about the family's relationship to the wider order. Each exudes a position toward the family that is importantly different or at least various. Theodore Mills Norton's essay is noteworthy for the central role it accords methodological concerns and the intensity of its focus on language, on human speech and communication. Norton insists that to be truly informative an analysis of the family and its relation to politics demands a critical, interpretive mode of inquiry. Such an approach is fundamentally at odds with behaviorist social science and structural functionalism of every sort, including its Marxist variant. The Frankfurt School and its thinkers— for this is the tradition Norton has tapped—promised an alternative to positivism and determinist Marxism. Norton accepts that this promise has largely been met, most recently in the distinguished body of work by the German social theorist, Jürgen Habermas.

The Frankfurt School began its work within a social context in which fascism was shortly to triumph. To account for the rise of fascism, for the triumph of this awful barbarism, the theorists of the Frankfurt School adopted both Marx and Freud as powerful theoretical bases in order to counter both positivistic social science and an overly optimistic faith in the future. Within this framework of methodological and political concerns, thinkers of the Frankfurt School, particularly Max Horkheimer, developed a set of arguments and conclusions about the classical, authoritarian bourgeois family, its collapse, and the concomitant rise of fascism. The human subject created in the family which superseded the classical bourgeois family was, according to Horkheimer, a perfect foil for fascist impulses, for he or she was all too willing and able to participate in setting up the terms of his or her own subjection.

Despite their claims to the contrary, the Frankfurt account of the relation of the family to the wider society wound up committing some of the mistakes of more deterministic and functionalist accounts. The family, for example, was conceived primarily as a key instrument in the legitimation of domination and the internalization of an ideological, distorted social norm. The approach in general wound up overassimilating the family into the terms of ongoing public social reality. It comes as no surprise that the political position secreted by this Frankfurt School analysis was one of pessimism and despair.

Habermas, to whom Norton turns for a resolution of the bind that thinkers like Horkheimer and Theodore Adorno got themselves into, has made a potentially important contribution to the ongoing enterprise of a theory of the family and politics in his notion of the ideal speech situation. Within an ideal speech situation (as a contrast model to the circumstances, familial and political within which human speech now occurs), no compulsion is present; domination is absent; and authentic reciprocity or "genuine symmetry" pertains between and among communicative participants. This poses problems immediately for the family, as children cannot enjoy a perfect symmetry of communicative competence with adults; nevertheless, the ideal speech situation conjures up a compelling picture of truth-telling and truth-seeking as vital human imperatives.

If one's purpose is in part the search for a language of human discourse, including politics, that does not silence particular persons or groups, nor proscribe particular topics, one must move out of immersion in the texts of the past (having engaged the past passionately and sympathetically) and enter the world of the complex modern subject. The "I" that I am grows out of a past that I can perceive but dimly, a past that can anger, enlighten, illumine, or mystify my thinking about what it means to be a male or female, a human being, a citizen, and a political theorist in our post-Holocaust, post-Hiroshima age. Norton's discussion suggests that the distorted communication of the present, between men and women, and citizens, provides nonetheless an anticipation and a presupposition that things could be different; that communication along the lines of an enhanced, reciprocal awareness is possible, if we can but move to create the conditions that allow for its emergence. This is the great challenge to theoretical and human renewal that Norton's reading of Habermas poses. Sadly, it is a challenge few feminist thinkers in our time thus far have taken up, as Jane Flax's critical essay, "Feminist Theories of the Family: An End to Ideology?," demonstrates.

Flax begins with the presumption that most of what exists to date is an uneven deconstruction by feminists of the old ideology of the family which was inimical, they insist, to the needs and interests of women as public and private beings. That deconstructive effort, however, is not sufficient in itself to comprise a full-blown feminist theoretical alternative. Such an alternative account—and by implication this holds for a general theory of the family and politics as well—must come to grips with human sexuality, child development, and those emotional and social needs linked with, and emergent within, kinship and familial ties and structures. Flax concludes her essay with a series of important questions she finds either unanswered or treated inadequately in feminist thought.

In addition to Flax's questions, there are other considerations of an explicitly political nature that remain underdeveloped in her essay. They go something like this. There is little doubt that the feminist movement has contributed to what Dorothy Dinnerstein, a psychoanalytic feminist, calls the "essential humanizing functions of stable, longstanding, generation-spanning primary groups."[13] The "reactive quality" of feminist criticism of the family has led to the creation of what I have termed a "politics of displacement."[14] A politics of displacement is nothing new under the political sun. Past examples that spring to mind include the policies of the Romanov czars who, over the years, implicated Russia in some external imbroglio whenever they wished to shift public attention away from their domestic politics. A more sinister instance is the use of German Jews as scapegoats for the widespread social dislocation and hardship that followed the end of World War I, a politics of displacement perfected by fascism. In the history of American capitalist expansion and labor strife, one finds the poor white and black unemployed frequently pitted against each other in such a way that each group saw the other as the source of its misery, and corporate oligarchs escaped serious political challenge. Feminism's politics of displacement reveals its true colors when feminist thinkers assault a social unit, already vulnerable and weakened by external and internal strains, as both cause and symptom of female subordination. In so doing, such feminists direct attention away from structural political imperatives and constraints and promote a highly personalized sexual politics that is simultaneously depoliticizing, individualistic, and potentially destructive in its implications. A theory of the family and politics must *account* for the emergence of a politics of displacement and go on to create a theoretical foundation that does not, as its implications are traced out, lapse back into a mode that is both depoliticizing and militantly over-politicizing at one and the same time.

A critique similar to the one I have offered of a highly personalized politics of displacement might be leveled at the radical psychiatrist R. D. Laing, but James Glass conjures up a different image—one that surely reflects the personal and political binds and confusions of our age even if it, finally, fails to resolve them. Glass sees Laing as one of a small number of modern thinkers courageous enough to bring us the bad news of the human condition. His essay presents a remorseless vision of the family as a system of torment and exchange that ushers, not infrequently, into madness and victimization for the family's more vulnerable members. For Glass, as for Franz

Kafka and R. D. Laing, a celebrant at one point in his career of schizophrenic "break-throughs," there is no authority except repressive and alienating authority—unjust power. The family serves to connect individuals to a wider system conceived in dire terms. What the family does, its "primary functions," is to "socialize the self into sado-masochistic patterns. . . . " Families are a schooling, not in freedom, as John Stuart Mill's ideal promised, but in the perfection of "destructive instincts."

Glass dissects Kafka's eerie short story, "The Metamorphosis," seeing in Gregor Samsa's horror a symbolic indictment of the hostile realities of the repressive bourgeois family. R. D. Laing's case for "schizophrenogenic" families receives a similar cogent and sympathetic treatment. There is something of Nietzsche in this radically deconstructive exercise. The full implications of Glass's analysis for politics, families, and political theory are best couched as a series of questions to ponder.

First, if we accept Glass's claim that schizophrenia is an "implicit attack on authority," does this make being a schizophrenic, as he suggests, in some ways a political act or activity? If so, does this not reduce politics to the crude level of any perceived "attack on authority" or traditional rules so that, finally, we cannot distinguish between an individual spitting on the living-room rug to protest parental "authority" and an organization of exploited workers striking to improve working conditions? In other words, if we construe political actions or acts with political meaning too broadly, do we not run the risk of destroying politics in the process? Glass clearly recognizes this danger and attempts to correct for it by claiming an analogy, not an identity, between schizophrenic dissociation and political rebellion; nevertheless, the force of his analysis tends to erode or downplay such distinctions. Second, if the isolation of those deemed "mad" is intolerable and unjust, what are the alternatives for individuals who have "opted out" or been "forced out" of the terms of shared social reality? Surely Laing's relabeling of the mad "sane" and the sane "mad" is no help at all in solving a real social dilemma of awesome and tragic proportions.

Finally, if the social system is one of torment and exclusion, "a depravity affecting everyone," how do we account for reciprocity, kindness, decency, affection, and acts of moral courage, both private virtue and public ethics? Things cannot be as terrible, either for families or politics, as Glass suggests or social life would be unlivable, even impossible. Glass's essay troubles because we know he has touched a raw nerve, yet we also sense that in his urge to give Laing a sympathetic reading and to assimilate Laing's views into his interpretation of Kafka's, certain vexing issues go unexplored and problems unexamined. Is it possible to create an alternative that incorporates Glass's sympathy for, and understanding of, society's personae non gratae without, at the same time, capitulating to madness oneself? And, if the family and all society is driving us mad, where then do we turn? I suggest we take a closer look at families from what might be called the child's-eye point of view.

Although political theorists have rediscovered the family, and made relations between men and women central to their concerns, children remain largely invisible. Of the essays in this volume, for example, only those by Krouse and Flax together with my second essay, " 'Thank Heaven for Little Girls': The Dialectics of Development," take up concerns with the child and moral development explicitly, if briefly. Glass's discussion is a rather special case, for in it he presumes that children are primarily, if not exclusively, victims of families and society alike. I place the development of the child at the center of a theoretical and political argument. My purpose in this is to appeal for a developmental perspective, grounded in the presumption of human sociality, as a necessary conceptual pillar in any attempt to understand and to interpret the links between the family and politics. Given the absence of children in traditional political thought and the limitations of the socialization literature, discussed briefly in the preface and more fully in this volume's final essay, it is necessary to create an approach that allows, even requires, that the theorist examine the child and politics in a manner that can incorporate the child's own self-understanding. Unless or until scholars acknowledge the child's inner reality and dignity as a human person, until we attempt to understand the fantasies, feelings, wishes, and fears of children, our conclusions on children will remain presumptuous. There are pitfalls in the conceptual and methodological moves I propose. Theorists might, for example, accept that the child's world is not their world in important ways tied to levels of cognitive and psychosexual development and identity. The inclination then might be to have the child express him- or herself in an open-ended fashion and to avoid making interpretations, judgments, and conclusions of one's own. This will not do as a viable alternative to current socialization research. A strictly "subjectivist" account runs the risk of simply replicating the "subjective truth" for each individual child without moving toward a coherent account of what this "truth" means in more general terms for an account of families, politics, and moral education. What is necessary, in order to do the research and articulate the theory I am calling for, is a framework of explanation that ties together first-person accounts (in this case by children) to theories of human identity and then goes on to wed both to political concepts and concerns.

Some of the questions *The Family in Political Thought* poses for future research and reflection are: What is the relationship between theories of human nature, developmental stages, the emergence of identity, and political life and culture? Is it possible to determine, with clarity, what is given in human nature and what the possibilities are for human growth and change given alterations in the political and social world? How do children acquire moral ideals and political values, and how do these ideals and values relate to their adult roles as active or passive, critical or comformist citizens? What is the connection between self-identity and the appropriation by children and adults of concepts with a social, public meaning? What is the impact of sex, race, and class differences on the emergence of political awareness and social identity? How, when, and under what terms do children come to identify with, or to repudiate, "others" or an Other beyond their own family, friends, and social group, particularly those of different classes, races, or nationalities? What changes in families, education, and politics might serve to create and to support a sense of social and political responsibility in children? What is the family's role, finally, in the child's adoption of a critical or non-reflective stand toward society?

This is a tall order, but, unless it is met, a theory of the family and politics will remain a series of intimations and the full meaning of the discursive collage framed within this volume will forever elude us.

Philosopher Queens and Private Wives: Plato on Women and the Family

☼ *Susan Moller Okin*

In his two largest political dialogues, Plato gives us an unusual opportunity to observe a political philosopher's mind at work on the subject of the family. While in *The Republic*, Plato abolishes the private family for the guardian class of his ideal city, in *The Laws*, the private family is not only reinstated, but is acknowledged as the foundation on which the second-best city is built. The following paper is concerned with the reasons for and the consequences of Plato's different proposals regarding the family. By considering Plato's proposals in the context of the society in which he was writing, we are able to increase our understanding of the relationships between the family and the purpose and characteristics of the political community, and, particularly, between the family and the position of women.

The aim of the true art of ruling, as Plato conceives it, is not the welfare of any single class or section, but the greatest possible happiness of the entire community.[1] "Happiness," however, can be a misleading word, for if it leads us to thoughts of freedom, individual rights, or equality of opportunity, we are far from Plato's idea of happiness (*eudaimonia*). Equality, liberty, and justice in the sense of fairness were not values for Plato. The three values on which both his ideal and his second-best cities are based are, rather, harmony, efficiency, and moral goodness; the last is the key to his entire political philosophy. Because of his belief in the intrinsic value of the soul and the consequent importance of its health, Plato does not think that happiness results from the freedom to behave just as one wants; it is in no way attainable independently of virtue. Statesmen, therefore, should "not only preserve the lives of their subjects but reform their characters too, so far as human nature permits of this."[2]

Though the ultimate aim of the true ruler is the happiness of all his subjects, the only way he can attain this is by raising them, by means of education and law, to the highest possible level of wisdom and virtue.

The gravest of all human faults, however, one considered by Plato to be inborn in most people, is that "excessive love of self" which is "the cause of all sins in every case." Worse still, whereas the soul and next the body should take priority, man's all too prevalent tendency is to give his property—in truth the least valuable of his possessions—his greatest attention. Thus, in *The Laws*, the currency and system of production, although allowing for private property, are so designed as to ensure that "a man by his money-making [will not] neglect the objects for which money exists: . . . the soul and the body. . . . Wherefore we have asserted (and that not once only) that the pursuit of money is to be honoured last of all."[3] Clearly Plato's citizens were never to forget that material possessions were but means to far more important ends.

The ruler's task in promoting his subjects' virtue is therefore twofold. He must aim to overcome their extremes of self-love and their fatal preference for material possessions over the welfare of their souls. A man who is to be virtuous and great must be able to transcend his own interests and, above all, to detach himself from the passion to acquire. As Glenn Morrow has noted, there is abundant evidence in both *The Republic* and *The Laws* that Plato regarded the maintenance of a temperate attitude toward property as essential for the security and well-being of the state.[4] It was acquisitiveness, after all, that had led the first city Socrates depicted—the simple, "true," and "healthy" city—into war with its neighbors and all the complications that this entailed. Again, corruption that results from increasing possessiveness is the recurrent theme of *Republic 8*, which analyzes the process of political degeneration.[5]

The Republic is an extremely radical dialogue. In his formulation of the ideal state, Plato questions and challenges the most sacred contemporary conventions. The solution he proposes for the problem of selfishness and divisive interests is that private property and hence private interests be abolished to the greatest possible extent. For in this city, not just harmony but unity of interests is the objective. "Have we any greater evil for a city," asks Socrates, "than what splits it and makes it many instead of one? Or a greater good than what binds it together and makes it one?" He concludes that the best governed city is that "which is most like a single human being." Nothing can dissolve the unity of a city more readily than for some of its citizens to be glad and others to grieve over the same thing, so that all do not work or even wish in concert. The highest possible degree of unity is achieved if all citizens feel pleasure and pain on the same occasions, and this "community of pleasure and pain" will occur only if all goods are possessed in common. The best governed city will be that "in which most say 'my own' and 'not my own' about the same thing, and in the same way."[6]

If he had thought it possible, Plato would certainly have extended the communal ownership of property to all the classes of his ideal city. The first of the "noble lies," according to which all citizens are told that they are one big family, can be read as the complete expression of an ideal that can be realized only in part. Because he believes in the tendency of most human beings to selfishness, Plato considers the renunciation of private property to be something that can be attained only by the best of persons. This is made clear in *The Laws*, where he rejects the possibility of eliminating ownership for the citizens of his projected second-best city, since tilling the soil in common is "beyond the capacity of people with the birth, rearing and training we assume."[7] What is impossible for the citizens of the second-best city, with all their carefully planned education, must regretfully be regarded as beyond the capacity of the inferior classes in the ideal city. Thus it is the guardian class alone that is to live up to the ideal of community of property and unity of interests.[8]

The overcoming of selfish interests is regarded as most necessary for those who are to have charge of the welfare and governance of all the other citizens—quite apart from their greater capacity for it. Since a person will always take care of what he loves, the guardians, especially, must love the whole community, and have no interests other than its welfare. Above all, then, the permitted property arrangements for them must be "such as not to prevent them from being the best possible guardians and not to rouse them up to do harm to the other citizens." Plato argues that the possession by the rulers of private lands and wealth would inevitably lead to their formation into a faction, whereupon they would constitute "masters and enemies instead of allies of the other citizens."[9] The combination of wealth and private interests with political power can lead only to the destruction of the city.

Plato's ideal for the guardians is expressed by the proverb, "friends have all things in common."[10] But if communal ownership of inanimate property is a great aid to the unity of the city, it appears to him to follow that communal ownership of women and children will conduce to even greater unity. It is clear from the way Plato argues that he thinks the communalization of property leads directly to the abolition of the family. He does not regard them as distinct innovations requiring separate justifications. In fact, he slides over the first mention of the abolition of the family, almost as a parenthesis,[11] and in both *The Republic* and the brief summary of this aspect of it presented in *The Laws*, the two proposals are justified by the same arguments and often at the same time. In *The Laws* especially, when Plato looks back to the institutions of the ideal city, women and children are frequently classified with other possessions. Thus he talks of "community of wives, children, and all chattels," and later, by contrast, of that less desirable state of affairs in which "women and children and houses remain private, and all these things are established as the private property of individuals."[12]

Women are classified by Plato, as they were by the culture in which he lived, as an important subsection of property.[13] The very expression "community (or common having) of women and children," which he uses to denote his proposed system of temporary matings, is a further indication of this, since it could just as accurately be described as "the community of men," were it not for its inventor's customary way of thinking about such matters.[14]

Just as other forms of private property were seen as destructive of society's unity, so "private wives" are viewed by Plato as diverse and subversive in the same way. Thus, in contrast to the unified city he is proposing, he points to those institutional arrangements that foster the ascendance of particularism and factionalism, with "one man dragging off to his own house whatever he can get his hands on apart from the others, another being separate in his own house with separate women and children, introducing private pleasures and griefs of things that are private."[15] Again, in *The Laws*, he strikes simultaneously against contemporary Athenian practices with regard both to private property and to women: "we huddle all our goods together, as the saying goes, within four walls, and then hand over the dispensing of them to the women. . . ."[16] It is clear that Plato saw conventional marriage and woman in the traditional role as guardian of the private household as intimately bound up with that system of private possessions that was the greatest impediment to the unity and well-being of the city.

In *Republic* 8, however, as Plato reviews the successively degenerate forms of the political order, we can see his association of private women with corruption at its most graphic. Just as women were communalized at the same time as other property, so are they now, without separate explanation, made private at the same time as other property, as the course of the city's degeneration is described. Once private, moreover, women are depicted as hastening the course of the decline, due to their exclusive concern with the particular interests of their families. First, when the rulers begin to want to own land, houses, and money, and to set up domestic treasuries and private love nests, they will begin to fail as guardians of the people, and the city will start to degenerate. Thereafter, private possession of women is depicted as a major cause of further corruption. The mother's complaints that her husband's lack of concern for wealth and public prestige places her at a disadvantage among the other women make the timocratic youth begin to despise his worthy father and to feel challenged into showing that he is more of a man. The wife with her selfish concerns, who "chants all the other refrains such as women are likely to do in cases of this sort," is, like Pandora, the real originator of the evils that follow.[17]

The fact that Plato identifies the abolition of the family so closely with the communalization of property, and does not appear to regard the former as a more severe emotional deprivation than the latter, must be understood in the context of the functions and status of women and the family in contemporary upper-class Athenian life. In view of the chattel status of Athenian women and the "peculiarly close relation thought to hold between a family and its landed property," Plato's blending of two issues, which to us appear to be much more distinct, is far from inexplicable.[18] There is abundant evidence in classical Greek literature that the women who were eligible to become the wives of Plato's contemporaries were valued for silence, hard work, domestic frugality, and, above all, marital fidelity. Confined to the functions of household management and the bearing of heirs, they were neither educated nor permitted to experience the culture and intellectual stimulation of life outside their secluded quarters in the house. Accordingly, it was almost impossible for husbands and wives to be either day-to-day companions or emotional and intellectual intimates.[19] Consequently, as recent scholars of Greek life agree, "the family does not bulk large in most Greek writing, its affective and psychological sides hardly at all," and "family life, as we understand it, hardly existed" in late fifth-century Athens.[20] The prevailing bisexuality meant that "two complementary institutions coexisted, the family taking care of what we may call the material side, pederasty (and the courtesan) the affective, and to a degree the intellectual, side of a man's intimate life."[21]

On the other hand, while the family was certainly not the center of the upper-class Greek's emotional life, it did function in ways that the modern family does not—ways that rendered it potentially far more socially divisive. The single-family household had emerged from the clan in comparatively recent times, and only gradually did the *polis* gain the loyalty that had once belonged to the autonomous clan. Antigone represents the paradigmatic example of this conflict of loyalties; there were, in fact, various areas of life where it had not yet become clear whether family or civic obligations should prevail. The extent to which the victim's kin, rather than the rulers, were responsible for ensuring that crime was properly avenged is well documented in *The Laws*.[22] Again, the predominance of duties to parents over any notion of legal justice is clearly indicated in the *Euthyphro*, where Socrates is incredulous that a man could even consider prosecuting his own father for the murder of anyone who was not a relative.[23] Despite its minimal functioning as an emotional base, then, the Athenian family of the early fourth century, as a firm economic entity and the focus of important duties, constituted an obviously divisive force and potential threat to civic loyalty.

Those scholars who have expressed profound horror at Plato's idea that the family be abolished and replaced by those mating arrangements designed to produce the best offspring seem to have treated the issue anachronistically, by neglecting the function of the family in Athenian life. When G. M. A. Grube, for example, objects to the system of temporary matings advocated for the guardians as "undesirable because it does violence to the deepest human emotions" and "entirely ignores the love element between the 'married' pair,"[24] he seems to be forgetting that at the time, the family was simply not the locus for the expression of the deepest human emotions. Even a cursory knowledge of the *Symposium*, with its deprecating comparison of those who turn their love toward women and raise families with those whose superior, spiritual love is turned toward boys and

philosophy, reveals that Plato and his audience would not have regarded the abolition of the family as a severe limitation of their intimate lives. Stranger still is the attitude taken by Leo Strauss, who not
only assumes that the family is "natural" and any move to abolish it
"convention," but makes the issue of whether the abolition of the
family is possible or not into an acid test for determining the feasibility of the entire ideal state.[25] Those passages of The Republic to
which he refers in order to demonstrate the supposed "fact that men
seem to desire naturally to have children of their own" are remark-
ably inadequate to prove his point. Moreover, his objection that
Plato's controls on heterosexual behavior mean that "the claims of
eros are simply silenced" implies a complete denial of the prevailing
homosexual eros of the time. It is very probable that Plato's listeners
would have regarded the ideal state's restrictions on their homosexual
behavior as far more repressive of their sexual feelings than the
abolition of the family and the controls placed on heterosexual intercourse.

The same scholars—Grube, Taylor, and Strauss—who reject the
abolition of the family as impossible, are those most intolerant of the
proposed alternative, in which partners are chosen for each other,
supposedly by lot but, in fact, for eugenic purposes. Those who reject
such proposals as quite impracticable, given human nature, because
of their "intolerable severity"[26] would do well to consider the position of respectable Greek women. For they were just as controlled
and deprived in their sexual lives as both sexes of guardians were to
be in the ideal city, and without having available to them the com-
pensations of any participation in life outside the domestic sphere.
The Greek woman was not permitted to choose her sexual partner,
any more than Plato's guardians were. Moreover, in her case the partner had not only the absolute right to copulate with and reproduce
by her for the rest of her life, but also all the powers that her father
had previously wielded over her. Once married, a woman had no
condoned alternative sexual outlets, but was entirely dependent on a
husband—who might have any number of approved hetero- or homosexual alternatives—for any satisfaction that he might choose to give
her. The extent of the double standard is brought clearly into relief
by the fact that the Greek word for adultery meant only sexual intercourse between a married woman and a man who was not her husband. Needless to say, the punishments were very severe. Even if her
husband died, a woman had no control over her life or body, since

she was returned to the custody of her father or guardian, who could remarry her at his pleasure. Alternatively, a citizen could give his sister or daughter into concubinage, from which she could be sent to a brothel without any reproach to her owner.[27]

If Athenian women of the highest class, living in one of the most highly cultured societies the world has known, could be controlled and deprived to this extent, it is hardly arguable that the exigencies of human nature render the Platonic mating system, with its requirement of supposedly "unnatural continence,"[28] impossible to enact. Women's sexual lives have been restricted throughout the greater part of world history, just as rigidly as Plato proposes to control the intimate lives of his guardians. "The claims of *eros*" have been "simply silenced" in women with considerable success. It is apparent from much of the history of the female sex that, with suitable indoctrination and strong sanctions, human beings can be conditioned to accept virtually any extent of control on their sexual and emotional lives. The point is, of course, that the scholars concerned have used the terms "human emotions" and "human nature" to refer only to men. What seems really horrific to Grube, Taylor, and Strauss is that whereas the Greeks, like many other peoples, merely reserved women for the production of legitimate issue and controlled their lives accordingly, Plato has dared to suggest that the sexual lives of both male and female guardians should be controlled for the purpose of producing the best possible offspring for the community.

The significance of Plato's abolition of the family is profound; the proposal has been echoed by a number of subsequent theorists or rulers of utopian societies that depend to a very high degree on cohesion and unity. As Stanley Diamond has asserted in an illuminating essay that analyzes the significance of Plato's treatment of the family, "The obvious aim is to disengage (the guardians) from all connections and motives which might diminish their dedication to the state. . . . Plato clearly sensed the antagonism between state and family, and in order to guarantee total loyalty to the former, he simply abolished the latter."[29] It is important to notice that Plato's revolutionary solution to the conflict was not to obliterate the primary ties of kinship, but to extend them throughout the entire ruling class. The guardians were in fact "to imagine that they were all one family,"[30] and it is stressed in many ways that the formation of the rulers into one family is to be no mere formality. They are required not only to address but to behave toward each other as brother, parent, and so on. "It would be ridiculous," Glaucon agrees, "if they only mouthed, without deeds, the names of kinship." Thus, the fear and shame associated with violence toward a parent will operate as an unusually strong sanction against attack on anyone at all of the older generation. Likewise, lawsuits and factional disputes will be no more common than they would be within a family, and the city's success in war will be in large part due to the fact that soldiers will be no more likely to desert their comrades than to abandon members of their own families.[31] Indeed, as Gregory Vlastos has concisely stated, "The ideal society of the *Republic* is a political community held together by bonds of fraternal love."[32]

The most radical implication of Plato's transforming the guardian class into a single family concerns the role of women. Rousseau, in the course of a bitter attack on Plato both for doing away with the family and for giving equal opportunities to women, nevertheless reveals a perceptive understanding of the connection between the two innovations. "I am well aware that in *The Republic* Plato prescribes the same exercises for women as for men," he says. "Having dispensed with the individual family in his system of government, and not knowing any longer what to do with women, he finds himself forced to turn them into men."[33] It appears that he is correct, except that in place of "men" we should substitute "people," since for Rousseau in many important respects only men were people. Scholars who have considered the connection between the first two "waves of paradox" of Book 5—the granting of equal opportunities to women and the abolition of the family—do not, however, agree. Some have stressed the independence of the two proposals, some have maintained that there is probably a causal link between them but have not committed themselves on its direction, and at least one has asserted, without giving any reasons, that it is the emancipation of women that renders necessary the abolition of the family.[34] For a number of reasons, however, it seems that to the extent that a causal relationship exists between the two paradoxes, its direction is as Rousseau states it.

In the ideal city, since there is no private wealth or marriage for those in the guardian class and since their living arrangements are to be communal, there is no domestic role such as that of the traditional housewife. Since planned breeding and communal child rearing minimize the unpredictability of pregnancy and the time demanded of mothers, maternity is no longer anything approaching a full-time occupation. Thus, women can no longer be defined in their traditional roles. However, every person in the ideal city is defined by his or her function; the education and working life of each citizen are to be dedicated to the optimal performance of a single craft.[35] If the female guardians were no longer to be defined in relation to particular men, children, and households, it seems that Plato had no alternative but to consider them persons in their own right. If they were to take their place as members of the guardian class, each must share in the functions of that class. Thus Plato had to convince his skeptical audience that women were able to perform tasks very different from those customarily assigned to them.

Socrates first reminds his audience that they have all agreed that each individual should be assigned work that is suited to his or her nature. But, he says, since none of them will claim that there is no difference of nature between the male and the female, they are in danger of contradicting themselves if they argue that the female guardians should do the same work as the male. However, there are many ways in which human beings can differ, and we do not regard all of them as relevant in assigning different functions to different persons. Socrates asserts that we have not yet considered "what form of different and same nature, and applying to what, we were distinguishing when we assigned different practices to a different nature and the same ones to the same."[36] But, he continues, is it not reasonable to consider only those differences and similarities that have some bearing on the activity in question? We do not worry about whether a man is bald or longhaired when assessing his capacity to be a good shoemaker. There is, therefore, no reason to consider the difference in procreative function between the sexes—"that the female bears and the male mounts"—as relevant in deciding whether they should play equal roles in the ruling class. Socrates lays the burden of proof firmly on whomever should claim that it is. He argues, rather, that since the characteristics of the soul determine whether a person is capable of a certain pursuit, and since sex is no more related to the soul than the presence or absence of hair, members of both sexes will be skilled in all the arts, depending on the nature of their individual souls. Thus, though he asserts that women in general are not as capable as men in general, especially in physical strength, individual members of both sexes will be capable of performing all functions needed by the city, including guardianship and philosophy. The only way to ensure that persons are assigned the jobs for which they are best suited is to assess the merits of each, independently of sex.

This argument, simple as it seems, is unique in the treatments of women by political philosophers, and has revolutionary implications for the female sex. Plato's bold suggestion that perhaps there is no difference between the sexes, apart from their roles in procreation, is possible only because the requirement of unity among the ruling class, and the consequent abolition of private property and the family, entail the abolition of wifehood and the absolute minimization of motherhood. Once the door is open, the possibilities for women are boundless. The annihilation of traditional sex roles among the guardians is total—even the earliest child care is to be shared by men and women. Plato concludes that, though females as a class are less able, the best of women can share with the best of men in the highest functions involved in ruling the city. The "philosopher monarchs," as they should always have been called, were to include both sexes.[37]

The overwhelming hostility from male scholars to Plato's first wave of paradox is fascinating in its own right, but this is not the place to discuss it. However, one charge that has been laid against him must be dealt with here. Leo Strauss and Allan Bloom have claimed that Plato's arguments for the equality of women depend on his "abstracting from" or "forgetting" the body, and particularly his "abstracting from the difference between the sexes with regard to procreation."[38] Clearly they do not. Plato is very careful to take into account those differences between the sexes that are palpably biological and therefore inevitable—pregnancy, lactation, and a degree of difference in physical strength. These scholars, in the company of millions of other people, mistakenly assume, as Plato very rationally does not, that the entire conventional female sex role follows logically from the single fact that women bear children. The real significance of the treatment of the woman question in *Republic* 5 is that it is one of the very few instances in the history of thought when the biological implications of femaleness have been clearly separated from all the conventional, institutional, and emotional baggage that has usually been identified with them. Plato's elimination of a private sphere from the guardian's lives entailed the radical questioning of all the institutionalized differences between the sexes.

During the argument about the proper education and role of women, Socrates twice indicates directly that these and the abolition of the family are really parts of the same issue. He talks, first, of the "right acquisition and use of children and women" and later of "the law concerning the possession and rearing of the women and children."[39] In addition, the way he introduces the emancipation of the female guardians is in itself significant. Having dropped in as an aside the proposal that the guardians will have women and children as well as their other possessions in common, Socrates is challenged, at the beginning of Book 5, to justify this important decision. In answer to this challenge, he embarks on his discussion, first, of the equal education and treatment of women and, second, of the communal breeding and rearing arrangements. It seems, then, that having decided to do away with the conventional role of women by doing away with the family, he feels impelled to support this proposal by demonstrating that women are capable of filling many roles outside their traditional sphere. A brief passage from *The Laws* shows how aware Plato was of the danger of freeing women from their confined, domestic role without giving them an alternative function. He thought the example of the Spartans should be enough to discourage any legislator from "letting the female sex indulge in luxury and expense and disorderly ways of life, while supervising the male sex."[40] Thus it was his dismantling of the family that not only enabled Plato to rethink the question of women and their potential abilities but forced him to do so.

Two additional arguments show clearly that it is the abolition of the family that leads Plato into emancipating the female guardians rather than vice versa. First, no mention is made of the women of the inferior classes. We are told that among these householders and farmers, private land, houses, and other property are to be preserved. The close connection between these things and the private ownership of women and children implies, though we are not specifically told this, that the family too is preserved among the lower classes.[41] Efficiency is no doubt one of Plato's primary aims in the organization of the artisans. But although the argument in Book 5 about women's talents is just as applicable to the other crafts as to that of governing the city, there is no suggestion of applying it to the women of any class but the guardians. The only possible explanation seems to be that where the family is retained, women continue to be private wives and functional mothers, so that their equality with men in other roles is not considered an open issue.[42]

Second, what happens to women in Plato's second-best city—that depicted in *The Laws*—overwhelmingly confirms our hypothesis. On the subject of women, Plato in *The Laws* presents a study in ambivalence. He is caught in a dilemma caused by the impossibility of reconciling his increasingly firm beliefs about the potential of the female sex with the reintroduction of private property and the family into the social structure of his city. On the one hand, having thought about women as individuals with vast unused talents, Plato seems to have been more convinced than ever, by the time he wrote *The Laws*, that existing practice with regard to women was foolish and that they should be educated and used to their greatest capacity. In theory, the radical statements about women from *Republic* 5 are carried in *The Laws* to new extremes. On the other hand, *The Laws* is a considerably less revolutionary document than *The Republic*; far from being "a pattern laid up in heaven," the second-best city is put forward as a far less utopian construct.[43] The very title of the dialogue, usually translated "Laws," is in fact more accurately rendered as "Tradition." A significant casualty of this "realism" is Plato's conception of the role of women. What is proposed for them in general terms is simply not fulfilled by the details of the society, in which they are again private wives and the functioning mothers of particular children.

Plato's arguments and conclusions in *The Laws* about the natural potential of women are far more radical than those of *The Republic*. He appears to attribute to the different rearing and education of the two sexes practically all differences in their subsequent abilities and achievements. Pointing to the example of the Sarmatian women, who participate in warfare equally with the men, as proof of the potential of the female sex, he argues that the Athenian practice of maintaining rigid sex roles is absurd. Only a legislator's "surprising blunder" could allow the waste of half the state's available resources, by prescribing that "most irrational" practice—"that men and women should not all follow the same pursuits with one accord and with all their might."[44] In addition, a few speeches before these striking assertions are made, Plato prepares for them with an elaborate metaphor about ambidexterity—a lightly veiled allusion to his belief that men and women, like right and left hands, would be fare more equal in ability if they received equal training.[45]

By the time he wrote *The Laws*, then, Plato had clearly come to recognize that female human nature was not fairly represented by the deprived and stunted women of his own society. Indeed, it was as yet unknown, although one could derive some impression of women's potential from the example of the female warriors who in other societies held their own with men in battle. However, in *The Laws*, the statements of general principle about women are far more radical than the actual details of the society as it is drawn up. Having made the

general proclamation that the law should prescribe the same education and training for girls as it does for boys and that "the female
sex must share with the male, to the greatest extent possible, both
in education and in all else"—should "share with men in the whole
of their mode of life"[46]—Plato's Athenian legislator fails to apply
these precepts, in many of the most crucial instances. In order to
understand the inconsistency between the general statements about
women and the detailed specifications given for the most important
of civic duties, we must turn to the effects on women of the reintroduction of private property and the family.

Though it is clearly a source of regret to Plato, he concedes that the
citizens of the second-best city, not being gods or sons of gods, are
not capable of holding their property in common. The reinstatement
of private property, one of the most far-reaching differences between
The Laws and *The Republic*, brings with it in the same paragraph the
reintroduction of marriage and the family.[47] It is clear from the context that the need for a property-holding man to have an heir requires
the disappearance of communal ownership of women and children
simultaneously with that of other property. However, the identification of women and children together with other possessions was so
automatic to the Greek mind that, again, no separate justification is
felt to be necessary. The failure to achieve communism of property,
it seems, entails the private possession of women.

The family, moreover, is the basis of the polity planned in *The
Laws*. As Glenn Morrow has noted, "the state is a union of households or families, not a collection of detached citizens," and "the
vitality of the family in Plato's state is evident at many points in his
legislation."[48] The existence of family shrines, the complexity of marriage and inheritance laws, the family's crucial role in the prosecution
of criminal justice, and the denial to sons of the right to defend themselves against their fathers—all these provisions indicate the central
and authoritative position of the family.[49] The marriage laws are the
first to be drawn up, and their repercussions for the position of women are immediate and extensive. In contrast to the temporary mating system of *The Republic*, in which neither sex had more freedom
to choose or refuse a mate than the other, the reintroduction of permanent marriage seems to involve, without any explanation, a very
different degree of choice of spouse for women and men. Marriage
is to be compulsory for all, since procreation is regarded as a universal duty. But whereas a man is subject only to the provision that

he seek a partnership that will result in the best offspring for his society and can decide whom he will marry, a woman is "given" in marriage. The "right of valid betrothal" of a woman belongs in turn to a long succession of male kindred, and only if she has no close male relatives at all can she have any say in choosing her husband. Ironically, considering this preemption of women's choice, Plato refuses to enforce legally the prohibition of unsuitable marriages, since he considers that to do so, "besides being ridiculous, would cause widespread resentment."[50] Apparently what was to be customary for women was considered intolerable control, if applied to men.

The treatment of women by the marriage laws is closely related to the fact that they are virtually excluded from property ownership. Even if she has no brothers, a daughter can participate in the inheritance of the family estate only by serving as the instrument through which the husband that her father chooses for her can become her father's heir, if she has no brothers.[51] *The Laws* documents the essential connection of property and inheritance to the marriage system and position of women. When a man owns inheritable property, he must own a wife too, in order to ensure a legitimate heir. The fact that women are private wives entails that in many ways they are treated as property rather than as persons. They themselves cannot inherit real property, which to a large extent defines personhood within the society (a disinherited son must leave the city unless another citizen adopts him as his heir);[52] and they are treated as commodities to be given away by their male relatives. With these as the basic features of the social structure of the city, it is not surprising that Plato, in spite of general pronouncements to the contrary, is not able to treat women as the equals of his male citizens. Their status as property seems to prevent the execution of his declared intentions.

Although the legal status of women in Plato's second-best city is an improvement on that in contemporary Athens, it is not one of equality with men. Glenn Morrow has said that "it is certainly Plato's expressed intention (though not fully carried out) to give women a more equal status under the law. . . ."[53] The proposed divorce laws, unlike the marriage laws, do treat women considerably more equally than did those of contemporary Athens; the criminal statutes enforce the same punishments for the wounding or murder of wives as of husbands, and they are generally applied without discrimination according to the sex of either plaintiff or defendant.[54] The most striking instance of equal treatment before the law is in the case of extra-marital intercourse, where the same penalties are extended to offenders of both sexes. This unusual departure from the double standard that one might expect to find in a society so firmly based on monogamy and inheritance can probably be explained by Plato's wish to make all the members of his city as virtuous and temperate as possible. After all, the standards are not relaxed for women, but they are considerably tightened for men. However, the Athenian concept of women as legal minors is still present in significant ways in *The Laws*. Besides not being eligible to own property, they are not allowed until the age of forty to give evidence in a court of law or to support a plea, and only if unmarried are they allowed to bring an action.[55] Women, especially if married, are still to a large extent *femmes couvertes*.

What begins to be revealed through the denial of important civil and legal rights to women is strongly confirmed by the roles allotted to them within the official governmental sphere. In *The Republic*, once we have been told that women of the guardian class are to share with men in every aspect of ruling and guarding, they are not specifically assigned to any particular offices, and there is no implication that they are ineligible for any. The only case where women are specifically mentioned as being eligible for office is at the end of Socrates' account of the philosophers' education. Here, presumably because the very idea must have seemed so outrageous, Plato feels it necessary to remind his audience that everything he has been saying applies equally to all women with the necessary abilities.[56] It is most unlikely that the women guardians, if allowed to compete for the highest rank of all, would have been excluded from any other office.

In *The Laws*, by contrast, in spite of the general pronouncements cited above, Plato both specifies when a certain function, such as the priesthood, is to be performed by persons of both sexes, and makes particular mention of women's holding certain offices, frequently with the strong implication that only women are eligible for them. Thus, it is women who supervise married couples, who look after infants, whose role in the educational system is to provide the children's meals and oversee their games—in short, who perform, in positions not of the highest rank, all those domestic, nurturing, child-oriented tasks to which women have traditionally been assigned. On the other hand, there is no hint of women's participation in the magistracy, or the "divine nocturnal synod," whose role parallels that of the philosophers in *The Republic*. The children are given their lessons by male educational officers; the post of supervisor of education is "by far the most important . . . of the highest offices of the State" and must be filled by "that one of the citizens who is in every way the most excellent," and it is explicitly laid down that its occupant be male, for he must be "the father of legitimate children."[57] This qualification adds weight to what is implied throughout the work—that in the second-best city, unless the eligibility of women is plainly mentioned, most offices, and especially high ones, are reserved for men.[58] Even for those in which she can share, a woman is not eligible until she is forty, whereas a man is eligible from the age of thirty.[59]

In spite of his controversial proposal in *The Laws* that, in the interests of order and discipline, even married women should take their meals communally, though segregated from the men, it is clear that Plato was ambivalent about the wisdom, or perhaps the feasibility, of bringing wives out of their domestic seclusion. Thus when he describes the funeral processions for distinguished citizens, women of child-bearing age are noticeably omitted from a list in which every other class of citizen has its place. They are similarly omitted from the choral competitions. Most remarkable, however, given his previous insistence that neither gymnastics nor riding are improper for women, and that trained women can perform in the military sphere equally as well as men, is the fact that, once the detailed regulations are being made, he exempts women almost entirely from military service. Young girls are to learn the military arts only "if they agree to it," whereas boys are obliged to study them. Then, although he makes the general provision that men, women, and children are all to participate in military training at least one day a month, when the details are given, women after the age of marriage (twenty at the latest) are again noticeably absent. They are not included either in races or in wrestling, both of which are integral parts of the training. As for horsemanship, it is decreed that "it is not worthwhile to make compulsory laws and rules about their taking part in such sports," but that they may do so "without blame," if they like.[60] It should be noted that Plato was not in the habit of making aspects of his educational systems optional—particularly those relating to the defense of the state.

Finally, whereas the term of military service for men is from the ages of twenty to sixty, "for women they shall ordain what is possible and fitting in each case, after they have finished bearing children, and up to the age of fifty, in whatever kind of military work it may be thought right to employ their services."[61] This means that for all the grand assertions about the necessity and rationality of women's being trained equally with men to share in the defense of the state, they are in fact allowed (but not compelled) to train up to the age of, at the latest, twenty; they are then excluded from most military activity until they are past the age of child bearing, and they are subsequently exempted again at fifty. In a society that condoned only conjugal sex, and where contraception was hardly in an advanced state, this could well mean an expectation of five years of military service from adult women. Surely this was no way to produce Amazons.

Despite Plato's professed intention of having the women of the second-best city share equally with the men in all the duties of citizenship, their role as private wives curtails their participation in public life for three reasons. The first is that they are subject to pregnancy and lactation, which is not controlled and predictable as it was in *The Republic*, where the guardians were to mate only at the behest of the rulers. In *The Laws*, since women are permanent wives, they are far less able to time or limit their pregnancies and cannot be held continuously liable for public and, especially, military duties. Second, the reinstitution of the private household makes each wife into the mistress responsible for its welfare, and it is clear that in *The Laws* a mother is to participate far more in early child care than did the female guardian, who was not even to know which child was hers.[62]

The third reason is that Plato found it inconceivable that women who are "private wives"—the private property of the male citizens—should play the same kind of public and, especially, military roles as the female guardians, who were not defined in terms of a traditional relationship to a man. Whereas the female guardians, like their male counterparts, could exercise naked, the young girls in *The Laws* must be "clad in decent apparel," as if a maiden who was shortly to become the respectable wife and private property of a citizen could hardly be seen naked by the world at large.[63] Plato seems to expect ridicule for his suggestion in *The Laws* that wives should dine at public, though segregated, tables, just as he had expected ridicule for his proposal in *The Republic* that all the guardians of both sexes should exercise together naked.[64] Although he thought it even more dangerous to leave women undisciplined than to neglect men, and insisted that women too should dine in public, he was well aware that, in the kind of society he was planning, there would be enormous resistance to such an idea. Consequently, although he deplored the fact that even the supposedly trained women of Sparta had panicked and run when an enemy invaded their city, and thought it folly that so important a potential for defense as the entire female sex should be neglected, he seems to have found it impossible to hold to his original proposal that women should participate in military activities equally with men. If the segregated public dining of private wives could cause a general outcry, there was no knowing what revolutions might be provoked by the proposal that men should mingle with other men's private wives on the battlefield. Despite all his professed intentions in *The Laws* to emancipate women and make full use of the talents that he was now convinced they had, Plato's reintroduction of the family has the direct effect of putting them firmly back into their traditional place.

In *The Republic*, because the abolition of property and the family for the guardian class entails the abolition of woman's traditional sphere, the difference between the sexes is reduced to that of their roles in procreation. Since the nature of the women of this class is declared to be the same as that of the men, the radical proposal that their educations and lifestyles are to be identical follows accordingly. Plato has prescribed an androgynous character for all the guardians; both male and female are to be courageous and gentle, and both, because of their education and continued fellowship, will hold precious the good of the entire community. For the purposes of this society, therefore, the abolition of traditional sex roles is declared to be far more in accordance with nature than is the conventional adherence to them.

In *The Laws*, by contrast, the reinstatement of property requires monogamy and private households, and thus restores women to their role of "private wives" with all that this entails. Although his general statements about women's potential are considerably stronger here than in *The Republic*, Plato *cannot*, because of the economic and social structure he has prescribed, carry out to any significant extent the revolution in woman's role that would seem to follow from such beliefs. In this society, the "nature" of woman must be different from the "nature" of man. She must be pure and respectable, as befits a private wife who is to ensure the legitimacy of the property owner's heir, while he is to retain the noble and courageous qualities that resemble those of the ideal guardian.

The striking difference between the roles of women in *The Republic* and *The Laws*, then, is not due to a change in Plato's beliefs about the nature and capacities of women. The difference is due to the abolition of private property and the family in the interest of unity in the former dialogue, and their reinstatement in the latter. When woman is once again perceived as the privately owned appendage of a man, when the family and its needs define her function, the socialization and regulation prescribed for her must ensure that her "nature" is formed and preserved in accordance with this role.

The family has often been virtually ignored by students of political thought. Simplistic distinctions between the public and the private, and narrow conceptions of the proper subject matter of politics have frequently resulted in its relegation to the sphere of the nonpolitical. As has been demonstrated, however, one ignores the family and philosophers' views of it only at risk of missing or misunderstanding other important, closely related, social and political issues.

Aristotle, the Public-Private Split, and the Case of the Suffragists

☼ *Jean Bethke Elshtain*

It is a part of the common wisdom of our political and historic past that the fight for female suffrage failed to alter significantly the system of social constraints that intertwined to oppress women in both the economic and political spheres. Admittedly, the majority of suffragists were engaged in a struggle for legal equality only—many in the hope that other changes would quickly follow upon the reform in statutes discriminating against women in the holding of property, in bringing action in civil suits, and in exercising the franchise. It is my contention that the suffragists' theoretical and political failure, in a wider sense, can be traced, first, to the manner in which they initially analyzed their dilemma and, second, to the proposed remedies that followed from this analysis. Indeed, I shall argue that, with few exceptions, the suffragists did not confront the full scope and basis of one of our system's basic incoherencies or "crimes of birth"[1] (that is, flaws of construction) and thus they were incapable of moving beyond the symptoms of sexual inequality.

An appreciation of the discursive background to suffragist thought and action necessitates a critical exploration of the theoretical and ideological split between what had come to be the public, political realm of immoral man and the private, apolitical realm of moral woman. To get at these mirror images I will first examine the notions of *public* and *private persons;* the relationship of these persons to systems of *public* and *private morality;* and the link of both to *politics* and that which is *not-politics.* I begin with the conceptual categories of Aristotle's *Politics.*

For Aristotle, the good life was possible only through participation in the life of the *polis,* the "final and perfect association." Man himself was "by nature an animal intended to live in a *polis*."[2] Although all associations aimed at some good, it was in the *polis* that the highest good was attained; therefore, only those persons who were its citizens achieved complete good.[3] Women, slaves, and children did not partake in the full realization of goodness and rationality that defined co-equal participants in the perfect association. There was an "essential" difference between greater (free, male) and lesser (unfree, female) persons, but these two classes of people were nonetheless linked together in relationships of *necessary* dominance and subordination. A nexus between "the naturally ruling element with the element which is naturally ruled" was essential to "the preservation of both."[4]

Aristotle rejected the notion that power over others was *automatically* tied to goodness. He urged instead that "the superior in goodness ought to rule over inferiors"; that power must be accompanied by goodness before it can become an element in a *legitimate* relationship between master and slave, or male and female; nevertheless, because the mere *fact* of such rule implied the existence of superior goodness in the dominant party, that is, a man could not be the slave of another were he not capable of becoming another's property and of apprehending the full reason and goodness in his master that he himself lacked,[5] power over another tended to accompany goodness in Aristotle's ideal.

The household comprised the nonpublic sphere within which the female was subsumed and which defined her. Because the good at which the household (*oikos*) aimed was a lesser good than that which was the end of the *polis*, the wife-mother achieved only the limited goodness of the "naturally ruled," a goodness different in kind from that of the naturally ruling. (Females possessed reason in a similarly incomplete, "inconclusive" form.) Aristotle states: "The ruler, accordingly, must possess moral goodness in its full and perfect form (i.e., the form based on rational deliberation), because his function, regarded absolutely and in its full nature, demands a master-artificer, and reason is such a master-artificer; but all other persons need only possess moral goodness to the extent required of them (by their particular position)."[6]

Aristotle's theory of citizenship emerges from his presumption that the life of the *polis* is superior to any other. A citizen in the strict sense (after paring away certain disqualifications or defects of youth, age, infirmity, and so on), is "best defined by the one criterion, 'a man who shares in the administration of justice and in the holding of office.' " The state "in its simplest terms" is a body of such persons adequate . . . for achieving a self-sufficient existence."[7] A good citizen isn't necessarily coterminous with a good man—not because there are divergent notions of "goodness," but because concepts of citizenship differ from state-to-state. The two can be linked, however, in the paradigm case of the good citizen living under an ideal constitution.

Where do "lesser" persons fit into this scheme of things? Aristotle makes a distinction between women, children, slaves, "mechanics and labourers," and citizens. The latter alone comprise the "integral parts" of the state. The former are its "necessary conditions" who, although they do not share in public life per se, nevertheless provide the basis or precondition upon which that public life rests. Aristotle compares rulers and subjects to flute players and flute makers; one makes use of what the other makes.[8]

What, to summarize thus far, emerges from Aristotle's discussion in terms of the questions posed at the outset concerning public and private persons, morality, and the connection of both to politics? Aristotle splits the public (political) from the private (nonpolitical) realm. There are greater (public) associations and lesser (private) associations. Fully realized moral goodness and reason are attainable only through participation in public life, and this involvement is re- served for free, adult males. Women *share* in goodness and rationality in the limited sense appropriate to their confinement in a lesser associ- ation, the household. Their relationship to the public realm is that of one of its "necessary" conditions rather than its "integral parts." In- deed, it can be said that women in Aristotle's schema are "idiots" in the Greek sense of the word, that is, persons who do not participate in the *polis*.[9] Politics—the life of rationality, responsibility, and the highest system of justice—is that activity that defines the *polis*. Aris- totle's views can be set forth as a series of dichotomies or "typologies" of persons, moralities, and public and private life.[10]

Public (Political)

Public persons are responsible, rational persons who share fully in both private life *and* the life of the *polis* and its *integral* elements (citizens). As citizens, such persons participate in the highest moral good and system of justice. In the ideal state, the good man and the good citizen are cotermi- nous. The life of the whole is superior in nature, intent, and purpose to that of all lesser associations.

Private (Nonpolitical)

Private persons are those who (for whatever reason) are not fully rational and who can only share in the limited goodness appropriate to their spheres. They are confined to these spheres and as such form a *necessary* condition for the superior public realm. The life of lesser associations, including the household, is inferior in nature, intent, and purpose to that of the more inclusive association.

The dichotomies are necessary ones given Aristotle's conceptual system that entails a rigid differentiation between all phenomena—biological and social—under his principle of entelechy. In Aristotelian philosophy, entelechy means "completed actuality" as opposed to "potentiality."[11] In simplest terms, what *is* is what *ought to be* because whatever *ought to be* has been actualized, that is, *is*.

The normative import of Aristotle's theories in terms of the actual operation of Greek politics lies in the fact that his concepts could be used to justify slavery, to defend the dominance of women by men, and to support as well the subordination of certain "underclasses." His concepts additionally strengthened the notion that Athenians, as superior participants in the ideal state, had a right to extend their sway over certain lesser, barbarous peoples.[12]

Aristotelian categories continued to exert great influence over subsequent discussions of public and private realms and of political personhood. Having put the proposition baldly, I would first like to lodge a partial caveat. A shift occurred in the work of postmedieval political theorists from a controlling definition of the political realm as an arena with intrinsic moral purposes, governed at least in part by moral rules and considerations, to one in which force alone constituted the final political appeal. Early modern political theorists, of whom Bodin and Machiavelli were the most important, responding to the growth in power and complexity of states governed by rulers who grew increasingly more secular, elaborated grandiose conceptions of political sovereignty and raison d'état. These theories, in turn, were used to rationalize and justify sovereign power and the use of force, and as such they became constitutive elements in its exercise.

The recognition that force is or can be the *ultima ratio* of politics was not, of course, new. St. Augustine observed it and, before him, Thrasymachus.[13] But with Bodin and Machiavelli politics was celebrated as the use of force *par excellence*. The state for Jean Bodin was an entity possessing perpetual, absolute sovereignty (*puissance souver-*

aine) with unlimited authority to make laws.[14] The perspective that had prevailed in medieval political theory, as well as in the thought of Aristotle, Plato, and the Stoic philosophers, did not separate politics from knowledge and pursuit of the good. The new definition of politics as the exercise of force on the highest levels, and of the state as (above all else) an organization of violence, perhaps tempered by law, reinforced Aristotelian distinctions between public and private persons and spheres, but invited a bifurcation *not* present in Aristotelian thought: the divorce of politics from moral considerations.

In order to be politically "good," that is, efficacious in the exercise of force, Machiavelli's prince had to be capable of being "bad" according to the standards of Christian morality. Machiavelli adjured that a good prince was one who could deliver the goods. This meant that a man could be a good ruler and a perfectly horrid person if private morality were set up as the criterion by which to judge his public actions—a concept that Machiavelli rejected.[15] Rules of conduct appropriate to the public sphere were inappropriate to the private one, and the obverse also pertained. The (im)morality of the public sphere as a competing system of morality—a "new" morality of politics, of rules appropriate to holding and exercising power on the macro-level, received full elaboration.[16] "Good" and "bad," as these terms related to what was public and private, political and non-political, lost any universalized meaning.

If the public and private spheres are radically separated, two divergent sets of stardards by which conduct in either realm is to be judged may be erected. The two realms become, in a real sense, incommensurable. But there is a complication in this tidy deal: individuals do not share equally in both spheres. Man has two statuses: as a public person and as a private person; therefore, men are subject to two disparate judgments in their capacities as public and private persons.

Woman, however, is totally immersed in the private, nonpublic realm and is judged by the single standard appropriate to that realm alone. She does not share in public life, hence she does not participate in the "good" (the competing standard of morality) of that life. According to this system, if a woman should "go public" (or attempt to) she is still to be judged as a private person. All that women were in private (kind, virtuous, loving, responsible) men could attempt to become with the aid and succor of women; but women could not "become" what men were (responsible public persons) without forsaking their womanhood by definition.[17]

The combined Aristotelian power politics perspective, a male-dominant system, is a set of partial or whole mirror images, each dependent on the other.

Public (Im)Morality

A "bad" man can be a "good" politician but he can also be a "good" man in private. What is moral in the public realm cannot be judged by the standards of private moral conduct; therefore, public persons are judged one way in their capacity as public persons and another way in their existence as private persons.

Politics

Politics is the realm of public power, the sphere of justice, and systems of law. The state is a body of citizens subject to laws. Political leaders are also subject to laws but not necessarily bound by them in the exercise of power. Women are not part of politics per se, but provide, in their capacities in the private sphere, a refuge from public life for men when they share in the private sphere.

Private Morality

A "good" woman makes a "bad" citizen by definition. The woman who is a "good" citizen cannot, in the private sphere, be a "good" woman. She is judged in each instance by standards of so-called private morality. She is not to share in public (im)morality. Women are morally "superior" because they are publicly inferior.

Nonpolitics

Nonpolitics is a private realm of feeling and sentiment, or moral suasion, not subject to laws and not judged by rational standards. If there is power in this sphere it is power as covert manipulation, deceit, and cunning. This realm is not properly part of the public sphere but provides a base for it. Women are part of nonpolitics, and so are men in their "private" capacities.

The political effect of these powerful typologies are incalculable. The splits were seen as necessary in order to maintain politics, law, order, justice, and sovereignty on the one hand, and to protect the innocent and helpless, preserve the home and its private virtues, and provide succor for those [men] seeking respite from the public world on the other. I shall now explore the influence of this particular version of the public-private split on the woman's suffrage movement.

On what terms did the suffragists lodge their battle for sexual equality? In what categories did they analyze their dilemma and propose remedies? With few exceptions, the suffragists accepted (implicitly if not explicitly) the presumptions of what might be called the Aristotelian power-politics paradigm even as they simply placed a different interpretation on certain of its features. Their arguments for the franchise involved some shifting and rearranging of terms but did not entail a paradigm shift.[18] Proceeding, in many instances, from the assumptions held by their opponents, the suffragists perpetuated the mystifications and unexamined presumptions that served to rig the system against them.

The following, for example, is a typical antisuffragist argument:

Man assumed the direction of government and war, woman of the domestic and family affairs and the care and training of the child. . . . It has been so from the beginning, throughout the whole history of man, and it will continue to be so to the end, because it is in conformity to nature and its laws, and is sustained and confirmed by the experience and reason of six thousand years. . . . The domestic altar is a sacred flame where woman is the high and officiating priestess. . . . To keep her in that condition of purity, it is necessary that she should be separated from the exercise of suffrage and from all those stern and contaminating and demoralizing duties that devolves upon the hardier sex—man.[19]

The statement sets into relief the notions that man and woman are different in essence and hence must have separate spheres of activity. (Or, man and woman have separate spheres of activity *because* they are different in essence.) Politics is by definition the man's sphere; it follows, a fortiori, that woman has nothing to do with politics. To the man alone lies those "stern . . . contaminating . . . demoralizing" duties. Woman had more important duties. Rev. N. J. Danforth, in a treatise called *The Ladies Casket*, proclaimed: "Oh, mother, acquit thyself well in thy humble sphere, for thou mayest affect the world." And one Rev. Harrington felt assured that most women, rejecting the suffragists, would cry: "Let the men take care of politics, we will take care of the children!"[20]

Women were separate but equal.[21] Suffrage opponents elaborated on this theme:

The Creator has assigned to woman very laborious and responsible duties, by no means less important than those imposed upon the male sex, though entirely different in their character. . . . While the man is contending with the sterner duties of life, the whole time of the noble, affectionate and true woman is required in the discharge of her delicate and difficult duties assigned her in the family circle, in her relations and in the society where her lot is cast. . . . I believe that they [women] are better than men, but I do not believe that they are adapted to the political work of this world. . . . I would not, and I say it deliberately, degrade woman by giving her the right of suffrage. I mean the word in its full signification, because I believe that woman as she is today, the queen of home and of hearts, is above the political collision of this world, and should always be kept above them.[22]

What was the response of the suffragists to arguments that woman was pure, private, and apolitical and man was immoral, public, and political (because his sphere was)? Rather than rejecting the conceptual system from which these notions were a predictable outgrowth, the suffragists frequently turned antisuffrage arguments upside down to serve as the basis for a prosuffrage plea. Yes, man was evil and bad and he had made something nasty out of politics. True, woman was purer and more virtuous—look at the way she had ennobled the private sphere. What must be done is throw the mantle of private morality *over* the public sphere by drawing women *into* it. Women would be politicized and politics would be transformed in one fell swoop.[23]

Elizabeth Cady Stanton, the most important of the early suffrage theorists, espoused the female-superiority view with vehemence in several speeches and essays:

The male element is a destructive force, stern, selfish, aggrandizing, loving war, violence, conquest, acquisition, breeding in the material and moral world alike discord, disorder, disease and death. See what a record of blood and cruelty the pages of history reveal! Through what slavery, and slaughter, and sacrifice, through what inquisitions and imprisonments, pains and persecutions, black codes and gloomy creeds, the soul of humanity has struggled for centuries, while mercy has veiled her face and all hearts have been dead alike to love and hope! The male element has held high carnival thus far, it has fairly run riot from the beginning, overpowering the feminine element everywhere, crushing out the diviner qualities in human nature until we know but little of true manhood and womanhood, of the latter comparatively nothing, for it has scarce been recognized as a power until within the last century. . . . The need of this hour is not territory, gold mines, railroads, or specie payments, but a new evangel of womanhood, to exalt purity, virtue, morality, true religion, to lift man up into the higher realms of thought and action. . . .[24]

The image enunciated by Stanton holds that the male element—destructive and selfish—is in control. The female element—loving and virtuous—is enslaved and intimidated. If social chaos is to be prevented, the balance must be tipped to the feminine element.

Theodore Parker, a male suffragist and a member of that group of New England transcendentalists that included Margaret Fuller, cast a backward glance at human history and observed that things would have been much different had women exerted political control.

If the affairs of the nation had been under woman's joint control, I doubt that we should have butchered the Indians with such exterminating savagery, that, in fifty years, we should have spent seven hundred millions of dollars for war, and now, in time of peace, send twenty annual millions more to the same waste. I doubt that we should have spread slavery into nine new States, and made it national. I think the Fugitive Slave Bill would never have been an act. Woman has some respect for the natural law of God.[25]

The following excerpts, from arguments for suffrage made in 1898 and 1905 respectively, echo one another in their celebration of woman's unique superior nature and sphere and of what her entry into politics would mean. "Wherever the State touches the personal life of the infant, the child, the youth, or the aged, helpless, defective in mind, . . . there the State enters 'woman's peculiar sphere,' her sphere of motherly succor and training. . . ."[26] "Does an intelligent interest in the education of a child render a woman less a mother? Does the housekeeping instinct of woman, manifested in a desire for clean streets, pure water, and unadulterated food, destroy her efficiency as a home-maker? Does a desire for an environment of moral and civic purity show neglect for the highest good of the family?"[27]

As the suffrage fight progressed women increasingly proclaimed their purity in religious terms and flatly contended that Christ himself received his "sweet, tender, suffering humanity . . . wholly from woman." Women, consequently, "have a greater share of Him than men have." If elected to public office, women would "far more effectively guard the morals of society, and the sanitary conditions of cities."[28] There were suffragists who admitted that the vote for women would not cure all society's ills, but they believed it would mean that governments responsible to women would be more likely to conserve life and preserve morals. Even the remedy for the evil of the liquor traffic lay in woman's suffrage. The social triumph of Christ's Golden Rule would be a corollary achievement.[29]

Why were suffragists constrained to celebrate their nobility and the purity of women? Why did they make such outrageous claims for the power of the ballot and their abilities to use the ballot to transform public life? They readily admitted to being "dreamers" (again the adoption of an epithet turned on its head to create a presumed virtue): "We are told that to assume that women will help purify political life and develop a more ideal government but proves us to be dreamers of dreams. Yes, we are in a goodly company of dreamers, of Confucius, of Buddha, of Jesus, of the English Commons fighting for the Magna Charta, . . ."[30] The answer to these troubling questions becomes somewhat clearer if one remembers that perspective they had implicitly embraced secreted controlling presumptions for both politics and the private realm. For women to reject its terms would have meant a rejection of the Victorian version of marriage and family life that revolved around the image of a saintly, sexless, wife-mother. The sexual Manicheanism[31] of the nineteenth century, reinforced by the interlocking images I have explored, was so deeply entrenched that the majority of suffragists could not and did not consider the manner in which this image served to reinforce male dominance.

Certain scholars see the emphasis by suffragists on woman's superior virtue as one indication of a shift in the movement from arguments for the vote based on "justice" to arguments based on "expedience." Aileen Kraditor contends that the early suffragist arguments demanded political equality "on the same ground as that on which men had based their demand for political equality with their English rulers two generations before."[32] I agree with Kraditor that a shift in emphasis did occur. But I do not see this, as she apparently does, as a major qualitative change; rather, it seems to me an altered emphasis within a complex tradition.

Kraditor herself points out that most of the suffragists belonged to the same native-born, white, middle to upper-middle class, Anglo-Saxon Protestant group as the male-dominant group of American society. She sees the expedience argument as one made to appeal to that group. Because the suffragists shared the same class status as the dominant males, they also shared identical class prejudices—without, however, sharing in the political power of the males of their class. The following statements are representative of the "expediency" approach to giving the vote to women.

You did not trust the Southern freedman to the arbitrary will of courts and States! Why send your mothers, wives and daughters to the unwashed, unlettered, unthinking masses that carry popular elections?[33]

We ask for the ballot for the good of the race. . . . When you debar from your councils and legislative halls the purity, the spirituality and the love of woman, those councils are apt to become coarse and brutal. God gave us to you to help you in this little journey to a better land, and by our love and our intellect to help make our country pure and noble. . . .

Woman's vote is needed for the good of others. Our horizon is misty with apparent dangers. Woman may aid in dispelling them. . . . She desires the homes of the land to be pure and sober; with her help they may become so. . . .

"Real democracy" has not yet existed and "never will" until women receive the ballot. Instead, "the dangerous experiment has been made of enfranchising the vast proportion of crime, intemperance, immorality and dishonesty, and barring absolutely from the suffrage the great proportion of temperance, morality, religion, and conscientiousness; that, in others words, the worst elements have been put into the ballot-boxes and the best elements kept out."[34]

We point to the official statistics for proof that there are more white women in the United States than colored men and women together; that there are more American-born women than foreign-born men and women combined; that women form only one-eleventh of the criminals in the jails and penitentiaries, that they compose more than two-thirds of the church membership, and that the percentage of illiteracy is very much less among women than among men. Therefore we urge that this large proportion of patriotism, temperance, morality, religion and intelligence be allowed to impress itself upon the government through the medium of the ballot-box.[35]

The shift in emphasis to rationales of expedience for women's suffrage is further evidence of the effects on women of their internalization of the terms of the Aristotelian power-politics perspective. The way in which the original argument for justice was framed contained the seeds of the expediency justification, for it meant the suffragists had implicitly adopted a set of beliefs about themselves and their society. Their failure lay in an understanding that was tied to the dominant ideology. With the achievement of suffrage, this ideology remained and continued to gloss over the deep structural binds of the system with the assurance that these inequalities emerged "naturally," or justifiably through "free" competition and therefore lay outside the sphere of politics. The majority of suffragists accepted their dematerialization, the terms of sexual Manicheanism. They wished to draw "their" men into this rarified realm and to exclude the more bestial and animalistic underclasses (whose "overbreeding" constituted a clear and present danger to Anglo-Saxon dominance). Dematerialization was a function of both their sex and their social class.

Political power—associated with war, force, and violence—was anathema to the suffragists. Such power was an aspect of the public, male sphere they wished to join and, by joining, transform. Rosemary Radford Ruether points out that by the mid-nineteenth century and the beginning of suffragist protest, the splits between public and private spheres and moralities had already had a devastating, impoverishing effect on both realms.[36] Moral virtues had been so "sentimentalized and privatized they ceased to have serious public power."[37] Morality was identified with the feminine sphere. In the rough and tumble world of politics, such morality was deemed "unrealistic."

The political world demanded "hard, practical aggressivity, devoid of sentiment or moralizing." A male participates in this world during the day; in the evening he repairs "to the idealized world of the 'Home' where all moral and spiritual values are confined."[38] What the suffragists did by accepting a definition of themselves that arose out of their powerlessness (which meant embracing their purity and victimization) was to reinforce a set of views that were strongly arrayed against full female political participation and socioeconomic equality.[39]

Suffragists' insistence on their purity and their dependence upon moral suasion as the means to reform meant they could gloss over a hard look at political power: What was it? How was it gained? To what ends was it (could it be) used? In their scheme of things, if women gained political power, that power would be transformed into a moral force. Women would not have to face issues arising from those ambiguous situations in which political judgments were made with no clear-cut array of the good and the bad on one side or the other. Women would use the vote to change society, but the vote would not change women.

That woman will, by voting, lose nothing of man's courteous, chivalric attention and respect is admirably proven by the manner in which both houses of congress, in the midst of the most anxious and perplexing presidential conflict in our history, received their appeals from twenty-three States for a sixteenth amendment protecting the rights of women.[40]

I will say to woman's credit she has not sought office, she is not a natural office-seeker, but she desires to vote. . . .[41]

Woman's work during the nation's various wars showed that "women were clearer and more exalted than the men, because their moral feelings and political instincts were not so much affected by selfishness, or business, or party consideration. . . ."[42]

Because the suffragists assumed that moral high-mindedness was almost exclusively a female trait, they could treat obliquely (or not at all) the argument that moving into public life would force women into a change of habits, attitudes, and standards. Women would remain guileless. Once the private had become public, politics in the traditional sense would come to an end. Operating within a male-dominant frame, the form, language, and mode of suffragist protest were set as much by their absorption in the sexual idealizations and mystifications of their time as by the objective conditions of female oppression.

That suffragists ultimately concentrated upon the trappings rather than the substance of male power indicates that the dominant perspective triumphed in the end. The result was the failure of the suffragists to achieve an original political vision. The suffragists said they wanted equality within the extant structure, but that structure was one of sex dominance by definition. They apparently did not see through the fact that the ideal of "woman," which they celebrated, included the idea of "man," which they denigrated, that these concepts were necessarily connected. The controlling images of "woman" and "man," in turn, were linked to a larger matrix, a social structure within which these relations made sense. As Peter Winch has pointed out, the idea we form of an object includes the idea of connections between it and other objects.[43]

The suffragists' ultimate conclusions were that private morality could be transferred to the public level; that public persons ought to be judged by the rigorous standards of the private sphere; that the public (im)moral qualities men exhibited were probably innate to the male character, but that they, too, could be transformed (as could public life by the entry of women into it); that the qualities women exhibited were innate and were not merely an outgrowth of their enforced domesticity; that these same qualities were the qualities that would invest the political sphere with a sanctified aura. In the suffragist future, if a man wished to be a good citizen he would have to take on the cloak of selflessness and private virtue. None of the suffragist conclusions, taken singly or together, comprised an *important* conceptual revolution. Most suffragists simply wanted to take the identifying terms of the private sphere in the reigning paradigm and ramify these terms into the public sphere.

A demoralization set in among suffragists when votes for women did not achieve the miracles they had claimed it would. Women could vote, but the system was largely unmoved; the ideas and the economic and political realities underpinning it retained their viability. Women did not vote as a bloc nor organize into political movements to promote their interests by translating certain needs into interests. All of this is unsurprising given the assumption that women were to stay pure and to purify politics at the same time. When the vote for women did not see the victory of private morality in the public sphere, it led to a reversion to the full defining terms of the public-private split with the single exception that women could vote without completely losing their femininity or claims to private virtue. (Participation beyond the level of the vote did present such a danger, however.)

What has the split between public and private morality and politics meant for political inquiry? American political scientists work within a polity in which political structures have been denuded of a shared set of public moral values; a polity in which self-interest is the penultimate guide to political activity and political behavior; a polity in which vast inequities in the distribution of goods and services are considered normal; a polity in which sex and race inequality is part of the status quo; and, finally, a polity in which the private sphere retains its importance both as a haven and as a solace for (mostly male) adults from the harsh realities of the competitive work-a-day world and as the one arena within which expression of sentiment and moral values is acceptable.

Given the interrelated set of presumptions or conditions I have set forth, what outcomes for politics should I expect? Does mainstream political science, for example, consciously or unconsciously, adopt certain norms or desired outcomes on these issues? I would anticipate, minimally, that an analyst who accepts all or a major portion of the rigid public-private split I have discussed would urge (a) a definition of politics that either clearly defines where politics and the private sphere begin and end, or, in some other manner, excludes by definition the familial, private sphere within which most women are located from political consideration or concern; (b) a concept of political participation that involves some standard of an active and aware political citizen and goes on to judge individuals against that norm without giving consideration to the factors that mitigate against participation or, having looked at those factors, decides that participation isn't necessarily desirable for all; (c) a focus on political interest groups (given the dogma of politics as the sphere for the achievement of individual self-interest);[44] (d) a trivialization of moral concerns or values as they relate to public, political matters; (e) a justification or rationalization of the various systems of stratification in a society (sex, race, class, age) as long as the systems' stability is unthreatened.

The conceptual and ideological vision that together forms what I have called the Aristotelian power-politics paradigm perpetuates an arbitrary split between that which is politics and that which is not, and promotes an ideology that severs politics from coherent moral consideration and moral issues from that which is explicitly political or public. Implicit within this framework is a concept of persons that admits into the privileges of full personhood—the notion of an individual who is rational, responsible, capable of making choices, and judged according to a known set of rules and standards— only those individuals who hold dual status as both public and private persons, and denies such personhood to those individuals with a single private status.[45] The single-status individuals are assessed as if they were fully public persons, however, in order to point out their limitations and inadequacies. Women face a perpetual double-bind. Concerns that arise "naturally" from their position in the private sphere, including the health, education, and welfare of children, are deemed private expressions of personal values, but any hard-nosed, realistic talk about power from women means they have forfeited the right to represent to the public sphere the private world that they have presumably forsaken.

Political and Marital Despotism: Montesquieu's *Persian Letters*

Mary Lyndon Shanley & Peter G. Stillman

Montesquieu's *Persian Letters*, although frequently read as simply a youthful novel prefiguring some of the themes of *The Spirit of the Laws*, is a sustained and profound meditation on the interrelationships of familial and political life.[1] That meditation is clothed in a witty and engaging story, which is readily summarized. Two Persian men, Usbek and Rica, leave Persia to travel to France in 1711; the following year they arrive in France, where they stay through 1720. The novel consists of their letters, those of their friends and advisers, and those of the members of Usbek's seraglio (or harem) in Persia. The letters depict some political events of the reign of Louis XIV and the first years of the Regency; they satirize French and Persian social, political, and religious mores; and they chronicle the decline and eventual dissolution of Usbek's harem. Over the nine years of Usbek's absence his wives become increasingly unhappy and unruly. Finally, the women revolt, and Usbek in fury writes the eunuchs ordering them to constrain the women by force. The head eunuch undertakes a violent revenge throughout the seraglio. Usbek's favorite wife, Roxane, having taken a lover, denounces Usbek and kills herself.

The portrayal of the decay of the harem constitutes one of the most dramatic pictures of the evils of political despotism in the history of Western thought. In addition, the *Persian Letters* is a devastating critique of perverse and destructive sexual and familial relations. The harem is an analogue for both the political realm and the family, and Montesquieu uses the "harem sequence" to show how political and marital despotisms share certain characteristics of jealousy, falsehood, distrust, and hatred. The implications of Oriental despotism stand as a cautionary tale for French political and familial life.

Although commentators have frequently seen in the decay of the harem an analogue for the evils of political despotism, anticipating the discussion in Book 5 of *The Spirit of the Laws*, only a few have treated Montesquieu's presentation of relationships among members of the harem as worthy of critical attention.[2] But this dimension of the work is nonetheless essential, because part of Montesquieu's criticism of political despotism is his conviction that it corrupts not only the public realm, but also intimate human relations like marriage and even the souls of individuals, including that of the despot himself. Usbek's world is one in which the private and public realms intersect and interact. Montesquieu is not a proponent of the social, or even the natural, equality of men and women, but he anticipates some important insights of contemporary feminist thought. The *Persian Letters* explores the psychological complexity and potentially corrupting aspects of certain male-female relations, suggests that neither a marriage nor a state can long survive when ruled by an absolute despot, and demonstrates the integral relationship between order in the familial and political realms.

Montesquieu certainly intends the seraglio to instruct readers about the dynamics and the evils of political despotism. In a despotism, Montesquieu observes in *The Spirit of the Laws*, "everything is reduced to reconciling political and civil government with domestic government, the officers of the state with those of the seraglio" (*SL*, 5:14). As if in echo, Usbek's first eunuch remarks that "in the seraglio it is as if I were in a small empire . . ." (9). Montesquieu wants to help the reader recognize the identity between familial and political despotism: to see in Usbek not only husband but prince; to see in the eunuchs who guard his wives not only domestic slaves but political ministers; to see in the women not only wives but subjects. Later we will discuss Montesquieu's views of the domestic or familial aspects of the seraglio; for the moment we examine the ways in which the seraglio instructs the reader about political despotism.

Montesquieu thinks that despotism, like every other form of government, should be analyzed according to its "nature" and its "principle." The nature of a government is "what makes it what it is"; the principle of a government is "what makes it act" (*SL*, 3:1). The nature of despotism is government where " 'a single man, unrestricted by law or other rules, dominates everything by his will and caprices' " (*SL*, 2:1). Whether in Turkey (19), Russia (51), Persia, or elsewhere, the despot's will appears unrestrained. Usbek remarks on "the unlimited power of our sublime sultans, which knows no other law than its own" (94).

The principle of despotism is fear. This is most evident in the subjects' terror of the despot's whimsical power. In a despotism, "the lot of man, like that of beasts, becomes nothing but instinct, obedience, and punishment" (*SL*, 5:10). Perhaps those closest to the despot are the most fearful of his ability to control their preferments and punishments, their lives and deaths. They have the most to lose, and at any time he can raise them up, bankrupt them, or kill them (e. g., 126). The despot must always have—and be known to have— "the capacity to wipe out all those who hold positions of leadership" (*SL*, 3:9).

In the seraglio, Usbek himself is the absolute ruler. He commands his wives with "unlimited power" and advises his eunuchs to make his wives "feel their utter dependence" (148 and 2). He wields similar power over his eunuchs. In one fit of anger, he writes the head white eunuch, "what are all of you [eunuchs] if not base tools that I can break at my fancy . . . ; you who exist in this world only to live under my laws or to die so soon as I shall order . . . ? I swear by all the prophets . . . that if you stray from your duty, I shall consider your life like unto the insects under my feet" (21). Enraged at another eunuch, he rails, "Miserable wretch that you are! . . . read . . . those orders [I have sent]; you will perish if you do not carry them out" (150).

Although Usbek holds ultimate power, the relationships of authority in the seraglio are complex. First, Usbek delegates great authority to the eunuchs who guard his wives. Like the ministers of absolute monarchs, the eunuchs are told to "command as master like myself" (2; see also 148). The first eunuch writes to a friend that he feels "born to command" the women (9). It is not surprising that the wives complain that the eunuchs are too harsh and abuse the authority Usbek has given them (4 and 9). The position of the eunuchs in the harem is like that which Montesquieu, in *The Spirit of the Laws*, attributes to ministers in a despotism: "In despotic government, when power is passed from one set of hands to another, nothing is held back. The vizier is the despot himself, while every subordinate officer is the vizier" (*SL*, 5:16).

The wives, however, are not passively obedient subjects. After all, the eunuchs are supposed to serve them, just as viziers are supposed to serve the despot's subjects. Even as the eunuchs command, they are required to respond to the "orders, commands, chores, and fancies" of the women. The eunuchs realize that "there exists between us something like an ebb and flow of dominion and submission" (9). But the women's greatest power lies in their ability to appeal directly to Usbek, and to bring down the wrath of the despot on his ministers. The chief eunuch describes a woeful instance when he was whipped because a wife had complained of his severity while lying in Usbek's arms (9).[3] Both wife and slave in a despotism are insecure since they are at the mercy of the despot's whim and of one another's intrigues.

Even the despot himself, for all his power, is not the invulnerable ruler he appears to be. Montesquieu sees that monarchs living under fundamental laws are happier than despots, for "despots have nothing . . . to moderate either the passions of their people or those of their own hearts" (*SL*, 5:9). Moreover, because his advisers fear him, the despot does not hear the truth from them, but only what they think he wants to hear. As a result, the despot knows little of the country he governs (140). Although he seems to be in total control, the despot is in fact dependent upon the loyalty of his ministers and the obedience of his subjects. Montesquieu understood perfectly the tenuous position of the despot: "no one can be a tyrant without at the same time being a slave" (*SL*, 4:3; see also 6).

Maintaining order in such a polity requires great skill. A eunuch must learn "the difficult art of commanding" and how to "conform to the maxims of inflexible government" (64). A skilled eunuch is essential to uphold the power of the ruler. But the eunuchs do not simply carry out Usbek's orders; they also manipulate him and his wives. The mechanics necessary to maintain a regime based upon fear reveal the ultimate weakness of despotic rule. Since despotism encourages the exercise of nothing but the passions, it gives people no chance to develop constancy, honor, or virtue (*SL*, 5:14 and 3:9). The grand eunuch advises his protegé to "make yourself master of the seraglio" by creating jealousy in the wives and fickleness in the master (Appendix, pp. 285–88). The chief eunuch has an adroit Machiavellian understanding of how to isolate the wives and pit them against one another. He creates in each of them a "more stringent need to please, less opportunity to band together . . ." (96).[4] The eunuch also explains how to keep the master from forming any real attachment to any of his wives, how to "wear away his heart so well, that he will feel nothing" (Appendix, p. 287).

The eunuchs are adroit at destroying any possibility for human relationships based on love, honor, and virtue, precisely because they have been so dehumanized. Their natural passions—not only sexuality but also love, friendship, and solidarity—have been repressed. Of the passions, they are left only with jealousy, ambition, and revenge. Dehumanized men, their chief means of action are through artifice and fraud (Appendix, pp. 285–88). They dissemble with their master and play on his inconstancy. They propagandize their subjects. They destroy friendship and community because they are a threat to them. Removed from the pleasures of fellow-feeling, they eliminate it in others (96).[5] But they do so bitterly and with unfortunate results for themselves. The first eunuch, for example, feels he is nearest to being a man when he is ambitiously ruling his little empire (9); Solim, the first eunuch at the book's conclusion, releases his rage at the society that has created him by loosing a bloodbath in the seraglio (160).

It is the eunuchs who realize and exploit the fact that the rhetoric of love is only a mask that hides the reality of fear upon which the seraglio is based. When Usbek is gone, the sham of the seraglio as a community of love breaks down and the wives revolt. In *The Spirit of the Laws* Montesquieu describes this process in general terms: "in a despotic government, when the prince momentarily relaxes his threatened use of force; when he momentarily is deprived of the capacity to wipe out all those who hold positions of leadership, all is lost. For the spring of government, fear, no longer exists, and the people no longer have a protector" (*SL*, 3:9). Uncertainty, whim, and caprice threaten every person living in a despotic regime, including the ruler himself. Fear maintains order only as long as it is joined to effective force; the minute that force relaxes, there is nothing to restrain the destructive resentment that fear itself has created.[6]

But Montesquieu sees that despotism exists not only in the Orient; European monarchies are in danger of becoming despotisms. Through Usbek, Montesquieu voiced his great concern that Louis XIV was moving toward despotic and arbitrary rule: "He governs with equal talent his family, his court, and his state. People have often heard him say that, of all the governments in the world, that of the Turks, or that of our august sultan would please him best—so much significance does he attach to Oriental politics" (37). Louis's apparent intentions and his explicit ideal were ominous, and the future of France under his successors was unclear.

The suggestion that Louis XIV was like the master of an Oriental harem and his ministers were comparable to eunuchs may have amused eighteenth-century readers of the *Persian Letters*. But Montesquieu himself was deeply concerned with the tendencies toward personal and arbitrary rule that he saw in France. Persuaded that monarchy was unstable (102), Montesquieu hoped that Frenchmen, appalled by the tale of collapse of Usbek's harem, would strengthen defenses against despotism in their own country.

Louis XIV, of course, encouraged personal rule. Usbek notes that the French king often acted by whim, showing preferment to "a man who undresses him or who hands him his napkin . . . over some other who takes cities for him and wins battles." Without inquiring whether the beneficiary was deserving, Louis assumed that "his choosing him will make him so" (37).

Of particular concern to Montesquieu was the fact that many checks against arbitrary rule seemed to be in eclipse. Usbek writes that "the *parlements* resemble ruins" upon the death of Louis XIV; they now "perform practically no function. . . . They have bowed before time, . . . and before supreme authority, which has swept all before it" (92). Rica later notes, in telling language, that the reason the *parlements* have become impotent is that when they exposed flattery and carried the sighs and tears of the people "to the foot of the throne" they were exiled and ignored by the Regency (140). (One recalls that Usbek is in exile from a despotic regime because he "carried truth to the very steps of the throne" of the Persian king [8].) Another possible check on arbitrary power—the aristocracy —has also been rendered useless and idle by Louis's arbitrary government. In France there are "people who are great by birth, but who enjoy no reputation from it," even while tax farmers and other lackeys are raised up and brought low by every turning of the wheel of fortune (88 and 98). Usbek notes that "there is no country in the world where fortune is as fickle" as France (98).

The great danger of such caprice is that moderating institutions are swept underfoot and moderating human virtues are given no chance to develop. If the king's favor is the source of all reward and punishment, then "fame and virtue are taken to be imaginary . . . unless accompanied by the prince's favor; for in it alone they have both birth and death" (89). One sees in Persia the result of these trends. In a state such as Persia, assassination and usurpation are enormous temptations (102 and 80). There is little to lose when life itself is at the mercy of royal caprice.

The danger to France is thus very real. The court is corrupt, and in Montesquieu's eyes corruption in government is bound to spread throughout the entire society. Usbek writes, "The greatest evil committed by a minister without integrity is not serving his prince badly and ruining his people. There is another ill a thousandfold more dangerous to my mind, and that is the bad example he gives" (146). Bad government erodes honesty and trust between business partners; it leads to rapaciousness and greed among fellow citizens; and it undermines respect for family ties. From Paris, Usbek writes his despairing observation of the present and it is all of France that he judges: "What will posterity say when forced to blush at the shame of its fathers? . . . I have no doubt but that nobles will slice off from their armorial quarterings an undeserved degree of nobility, which does them dishonor, and will leave the present generation in the frightful void where it has put itself" (106).

Despotism exists not only at the level of government. It is clear from both the *Persian Letters* and *The Spirit of the Laws* that Montesquieu believes that "if the people as a whole is directed by a single principle, so too will be the private families that are its constituent parts" (*SL*, 4:1). The *Persian Letters* is an analysis of marital as well as political despotism; the seraglio is a family as well as an analogue for a political system.

A seraglio is intended to be a place of sexual enjoyment and love. As David Kettler points out, Montesquieu celebrates sexual pleasure as a component of love: "Man's love is not directed towards Platonic ideas or the Christian God; its object is woman."[7] Members of the seraglio make it appear—both to others and to themselves—a true romantic retreat. Usbek's wives repeatedly recall their love and declare it anew. An early letter from Zachi laments Usbek's departure: "The seraglio fairly breathes with love and your unfeelingness takes you ever further from it!" (3). Zephis, chastised by a eunuch for familiarity with her female slave, declares that she desires "no other guarantee of my conduct save yourself, save your love, save my own . . ." (4). Melvin Richter believes that the remembrances of loving nights and the declarations of affection between Usbek and his wives reveal that "even the obedience of the women to the eunuchs and to their husband, depends upon love," and that to some extent at least the wives acknowledge Usbek's authority as legitimate and consent to it.[8] Although Richter is right in pointing out that Usbek's wives do not live in conscious fear of Usbek's power, it is also true that their complicity in his rule is based not on love itself but on the delusion that they love rather than fear their master. The illusion that the seraglio is filled with love is based on and maintained by spirals of deception and self-deception. The wives participate in creating that illusion, and find solace in their fantasy.[9]

Although the women in the seraglio engage in perpetrating the lie, each at times clearly knows better. About halfway through the text, Zelis refers to Usbek's seraglio as "this very prison where you hold me" (57). When the seraglio crumbles at the book's end, she asserts that it is not the eunuch, but "the tyrant [himself] who offends me" (158). As Roxane dies, she writes defiantly, "Yes, I have deceived you. . . . Out of your horrible harem I managed to make a place of pleasure and delight by taking a lover. . . . But for a long time you have had the good fortune to believe that a heart like mine was submissive to you. We were both fortunate: you thought I was deceived, and I was deceiving you" (161). And Roxane is right: Usbek was deceived by her (26 and 148).

Indeed, Usbek deceives himself as well. Early in his journey, he writes Roxane, as if he is trying to convince himself that what he suspects even then is not true: "I cannot imagine that you have any other motive save that of pleasing me. And when I see you blush modestly, when your eyes seek mine, when you steal your way into my heart with your sweet and flattering words, then, Roxane, I could not possibly doubt your love" (26). A year later he is more forthright and clear sighted, acknowledging that "the seraglio is made more for hygiene than for pleasure. It is a uniform existence, without excitement. Everything smells of obedience and duty" (34). Despotism in the political order produces in marriage a despotism that promotes neither constancy nor love but only dutiful compliance with command.

Obedience and duty in the harem make love impossible, for, as David Kettler says, "love implies at least the possibility of reciprocity and an essential equality between men and women. The love which enhances humanity presupposes a modicum of humanity. . . ."[10]

Reciprocity and equality are virtually impossible within the seraglio, and beneath its surface show of passion and devotion it is a singularly loveless place.

As equals, men and women must be able to give and receive love freely and knowingly. This possibility is lacking in the harem and thus Usbek's seraglio is doomed. Not only are the eunuchs slaves; the wives are no more free than the eunuchs. The wives are bought and sold (89). They have no choice but to "love" Usbek (161). For instance, when Roxane married Usbek, she resisted his advances for two full months; at one point she "seized a dagger and threatened to immolate [immoler]" him (26). Although Usbek sees Roxane's behavior as "an obstinate refusal occasioned by alarmed chastity," her behavior might also be motivated by a genuine abhorrence of Usbek "as an enemy who had outraged" her. In fact, in moments of honesty and insight, Usbek acknowledges that his wives are not free in their loving. He berates Zachi after she has been found alone with a eunuch: "You will perhaps tell me that you have always been faithful. Come now! Could you have been anything else? . . ." (20).

The women's lack of knowledge of men intensifies their enslavement. Even while assuring Usbek of her love, Fatima remarks, "When I married you, my eyes had never yet beheld a man's face. Yours is still the only one I have been permitted to see" (7). Like nuns, the women of the harem are kept in a "sacred temple" (20). When they travel, they cannot even glimpse other men: Usbek writes, "O happy Roxane! Whenever you go to the country, you have always had eunuchs to walk ahead of you and reduce to death all such insolent ones as fail to avoid sight of you" (26). The men in Persia also lack knowledge of women. After two years in Paris, Rica writes that "I can really say that I have known women only since I've been here. I have learned more about them in a month than I would have learned after thirty years in a seraglio" (63).

There are three features of note about the corruption of the despotic marriage, each of which reminds one of similar evils caused by rule based on fear in the political realm.[11] First, where there is no freedom, there can be neither virtue nor love. The wives never have the opportunity to exercise free choice and thus to demonstrate their virtue. In the seraglio, they dwell "as in a continuing state of innocence, far from the reaches of all human beings. [They] are in a joyful state of happy inability to transgress" (26). When they vaunt their chastity, Usbek declaims in anger, they "vaunt much a virtue that is not free"

(20). When the external controls that bound them weaken in Usbek's absence, they immediately plot against the eunuchs and take lovers, just as when the iron hand of the sultan relaxes, he is liable to face armed rebellion and bands of assassins.

Second, in the despotic marriage, the pleasures and joys of love "are practically never relished except as manifestations of authority and subservience" (34). Sexual politics as manipulation and coercion, dominance and submission, corrodes love relations. As Zachi describes her feelings in the contest among wives:

Happy Usbek, what charms were displayed before your eyes! . . . in a trice, you made us assume a thousand different positions—ever a new command and ever a new submission. I confess it to you, Usbek: a passion much more keen than ambition made me want to please you. I saw myself surreptitiously becoming the mistress of your heart. . . . The triumph was all mine, and disappointment the lot of my rivals. (3)

But Zachi's momentary triumph, won through humiliation, is only of fleeting sensual pleasure to herself (because Roxane soon supersedes her in Usbek's favor), and a source of bitter frustration to the other wives. In a moment of insight, Usbek himself notes that women under polygamy are "constrained to an artificial continence" (64), and the majority live most of their lives under a regime of enforced chastity and repression. Fatima's complaint to Usbek is telling: "You men are very cruel: You are delighted that we should have passions we cannot satisfy. . . . It is easier for you to glean from the affliction of our senses what you dare not expect from your own worth" (7). And despite his ability to dominate his wives, Usbek is not happy. He is "devoured by grief," and a "secret jealousy" assails him (6 and 27). He is even denied sexual satisfaction in the harem: "I find myself in a state devoid of feeling . . . with no desires at all" (6). He fears that upon his return "the embraces of my wives shall relieve me no whit; in my bed, in their arms, I shall find joy only in anxiety . . ." (65).

Although they are unhappy, Usbek and his wives are incapable of considering the possibility of reciprocal and equal love relations. This is most ironic because Usbek's favorite wife is Roxane, a woman he respects because she stood up to him by defending her virginity. It is she whom Usbek most nearly regards as an equal: she is the only member of his seraglio whom he addresses with the respectful "vous" (26). But the corrupting dynamic of super- and subordination in the seraglio is too well set. Between the husband and his wives, eunuchs

and their charges, and political despots and their subjects, the effort
to maintain absolute rule establishes an ineradicable "ebb and flow
of dominion and submission" (9).

A third feature of the despotic marriage, closely related to sexual
politics, is that it forces the participants into self-destructive responses. Usbek's self-induced jealousy and anxiety are the major examples of this phenomenon. But there are others. Zachi, who stead-
fastly maintains her "love" for and subservience to Usbek and his
whims, is passionate but frustrated (47 and 157). In winning the
beauty contest among the wives (a contest she titillatingly describes
[3]), she arouses her own sexual passions to such a pitch that shortly
after Usbek leaves she goes to bed with a white eunuch (20). Later,
she is discovered "in bed with one of her women slaves" (147). Both
acts are "strongly prohibited by the law of the seraglio" (147).
Roxane, on the other hand, takes revenge on Usbek by deceiving him
throughout their marriage and taking a lover at the end. But the
despotic marital life into which she has been thrust wreaks its revenge
upon her. Her lover is killed by the eunuchs and she commits suicide.
As usurpation and assassination tend to repeat and perpetuate themselves in the political realm, so deception and revenge in the seraglio
ultimately multiply and are self-defeating.

That Montesquieu meant to characterize and criticize more than
Oriental marriages is clear. Even as he worried about the political
future of France, he was troubled about the future of the French
family. Although the French family was not tyrannical, it, like the
seraglio, lacked mutual respect and reciprocity, contained unnatural
and coercive elements, and usually failed to produce virtuous spouses.

A series of letters shows the reader that little respect and reciprocity infused French life. Rica writes about seductions (28), the vanity
of women in fashion (52), prostitution (56), and the scandals of the
family court, "the sacred place where all the family secrets are dis-
closed and where the most secret actions are brought out into broad
daylight" (86). Usbek learns of the insidious role played by the personal confessors of French wives; like the eunuchs in a seraglio, the
priests know "the women's weaknesses" and manipulate them (48).

French marriage law and custom contain one particularly unnatural
element: divorce is forbidden. Usbek's enlightened opinions are
strongly put. By forbidding divorce,

not only was . . . sweetness taken away from marriage, but its very end
as an institution was threatened. By wanting to tighten its bonds, they

[i.e., Christians] loosened them, and instead of bringing hearts closer together as they claimed, they separated them forever.

Into such a free action, where the heart should play so important a role,
restraint, necessity, and the very fatality of destiny were introduced. . . .
They tried to stabilize the heart—which is to say, the thing in human
nature that is the most variable and inconstant. (116)

On the whole, however, both Persian tyranny and French licentiousness result in marriages in which there is little mutual involvement
and few common purposes between spouses. In neither society is there
that sharing of activities, concerns, and goals that allows each partner
to become a being of unique worth to the other. Persia's marital
tyranny deserves the blunt condemnation Montesquieu delivers in
the final harem letters. France's egalitarian licentiousness in marriage
is less cruel; it therefore deserves and receives light but pointed satire.
Both are far from the reciprocal equality and virtue characteristic
of Montesquieu's Troglodytes (12–13) and Astarte and Apheridon
(67).

Furthermore, the "Oriental politics" of Louis XIV poses a clear threat
to the French family as it does to the French court and the state.
Licentiousness is close to tyranny, as Plato's *Republic* suggests in its
description of the development of the tyrannical man from the unruly
egalitarian democrat (Book 9). If moderation continues to decline in
France and Oriental despotism to increase, Montesquieu fears the
effects on the French family.

The destruction of Usbek's seraglio represents the collapse of both
political and familial order and reveals the full horror of despotism.[12]
Nine years after Usbek has departed, his wives rebel openly against
the eunuchs' role. The ministers are no longer able to persuade or
to impose order in their master's name, and Usbek finally delegates
his authority to a eunuch who can see nothing to do but end the
rebellion by shedding blood. The deaths occasioned by the collapse
of the seraglio are tragic, but the death of human emotion and
freedom under Usbek's marital despotism was also tragic. Despotism,
it seems, must inevitably produce tragedy: if a despotic regime
endures, it truncates the human spirit; if revolution breaks out, a
bloody loss of life ensues.[13] Nonetheless, Roxane's rebellion is clearly
heroic. Her taking a lover and even her suicide are assertions of the
self that life with Usbek in the seraglio had made impossible. In
Usbek's absence the women have forged bonds of mutual regard

and friendship, which at the end sustain each of them in asserting her freedom from the eunuchs' and Usbek's rule (147, 151, and 152). With Usbek at home the wives were guilty of complicity in their own subjection as their competition for his favor kept them apart. With Usbek gone, however, those ties of friendship and solidarity—which were banished from the seraglio by jealousy, envy, and resentment— began to develop. Their friendship is ultimately shown to be much stronger than the supposed passion each wife felt for Usbek. Thus Roxane's rebellion is not just a personal act of defiance; it is a demonstration of the strength that community gives to individuals seeking freedom.

Precisely because Usbek is in many respects a congenial, intelligent, and even admirable man, Montesquieu's condemnation of the corruption that domestic tyranny works on otherwise good men is all the more compelling. Usbek is clearly a man of enlightenment.[14] He undertakes his voyage to escape retaliation for having "spoken the truth" at court, and develops a genuine love of learning (8 and 48). Perceptive, witty, and tolerant, he subjects the customs and institutions of both France and his native Persia to meticulous scrutiny. He seems to be a good and generous friend: Ibben writes him warmly and faithfully for nine years, and entrusts his nephew Rhedi to Usbek's care when Rhedi travels to Europe. Usbek is humane, at least by Persian standards: he will not force castration on a slave who does not wish it (41–43).

But in his domestic life Usbek is a despot, and in the end he is unable to extricate himself from the inevitable dynamics of despotic rule. A despot, however enlightened, must rule by fear. Usbek's early efforts to hold the seraglio together by appealing to his wives to mend their ways out of love and "consideration for me" only hasten the demise of the seraglio (65, 149, and 153). With the seraglio in chaos, Usbek resorts to those tools of coercion and fear that he had learned to wield so effectively. He writes to his wives that his word must be for them "like unto the thunder that falls in the midst of storms and flashes of lightning" (154). Trapped by the inexorable workings of the institutions of absolute rule, Usbek can bring no warmth to his own seraglio. As Mark Hulliung says, the bloodbath at the end of the novel is a reflection of "the destruction rampant within Usbek's psyche."[15] Certainly Usbek is incapable of transferring to his rule of the seraglio the more humane and liberal principles he has embraced on his Western journey.[16] Usbek can leave Persia, but he cannot escape the influence of the institutions that have formed him and that he has helped to perpetuate.

For Montesquieu, the nature and principle of a society's political order shape its social institutions and its family relationships. Like Plato, Montesquieu sees tyranny as the worst possible form of polity, for it corrupts the individual as surely as it corrupts the city. The relationships of domination and submission that characterize despotism, and the use of fear to maintain order in despotic regimes, penetrate the walls of private homes and shape the very personalities of its members. The continuing corruption of despotism is inevitable and inescapable, as fear and caprice work without cease to corrode and eventually destroy all traces of virtue, duty, or love. The harem's fate—and Usbek's own—are reminders of the evils of despotism, the dangers of power unrestrained by moderating institutions, and the hazards of capricious activity by the ruler. In the *Persian Letters*, Montesquieu helps his reader understand and feel the deep effects of the many horrors—in government and marriage—of despotic rule.

Marriage Contract and Social Contract in Seventeenth-Century English Political Thought

☸ Mary Lyndon Shanley

Seventeenth-century English liberal political theory asserted that human beings were free and equal in the state of nature. But in the everyday experience of most seventeenth-century Englishmen, the vast majority of social relationships took place between persons who believed themselves to be unequal. Indeed, wellborn and lowly alike thought that hierarchy in human relationships was essential to the maintenance of social order: magistrate must rule over subject, minister over congregation, master over servant, parent over child, and husband over wife. Most people regarded these hierarchies as integrally related: each was governed by God's command to "Honor thy father and thy mother." So important was status to social order that disruption in any one relationship could produce ill effects in all the others: the Puritan Divine Richard Baxter was convinced that "most of the mischiefs that now infest or seize upon mankind throughout the earth, consist in, or are caused by the disorders and ill-governedness of families."[1]

The ideas of status by ascription and of the similarity of all authority were not, however, immutable. Some seventeenth-century theorists advanced the proposition that the only legitimate basis for relationships of super- and subordination was the free consent of the individual. While contractarian ideas first developed in analyses of the proper basis of authority, they gradually began to appear in discussions of other human associations as well.

One of the most striking instances of the extension of this conceptual revolution was the change that took place in the conceptualization of the marriage contract in the course of the seventeenth century. In 1640 virtually all writers still spoke of the "contractual" element in marriage as being simply the *consent* of each party to marry the other. Both man and woman consented to take on the rights and obligations of their respective stations. The man's role was that of head and governor, the woman's role that of obedient follower. To contract a marriage was to consent to a status that in its essence was hierarchical and unalterable. By 1690, however, John Locke suggested that if marriage were a "contractual" relationship, the terms of the contract as well as entry into the relationship were negotiable. Nothing inherent in the contracting of marriage dictated woman's subordination to man. Women, like men, were free beings able to define their relationship to others by their own wills and consent. Moreover, the marriage contract did not need to be lifelong or unchangeable.

Much of the shift in thinking about the basis of the marriage relationship was provoked or inspired by the political debates of both the Civil War and the Restoration. The Royalists thought they had found in the marriage contract a perfect analogue to any supposed contract between the king and his subjects, for marriage was a contract but was in its essence both hierarchical and irrevocable. Parliamentarian and republican writers were forced by these arguments to debate the royalist conception of marriage as well as of kingship. They gradually extended their individualistic premises into the depiction of domestic order. The parliamentarian discussions, however, were beset by various inconsistencies. It was John Locke who, more clearly than his predecessors, saw the implications of contractarian ideas for marriage, and who attempted to solve several of the dilemmas that had beset earlier attempts to compare the marriage bond to the social contract.

These changes in the conceptualization of the marriage contract provide an excellent example of the role of analogy in political discourse. The course of the argument between Royalists and Parliamentarians illustrates the ways in which an analogue—initially introduced to support one argument—may itself become a focus of debate. If the analogue is a powerful one, both sides will attempt to control it and bend it to their respective purposes. In the process, the image itself may be altered or transformed. This is precisely what happened with the notion of the marriage contract in the course of the seventeenth-century political debates in England. The theoretical arguments that emerged from these debates over political sovereignty eventually—although very slowly—became the bases for liberal arguments about female equality and marriage.[2]

Although the development of contractarian thought in England is usually associated with advocates of parliamentary or popular rights, by the early seventeenth century "contractarian principles had taken firm hold of nearly all political thought." Although supporters of Charles I relied upon patriarchal and divine-right arguments to support their position, they also used the notion of contract to argue that the people had ceded their rights to the original monarch in a contract of submission, and "had no right to do anything but endure [even] the tyranny of a lawfully constituted ruler."³ Therefore when the Parliamentarian Henry Parker claimed that since power had originally conveyed from the people they could take it back, Sir John Spelman replied, "I should rather think if Regall power were originally conveyed from the people, they by conveying it over have divested themselves of it."⁴ Sir Dudley Digges, joining the fray against Parker, argued that civil government was created by "a consent and mutual obligation . . . of [men] not using their natural power but only as the law shall require, that is, of not resisting that body in which the supreme power is placed." So it comes about, Dudley continued, that "in acquittal for our submission of our private strength, we are secured by the united power of all and the whole kingdom becomes our guard."⁵ By 1640, part of the debate between Royalists and Parliamentarians was being waged over the nature of English monarchy's ancient compact with the people, which was ratified by every ruler through the coronation oath.⁶

Because it suited their purposes admirably, Royalists introduced and initially profited more from the analogy between social contract and marriage contract than did their opponents. The marriage contract was useful to Royalists because it provided an example of a contract that established a relationship of irrevocable hierarchical authority between the parties. Supporters of Charles I pointed out that marriage was a relationship that both man and woman entered by free consent, but in marriage God established the husband in a position of rule over his wife. Neither the spouses' own agreement nor a violation of God's ordinances concerning marital duties could alter that relationship or free husband and wife from their obligations. Similarly, men might originally have agreed freely to establish a monarchy, but once the agreement was struck the sovereign's powers were as fixed as those of the husband.

Henry Ferne, for example, used the marriage contract to ridicule the notion that Parliament holds some sort of "reserved power" to judge the actions of the king. Such an idea was a pernicious and harmful doctrine, "a very seminary of jealousies and seditions. . . ." To give Parliament such powers was

as if, in Matrimony (for the King is also *sponsus* Regni, and wedded to the kingdom by a ring at his Coronation) the parties should agree, on such and such neglect of duties, to part a sunder . . . ; what our Savior said of their light and unlawfull occasions of Divorse, *non suit ob initio*, it was not so from the beginning, may be said of such a reserved power of resistance, it was not so from the beginning. . . .[7]

In the same way, Dudley Digges considered absurd the parliamentarian contention that "there is a mutuall contract between King, and subjects, and if he breake the covenant, He forfeites the benefits of this agreement, and He not performing the duty of a King, they are released from the duty of Subjects." Digges marshaled evidence from both scripture and family conduct to show that the existence of an initial contract does not mean that the respective parties to the contract, even those who are seriously abused, have the right to rescind the compact or withdraw from it.

The Jewes could have made this plea, grounded in the nature of a Covenant, the breach of which (though instituted by God betweene King and People, Deut. 17.) was no dispensation for them to Rebell, as was evidenced formerly. . . . So there is a contract between Husband and Wife, the violation of which on the man's part doth not bereave him of his dominion over the woman. I confesse, a great obligation lyes upon Kings. . . . And if they abuse their power, God's punishment will be as high as their ingratitude.[8]

Political resistance was forbidden. The notion of justifiable rebellion was as ludicrous as the notion that a wife might be released from subjection to her husband either by their mutual agreement or because of his abuse.

According to the Royalists, thinking about marriage in terms analogous to those used when thinking of political authority made it possible to argue that consent, once given, establishes an unalterable relationship. Digges insisted that no person then living in England partook of the original freedom of the state of nature: "Else no contracts could be of force, because by the law of nature men were free. . . ." People lost that freedom through their civil compact "which it was in our power to make, but having once made it, we have tyed our hands from using positive liberty."[9] Or, as

Ferne explained it, "many things which are altogether in our disposing before we part with them, are not afterward in our power to recall. . . ."[10] Consent might have indicated initial freedom, but it did not guarantee continuing choice.

The usefulness of the marriage contract as an analogy for the social contract was not lost upon supporters of Charles I. They saw in it a means to demonstrate to those who prattled about "natural freedom" and of the "original compact" between king and people, that bonds created initially by free consent are not necessarily either alterable or revocable. The Royalists' use of the marriage contract to support absolutist arguments posed a difficult challenge for republican theorists.

As defenders of the absolute and inalienable authority of the king tended to argue that God had commanded wives to be subject to their husbands, that men were by nature superior to women, and that the marriage contract once made could not be broken, so advocates of parliamentary or popular checks on the king's prerogative tried to paint the marriage relationship as one in which the authority of husbands over wives could be limited or even broken. To answer the Royalists' claims concerning kingly authority, the Parliamentarians had to debate their conception of marriage as well.

The parameters of the Parliamentarians' arguments concerning marriage were set by prevailing notions of marriage and divorce.[11] Under canon law, true marriage was held to be a sacrament. There could be no divorce in the sense of a real dissolution of marriage with the possibility of remarriage. Divorce was only *a mensa et thoro* (separation from bed and board), and even this only by the sentence of an ecclesiastical court. In pre-Reformation England, the grounds of judicial separation were limited, more restrictively than elsewhere, to adultery and cruelty.

Many Protestant reformers, from Luther on, favored granting divorces for adultery, with permission for the innocent party to remarry. The Ordinances of Wittenberg (1553) and of Geneva (1561) recognized both adultery and desertion as valid grounds for divorce. In England a proposed *Reformatio Legum Ecclesiasticarum* in 1552 reflected a similarly liberal point of view. Although Henry VIII died before he could force this act through Parliament, and the House of Commons defeated it under Edward VI, the reform principles apparently received considerable acceptance throughout the Elizabethan period. From the beginning of the seventeenth century, and especially under Archbishop Laud, however, a contrary trend prevailed. The *Constitutions and Canons Ecclessiasticall* published in 1604 urged closer adherence to the pre-Reformation practices, declaring that ecclesiastical courts should grant separations only with the utmost caution and only after the parties posted a bond that neither would remarry during the other's lifetime.[12] Jurisdiction over all separations remained with the ecclesiastical courts.

The Puritans resisted this trend backwards toward the canon law. In the early seventeenth century a split developed between those Puritans who permitted remarriage after divorce (divorce *a vinculo*) and those who only allowed divorce *a mensa et thoro*.[13] Even those who favored divorce *a vinculo*, however, narrowed Luther's list of grounds to encompass only adultery and desertion.[14] Despite the Puritan reform movement, during the first half of the seventeenth century the dominant opinion and practice among Puritans and Anglicans alike were that divorce could only be granted for adultery, that such divorce was only *a mensa et thoro*, and that it did not dissolve the marriage bonds nor permit remarriage even of the innocent party.

It was in this context that the parliamentarian pamphleteers attempted to convert the analogy between marriage contract and compact between king and people to serve their purposes as effectively as it had the Royalists theirs. Two main strategies appeared in parliamentarian pamphlets. Parliamentarians agreed with Royalists that the husband was superior to the wife in marriage. But some argued that despite the husband's superiority there were *inherent* restrictions on his power. Bolder writers enlarged on this and asserted that if a husband transgressed certain limitations, his wife had the right to oppose him and in extremity to separate herself from him.

William Bridge argued the position of inherent limitations on husbandly power to refute the absolutist claims of Henry Ferne, supporter of Charles I. One of Ferne's arguments in *The Resolving of Conscience* had been that if there was an original convenant between king and people, then its terms (as evidenced by the Coronation Oath) made no provision for resistance by Parliament.[15] Bridge replied that "though there be no such words expressed . . . , *ratio legis* being *lex*, in reason that must be implied," and relied on a comparison between marriage and government, two institutions equally ordained by God for man: "there is a covenant stricken between a man & an woman at Marriage; when they marry one another it is not verbally expressed in their agreement, that if one commit Adultery, that party shall be divorced; and yet we know that that covenant of Marriage carries the force of such condition."[16] Although Bridge did not explicitly contend that if God, in establishing marriage, provided the remedy of separation, so in creating government He must have proffered a similar remedy, that was the implication of his argument. Others might, and later did, draw upon his tacit suggestion.

Henry Parker had much the same objective as Bridge—to argue for implicit restraints upon the power of the king—when he wrote of the relationship between marriage contract and social contract in *Jus populi*:

In Matrimony there is something divine . . . but is this any ground to infer that there is no humane consent or concurrence in it? does the divine institution of marriage take away freedome of choice before, or conclude either party under an absolute formalization? . . . And if men, for whose sake women were created, shall not lay hold upon the divine right of wedlock, to the disadvantage of women; much less shall Princes who were created for the peoples sake, chalenge any thing from the sanctity of their offices, that may derogate from the people.[17]

The argument that scripture countenanced no absolute coercion by husbands was directly relevant to Parker's contention that comparing the power of a husband to that of a king showed that there must be limits to kingly authority.

Herbert Palmer and his co-authors of *Scripture and Reason Pleaded for Defensive Armes* carried Bridge and Parker's argument about inherent limits to authority a step further. They reasoned that if a husband or king transgressed the implicit limits of his respective office, *active resistance* in home or state was justified. Using the notion of self-preservation, Palmer introduced the concept of individual rights into the discussion of marital obligation:

A Wife is tyed to her Husband by the Covenant of God, (so called *Prov.* 2.) and by the Ordinance of God more ancient, and no lesse strong then that of Politick Government. She cannot recall wholly her Husbands Authority over her. . . . *Yet for her necessity, she may* by the Law of God and Conscience . . . *secure her Person from his violence by absence* (though it ordinarily be against the Law of Marriage, and the end of it.) or *any other meanes of necessary defence.*[18]

Palmer and his associates argued that the right of self-preservation gave an abused spouse the right to separate, just as the right of self-preservation gave Parliament the right to raise an army under defensive arms.

John Milton, more clearly than other Parliamentarians, saw what the political debates implied for the understanding of marriage. Milton, himself anxious for release from an unhappy marriage, used the fact that Parliament was in arms to argue for divorce *a vinculo*. Where the political pamphlets had argued that the social contract was like the marriage contract, Milton *reversed* the terms of the analogy and argued that understanding the political bond can help one to understand the nature of marriage. His dedicatory letter "To the Parliament of *England* with the Assembly," prefaced to the second edition of the *Doctrine and Discipline of Divorce* (1644), was a brilliant appeal to a body that was in arms against the king:

Advise yee well, supreme Senat, if charity be thus excluded and expulst, how yee will defend the untainted honour of your own actions and pro-ceedings: He who marries, intends as little to conspire his own ruine, as he that swears Allegiance: and as a whole people is in proportion to an ill Government, so is one man to an ill marriage. If they against any authority, Covenant, or Statute, may by the soveraign edict of charity, save not only their lives, but honest liberties from unworthy bondage, as well may he against any private Covenant, which hee never enter'd to his mischief, re-deem himself from unsupportable disturbances to honest peace, and just contentment. . . .[19]

Milton, with a boldness matched by none of his contemporaries and roundly condemned by most of them, used this notion of saving "honest liberties from unworthy bondage" to argue for divorce *a vinculo* for any incompatibility that made the marriage partners unsuited to be true companions and unable to be true helpmeets.[20]

Challenged by the Royalists to show why resistance to authority was any more justifiable in politics than in marriage, the parlia-mentarian pamphleteers were forced to consider what, if anything, could limit a husband's authority over his wife or authorize resistance to his power. The Civil War political debate therefore generated a secondary debate on the nature of the marriage bond itself. Apologists for resistance to Charles I were required to take more liberal positions with regard to marriage and divorce than were widely acceptable.

Despite the efforts of men such as Bridge, Parker, and Palmer, the Parliamentarians had difficulty turning the image of the marriage contract to their own use. Their assumptions about marriage did not accommodate their rapidly developing arguments about legitimate political authority. Parliamentarians, like Royalists, believed that women were naturally inferior to men and were commanded by scripture to be subject to their husbands in marriage. Although Parliamentarians continued to accept the injunction "Wives, be subject to your husbands," many wished to argue that Parliament shared authority with the king. Parker was almost alone in allowing a wife any resistance to a violent husband other than absence, but many argued that men might take up arms against the king. Although the Parliamentarians eventually argued that if the terms of the political contract were abused and broken then the contract must be revocable, they had serious doubts about divorce *a vinculo*. Had the victory in the war between Parliament and king gone to the party best able to turn the image of the marriage contract to the service of its position, Charles I would not have become a royal martyr.

During the reign of Charles II when Parliamentarians and Royalists resumed their political debates, they continued to deploy marriage as an analogue for the proper relationship between king and Parliament. The antiroyalist tracts during the Restoration, however, were more clearly influenced by social contract reasoning than those of the Civil War years had been. This shift to social-contract theory occurred as arguments from natural law began to replace those based upon scripture. Scripture had been adequate to prove that God had intended subjects to be subordinate to the prince and wives to be subject to their husbands, but it was now necessary to demonstrate that both kinds of authority were based upon free consent. In the political debate this meant that it became possible to argue for parliamentary limitations on royal prerogative. In the discussion of marriage, contract theory called into question the natural hierarchy of husband over wife that both parties to the Civil War debates had taken for granted.

The work of James Tyrrell reflected the new concerns of liberal theorists during the Restoration. Tyrrell, a lifelong associate and correspondent of John Locke, sought to demonstrate that patriarchal justifications for royal authority were absurd.[21] Tyrrell argued that "a man without his own act or consent can never lawfully fall into the power or possession of another."[22] Since patriarchal theory asserted that the authority of the king in the state was like that of the father in a family, Tyrrell attempted to show that male rule in the household was based upon consent. Where many Civil War pamphleteers pondered whether the power that husbands naturally exercised over their wives could be revoked if it were abused, Tyrrell aimed to justify the hierarchical relationship itself.

Tyrrell's work was indebted to the Continental natural-law theorists who insisted that consent—not nature or scriptural admonition alone—established the relationship of super- and subordination in marriage. Grotius believed in the natural "superiority of [the male] sex," and argued that "the difference in sex" gives the husband authority over the wife even in the state of nature.[23] Pufendorf, however, substituted the voluntary origin of woman's secondary position in marriage for assumptions about her "natural" subjection.

We presuppose at the outset that by nature all individuals have equal rights, and no one enjoys authority over another, unless it has been secured by an act of himself or the other. For although, as a general thing, the male surpasses the female in strength of body and mind, yet that superiority is of itself far from being capable of giving the former authority over the latter. Therefore, whatever right a man has over a woman, inasmuch as she is his equal, will have to be secured by her consent, or by a just war.[24]

Tyrrell's reflections on the authority of husband over wife were beset by ambivalence. On the one hand, he argued that a wife's subjection to her husband had to be established by her own consent. Discussing parental authority, Tyrrell stated that "the power of the Father does not commence barely from Generation, but is acquired from the Contract of Marriage; which (till I meet with some reason to the contrary) I see not why it might not be so agreed by the contract, that the Father should not dispose of the Children without the Mother's consent. . . ."[25] This implied that the marriage contract involved something more than the consent to marry and might contain stipulations about the terms of the relationship. Tyrrell made a serious effort to shift the ground of woman's subordination in marriage from scripture to nature and finally to her own consent.

On the other hand, Tyrrell also asserted that "the woman, as the weaker vessel, is to be subject to the Man, as the stronger, stouter, and commonly the wiser creature." Such an argument from nature seriously undercut his contractarian impulses. Even when Tyrrell tried to bring these two points of view together by insisting that women accepted their own inferiority when they agreed to marry, he allowed that a woman, subjected to her husband, became "as a Slave."[26]

Tyrrell's effort to ground familial as well as political authority in consent was not, finally, wholly successful. Despite his contractarian convictions, Tyrrell believed that both God and nature dictated that men should rule in their households. Further, while Tyrrell thought the political contract was revocable, he, like his Civil War predecessors, could not bring himself to sanction divorce. He insisted that "Christ hath taken away the liberty of divorce," which even in Mosaic law existed only for adultery. Indeed, Tyrrell concluded that husbands should be allowed to chastise their wives without incurring reproof or hindrance precisely because they do not have the recourse of divorcing them.[27]

Tyrrell is typical of the liberal thinkers who wrote in the period between the Civil War pamphleteers and John Locke. His adoption of natural-law reasoning allowed him to resolve certain problems that had beset the former when they compared the marriage contract to the original pact between king and people, but he continued to adhere to a patriarchal conception in marriage. It remained for John Locke to draw out the implications of the contractarian image of marriage.

Locke moved to resolve the dilemma faced by those Parliamentarians who attempted to argue against royalist theorists over the nature of the marriage contract. Locke did not so much make a sudden departure from earlier thought about the family as he took the premise of the natural freedom and equality of all family members more seriously than had previous thinkers. In doing so, he strengthened liberal arguments concerning the voluntary origin of all obligations. Nonetheless, even as he resolved certain of the conceptual dilemmas that permeated early liberal discussions of the relationship between marriage contract and social contract, Locke rejected emphatically the notion that familial and civil authority were analogous. Locke's individualist assumptions and his repudiation of the family/state analogy were to affect subsequent discussions of marriage and the family.

Use by the anti-Royalists of the marriage contract/social contract analogy, remember, had floundered on the assumptions that even though men and women possessed the same rights in the state of nature, husbands were superior to wives in marriage; that it was impossible to make stipulations to alter the hierarchical relationship; and that the parties enjoyed no right of revocation of their marriage contract no matter how discomfiting it became. A theorist who took this view of the marriage contract, and held it to be analogous to the political contract, could find no justification for resistance to Charles I or for the Glorious Revolution.

Locke's first step in resolving this difficulty was to abandon unequivocally reasoning from scripture in favor of natural-law theory. Locke admitted that scripture might be a guide to God's will, but he rejected reliance upon biblical writ as sacrosanct authority on the proper basis of human relationships. This freed him from debates over the correct interpretation of contested biblical passages, and allowed him to consider afresh and more radically both political and marital bonds.

Locke began his reconsideration of marriage and the marriage contract indirectly through his analysis of patriarchal ideas concerning parents and children. He rejected the patriarchal premise that generation creates paternal rights that last until the father dies or surrenders these rights voluntarily. Although children are born dependent upon their parents, this temporary dependency is not the same thing as lifelong subordination. Children cast off subordination to their parents as they cast off their swaddling clothes: "Age and Reason as [children] grow up, loosen [the bonds of subjection to parents] till at length they drop quite off, and leave a Man at his own free Disposal." Children have no *duties* until they know the law of nature, and then their duty is to owe "honour, respect, gratitude and assistance" to their parents;[28] parents, on the other hand, have the duty to nurture and educate their children.[29]

Locke's consideration of parents' duties to care for their children led him to discuss the relationship between father and mother, husband and wife. He insisted that *both* parents are required by the Law of Nature to care for their children. Attributing parental duties to mother and father alike served Locke well in his argument against the patriarchalists,

for it will but very ill serve the turn of those Men who contend so much for the Absolute Power and Authority of the *Fatherhood*, as they call it, that the *Mother* should have a share in it. And it would have but ill-supported the *Monarchy* they contend for, when by the very name it appeared that the Fundamental Authority from whence they would derive their Government of a single Person only, was not placed in one, but two persons jointly.[30]

It might appear that Locke's attribution of parental authority and responsibility to mothers was simply an expedient of the anti-patriarchal argument. After arguing that mothers share in parental authority he quickly slipped back into using the common phrase "paternal" power rather than "Parental" power,[31] or deployed the terms as if they were interchangeable.[32] On balance, however, I think that this is simply Locke's falling into customary usage, perhaps unconsciously. He made his *theoretical* point self-consciously when he asserted that "paternal" power should be termed "parental," and that "whatever obligation Nature and the right of Generation lays on Children, it must certainly bind them equally to both the concurrent Causes of it."[33]

To argue that the child is obligated to mother and father alike showed only that a woman could exercise authority over her child; it did not say anything of her relationship to her husband if the child were not involved. Locke based his analysis of the origin and nature of "conjugal society" upon the contractarian model of the natural-law theorists. Conjugal society is formed by "a voluntary Compact between Man and Woman."[34] In contrast to those who argued that marriage was the result of contract, meaning thereby consent to the pre-established duties of the marital state, Locke extended the contract analogy and suggested that the parties themselves might not only agree to marry, but might set at least some of the terms of their relationship.

Locke rejected explicitly the notion that marriage requires the absolute sovereignty of the husband: "the ends of Matrimony requiring no such Power in the Husband, the Condition of *Conjugal* Society put it not in him, it being not at all necessary to the State."[35] The only thing that nature does dictate about marriage contract, in its essence, therefore "consist[s] chiefly in such Communion and Right in one anothers Bodies, as is necessary to its chief End, Procreation," along with "mutual Support, and Assistance, and a Communion of Interest too, as necessary not only to unite their Care, and Affection, but also necessary to their common Off-spring, who have a Right to be nourished and maintained by them. . . ."[36]

It is the exigencies of the care of children, not any particular attribute of either sex, that set the only natural or prima facie terms to the marital relationship. Therefore, argued Locke, many of the conditions that now *seem* to be intrinsic to the marital state, need not be so at all. Stipulations concerning any of these conditions might themselves be set by contract. "Community of Goods, and the Power over them, mutual Assistance, and Maintenance, and other things belonging to Conjugal Society, might be varied and regulated by that Contract, which unites Man and Woman in that Society, as far as may be consistent with Procreation and the bringing up of Children. . . ." Locke carried the implications of his contractarian view of marriage to the point of insisting not only that the terms of the relationship could be set by contract, but also that once the ends of the contract are fulfilled, the contract itself might be terminated.

It would give one reason to enquire, why this Compact, where Procreation and Education are secured, and Inheritance taken care for, may not be made determinable, either by consent, or at a certain time, or upon certain Conditions, as well as any other voluntary Compacts, there being no necessity in the nature of the thing, nor to the ends of it, that it should always be for Life.[37]

Beginning from the premises that the end of marriage is the procreation and nurture of children and that marriage is a contractual relationship, Locke concluded that husband and wife might set whatever terms they wished to their relationship as long as these were conducive to the care of their young.

Locke did not, however, abandon completely male supremacist notions with regard to marriage and the family. Marriage, he thought, could not be a completely egalitarian relationship because it took two—and two only—to make a marriage. If husband and wife disagreed on anything concerning the management of the family, their differences could not be decided by majority rule. "But Husband and Wife, though they have but one common Concern, yet having different understandings, will unavoidably sometimes have different wills, too; it therefore being necessary, that the last Determination, i.e., the Rule, should be placed somewhere, it naturally falls to the Man's share, as the abler and the stronger."[38] This sounds like parts of Grotius, Pufendorf, and Parker, not to mention Filmer and Digges.

There are, however, two qualifications to Locke's bow in the direction of male superiority. First, Locke qualified this grant of power to reach only "to the things of their common Interest and Property." Where husband and wife disagree about their domicile or the purchase of household goods, for example, the husband has the final say. Nonetheless, even in these cases, the matter could be regulated by contract.[39]

Second, other aspects of Locke's theory seriously mitigated the idea of the husband's superiority over his wife. At the outset of the *Second Treatise* Locke asserted that "men live together by no other Rules but those of Beasts, where the strongest carries it . . . ," thus rejecting emphatically the proposition that strength gives any right to rule.[40] Locke's qualification of the sphere of husbandly power reflected his (perhaps unconscious) discomfort with assigning a "natural" dominance of one being over another when both were free and equal in the state of nature.[41] It was a position his own theory could not support fully.

Locke carried the notion of the contractual nature of marriage close to its logical conclusions. If all beings were free and equal in the state of nature, then when they agreed to marry they were free to set whatever terms they wished, as long as these were consonant with the procreation and care of children. Locke did not take his voluntarism to the point of saying that the purpose of the association also had to be set by contract (a popular assertion today),[42] but he imposed no other absolute limits on the couple's freedom. In Locke's view, the marriage contract was revocable, and its terms were negotiable. Locke's picture of marriage eliminated the embarrassments that earlier antiroyalist writers encountered when they wrote of the analogy between the social contract and the marriage contract.

Although Locke had finally made the marriage contract compatible with parliamentarian ends, he broke with earlier theorists in rejecting the ideas that the family was analogous to civil society, and that the justification of authority in one realm was therefore identical to the justification of authority in the other.

I think that it may not be amiss, to set down what I take to be Political Power. That the Power of a *Magistrate* over a Subject, may be distinguished from that of a *Father* over his Children, a *Master* over his Servant, a *Husband* over his Wife, and a Lord over his Slave . . . it may help us to distinguish these Powers one from another, and show the difference betwixt a Ruler of a Commonwealth, a Father of a Family, and a Captain of a Galley.[43]

This was part and parcel of Locke's liberal politics—the family was a private association that preceded civil society, therefore the state had no right to intrude upon or into it. Precisely because he viewed marriage as distinct from political association, Locke was able to maintain that the husband should exercise rule as "the abler and the stronger," even as he rejected any such argument with respect to political authority.

Despite his partial capitulation to patriarchal ideas about male superiority, Locke anticipated important reforms in marriage law and practice. His notion that contract might regulate property rights and maintenance obligations in marriage was an astonishing idea for the seventeenth century and subsequent centuries. It was only with the passage of the British and American Married Woman's Property Acts in the latter half of the nineteenth century that either English or American law allowed that "Community of Goods, and the [husband's exclusive] power over them" was not a necessary part of the marital order.[44] This law continues at present to hold that mutual assistance and maintenance by the husband are essential to the marriage relationship.[45] Similarly, Locke's notion that marriage might end "by consent, or at a certain time, or upon certain Conditions" anticipated reforms of our own day: limited-term marriage and "no-fault" divorce. When opponents of patriarchal practices in later centuries attacked both the formal (mainly legal) and informal underpinnings of the patriarchal family, among their most powerful weapons were the individualistic premises that Locke incorporated into both his political theory and his depiction of marriage.

John Locke sought to resolve the dilemmas of earlier Parliamentarians who had attempted to incorporate a view of marriage as a hierarchical and irrevocable relationship into an emerging liberal political framework with which such views were held in tension. Locke's deep voluntaristic convictions and his sensitivity to more affectionate and egalitarian human relationships also influenced the terms in which people subsequently discussed marital rights and duties.[46] In this sense the analysis of marriage in the *Two Treatises* both culminated fifty years of changing images of marriage in political discourse, and laid the groundwork for ensuing debates concerning the "contractual" nature of marriage.

Julie and "La Maison Paternelle": Another Look at Rousseau's *La Nouvelle Héloïse*

✿ Tony Tanner

> *For in the state of the families, which was extremely poor in language, the fathers alone have spoken and given commands to their children and* famuli, *who, under the terrors of patriarchal rule . . . must have executed the commands in silence and with blind obsequiousness.*—Vico, The New Science

If, *as is my impression,* not many people actually read through Rousseau's *La Nouvelle Héloïse,* one reason might be that, in a sense, we have all read it hundreds of times even before picking up the actual text. If we do not have some vague secondhand, or hundredthhand, sense of the story of Julie and her tutor Saint-Preux and of the scenery—the two young lovers so chastely passionate who are allowed to marry, the house in the beautiful setting at the foot of the Alps near Lake Geneva, the enforced separations and anguished letters, the calm reunion when youthful passion has been transformed into a mature affection and sincere piety—we still will have read many other books that have been influenced indirectly by the modes of feeling that Rousseau outlined and indulged in this book. In turning to this one, we may wonder a little at the enormous impact of this recorded series of specious and self-induced intensities and often quite interminable lexical dalliances with almost decontextualized emotion—feeling feeling itself feel, as it were. Yet a somewhat more careful reading reveals a rather different book, a book that not only bespeaks some kind of imminent crisis in the particular family structure on which Western society was based, but carries within it a sense of doom concerning the very emotions and institutions that the book strives to celebrate. There is, of course, a similar sense of the problematics of the family in *Clarissa,* and it is well known how much Rousseau admired that work. But Rousseau, in apparently working for a happier ending, if anything reveals—no matter how implicitly or unintentionally—potentially more ominous signs of things amiss. It is almost as if, on the eve of what we roughly think of as the great period of the consolidation and domination of the bourgeois class and its growing belief in the myth of its own "perenniality" (Sartre's word), Rousseau wrote a book that had a manifest content of *l'amour* in all its more piercing, poignant, and plangent forms, and a latent content that said the bourgeois family would not work. But let me turn to some details from the book.

The first embrace between Julie and Saint-Preux takes place in a charming "arbor" (*bosquet*) in a grove that lies close to Clarens, the house in which Julie lives. She herself selects the spot and prepares him with a tantalizing hint which mingles topographic specificity with promissory vagueness and ordained constraints. "Among the natural arbors which make up this charming place, there is one more charming than the rest, with which I am most delighted and in which, for that reason, I am reserving a little surprise for my friend . . . I must warn you that we shall not go together into the arbor without the inseparable cousin [*l'inséparable cousine*]."[1]

The choice of an arbor for a secret rendezvous is appropriate enough, but I want to note that their unlegalized sexual embrace takes place very near the house that Julie, effectively, will never leave—the house of her father. The insistence on having the *inséparable cousine* (Claire) present when she is to give Saint-Preux his "surprise" is indicative of Julie's wish somehow to combine intrafamilial love with extrafamilial passion: the cousin, as "cousin," is to be a mediator between filial devotion and female sexuality, between the father and the lover, between what is in the home and what is not in the home. As cousin she stands exactly in relation to Julie's family (in the restricted sense of parents and their children) as the arbor does to the house: that is, not actually inside it, but not totally outside it either, not completely unconnected and foreign. Arbors (and related topographical phenomena) play a frequent role in the long iconological history of that topographical middle ground between culture and wild nature where the two may meet, and for Julie it is clear that her cousin represents a relational middle ground that she herself hopes to be able to maintain between daughter and lover. Of course it proves to be impossible; but the desire and attempt to keep everyone and everything together, connected, related, unsundered and inseparable, literally in one place, as well as emotionally, mentally, and even, at times, perceptually indistinguishable and merged, is the dominant drive in Julie's existence. She eventually wants to internalize the external, as it were, and "enhouse" the unhoused elements of existence. It represents a dream of *total* harmony, of complete incorporation and domestication, which at the same time wishes to maintain that it is totally *natural*; as if to maintain that nature *is* culture and culture nature (not a relationship but an identity).

The relationship of this complex and impossible dream to the developments in the thought of the Enlightenment is obvious. But in terms of sexual/familial relationships such a dream can lead to strange displacements or confusions. *La Nouvelle Héloïse* is indeed a novel about love above all else, but the most powerful love relationship is between Julie and her father. Saint-Preux is an adopted child. The novel sedulously avoids adultery, but it is marked by all-pervasive feelings of incest (emotional and mental incest of course, though in one extraordinary episode it is almost as if the father brutally "rapes" Julie). By comparison, the most physical action of Saint-Preux to appear in the text is a feverishly excited manual exploration of Julie's clothes and underwear (in her absence), in an equally extraordinary incident of quite astonishing prurience. Julie's dream is, in certain important ways, a dream of total incest. The ultimate utter failure and collapse of this dream are a crucial prelude to many of the great novels—often novels concerning adultery—that were to follow it.

What apparently happens in the arbor on that first occasion is that the "inseparable cousin" first asks Saint-Preux for a kiss with a contradictory air of droll imploring, and a "cousinly" embrace ensues. It is now Julie's turn (it is all rather like the kissing games played at children's parties, as if Julie wants to defuse sexuality by infantilizing it), and she bestows a distinctly uncousinly kiss on the understandably "surprised" Saint-Preux. She then returns to the arms of the inseparable cousin and proceeds to faint. It is small wonder that Saint-Preux registers a certain degree of mystification in the scene, and we may adjudge it a considerable understatement when he subsequently refers to "the test of the arbor." He is immediately afterward ordered by Julie to leave the house and travel, which, being the bemused, compliant figure that he is, he promptly does. Shortly thereafter he refers to the "delirium" of the arbor. At this point Julie falls hysterically ill and Saint-Preux is summoned back, and in the very next letter

Julie tells the absent Claire that the moment of "crisis" has arrived and begs her to return. From the next letter we infer that she has capitulated sexually to Saint-Preux—it can only have been in the arbor and only because the inseparable cousin had become separate. Julie has yet to learn that there is no such thing as an inseparable person because separation is not a function, but a condition, of individual existence.

Just as it was Julie who made the appointment for the initial embrace in the arbor, so she decrees their next venue—a remote chalet in the country near the source of the Vevaise. (Saint-Preux is never allowed to initiate any meeting, decide on any venue, fix on any abode. His life is entirely shaped and directed by others, starting with Julie. In innumerable ways he is constantly being reminded of the complete helplessness of his social position and of his entire dependency on others for just about everything, including his identity. There is one strange letter from Julie in which she upbraids him, at considerable length, for indulging in what we infer to have been obscene language and perhaps swearing. There are also reports in other letters of outbursts of anger that are clearly tantrums. These are symptoms of the frustration of a child who is deliberately not being allowed to grow up.) This is how she outlines their proposed meeting at the chalet. Having described the setting, she refers to the remote village that "sometimes is used as a shelter for hunters but should only serve as a refuge for lovers." We can notice here a sign of that strategy of accommodation by rebaptism that in various ways comes to dominate the novel (i.e., she renames the "repair aux chasseurs" as "asile aux amants"; the significance of transforming a space connected with hunting into one dedicated to loving will not go unnoticed). Julie continues:

At the invitation of Monsieur d'Orbe, Claire has already persuaded her papa to go with some friends to hunt for two or three days in that area and to take along the inseparable cousins. The inseparables have others, as you know only too well. The one, representing the master of the house, will naturally do the honours of it; the other with less ceremony will do those of a humble chalet for his Julie, and this chalet sanctified by love, will be for them the temple of Cnidus.

Monsieur d'Orbe is the accepted suitor of Claire and is to be her husband. Thus he may represent "the master of the house," i.e., her father. This is the one position that Saint-Preux is never to be allowed to occupy; at most he will be a child of the house, never the master—never, that is, the father's representative.

Saint-Preux can only do the illusory honors of the chalet, and necessarily with less éclat than the appointed representative of the master of the house, since one aspect of his helpless position is that he is permitted almost no access to social éclat of any substantial kind. He can hardly shine, because he can hardly show—hardly, in fact, appear at all. Thus, the lovers are thrown back on private, temporary improvisations, making chivalric courts out of bourgeois bedrooms and temples out of chalets. Since these transformations have no social validation, they must necessarily be entirely provisional and ephemeral. Building on nothing, Saint-Preux and Julie can only build nothing, and it is hardly surprising that one of Saint-Preux's torments is that he lives for a series of discontinuous and randomly spaced ecstatic moments separated by voids of tedious intervals. He is not permitted to experience anything additive or cumulative. Since he and Julie are not permitted to be coadunate in any socially recognized way, he is constantly falling into or being pushed into mere apartness—the other side of the house, the other side of the world—from which he is occasionally, unpredictably, and on perpetually changing terms not of his making, summoned back. It is almost as if, outside the "house of the master," time loses its continuity and relatedness. Because of his excluded position, Saint-Preux's experience is deprived of its durée; when he is allowed in, it is for the most part an illusory inclusion—a momentary contact in an improvised frame.

As it transpires, there are always factors preventing Julie from meeting Saint-Preux in the proposed chalet—one might say that it turns out to be too far from home. But, she writes to the understandably somewhat desperate Saint-Preux, it should surely be possible to create "a chalet in the town." The phrase points to the paradoxical strategy to which they have to have recourse. In general it implies that the unlegalized lovers must establish their own fantasy spaces (chalets) inside the socialized space within which they have to live. It is as though there were no genuine "outside" left for them, a worrying phenomenon which was increasingly to attract the attention of nineteenth-century writers. Inside these temporary private chalets the unsanctioned sexual embrace may be enjoyed without any disturbance of—or departure from—the existing society. And the place that Julie decrees will serve as a chalet in the town could hardly be more revealing, for it is nowhere less than the house of the father—*la maison paternelle*.

In the letter in which Julie explains the layout of the house and just when and where Saint-Preux should come to her, she is at considerable pains to stress the danger of the proposed encounter—more so than the bliss it may promise.

No, my sweet friend, no, we shall not leave this short life without having tasted happiness for an instant. But yet remember that this instant is surrounded by the horrors of death; that to come is to be subjected to a thousand hazards, to stay is dangerous, to leave is extremely perilous. . . . Let us not deceive ourselves. I know my father too well to doubt that I might see him stab you to the heart immediately with his own hand, if indeed he did not begin with me; for surely I should not be spared, and do you think that I should expose you to this danger if I were not sure of sharing it? Still, remember that it is not a matter of depending on your courage. You must not think of it and I even forbid you quite expressly to carry any weapon for your defense, not even your sword. Besides, it would be perfectly useless to you, for if we are surprised, my plan is to throw myself into your arms, to grasp you strongly in mine, and thus to receive the deadly blow so that we may be parted no more, happier at the moment of my death than I was in my life.

The length of the quotation is necessary to reveal the main source of Julie's emotional excitement. Even a casual glance at the letter would give one the sense that it is hardly calculated to encourage the summoned lover; but a more careful reading reveals that the summons amounts to an emasculation. He is to bring *no* weapons—not even his sword. All those hazards and dangers she refers to pertain to one thing; they are the aura or atmosphere of the *maison paternelle*—the terrible presence of the father. And it is clear that Julie's imagination is fixed much more on the "sword" of the father than of her lover. Her fantasies center on seeing her father stab the unarmed lover (no question of the father not having *his* sword to hand): then it becomes clear, the root fantasy is of herself being stabbed by her father. That is the dreaded/desired penetration. Saint-Preux is invited into her bed, not so much to satisfy her love for him as to indulge her imagination of the aroused and irresistible father.

If this seems excessive, let me justify my contention that the most physical contact or encounter actually described in the book is not between Julie and Saint-Preux but between Julie and her father. The extraordinary letter in which Saint-Preux describes his waiting moments in Julie's room prior to her arrival reveals him in the posture of a feverish fetishist. Quite apart from the awkwardness inherent in the epistolary mode, the letter conveys the excitement of a man who derives his sensual satisfactions from associations. Because essentially he has been forbidden to have direct access to the body of Julie, as he is summoned in swordless secrecy, it is hardly surprising that his feelings should have been displaced from the person—whom he constantly sees but from whom he is as constantly debarred—to her accessories. So it is that he seems to be deriving his most sexual excitement from rummaging through her clothes which he itemizes almost while fingering them. "All the parts of your scattered dress present to my ardent imagination those of your body they conceal." The excitement mounts until he is passionately kissing the whalebone of the corset that has taken the imprint of her breasts. At this stage he is clearly on the point of involuntary orgasm or masturbation. Then— and we should not attribute this to the exigencies and constraints of the epistolary mode—he seeks relief in writing. "What good fortune to have found ink and paper! I am expressing my feelings in order to temper their excess; I moderate my ecstasy by describing it."

To a modern reader this moment is comic indeed: but in fact it has far-reaching reverberations. Saint Preux is forced away from the body of the loved other and into writing, an inherently solitary activity. *Donner le change* is effectively to "sidetrack" or "put off," as when putting dogs on the wrong scent, and for Saint-Preux to state that he is putting his emotions on the wrong scent or track by describing them gives us a clear picture of his position and behavior, which clarifies not only his position in Julie's room at that particular moment, but his position in the whole society throughout the book. He epitomizes the man who is forced to deflect and pervert his feelings into writings—hence, among other things, the extraordinarily long and often seemingly semantically depleted letters he writes. They are a kind of onanism, and for him, there clearly are many times when what matters is not *what* he is writing but *that* he is writing. It is almost all he is permitted to do by the rules that determine all the relationships in the society in which he lives. As the moment approaches for Julie's arrival, Saint-Preux seems on the verge of impotence. He thinks he hears a noise and immediately wonders whether it is Julie's cruel father, as well he might after her encouraging letter, and then as the door opens and he actually sees her—"c'est elle! c'est elle!"—he would seem to be about to collapse, indeed to be collapsing to the degree that collapsing is compatible with letter writing. "My heart, my feeble heart succumbs to so many agitations!" ("Mon coeur, mon faible coeur, tu succombes à tant d'agitations!"). In all seriousness, a reader might very well wonder whether that feebleness was not impairing other organs as well. And the feebleness of the lover is in direct correlation to the power of the father.

I do not think that it is any spirit of disappointed prurience that causes me to maintain that after the conclusion of this letter there is no *sense* of any real sexual connection and experience between Saint-Preux and Julie. It is, indeed, almost as if it never happened. What very certainly does happen, and it takes on a vivid position in the text, is the father's attack on Julie, and their subsequent embrace. Again I must quote at length since, among the hundreds of thousands of words exchanged by the lovers in letters, this is the one brute act that asserts a total dominance over the inferior power of the word. The episode takes place shortly after Lord Bomston, the English aristocrat, has offered to bestow a fortune and an estate on Saint-Preux, thereby hoping to qualify him as an acceptable suitor in Julie's father's eyes. The father dismisses the idea with angry contempt, for reasons to which I shall return; but as a result of all the rational persuasion that people are bringing to bear on him—what, after all, *can* he have against the marriage after Lord Bomston's offer?—his irrational anger mounts until he falls on his daughter and spills his rage on the person at whom it has really been aimed all along.

At that moment, my father, who thought he felt a reproach in these words and whose fury awaited only a pretext, flew upon your poor friend. For the first time in my life I received a blow; nor was that all, but giving himself up to his fit of passion with a violence equal to the effort he was making, he beat me mercilessly, although my mother had thrown herself between us, covered me with her body, and received some of the blows which were intended for me. In shrinking back to avoid them, I stumbled, I fell, and my head struck the leg of a table which caused it to bleed.

The attack could hardly have been more sexual, albeit specific incestuous lust has been translated, or distorted, into violent anger which is permitted to the father simply because he is the father. The fact that at one point he is hitting Julie and her mother indifferently adds to the clarity of just what kind of passional energy he is releasing. Psychoanalysts refer to the figure of the mother and father copulating as "the combined object" in the eyes of the child. Here the wife and daughter form another "combined object" in the eyes of the father—eyes dazed with lustful anger, angry lust. And it is only when he has drawn blood that the father's orgasmic eruption is over, and "the triumph of anger" finished.

There follows the reconciliation. Before describing it, Julie discusses "paternal dignity" and makes the assertion that "a father's heart feels that it is made to pardon and not to have need of being pardoned." All this points to the fact that for this family/society, all power, both to punish and to pardon, flows in one direction—*from* the father. In his way he directly and indirectly controls, one might say owns, the permissible reciprocities of all those in any way connected to him. What has Saint-Preux to offer that can compete with this power? The answer, or one answer, would have to be "words" or more generally the pleasures and persuasions of language. But the father has no need of language: he can just reach out and take what he wants. Thus Julie's account of the scene after the climax—a scene pervaded with a distinctly postcoital silence and exhaustion—continued. The father does not speak to her, but this is what happens after dinner as Julie and her parents are gathering round the fire:

I was going to get a chair in order to put myself between them, when, laying hold of my dress and drawing me to him without saying anything, he placed me on his knees. All this was done so suddenly and by a kind of quite involuntary impulse he was almost regretful the moment afterwards. . . . I do not know what false shame prevented those paternal arms from giving themselves up to these sweet embraces. A certain gravity which he dared not abandon, a certain confusion which he dared not overcome put between the father and his daughter this charming embarrassment that modesty and passion cause in lovers. . . . I say, I felt all this, my angel, and could no longer hold back the tenderness which was overcoming me. I pretended to slip; to prevent myself, I threw an arm around my father's neck. I laid my face close to his venerable cheek, and in an instant it was covered with my kisses and bathed with my tears. I knew by those which rolled from his eyes that he himself was relieved of a great sorrow. My mother shared our rapture. Only sweet and peaceful innocence was wanting in my heart to make this natural scene the most delightful moment of my life.

I want to stress again that nothing remotely comparable in physical contact is ever evoked as occurring between Julie and Saint-Preux. More than that, we may note from her ecstatic description of this "moment" that by a potentially perverse inversion of roles, it is no longer the father who is an interfering obstacle between the daughter and lover, but rather the lover who, by his violation of the girl's "innocence," is the source of a contaminating self-reproach in the otherwise blissful relationship between the daughter and the father. With the beaming mother looking on, this truly does offer a spectacle or scene that is pervaded with latent—and not so latent—incestuous feelings. (I am not so foolish or out of the world as to imagine that there is really no such thing as a family quarrel and a joyful reconciliation but only transformed incestuous to-ings and fro-ings; but here the physical detailing is so excitedly minute in a way that is so missing from Julie's letters to Saint-Preux that it seems permissible to perceive the scene and the attendant emotions it aroused in terms of barely controlled incest.) Julie revealingly goes on to add: "For myself, as I told him, I should think myself only too happy to be beaten every day for this reward, and there was no treatment so harsh that a single caress from him could not efface it from my heart." After this, what chance has Saint-Preux? He may be her lover but, more important, he is not, and cannot replace, her father. The lover's words are powerless beside the father's arms (*"bras paternels"*). Julie herself notes that a "revolution has taken place within me" and asks Claire a key question: "It seems to me that I look with more regret upon the happy time when I lived tranquil and content in the bosom of my family, and that I feel the weight of my fault increase along with that of the blessing it has caused me to lose. Tell me, cruel one! Tell me if you dare, is the time of love gone, no longer to return?" The answer to this question in one very real sense is "yes," and from this point, with no matter what delays, hesitations, and resistances, Julie turns her passional energies toward reachieving a kind of total family structure or situation that will reproduce in extended form the happy family circle that Saint-Preux so imperfectly penetrated and for a brief time almost broke.

There are two more points concerning this remarkable letter that I wish to make, and by way of explaining the detail into which I have gone concerning this letter (Letter 63 in the first part), I should perhaps say that I regard it as the most important one in the whole book. After what is effectively a decisive capitulation to the will and orders of the father (it is on this occasion that he names the husband she will marry), Julie indulges in some of her earlier feelings for Saint-Preux, asking Claire to tell him not to despair or give up hope (though on what he could conceivably base any hope it is hard to see), and reiterating an earlier belief that Heaven made them for one another: "Yes, yes, I am sure of it: we are destined to be united. . . . Is not such assurance firmly rooted in our hearts? Do we not feel that they are inseparable and that we no longer have but one between us?" Julie calls Claire her "inseparable"; from Saint-Preux she feels "indivisible"; and her dreams, fantasies, and aspirations all tend to the one article of faith that all the people she loves or cares for are "destined to be united": the arbor, the chalet in the town, and her cousin's habitation are somehow to be reclaimed and, after necessary purifications or modifications, to be brought together and contained in la maison paternelle. But the father is, among other things, he who separates. In the Oedipal situation, it is he who separates the mother from the child, thus standing as the obstacular presence that prevents the child from returning to a state of blissful unseparated oneness with the mother, which is, they say, a primal desire and fantasy. In this particular case we may say that it is the father who separates Julie from the desired sexual partner and lover. But more than that, it is the father who institutes and introduces all those divisions and separations and distances that the child has both to negotiate and to employ as he grows up and out and into the world—spatial (who and what goes where), legal (who and what may and may not be related, as Julie's father at the same time names her husband and bans her lover), and linguistic (the source of the names and the namings of people and things).[2]

Thus the father, as a presence, is the source of all those separations and divisions that ultimately derive from the prohibition of an incestuous return to undifferentiated oneness with the mother. Julie's dream of total union is a projection into the future of a totally regressive urge. What she has to learn, though she resists it in every way she can, is that the world is a place of separations and divisions. Or, to put it another way, one may curl up in the arms and on the lap of the father for ecstatic moments, but one cannot do it forever.

The second point concerns the postscript. Its very delegation to that subsidiary area of the letter is itself significant because in this way it is separated from the otherwise blissful aspects of the paternal beating and embrace. I shall quote it in full. "P. S. After I had written my letter, I went into my mother's room and there became so ill that I was compelled to return to my bed. I even perceived . . . I fear . . . ah, my dear! I quite fear that my fall yesterday may have some consequence more disastrous than I had thought. Thus all is finished for me; all my hopes abandon me at once." Although pregnancy is never mentioned and this shy allusive hint is a deliberate kind of mystification, one does not have to read too far between the lines, or rather along the dots, to infer that Julie has suffered a kind of miscarriage. This is borne out by a letter shortly afterward.

Thus it is clear that in his assault on his daughter the father also killed the prospective child she would have had from her lover. It is as though such is his power and his anger that he can reach into the latent future and eradicate a life that has already been engendered. In this way he effectively cancels the fertility of the lover, annuls the potency of his inseminations, and leaves him and his life sterile. Saint-Preux is quite right to claim that his *bonheur* has disappeared like a dream leaving no earthly monument, for the one unmistakably concrete evidence and fruit of his union with Julie has been blotted out. In this way such physicality as their relationship enjoyed is rendered effectively nonexistent. The father has attacked that, to him unacceptable, reality and rendered it unreal—as though it had never *been* real. The father can also reach into the past and eliminate a sexuality concerning his family that had neither his sanction nor his license. Such a father is indeed close to the awesome figure dominating the primal horde in Freud's vision of the powers of the primitive father.

All this might seem to be attributing too much to the father, but the effects of his presence in this book (and the differing degrees of the father's absence in later works) are so crucial that a fairly careful consideration of his role and power is justifiable. The references to the father are not literally innumerable, but they are so plentiful as to give the impression of recurring constantly. They range from references to his body—*le sein d'un père, le cou de mon père, les bras paternels, la main de son père*—to descriptions of his temperament and will— *l'inflexible sévérité de mon père, les préjugés de ton père, le volonté de mon père, le discours de mon père, la violence de ton père, ton inflexible père, la dignité paternelle, des violences d'un père emporté, la vanité d'un père barbare, la défense de mon père, l'esprit de votre père, l'amour paternel, les volontés d'un père, la tyrannie de votre père, la complaisance de mon père* (a good humor or obligingness of a somewhat debatable kind because its existence is dependent upon the will of the father being obeyed in all things. It would be "abused" if Julie left the *maison paternelle* because then, of course, he would have to go, too, in the event the world comes to Clarens, not the other way around). And after Julie's death, there is *la douleur d'un père infortuné*. Recurrently this violent, barbarous tyrant becomes rather litanously *le meilleur des pères* and, after her marriage to Wolmar, Julie refers with grateful compliancy to *la bonne intention des pères* (good intentions that, she says, are guided by Heaven). And, although he says very little (in effect he says only two things—Julie will not marry "that man"—he refuses even to name Saint-Preux—and "Julie will marry Wolmar"), there is above, or behind, everything *la parole du père: la parole de cet homme inflexible est irrévocable*. Not the words (Saint-Preux, we may say, has the words, particularly the written words), but the Word. The Word as spoken by the father is irrational, arbitrary, prejudiced, but it is inflexible, irrevocable, abso-lute. It is also, in Foucault's terms, *la parole dont la forme première est celle de la contrainte*. Julie's most powerful experience of *la parole du père* is as an interdiction, a prohibition—*la défense du père*.

In this context, let us consider a little more closely the grounds of his utter rejection of Saint-Preux. An early hint, perhaps, occurs when we learn in a letter from Julie that her father is very content with her skill in everything "except heraldry, which he thinks I have ne-glected." Inasmuch as the study of heraldry involves the tracing and recording of genealogies, it is devoted to a respect for the position, power, and prestige of long lines of the fathers and the names of the fathers; it also means a recognition of the *symbols* of that position and power—armorial bearings, coats of arms, and the like. As an ob-ject of study it has no use beyond that, no application to other aspects of life and learning; it involves no knowledge of history, and has no educative potential. It is really a kind of fetishism, involving a pro-longed and respectful mediation on the titles and trappings of the fathers.

Another hint, a stronger and more obvious one, is given when we learn that Julie's father once killed a friend in a duel and, some years later, lost his only son, which he saw as a punishment for the deed. The paragraph is remarkable, for again it evokes very vividly the physical power, the blood-letting barbarity of the father, and I will quote it at length.

You know that my father had the misfortune in his youth to kill a man in a duel. This man was a friend; they fought reluctantly, compelled by an absurd point of honour. The fatal blow which deprived one of his life robbed the other of his peace of mind forever. Since that time, painful remorse has never left his heart. Often we hear him cry and lament in private; he thinks he still can feel the blade thrust by his cruel hand into his friend's heart. In his nightmares he sees the pale and bloody body. Trembling he gazes upon the mortal wound; he would like to staunch the flowing blood; terror seizes him; he cries out; the frightful corpse does not cease pursuing him.

That this is in a letter to Saint-Preux can hardly give him confidence in his suit for Julie. But the key observation concerning the duel is that they were "compelled by an absurd point of honor" (*l'insensé point d'honneur les y contraignit*). *Insensé* is mad, insane, literally without sense. The code behind this kind of point of honor—the content is not specified and is irrelevant—is irrational, arbitrary, and prejudiced, but (and by the same token) it is inflexible, irrevocable, absolute—that is, it is exactly similar to the Word of the father as I have just described it. And its imperative asserts itself in the rent body and flowing blood of a friend, just as the imperative of the Word of the father expresses itself in the beaten body and flowing blood of a daughter. The Code and the Word are absolute *because* they are irrational and vice versa. Their authority cannot be questioned because they cannot be questioned. Their power does not have to be sanctioned, because theirs is the sanctified, and sanctifying power. The orders, edicts, and constraints of these powers can only be obeyed. The alternative is to deny, destroy, or abandon the Code—and the father.

But let me return to Julie's father's rejection of Saint-Preux. Lord Bomston has not only offered to give Saint-Preux money and property; he has also attacked the pointless irrationality of Julie's father's attachment to the idea of a noble title as essential for any potential husband for Julie. Thus Bomston, the cool, rational Englishman: "Nobility? An empty prerogative in a country where it is more injurious than useful. But he [i.e., Saint-Preux] has nobility even so, do not doubt it, not written in ink on old parchment but engraved on his heart in indelible characters. In short, if you prefer reason to prejudice, and if you love your daughter better than your titles, you will give her to him." This argument carries a multiple sting because, in addition to putting the father in the position of valuing his titles more than his daughter and esteeming an ink-and-parchment nobility more than a nobility of the heart, it attacks the substance of his own title. Here I will simply quote from the note provided by Judith McDowell as a gloss on the first point Bomston makes in the passage quoted above concerning the "empty prerogative" of the nobility of Julie's

father. Daniel Mornet gives the following explanation for this remark: "Berne had conquered the Vaud region, after which all the
Vaud nobility had been excluded from public office; since there was
little commerce or industry in which they cared to engage, they were
reduced to a life of idleness or expatriation." In other words, Julie's
father's noble title is *only* a title, no longer referring to or connoting
some kind of service or function in the land as, Lord Bomston points
out, titles of nobility usually do. This only serves to sharpen the focus
on the *total* irrationality of the father's ferocious attachment to his
name.

Here is part of his answer, or rather reaction, since Bomston's
points are unanswerable. "What! My Lord . . . can an honourable
man like yourself even think that the last surviving branch of an
illustrious family might lose or degrade its name by taking that of a
nobody [*d'un quidam*], without a home and reduced to living on
charity?" Since Bomston has just offered to bestow a home and
money on Saint-Preux, the father's last two objections about him do
nothing except reveal the father's wild impenetrability as he flails
around trying to produce "reasons" for that which has no reasons,
and, as far as he is concerned, required none. For him it all comes
down to the opposition *nom/quidam*. *Quidam* is precisely "some person," an unnamed individual, or as Harrap's dictionary puts it, "Person (name unknown)." Julie's father refuses to recognize Saint-Preux
as having "a name." Of course he does have one (just about—you can
read a very long way into the book without finding what it is; his
letters are always "A Julie" or "Réponse" and so on), but it is one
that the father effectively nullifies by his withholding of ratification.
He is forced into the ontological category of quidamity (the word
exists)—"person (name unknown)." Against that, the father upholds
the name of the family, which is of course *le nom du père*; not this
or that name in particular (indeed, to be honest I cannot recall
whether we ever learn his name as opposed to his title, "Baron"). The
father's unarticulated dread is two-fold: of a daughter taken over by
a quidam; of a world taken over by quidams, which would render
his name, his role, his being, all equally meaningless.[3]

Once married to Monsieur de Wolmar, Julie wants Saint-Preux to
assume "a submissive and compliant manner with my father" and in
the move toward consensus and what I call "ensemblization," which
dominates the later parts of the book, even he comes round to respecting and admiring the father, despite what he rather nicely calls *la*

bizarrerie de ses préjugés. Bizarre indeed they are, and it is perhaps
more than a happy accident that etymology of that word not only involves the Italian *bizzaro*, "angry," but may also involve the Basque
bizarra, "beard," thus suggesting a particular kind of male choler as
well as the more general sense of the odd, singular, or whimsically
strange. The father's prejudices are bizarre, but, as I have stressed,
they are totally binding, on the father himself as well as on those
within his jurisdiction. Julie, in her most distraught moment of conflicting urges and imperatives, attempts a kind of psychic fragmentation whereby she will let love dispose of her heart but allow her
father to dispose of her hand. "Let a father enslaved by his promise
and jealous of a vain title dispose of my hand as he has pledged; let
love alone dispose of my heart." Julie has complained that she is enslaved by her father; he in turn is enslaved by his own word. Thus
the father is both the source and the slave of the Word. And there is
a very important aspect of this double relationship he has to the
Word. It is often noted in the book that Julie's father is blind, as well
as irrational, given to foolish ideas and to a general *bizarrerie* in his
prejudices; there are references to his not knowing what is going on.
It is as though he has the most power but sees the least. And this is
not attributable to *what* he is by temperament so much as *where* he
is by role. That place, to use a phrase from Lacan, entails blindness
(*cette place comportait l'aveuglement*).

This comes from Lacan's famous "Séminaire sur 'la Lettre volée' "
from which I quote one more paragraph:

Rex et augur, the legendary, archaic quality of the words seems to re-
sound only to impress us with the absurdity of applying them to a man.
And the figures of history, for some time now, hardly encourage us to do
so. It is not natural for man to bear alone the weight of the highest of
signifiers. And the place he occupies as soon as he dons it may equally be
apt to become the symbol of the most outrageous imbecility. Let us say that
the King here is invested with the equivocation natural to the sacred, with
the imbecility upon prizes none other than the subject.[4]

In the world of this book, Julie's father occupies that role described
by Lacan as bearing the "highest of signifiers," and we may well feel,
as most of the figures in the book do, that over the central issue he
displays what at the time seems to be "outrageous imbecility," just
that imbecility characterized by Lacan as involved with being the supreme authority.

In all this, Rousseau's book is focusing on something quite extraordinarily crucial in the history of Western society. The Word of the father is, we have noted, bizarre but binding, not because of what it says but because of where it comes from. The father is the ultimate sanction, the absolute "referential" in Lefebvre's sense of the term, the fixed point beyond rationality, from which flows power, to which can only flow obedience; the figure speaking a language of pure command and taboo, the source of nomination (*le nom du père*) and prohibition (*le "non" du père*). Because of the father and his inflexible command and irrevocable world, it seems as if the established institutions are secure and can endure; the momentary fissures of passion are blocked, and marriage, the family, and the whole way of life connected with these institutions as practiced in that society are celebrated as achieving an ideal of incorporative harmony and functioning with serene efficiency. *The father makes the contracts, and the contracts hold.* But, as we have noted, the Word of the father is even here in a very imperiled condition. His family name and title are becoming meaningless, based on functions, distinctions, and differences that were ceasing to exist. If the apparently "full" word of the father is listened to carefully and discovered to be in fact an "empty" word— what then?[5] What becomes of all the dependence structures and binding contracts—not only between parents and children, husbands and wives, but also between words and meanings, signs and things?

With the nineteenth century, despite those grim images of the cruel authoritarian father such as Thomas Arnold—and indeed during the eighteenth century as well, from around the time of Rousseau's novel (1761, but of course such phenomena have no date of origin)—we are entering a period in which the Word of the father and all that it implies start to come into question, and if it may be said that the Word in varying ways ceases to "enslave," it must also be added that it comes to be a problem to establish just what, if anything, it can bind or hold together. (It would be a matter for a separate study to consider the figure of the father in nineteenth-century fiction, but as random examples of the weakened figure of the father we can readily think of those comatose, ailing, or absent fathers in the works of Jane Austen, and remember that Emma Bovary's father enters literature with a broken leg, and look ahead to the veritable child-father in *The Golden Bowl*.) Instead of the *nom du père* there is a growing sense of the *"non" du père*, not in the sense of the paternal prohibition, but rather implying the absence of the father, or the father as absence. It is in this sense that Foucault uses the phrase in his essay concerning Hölderlin (see above, n. 2). There he also refers to the phenomenon of *l'absence ravageante du père*, that father who, at the decisive moment in Julie's life, was so "ravagingly" present for one last display of blind, awesome power and fury, which was perhaps in part provoked by a sense that that power was being in some indiscernible way undermined, and by the as-yet-unconscious dawning of an unformulable apprehension that it was on the verge of an irreversible decline.

For a long time Julie seems torn at having to choose between "lover or father." But there is never any real chance of her abandoning the father for the lover. This is made very clear when Lord Bomston offers what would appear to be a perfect solution for the two lovers. Having attempted in vain to argue against the irrational prejudices of her father, and in vain having offered to make Saint-Preux both propertied and wealthy, this inexhaustible source of rational beneficence offers what would seem to be an impossibility—the legitimization of their passion in a new country. It is obvious that Lord Bomston acts and wishes to act as a father figure to the two young lovers; what should be noted is that he is trying to compensate for the blind irrationality of the real father by being the incarnation of *rational* paternity. Julie's father works with fists, threats, and interdictions; Lord Bomston, with kindness, praise, and facilitations. Thus, he writes to Julie to invite her to join Saint-Preux in England—a very mythical England drawn from an atlas of imagined wish fulfillments. He writes as a votary of romantic and passional love rather than familial devotion, and urges Julie to be true to the emotional condition of her heart. Because, he argues, this condition cannot be altered, there is only one thing to do—"you must make it legitimate." He then describes a beautiful estate he has in Yorkshire, with a fine old mansion, grounds and a running river, an ample self-supporting economy, peaceful contented inhabitants, and a complete absence of "hateful prejudices." It is indeed "a happy country" familiar from pastoral-utopian modes, dream geographies, and golden-age literature since time immemorial. And, he tells Julie, it is all hers.

It is, certainly, the ultimate invitation to two young lovers, kept apart by parental edict. "Come, unique pattern for true lovers. Come, charming and faithful couple, and take possession of a place made to serve as the refuge of love and of innocence." Whether there is or can be such a place is a question, or a quest, pervading literature of all ages. The important aspect of it in this context is that it offers not only an ideal setting, subsistence, and so on, but also and most particularly a *legitimization* that had been withheld by the real father. If Julie accepted the invitation she would be acknowledging that there could be a source other than her father for the legitimization of her relationships, and indirectly asserting that not all authority and sanctions come from the father, that there is a space, a law, and a language beyond his jurisdiction. Lord Bomston's final appeal would seem to be irresistible: "The tyranny of an obstinate father will plunge you into the abyss, which you will recognize after your fall . . . you will be sacrificed to the chimerical distinction of rank." But just at this point Rousseau interrupts with a footnote: "The chimerical distinction of rank! This is an English lord who is speaking in this way! Must not all this be fictitious? Reader, what do you say about it?" What is notable about this particular interruption or interpolation is that it impugns the credibility of Lord Bomston's offer, rational and indeed very Rousseauistic though his sentiments and beliefs are. What Rousseau is effectively marking with his marginal murmur of incredulity is not the fictitiousness of his work but the essential fictitiousness of Lord Bomston's offer. The "tyranny of the father" is real enough. It is that place of refuge for love and innocence, that *heureuse contrée* beyond all prejudices that is, alas, only a fiction. We readers, don't we think so?

Of course Julie declines the invitation. To Claire she writes that although the idea of "conjugal fidelity" fills her with inexpressible delight, she could not be an "ungrateful and unnatural daughter" particularly in view of the "blind fondness of a doting father and mother." To Lord Bomston she writes with lucid gratitude and absolute firmness, concluding her rejection with a ringing affirmation of what she knew all along even if she didn't know that she knew it: "I shall never desert my father's house." This declaration is reaffirmed to Saint-Preux many letters later when Julie, making use of a schizophrenic strategy by which she tries to combine the mutually exclusive lover and father, declares that she is his forever but will never leave home. "Do not think that to follow you I shall ever abandon my father's house" (*Ne pense point que pour te suivre j'abandonne jamais la maison paternelle*). The arbor and the chalet are insubstantial, dream stuff: ultimate power, authority, and reality reside in, and only in, *la maison paternelle*.

So there Julie stays, marrying the man her father chooses for her.

This man, Monsieur de Wolmar, is all too obviously a surrogate father, of similar age and with no previous involvements or attachments before the father's imperative was extended to him and he obeyed, "seconding my father's intentions," as Julie revealingly writes to Saint-Preux. At the same time, he is a cool, passionless figure, the incarnation of arid voyeuristic rationality, sexually an entirely negative figure toward whom the displaced passionate father could feel no jealousy. For Julie he offers a reprieve from love, which—she writes to Saint-Preux—so far from being necessary to a happy marriage, is precisely what opposes or prevents it. "Love is accompanied by a continual uneasiness over jealousy or privation, little suited to marriage, which is a state of enjoyment (*jouissance*) and peace." *Jouissance* can refer to the pleasure of orgasm but this is hardly its connotation in Julie's calm rationale for abandoning love. The stress is on peace, and it would seem that Julie's ambition is to turn her marriage into a condition of continual rest, or "arrest," in the interests of "peace." But what kind of life is it that is drained of all inquietude? "Death" is quite obviously the abrupt and only completely accurate answer, and what Julie is searching for could be seen as a kind of death-in-life, a permanent stasis in which everyone has come together and no one need move again. She names her garden—a strange enclosed world of her own making in which nature is not so much domesticated as bourgeois-ified—"Elysium," quite aware that it refers to the abode of the blessed after death. And the economy of her household, described at a length inordinate even by Saint-Preux's standards, is organized, routinized, and supervised down to such detail that one feels that in such a place the involuntary, the unpredictable, the "unquiet" would never happen again.

The first letter Julie writes after her marriage (beginning of Book 4) is to her cousin Claire urging that they annul the distinction between their two houses by conflating them, since Claire's husband, another somewhat senior citizen, has recently died. Julie is embarking on her grand dream of rehousing the world in her home, the house of the father. The attempt at ultimate synthesis has begun. And one of her reasons for pressing Claire to join her in her home is worth noting. Something is lacking. Her husband is unresponsive, his tenderness is *too* reasonable. But Julie can hardly wish for an inrush of unreason since that would be to seek the very inquietude she has chosen to leave behind. She refers to "all these voids," voids specifically left by her mother's death and the death of Claire's husband, but more generally by the fact that, as her children are too small for the kind of reciprocal love she needs, there is no one on whom she can lavish the full energies of her love and receive love in return. It is this role she wants to be filled by her cousin, the inseparable. Yet clearly the void is hardly one that can be filled by a cousin; indeed it could be said to be an ontological void. But there is no need to go so far to comprehend what Julie is lacking. It is not necessarily Saint-Preux himself, but the passional irregularities, intensities, frictions, and reciprocities—which can only be experienced in that *inquiétude continuelle* that she formally put behind her when she chose to reject him. It would seem that marriage as conceived by Julie has its privations as well as its peace; perhaps, even, it is its peace that is part of its privation.

Having brought Claire into the house, Julie extends her plans for inclusion. Her husband writes a courteous and generous letter inviting Saint-Preux to come and share their house, and he accepts, content to feel like "the child of the house." The father, temporarily absent because he is involved in a lawsuit (and one may imagine that he was often involved in such eristic errands, given his temperament), rejoins them. Even Lord Bomston is brought in, so that in a very real sense we may say that it is as if they are all there together in *la maison paternelle*, all united, and all so harmonious that Wolmar insists that Saint-Preux should embrace Julie, while Saint-Preux comes to love and respect the very father who ruined his life. There is no friction, and reconciliation and homecoming are everywhere. This may seem like a version of the commonplace "they all lived happily ever after" dream. But there is one aspect of this "ensemblizing" drive that is worth special attention. It concerns the move toward indistinguishability between Julie and Claire, particularly as mothers, a move that extends toward their children as well. It entails at times what amounts to an interchangeability of selves, so that the I-Thou disjunction/conjunction is dissolved. Thus Julie: "I feel that I doubly enjoy my little Marcellin's caresses when I see you sharing them. When I embrace your daughter, I imagine I am pressing you to my bosom. We have said a hundred times, as we see our little babies playing together, that our united hearts mix them, and we no longer know to which one of us each of the three belongs." Saint-Preux, writing about Claire's daughter Henriette, refers to her mothers: "I say her *mothers*, for to see the manner in which they act with her it is difficult to distinguish the real one, and some strangers who arrived today are or seem to be still in doubt on the matter. In fact, both call her *Henriette* or *my daughter*, indifferently. She calls one mama and the other little mama." And later he writes to Claire: "You are both more dear to me than ever, but my heart no longer distinguishes between you and does not separate the inseparables." However, this same letter contains an account of a very ominous dream, to which I shall return.

At the conclusion of Book 5, Julie effectively suggests that Claire should marry Saint-Preux, and it is hard not to assume that, given their feelings of interchangeability (if not actual identicality), this would permit some vicarious indulgence in what might be expected to be the customary sexual embraces that would then legitimately ensue.

Ah cousin! What delight for me to unite forever two hearts so well formed for each other, who have been joined for so long in my own. Let them be even more closely joined in it, if possible. Let there be but one heart for you and me. Yes, my Claire, you will still serve your friend by indulging your love, and I shall be surer of my own sentiments when I shall no longer be able to distinguish between him and you.

The suggestion is firmly declined, but it testifies to an inclination to live in a kind of emotional blur in which her feelings can only be sure of themselves when they are no longer able, or constrained, to distinguish between their objects. From one point of view this desire to establish an inclusive happy-family pile in which, at least emotionally speaking, the various figures—cousin, lover, friend, father— are heaped indistinguishably together, is an attempt to realize a dream of total harmony in which all the oppositional elements in human relationships—familial, passional—have been eliminated and all the different parties can come together to live for ever and ever in peace and concord, never to part again. As Saint-Preux puts it, writing in the optative mood, if he can just see his friend Edward (Lord Bomston) happy, "we will all rejoin each other never to part again," though, as he notes in passing, if that state of perfect happiness were achieved, there would not in fact be much else for him to wish for, or to vow to do. Such a vision of human and humane harmony is from this point of view the acme of Enlightenment thought. From another point of view, Julie's dream (shared by others, but originating with her, or with her and Claire) involves an abandoning of distinctions, a loss of a sense of difference, which could be seen to point the way back to that "infamous promiscuity of things and women" which for Vico was the abhorrent state from which civilization had to emerge, that incestuous *ur*-confusion we think of as the primordial reign of chaos and old night. That, at its height civilization should start to look, albeit obliquely and very indirectly, longingly back to the precivilized state from which it emerged is a phenomenon of some considerable implications. And that this incestuous dream is engendered in, and arguably engendered by *la maison paternelle*—the paradigm locus of authority in society—is perhaps even more thought-provoking. The father, he-who-separates, produces a daughter who wishes to be she-who-brings-everyone-together-again. The rule of law engenders a dream of indistinguishability. Rousseau lays bare the outlines of a paradox that has more profound implications than he himself, perhaps, could guess.

But for all the aura of loving harmony, all is not quite well at Clarens and in Elysium, and this brings me back to Saint-Preux's nightmare. Saint-Preux has the dream after he has been established in Clarens but is setting out on a journey with Lord Bomston. In the dream he thinks he sees Julie's mother on her deathbed and Julie on her knees beside her, weeping and kissing her hands. Some remarks are exchanged which conclude with the mother saying:

"You will be a mother in your turn. . . ." She could not finish. . . . I tried to raise my eyes and look at her; I saw her no more. In her place I saw Julie. I saw her; I recognized her although her face was covered with a veil. I gave a shriek, I rushed forward to put aside the veil. I could not reach it. I stretched forth my arms, I tormented myself, but I touched nothing. "Friend, be calm," she said to me in a faint voice. "The terrible veil covers me. No hand can put it aside." [He has the dream three times.] Always the mournful sight, always that same appearance of death, always that impenetrable veil eluding my hands and hiding from my eyes the dying person it covered.

One might speculate endlessly, and perhaps fruitlessly, about the interpretation of this dream (how to read dreams *within* fictions is an interesting matter in its own right). But that veil subsumes a very clear symbolic form a great deal; all that has indeed separated Julie from her lover, all that she has allowed to come between them, and all that she has interposed between them herself—the inseparable cousin (at the beginning), the Word of the father, *la maison pater-nelle*, the *chaîne indissoluble* of her marriage, the rigid and powerful *cortège* in which she is fixed as the mother. All these have meant that when Saint-Preux has attempted to "reach" her, no matter how much he has stretched out his arms and tormented himself, he has always and inevitably (after the very brief and apparently soon-regretted affair) touched nothing, because of that veil *redoutable* and *impénétrable*. It is also, of course, the bridal veil which, worryingly enough, has turned into a shroud. So disturbing is the dream that Saint-Preux rushes to wake up Lord Bomston, who delivers the usual scolding: "you are worthless," and then drives Saint-Preux back to Clarens where he can sneak a glimpse of Julie and tear away "that fatal veil which is woven in your mind." Ashamed as usual, Saint-Preux only pauses to hear the voices of Julie and her cousin coming from Elysium and returns to his travels quite happy, feeling that he has at least done the honor to himself as Edward's friend of "getting the better of a dream." But, in a sense, it is the dream that has got the better of him long before he had it, and in any event, it is the dream that gets the better of them all in a way that I describe in the concluding part of this essay. Claire, in her answering letter in which she urges them both to hurry back to their "little community" registers her sense of the ominousness of the dream. "That veil! That veil! . . . There is something indefinably sinister in it which disturbs me each time I think of it." The implications involve the unconfrontable and unthinkable fact of Julie's death and her disappearing into eternal unreachability.

At one point Monsieur de Wolmar announces his intention to go on a trip which will keep him away for a few days. He asks whether Saint-Preux would like to come with him or stay at Clarens with Julie (as Julie writes to her cousin, her husband seems "determined to drive me to the limit"). Saint-Preux promptly states his preference for remaining, an answer that deeply pleases the perversely rational husband. However, the prospective situation disturbs Julie, and she communicates her anxieties to her cousin, registering her concern about her own latent instabilities. "Whatever you think of yourself, your mind [*âme*] is calm and tranquil, I am sure. Objects present themselves to it such as they are, but mine, ever agitated like a moving wave [*comme une onde agitée*], confounds and disfigures them." Whether we decide to translate *âme* as "soul" or "mind," it refers to some absolutely central governing spirit or prime mover, and for Julie to say that hers is constantly agitated *comme une onde agitée* is to reveal an aspect of her character of far-reaching significance. For if she is watery at the center, fluid, labile, potentially "thalassic," then all the meticulous structuring and architecture of her life, starting with her complete submission to her father/husband (he's not fluid at the center—he is empty, a very different matter) and extending to the meticulous routinizing of life at Clarens, can be seen in another light. To some extent, perhaps a large extent, they may be motivated by a fear of internal dissolution, a kind of passional liquefaction in which she would lose herself and drown. By the time we reach the height of the Romantic era, however we wish to date it, we find many metaphors for yearning to dissolve and merge with the elements, other people, the universe, whatever. The "flow" seems to have lost its terrors and revealed its enrapturing allure. But for Julie it is still a source of worry. Her carefully constructed life may be seen as, in part, a dike erected against the possible flood tides within her, just as her marriage, as she clearly indicated, was not a way of releasing passion but of escaping it. The problematical relationship (or opposition) between the dissolving liquefactions of passion and the binding structurations of marriage is at the very heart, or *âme*, of the great bourgeois novels of adultery of the nineteenth century.

Claire is not liquid and she writes back promptly with some sensible-seeming advice to Julie. She reminds her that she loved as Héloïse did and that, like her, she is now "pious." If Julie is worried about being alone with Saint-Preux, then make sure the children are always around and go off for some excursions—boat rides, for instance. "You like boat rides; you deprive yourself of them for the sake of your husband who fears the water and for the children whom you do not wish to hazard on it. Take advantage of the time of this absence to indulge yourself in this amusement, leaving your children in Fanchon's care [Fanchon Anet is Julie's closest attendant]."

It is revealing indeed that Monsieur de Wolmar is frightened of water, but it is perhaps not exactly the most prudent recommendation that the watery-centered Julie go for boat rides with her former lover. Her justification that they will always be under the protection of the boatmen seems a little feeble. There are a large number of very important boat rides in the history of the novel, but the figure of the protective boatman is conspicuously absent. There may be boatmen but they do not protect. And indeed if the really dangerous "waters" are internal, it is hard to see how they could.

The excursion by boat is duly taken and described by Saint-Preux in a letter that concludes Part Four. It is a trip laden with omen—indeed, it is effectively all omen, starting even from the base topography, for Julie's *house*, Saint-Preux reminds Lord Bomston, is *not far from the lake* and she likes being on the water. This basic house/ water topography could hardly appear more naturally than it does in Rousseau's book; at the same time it could hardly acquire more symbolic implications than it finally does. For Julie, householder and gardener supreme, is doomed to die by water. To select a few of the more notable details from this seminal boat trip, Saint-Preux steers the boat into the middle of the lake, i.e., as far from the shore as possible; a gale blows up and soon the waves are terrible; the frail boat cannot resist them, and it is driven to the opposite shore. There it is impossible at first to find any shelter or a place to land, and Julie is seized with sickness and almost faints at the side of the boat. Fortunately she is "used to the water" and this condition does not last long. She then acts as a kind of lacustrine Florence Nightingale and goes around wiping brows and dispensing water and wine. There is just one moment when two planks are opened by a particularly deluging shock and it seems as though the boat might indeed founder; the recorded reactions are revealing:

For an instant, two planks being partly opened in an impact which wet us all, she thought the boat broke to pieces, and in an exclamation from this tender mother, I distinctly heard these words: "Oh my children, must I see you no more?" As for myself, whose imagination always exceeds the peril, although I knew the real state of the danger, I expected to see the boat swallowed up at any moment, that affecting beauty struggling in the midst of the waves, and the pallor of death dulling the roses of her cheeks.

Comment on Saint-Preux's morbid imaginings is redundant (notice he does not imagine trying to save her but only watching her drown!), though to the extent that they are perverse it must be admitted that his treatment by society goes some long way to explaining why they should be so (you surely can't be treated as a quidam in a hierarchical society for very long without some perversion of the imagination taking place). On this occasion the boat reaches the shore safely, but his vision of *le bateau englouti* and the lovers (once-lovers, if you will) "drowning" together, is one that in varying forms haunted the European imagination for well over a century after this.

Julie herself maintains that their love is not repressed passion but purified passion and this is the rarity of her relationship to Saint-Preux. She insists that they have managed to transform *amour* into *amitié* and that as a result they can "spend our life together in fraternal familiarity and peaceful innocence." Despite the length, or

rather perhaps because of the length, at which they reassure and con-
gratulate each other on these purifications and transformations, one
registers both their precariousness and their latent perversity—to treat
an ex-lover with "fraternal familiarity" because that falls within the
bounds of the legitimate is, as I have suggested, to repress adulterous
feelings only to allow them to be reinstituted as incestuous ones. It
is a situation of uneasy equilibrium which, in effect, can only wait
for whatever will precipitate its inevitable disintegration—dangerous
waters within or without. In any event, it is once again the external
lake that precipitates a crisis, and this time one that is terminal.

On an expedition to the castle of Chillon on the lake, Julie's young
son falls into the water and she runs back like an arrow and throws
herself in after him. The account of the accident is in a letter from
Fanchon Anet, the attendant mentioned earlier by Claire:

we had neither servants nor a boat there; it took time to get them out . . .
the child is recovered, but the mother . . . the shock, the fall, the condition she was in . . . who knows better than I the dangers of such a fall!
. . . She remained unconscious for a very long time. . . . From some
orders she has given me, I see that she does not believe she will recover.
I am too unhappy; she will not recover. Madame d'Orbe is more altered
than she.

And it is that separated inseparable and much changed cousin who
informs Saint-Preux of Julie's death in brusque terms, which are indeed appropriate from someone stunned with grief, but which nevertheless carry something of the tone of a reproach as though it were
somehow all his fault, both for loving her and for having the dream
about the veil. "It is over. Impudent, unfortunate man, unhappy
dreamer! You shall never see her again . . . the veil . . . Julie is no
more. . . ." We are given no detail of Saint-Preux's reaction, but we
learn that Claire goes literally out of her mind, rolling about the floor,
mumbling and gnawing on the legs of chairs, a demonstration of an
intensity of grief, indeed of sheer uncontrolled passion, which is
scarcely to be matched by any of the other signs of feeling in the
entire book—perhaps only by the wild outburst of anger of Julie's
father. It is the grief of the "inseparable" who finds herself truly
and irrevocably separate; the response to a forced and final breaking
of a bond so close and so deep that it seems to me to bespeak that
primordial urge to merge back into intrafamilial oneness that goes
under the name of incest. It is with no intention of suggesting any

actual sexual perversity that I point out that from the long account of Julie's dying, written by her husband, it transpires that not only will Claire not leave Julie's bedroom, but Julie invites her to share her bed, while the tired husband is sent away.

Saint-Preux is not heard from again, though we gather he is temporarily prostrated with grief. But enclosed with Wolmar's letter is a last letter from Julie to Saint-Preux which reveals that there was indeed something wrong with her "project," i.e., her dream of ensemblization. "We must give up our projects. All is changed, my good friend. . . . We dreamed of rejoining each other. *That reunion was not good* [my italics]. It is Heaven's blessing to have prevented it, thereby, without a doubt, preventing misfortune." This is tantamount to saying that adultery would have been inevitable (and for Julie, of course, death is far preferable to such a dishonor); but more, it is a revocation of the whole dream of union or rather multiple reunion itself. It does not work. As Julie reveals, there was a split between "will" and "feeling" that was permanently there. "This sentiment, nourished despite myself, was involuntary; it has cost my innocence nothing. Everything which was dependent on my will was devoted to my duty. If my heart, which was not dependent on it, was devoted to you, that was my torment and not my crime." The House of Clarens, then, was built on repression and a secret "torment." No wonder it was bound to fall.

In her last letter, it is clear that Julie is still thinking in terms of some kind of total union of all her loved ones. "Would that I could invent still stronger bonds in order to unite all who are dear to me." But, as Claire reveals in the last letter of the book, there is no union left, only despairing fragmentation and monadic misery. This letter effectively outlines the fall of the House of Clarens, a fall, to my mind, of inestimable importance for the subsequent history of European literature. She writes to Saint-Preux.

You will see here only grief and sorrow; and perhaps our common affliction will be a solace for your own. In order to be given vent, mine needs you. I alone can neither weep, nor cry out, nor make myself understood. Wolmar understands me but does not respond to me. The sorrow of the unhappy father is buried within himself. . . . My children affect me but are incapable of pitying me. *I am alone amid everyone* [my italics].

By the end of the letter, which is the end of the book, Claire, writing in a state of distracted discontinuity, reveals her sense of the utter void that has been left by Julie's death and her desire to rejoin her inseparable cousin in the grave as soon as possible.

Perhaps, when I stated earlier that the book was primarily about a love affair between father and daughter, I should have added, "and between cousin and cousin." As far as the book is concerned, when Julie dies, Saint-Preux vanishes. But the most moving and significant statement in the whole letter is the one I have italicized. This enormous book is for the greater part concerned with an extensive dream of union whereby the family house can be extended and modified to contain everyone (and everything) that Julie loves in different ways within it; a dream of achieving a lasting tranquillity within which varying, and latently oppositional, relationships may be enjoyed in a kind of steady state of constant calm, with no friction. In a sense it is a dream of the world itself as one unchanging and contented family. But there is that agitated water . . . unacknowledged sexuality . . . and death. At the end, all the bonds have snapped: father, husband, cousin, lover, children, thrown back or turned in upon themselves, wandering around in a daze of misery without communication. Instead of the world as family, we have the family as isolation: *Je suis seule au milieu de tout le monde.* There is a glimpse here of that unspeakable solitude at the heart of all relationships which every other page of the book works to transcend or conceal or deny. After the fall of the House of Clarens—which is the paradigm fall of *la maison paternelle*—that glimpse would, in time, be extended into a scrutiny that was to characterize some of the greatest European novels of the nineteenth century.

Hegel's Conception of the Family

⚙ *Joan B. Landes*

A central theme of political philosophy concerns the relationship between the family and political life. G. W. F. Hegel's position on this subject merits special consideration. The family he envisions is not a simple model for politics. He therefore rejects the idea that authority relationships throughout society are homogeneous, a view that underlies the patriarchalist argument that the father's relationship to his wife and children is analogous to the king's relationship to his subjects, the Hobbesian contention that all relationships (even that between parent and child) are conventional, and the contemporary radical feminist assertion that the exercise of male power occurs in an identical fashion in family and society.[1] Similarly Hegel does not subscribe to a simple political socialization model whereby discipline and authority learned in the family can be directly applied in citizenship roles within the political realm. Although Hegel does attribute an important educative role to the family, he distinguishes between the social relationships that obtain in the family, society, and the state. Like the partriarchal model, the political socialization thesis errs by failing to discriminate between the quality of human relationships in each (partially independent) sphere of social life. On the other hand, Hegel rejects the proposition that the family constitutes a wholly independent sphere of social existence, a refuge from an unpleasant social world.[2]

Hegel insists that the modern family is (or should be) an "ethical root of the state."[3] The family is a partial sector of the political world, but it cannot be reduced completely to the logic of political or economic relationships. Within the family, individuals first learn to orient their activity toward the whole. The family member in modern society is simultaneously a member of civil society and the state. The three moments of ethical life—family, civil society, and state—exist in opposition to or in tension with one another; at the same time, they are united in a totality whose highest expression is the constitution of the state.[4]

Hegel's theory of family life cannot be understood except in light of his attempt to forge a new unity between ethical and political life in the face of the social fragmentation that has resulted from the rise of modern economic relationships. He regards the Athenian *polis* as an ideal form of *Sittlichkeit* (ethical life) whose foundation was a kind of living interaction between public and private existence.[5] He retains the standpoint of ethical family life in his discussion of the modern family, stressing that the family must coexist with the social consequences of egoistic individualism, property and class divisions, as well as the claims of private conscience. Family life in modern times, unlike the ancient *polis*, must conform to the fact of the modern individual. According to Hegel, the full or authentic individual is at once a family member, a bourgeois or member of civil society, and a citizen. An individual's relationship to any one sphere of ethical life is always mediated by his relationships to each other sphere.

Modern subjectivity, the individual's consciousness of himself as a moral agent, is a product of the social experiences between self and others, both inside and outside the family. The family provides a material and ethical basis for individuality. At the same time, Hegel criticizes the existing forms of subjectivity and individualism that prevail within the modern world. He envisions the possible realization of free subjectivity which, rather than presupposing antagonisms between individuals, might form the basis of a genuine public community. The generation of a higher form of communal life culminates in the ethical state, an institution that would be a great deal more than an artificial mechanism for resolving differences between antagonistically related egoistic individuals, as is described in the Lockean or Hobbesian versions of political life. The ethical state is not an isolated institution. It is grounded in the family as well as in certain social institutions of civil society.

The immense appeal of Hegel's conception is marred by a series of internal contradictions that will be explored in this article from the standpoint of family life. Broadly speaking, they concern the relationships between family and property, the family and love, the position of women, and the inevitability of the historical form of the family associated with the rise of industrial capitalism. The *Philosophy of Right* contains Hegel's most mature statement of a theory of family life. It will provide the focus for the following discussion, but other texts will be referred to in order to achieve a broader understanding of Hegel's perspective.

1   The Family and Property

Hegel strictly delimits the arenas of social life in which contractual relationships between persons prevail. In particular, he exempts both family life and the state from the sphere of contract (para. 75R). As Hegel remarks, "though marriage begins in contract, it is precisely a contract to transcend the standpoint of contract, the standpoint from which persons are regarded in their individuality as self-subsistent units" (para. 163R).

Hegel's noncontractual view of the family is not the result of a simple arbitrary desire to uphold ethical sociality inside the family while anarchic egoism reigns unchecked in the disagreeable world of civil society. Rather, the argument that the family is an ethical legal relationship follows directly from Hegel's views on contract, property, personality, and individuality. The noncontractual view of family life emerges in terms of a three-pronged critique of Roman law, the institution of slavery, and Kant's philosophy of law. Hegel distinguishes the human world from the animal world as well as the world of external objects. He rejects all arguments used to justify slavery that "depend on regarding man as a natural entity pure and simple, as an existent not in conformity with its concept . . ." (para. 57). Likewise, he insists that human beings cannot be degraded to the level of mere "things." The latter premise is the point of departure for an attack on Roman law wherein children, like slaves, were treated as the legal property of the father and, from his point of view, as "things" (paras. 43R and 40R).

The restriction that Hegel places on a person's ability to own another person is seen even more clearly in his critique of Kant's philosophy of the family. Hegel objects to Kant's statement that "Personal right of a real kind is the Right of the *possession* of an external object as a THING, and to the *use* of it AS A PERSON," where Kant is referring to a man's right over his wife, children, and domestic servants.[6] According to Hegel, Kant confuses rights that presuppose substantial ties, as in the family and the political sphere, with rights that concern abstract personality as such (para. 40R). For Hegel, the family—that is, its substantial basis—involves the sacrifice of personality. A full understanding of this perspective requires a brief review of the opening section of the *Philosophy of Right*, entitled "abstract right."

Personality, in Hegel's view, is an important but partial aspect of individuality—the most distinctive trait of the modern world. It is an abstraction that one-sidedly emphasizes the characteristics of arbitrary free will and the capacity for rights. At the level of personality, the will is present only as "desire, need, impulse and casual whim" (para. 37). Although Hegel insists that persons possess formal rights, he captures the purely negative character of rights in the dictum, " 'Do not infringe personality and what personality entails' " (para. 38). The personality asserts its rights and freedoms only through its opposition to other persons. Freedom, in the sphere of abstract right, is a wholly negative concept that describes the acquisitive relationships between persons who wish to possess all things within their purview.

According to Hegel, even a person's body and mind are initially external embodiments for the person which, like all other external things, only become his once he deposits his will into them. Whereas early liberal theorists had assumed that a person's body is given by either nature or God to that individual, here this relationship is regarded as complex and problematic.[7] The person must take possession of his own self. Property in one's own person is to be achieved, not assumed. But even depositing one's will in a thing is not by itself a sufficient basis for the existence of property. A further requirement is that of recognition by others. Recognition is confirmed in contracts that transform mere possession into private property. Thus, property presumes and requires the existence of social relationships between persons, themselves bearers of formal rights. At this stage, persons enter into social relationships in an external manner, that is, at the level of abstract right, social relationships are contractual relationships.

However, a person does not possess the right to alienate his entire person through a contract. Hegel insists on the distinction between the alienation of certain skills or powers for a limited period of time and the alienation of one's person; the latter would be a condition of servitude or slavery. On the basis of this distinction, Hegel argues against Kant's view of the family stated above. Hegel contends that the Kantian definition of personal right of a real kind obscures the fact that "a right arising from a contract is never a right over a person, but only a right over something external to a person or something which he can alienate, always a right over a thing" (para. 40R). By viewing marriage as only a civil contract, Kant degrades marriage to the level of a contract for reciprocal use (para. 161A). Furthermore, Kant fails to understand that contract never entitles one person to rights over another person. He neglects the fact that there are certain inalienable aspects of personality, e.g., "universal freedom of will, my ethical life, my religion" (para. 66). And perhaps most important, property by its nature is something "immediately different from free mind . . . [something that is] external pure and simple, a thing, something not free, not personal, without rights" (para. 42). For Hegel, marriage transcends the standpoint from which man and wife are deemed to have property in each other, especially in one another's sexual faculties.

In contrast to the Roman and the Kantian views of marriage, Hegel insists that not all social relationships between individuals are contractual relationships. Or, to state it in the reverse, the contractual relationship is not the only possible human relationship. Indeed, there are some relationships that require the *Aufhebung*, that is, cancellation, preservation, and transcendence, of the standpoint of contract and the "sacrifice of personality" (para. 40R). There are, according to Hegel, spheres of social existence in which "contract and its concomitants—like the *Versachlichung* . . . [reification] of human relations . . . do not prevail, where feeling and community may have scope, and where human, not merely personal, characteristics exist."[8]

2 Alienated Family Life

Certain difficulties arise with respect to Hegel's efforts to rescue the family from the alienation of civil society. The charge could be made that Hegel is merely an ideologist for the bourgeois family in that he projects an illusory and mystified view of the real—property—basis of family relationships.[9] Strikingly, however, Hegel himself acknowledges the property character of the family: "The family as person has its real external existence in property [*Eigentum*]; and it is only when this property takes the form of capital [*Vermögen*] that it becomes the embodiment of the substantial personality of the family" (para. 169; see also para. 170).

The English-speaking reader is hampered by the Knox translation of these passages, for Knox translates *Vermögen* as "capital" rather than "estate" or "material possibilities." In fact, Hegel reserves the term *Kapital* for later sections of the text where he is more precise about its meaning.[10] This is significant because it would be too easy to conclude from the Knox text that Hegel means to limit his discussion to only the bourgeois class. But his usage here is much broader. He is referring to the property-owning classes in their widest range and even suggests that this might include certain privileged groups among the wage-earning classes as well as the capitalists, landed aristocrats, and civil servants.[11] Each of these groups and classes has permanent and secure possessions that give an "external reality" to the family's otherwise interior existence. The family, through its possession of property, acquires the status of personhood. It possesses formal rights grounded in its ownership of property. It even possesses rights over and against the rights of individual family members.[12]

The family's unity or its existence as a "universal and enduring person" is only temporary. Hegel understands that the ethical dissolution of the family occurs when the children have come of age and are recognized as persons before the law, capable of holding property and of marrying: "the sons as heads of new families, the daughters as wives" (para. 177). The "natural" unity of the family disintegrates through death, inheritance, or divorce into acquisitiveness and competitive struggle; all ethical concerns seem to disappear. Paradoxically, property, which was hitherto presented as the basis of family unity, and its legal correlate, personality, are now identified as corrosive forces that undermine this unity. The acquisitive, egoistic, and negative characteristics of persons already treated by Hegel in his discussion of abstract right now reassert themselves and destroy the universality that exists within the first form of common ethical life experienced by individuals. This development is also given a historical basis as the necessary result of the shift from rural agrarian society to urban industrial life.[13]

Originally the family is the substantive whole whose function it is to provide for the individual. . . . But civil society tears the individual from his family ties, estranges the members of the family from one another, and recognizes them as self-subsistent persons. Further, for the paternal soil and the external inorganic resources of nature from which the individual derived his livelihood, it substitutes its own soil and subjects the permanent existence of even the entire family to dependence on itself and to contingency. Thus the individual becomes a son of civil society which has as many claims upon him as he has rights against it. (Para. 238)

Hegel sees another important function of the relationship between property and family life in the modern industrial period. The family serves to moralize and communalize property, elevating it above mere selfishness and greed.[14] This function of the family grew in importance as the propertied classes of industrializing nations were forced to confront the antagonistic products of the development of private wealth. In Hegel's own words, the massive pauperization of large numbers of people "brings with it, at the other end of the scale, conditions which greatly facilitate the concentration of disproportionate wealth in a few hands" (para. 244). He acknowledges that capitalist development leads to crises of overproduction and produces massive poverty among large sectors of the population.

Historically, the bourgeois family provided a physical and spiritual retreat from the uglier side of social life in the "economic sphere"—as it came to be understood. In the nineteenth century, home and community were presented as attainable ideals to the discomforted individuals of the propertied classes. Because of its moral character, the family represented a domain where sentiment and love might prevail, and these feelings obscured the ugliness of the alienated world of civil society but also sought to purify that world as well. The woman, as the central figure in the family household, represented spirituality, beauty, and ethical good.[15] By demonstrating how the family serves to moralize property, Hegel seems to implicitly recognize that the bourgeois family simultaneously mirrors and attempts to conceal from its members the alienated order of property within industrial capitalist society.

3   Authority Relations in the Family: The Position of Women

Hegel comprehends the historical shift toward a new position or role for the male family head. The father in the urban bourgeois industrial household no longer unilaterally "owns" the family resources, nor does he "own" his wife and children. Nevertheless, Hegel insists that for legal purposes the family is to be represented by its head, the husband. Moreover, Hegel specifies that it is the husband's prerogative to go out and work for the family's living, attend to its needs, and to control and administer its capital (para. 171).

The social order associated with the rise of modern industry has transformed the older, "natural," and patriarchal society rooted in agricultural life. The new family, unlike the old, is dependent, subordinate, and contingent.[16] Alone, it can no longer provide for the economic livelihood of its members. Instead, it offers the individual a realm in which subjective feeling is revered. This family is associated with a class whose mind is "concentrated on the struggle for riches" (para. 203A). In the industrial bourgeois family, the father's hegemony is still economically based. However, his familial position is no longer a result of his direct control over the labor of other family members. Hegel also recognizes the significance of the removal of production from the family and its relocation in factories.

Hegel interprets these facts to mean that the family is no longer patriarchal in any classical sense. His discussion of patriarchy is further illuminated by several unusual insights into the varying historical forms of patriarchal society. He anticipates many later discoveries on the character of kinship society as well as the relationship between private property, monogamous marriage, and the rise of the state that we now associate with the writings of Bachofen, Morgan, and Engels.[17] For example, Hegel admits of no natural foundation for restricted sexuality, monogamous marriage, or private property. All are conceived as historical products of different stages of social life. It is significant that the organization of sexual life within the family is related intimately to the organization of production and the political order of society. Thus, Hegel states:

The real beginning and original foundation of states has been rightly ascribed to the introduction of agriculture along with marriage, because the principle of agriculture brings with it the formation of the land and consequently exclusively private property; the nomadic life of savages, who seek their livelihood from place to place, it brings back to the tranquility of private rights and the assured satisfaction of their needs. Along with these changes, sexual love is restricted to marriage, and this bond in turn grows in an enduring league, inherently universal, while need expands into care for a family, and personal possessions into family goods. Security, consolidation, lasting satisfaction of needs, and so forth—things which are the most obvious recommendations of marriage and agriculture—are nothing but forms of universality, modes in which rationality, the final end and aim, asserts itself in these spheres. (Para. 203R)

The organization of family life corresponding to an agricultural class society is subsequently undermined by social and economic changes. In Hegel's view, the family's development parallels the development of subjectivity and modern economic life. The individual family unit—what today might be termed the nuclear-family form—supersedes the much older clan (or kinship) organization. Thus, in the modern period, the families of origin of the husband and the wife become less important and the clan itself becomes an abstraction, devoid of rights (para. 177).

Yet Hegel resists implying that these changes should result in absolute social equality between man and wife within the family—an implication that he would have associated with the views of romantics or libertines. The father's continued authority in the new nonproductive, sentimental family household is grounded solidly in two salient facts. First, the father has administrative control over family resources, including the final determination of that property through the inheritance.[18] Second, the father alone enters civil society and there represents the other nonparticipating family members. The father, in this way, negotiates with outsiders on behalf of those family members who are restricted to its interior. Although sons at least have the promise of such activity to look forward to upon reaching their majority, daughters and wives are expected to play out their lives within the family setting. The father brings back economic resources to sustain the other family members who are now divorced from social production and this provides the social basis for his continued hegemony within the family.

Women's activities, involved with the bearing and care of children and the supervision of domestic employees, are not of any direct economic significance. Lodged within the family, women can generate no new wealth or continuing income. The modern woman is dependent upon her husband and his activities in civil society for her economic survival. In Hegel's account, women never enter—nor do they have to—the sphere of need (civil society).[19] Hegel grasps, of course, both the new social division of labor within the bourgeois family and the social division of labor between family and society that is characteristic of the period of industrial capitalism. He recognizes the historically novel form of family life that develops within bourgeois society. His approach to the family as an ethical unity outside of the contractual relations that predominate in the sphere of civil society is qualified, as we have seen, by the extent to which the family itself is determined and permeated by property concerns. Nevertheless, his theoretical position reveals the ideological importance of the new family form that predominates in the modern world.

Furthermore, Hegel's elevation of the family above civil society is compatible with efforts to award women positions of spiritual reverence and authority quite out of accord with their actual social status. His theory of the family, therefore, could be used to legitimate the practice, common to most nineteenth- and early twentieth-century liberal industrial societies, of denying women full civil and political rights. In these ways, Hegel's conception of family life is consistent with the requirements of capitalist social organization. But his theory of family life and of women's role within it is also grounded in a critique of bourgeois subjectivity. Accordingly, Hegel's view of women's position in the family becomes an integral feature of his compelling attack on egoistic individualism and modern morality as well as a basis for his efforts to restore an ethical dimension to the modern world. Paradoxically, the conservative contents of Hegel's arguments are tied to a radical social critique. In his view, to allow women to adopt the standpoint of personality and rights in the sphere of civil society would constitute a further regression from the ethical achievements of the ancient *polis* by accentuating and expanding what he regards as the limited form of bourgeois subjectivity. Therefore, he would have modern women reject the very standpoint of individuality and become embodiments of universal family law like Sophocles' Antigone.[20] In summary, the authoritarian dimension of the family is made necessary by the antagonistic property structure of civil society. The continuing authority of the father within the nuclear family is a product of the social division of labor associated with the rise of industrial capitalism. At the same time, elements appear within Hegel's theory of the family that are incompatible with the order of civil society and point toward a more humane form of social life. These elements will now be examined from the standpoint of love, the substantive basis of the sentimental family.

4 *The Family and Love*

In Hegel's words, the family is "ethical mind in its natural or immediate phase" or "mind's feeling of its own unity" (paras. 156 and 158). The characteristic determination of the family is love. It is through love that family members are linked as each member achieves a self-consciousness of his own individuality. Love is primarily a feeling. Thus, according to Hegel, at the level of the family, social morality appears to us in the form of something natural. In contrast, "In the state feeling disappears; there we are conscious of unity as law; there the content must be rational and known to us" (para. 158A). Also, the universality achieved in the family through love remains trapped in the particular due to love's exclusiveness.

Through love the individual achieves a consciousness of his unity with another. In this unity each person transcends his own egotism. The individual comes to self-consciousness, then, only through a renunciation of his independence, which is at the same time knowledge of his self as a unity with another and of the other with him. Love involves a simultaneous limitation upon and liberation of one's individuality. In the act of loving the individual desires to abandon the standpoint of personality appropriate to the sphere of abstract right as well as the standpoint of the isolated subject that prevails in the sphere of civil society. Within the family, individuals who love become real social beings, living in and through one another.

Hegel proposes that the family limits the right achieved by the individual on the basis of the family's unity, that is, through that individuality first attained in familial sociality. Thus, individual right "takes on the *form* of right (as the abstract moment of determinate individuality) only when the family begins to dissolve." In other words, the right of the family, "a right against externality and against secessions from the family," takes precedence over the rights of individuals (paras. 159 and 159A). The latter remains wholly potential until the moment of the family's dissolution through death or divorce or as the individual members of the family pass over into the sphere of civil society and the state. "In this process of familial disorganization, the individuals who ought to exist as members in the family, become independent persons, subjects, bourgeois and citizens in their mind as well as their reality."[21] After the disintegration of the family the members each receive a proportionate share of such things as money, food, educational expenses, alimony, and so on, the external aspects of what was once the family's unity.

The right of the family is a right against the externality of nature, civil society, and state.[22] It is a right against individuals leaving the unity of the family. But such right is helpless ultimately against the subjective demands of love. Hegel, therefore, concludes that "the demand for unity can be sustained, then, only in relation to such things as are by nature external and not conditioned by feeling" (para. 159A). In other words, the right of the family—which ultimately resides in the father's authority over other family members—can extend only to property matters. It is powerless against the subjective desire of individuals to embrace one another in a love union. Hegel's analysis captures the inherent tension in the bourgeois love match between the demands of the heart and the considerations of property, a recurrent theme in the fiction of the eighteenth and nineteenth centuries.

According to Hegel, love possesses an internal contradiction from which the lovers are never free.

The first moment in love is that I do not wish to be a self-subsistent independent person that, if I were, then I would feel defective and incomplete. The second moment is that I find myself in another person, that I count for something in the other, while the other in turn comes to count for something in me. Love, therefore, is the most tremendous contradiction; the Understanding cannot resolve it since there is nothing more stubborn than this point (*Punktualität*) of self-consciousness which is negated and which nevertheless I ought to possess as affirmative. Love is at once the propounding and the resolving of this contradiction. As the resolving of it, love is unity of an ethical type. (Para. 158A)

In the first moment of love the individual rejects the standpoint of the bourgeois who wants nothing more than to pursue his own self-interest. Likewise, the lover transcends the standpoint of formal or abstract right that allows only for one-sided, acquisitive, and egoistic individuality. The lover strives to achieve self-consciousness by denying his own self-interested and egoistic character. In love's first moment individuality requires the denial of self. But in the second moment, the negative determination is transcended and the individual recovers himself through another, who simultaneously achieves her individuality through him. In the process of love, the individual is first negated and then returned to himself, but on a higher level. This dialectic explains how Hegel came to view the relationship between man

and wife as "the primary and immediate form in which one consciousness recognizes itself in another, and in which each knows that reciprocal recognition."[23] In the process of love, individuality is attained
in and through another person. Individuality, in this account, is simultaneously sociality, and the family is situated as an important moment
in the development of self-consciousness.

The dialectic of love that Hegel outlines presupposes a relationship
between equals in a monogamous love match. Indeed, Hegel argues
that "in essence marriage is monogamy because it is personality—immediate exclusive individuality—which enters into this tie and surrenders itself to it. . . . Personality attains its right of being conscious
of itself in another only insofar as the other is in this identical relationship as a person, i.e., as an atomic individual."[24] In Hegel's view,
therefore, monogamy imposes a certain measure of equality between
man and woman. Unlike Aristotle who conceived of woman only in
terms of the economic life of the *oikos* or the medievals who defined
woman through her sexuality, Hegel proffers a noneconomic, almost
transsexual definition of woman who achieves her equality with man
as a whole individual and partner in love. Here Hegel is much closer
to the Protestant conception of women which challenged the medieval
Christian morality and required mutual chastity of man and wife,
situated love wholly within the marital bond, founded the father's
authority within the family on covenant or agreement, embraced
"natural" forms of sexuality—i.e., sexuality contained within the family and oriented toward reproduction—and, finally, viewed marriage
as a partnership and the wife as a companion or "helpmate."[25] Hegel,
by secularizing these early Protestant notions, advances a positive
conception of family life and women, and an idea of love in which
the male and female partner are seen as "living subjects who are alike
in power and thus in one another's eyes."[26]

Nevertheless, love also possesses a negative moment. As we have
already established, the male is the dominant partner in the monogamous bourgeois family of which Hegel writes. His authority is
grounded in control over family property and the social division of
labor between family and economy. But Hegel compounds the inequality between husband and wife that derives from these social
facts by arguing that men and women possess separate (and unequal)
natures.[27] Man is portrayed as a creature of reason, woman as a creature of intuition: man is powerful and active, woman is passive and
subjective.

. . . It follows that man has his actual substantive life in the state, in learning, and so forth, as well as in labour and struggle with the external world and with himself so that it is only out of his direction that he fights his way to self-subsistent unity with himself. In the family he has a tranquil ethical life on the plane of feeling. Woman, on the other hand, has her substantive destiny in the family, and to be imbued with family piety is her ethical frame of mind. (Para. 116)

Woman, in Hegel's view, is determinately limited. She is denied the right to participate in the highest activities of reason—art, religion, and philosophy—as well as in the highest forms of ethical life—civil society and the state. Her substantive destiny lies within the family. Only woman is singularly destined to experience the passive stance in love, to both lose and achieve her individuality in and through another person, the man; while he, according to his separate nature, is allowed to transcend mere loving in order to participate in the "substantive life in the state, in learning . . . and in labour" (para. 116). The woman, in other words, achieves her full individuality in a passive manner, always in and through another's free subjectivity. Once she enters the marital bond for which her whole life is destined, she never leaves the family. Only the girl loses her honor "in surrendering her body" in sexual relations. As Hegel states: "A girl is destined in essence for the marriage tie and for that only; it is therefore demanded of her that her love shall take the form of marriage . . ." (para. 164A).

In Hegel's view, man and woman belong to separate spheres. This is a result of their different natures. Woman is destined to be a mother and a wife. Her sexuality is appropriated by the male in marriage. Woman is an incomplete individual or ethical subject and an inferior creation of mind. Hegel remarks:

Women are capable of education, but they are not made for activities which demand a universal faculty such as the more advanced sciences, philosophy, and certain forms of artistic production. Women may have happy ideas, taste, and elegance, but they cannot attain to the ideal. The difference between men and women is like that between animals and plants. Men correspond to animals while women correspond to plants because their development is more placid and the principle that underlies it is the rather vague unity of feeling. When women hold the helm of government, the state is at once in jeopardy, because women regulate their actions not by the demands of universality but by arbitrary inclinations and opinions. Women are educated—who knows how?—as it were by breathing in ideas, by living rather than by acquiring knowledge. The status of manhood, on the other hand, is attained only by the stress of thought and much technical exertion. (Para. 166A)

Viewing family life from the standpoint of love points up the contradiction of Hegel's attitude toward women, a contradiction that he shared with the Protestant bourgeoisie of his own epoch. On the one hand, woman is an individual subject who possesses rights and transcends the standpoint of formal personality when she recognizes and is recognized by another individual within the love union. On the other hand, woman remains inferior, trapped in the immediacy and contingency of natural life rather than social order. As a result, monogamous marriage, which is predicated on the "free surrender by both sexes of their personality" (para. 168), a fundamental element in Hegel's theory of ethical life, is marred by the subordinate status and incomplete individuality of the woman. Hegel's statements on women illuminate his argument that the family remains an ethical unity on the level of feeling rather than conscious reason. Woman, the major figure in the family landscape, is passive and subjective, capable of achieving self-consciousness only on the level of feeling but not through conceptual thought. As one commentator remarks, for Hegel "Love between man and wife is the highest moment of natural life."[28] But this is precisely the significant point. Only woman's nature is stamped by an association with the natural order; only woman can never transcend the level that spirit achieves in the first moment of objective ethical life. Trapped within the family, woman is denied the benefits of civil society, economic independence, and social awareness through labor and human interaction. Similarly, she can never experience the highest order of freedom, for she is denied a space within the public realm.

5   The Family and Sexuality

The family seen through the lens of Hegel's social philosophy is a rational institution that, at the same time, serves to institutionalize certain aspects of the natural world. Whereas slavery and subjection have been replaced by rational considerations, inequality persists. Because the modern family is no longer viewed as a wholly natural institution but as one that also conforms to the demands of reason, family

members are prone to accept as "natural" and "reasonable" the facts
of male superiority and female inferiority. The actual social relations
between man and wife are reproduced and anchored in the family
member's consciousness as a rational product of the natural differences between the sexes. Therefore, the exclusion of women from economic and public life in the industrial capitalist world is considered
to be a necessary result of the natural hierarchical division of the
human species. The actual historical trajectory of woman's seclusion
in the family is lost from the conscious memory of the modern individual. Under these circumstances, reason opposes historical truth; it
masks the truly irrational content of the organization of modern
family life and presents it to consciousness as the result of demands
that nature places on the social and historical order. In this context,
love has a contradictory character. On the one hand, love preserves
the promise of free subjectivity within a truly rational social order;
but on the other hand, it embodies the psychic internalization of
domination in the irrational order of the present.

The contradictory character of the relationship between man and
wife is a central, not a peripheral consideration for a critical appreciation of Hegel's social thought. As Marx understood, the relationship
between man and woman is a direct expression of man's whole relationship to nature.[29] In the modern sentimental love family that Hegel
portrays so compellingly, woman becomes a symbol for the social domination of nature. Although she is tied to ethical existence and moral
community through marriage, she continues to represent the natural
order within the social universe. In this sense, she is "re-naturalized."
The image of nature contained in the figure of woman is one of nature
transformed, tamed, and subjugated. In fact, the woman is the paradigmatic figure of a world in which both external nature and human
nature are dominated.[30] The treatment of woman in Hegel's theory of
family life reveals, in Max Horkheimer's unforgettable phrase, that
the "domination of nature involves the domination of man. . . ."[31]

One might say that Hegel accepts unquestioningly what Freud later
recognized as the underlying necessity for sentimental love to sub-
limate erotic desire, to imprison women in the family, and to limit
her sexual desires to those that are in the "family's interest." In short,
sentimental love—the hallmark of modern civilization—requires the
restriction of sexual life to a single kind of sexual gratification, heterosexual love, which is itself further bound by the rigid standards of

legitimacy and monogamy.[32] For Hegel, the repression of free sexuality is a prerequisite for the achievement of ethical family life. Accordingly, he presents marriage as a spiritual union in which "physical passion sinks to the level of physical moment, destined to vanish in its very satisfaction" (para. 163; see also para. 164). He stresses the importance of the marriage ceremony, for it assures that the love union is recognized and confirmed by the lovers' families and the larger community. Physical passion, in Hegel's view, is a contingent and capricious element in marriage, which, in the successful ethical family, is suppressed and limited to a subordinate moment by serving the necessary aim of human reproduction.

Hegel quarrels on this point with the romantics who, he charges, absolutize the subjective and individual aspects of love. He viewed their philosophy as a product of bourgeois subjectivity that could conceive of love solely in terms of subjective motivations without understanding its social determinations. For Hegel, marriage is an objectively appointed end and an ethical duty for each individual. The family is not for Hegel as it is for Kant a result of individual free choice or individual morality. One is born into a family and this implies certain duties. Moreover, one's future family life in a newly created sentimental love unit is predetermined. According to Hegel, ethical love supersedes individual morality. Marriage requires a necessary self-restriction from the standpoint of subjective desire, but it simultaneously offers a liberation because through it the lovers acquire substantive self-consciousness (para. 162).

6 The Family and Ethical Life

Hegel attempts to restore to the modern secular family of the Continental bourgeoisie a religious dimension. In the *Philosophy of Right* he speaks of family piety (*pietas*) and the *Penates* or guardian deities of the household. He thereby recalls to the modern reader aspects of the ancient family and *polis* as a lost norm against which modern family life is measured. The subjective love philosophy of the romantic movement and the genital contractualism of Kantian philosophy are, in Hegel's view, both reflections of the invasion of modern family life by the worst aspects of bourgeois subjectivity and egoistic individuality. Potentially free subjectivity is increasingly undermined by the negativity, particularity, egoism, and selfishness of civil society; in short, by the most characteristic social products of capitalist society. This, then, is the radical thrust of Hegel's interpretation of the modern world. As a recent critic observes, "Today there is 'no' subjectivity."[33] To an important extent, Hegel also believes that subjectivity in the modern world remains to be realized or liberated.

The argument here is complex. In a dialectical manner, Hegel suggests that the creation of the individual (not mere feeling or sexual love) is the goal of ethical life within the family; but that individualism, "the right of the subject's particularity, his right to be satisfied, or in other words, the right of subjective freedom," is the most distinctive negative characteristic of modern life and therefore also of the modern family (para. 124R). Since the modern family educates its children toward freedom of personality at the time when they come of age and become recognized as persons, the family ultimately exists for civil society, and its unity remains at best fragile and temporary. It lacks the overall unifying quality of Greek family life which was one moment in the larger totality of the *polis*. Likewise, the modern battle of the sexes is seen by Hegel as a degraded substitute for the conflict in ethics and tragedy between family piety (the law of woman) and public law (the law of the land and of man). The modern figure of emancipated woman who strives to achieve a formal equality with man in the sphere of bourgeois or civil society is for Hegel a pale image before the grandeur of Sophocles' Antigone.

The most conservative aspects of Hegel's arguments, then, seem to be introduced as a way of restoring communal ethical existence in the face of limited or bourgeois subjectivity. The family, like the corporation, is seen as an ethical root of the state. Hegel agrees with Plato that a good citizen must be a member of a good state. He argues that human community persists in time and in space. There is a continuity with the dead ancestors of the present citizens. The communitarian aspect of political life in the modern state is founded in other, more permanent bonds of community. The state does not arise mechanically or artificially on the basis of externality and egoism. Accordingly, Hegel rejects the contract view of the state that attracted earlier, especially seventeenth-century, liberal theorists. Likewise, he has no use for patriarchal genetic views of the state's origins that posit an undifferentiated continuity between family life and the state.[34] Rather, he offers a third position that the family is an ethical root of the state. In the modern period, the economic structure of civil society mediates between the family and the state. Thus, the direct conflict of the Greek period between family law and public law is circumvented to some extent. But the family also mediates between civil society and the state, especially through its educatory and psychic mechanisms. The family organizes personal life through the ideology of love and the sexual division of labor. As a result, the history of the individual is foreshadowed in the history of the larger society. Like Freud's superego, the family represents a tool of the past anchored in the present.

In short, the principle of individual freedom that is objectified in the state requires the training of individuals from the time of their birth. It is this important function that the modern family serves. It reproduces certain authority relations and anchors them in the developing individual.[35] At the same time, there is an emancipatory potential contained within the conflict between family and state and in the sexual struggle between woman and man. Even within the ideology of the past that the family transmits to future generations the potential exists for a more communal, nonantagonistic future form of society. It is for this reason that Hegel's theory of the family as an ethical root of the state demands our continuing attention.

In a positive fashion, Hegel attempts to contain the anarchic, disintegrative, and egoistic tendencies of modern civil society by preserving a social sphere that is free from its most acquisitive and egoistic characteristics. But, negatively, the ethical character of the sentimental family and its function as a refuge from bourgeois society is grounded in the subordination of women and the repression of sexuality. Hegel's conception of the family leads him to oppose the arguments of proto-feminists, sexual radicals, romantics, and Kantians. For him, all are guilty of an excessively subjective morality that promises no more than the extension of formal abstract rights to women and the dissolution of the important distinction that Hegel has erected between family life and civil society. At the very least, we should allow for the possibility that some (if not all) of these perspectives simply reproduce the social relations that they purport to oppose.

In conclusion, the modern critic of Hegel's theory of family must confront the fundamental issues he poses for those who would offer a vision of equality and liberation that remains trapped within the limits of egoistic individualism. These limits sacrifice the content of free subjectivity and ethical community life which Hegel sought to establish. For Hegel the latter could only be achieved on the basis of woman's imprisonment in the family and her social subordination. It is still not clear whether the insights that Hegel offers into the practice and consciousness of communal existence can be retained without accepting his more pessimistic conclusions.

Patriarchal Liberalism and Beyond:
From John Stuart Mill to Harriet Taylor

🌞 *Richard W. Krouse*

This essay will trace the development of the concept of the family in liberal political philosophy from its foundations in seventeenth-century consent and contract theory, through the social and political thought of the early English utilitarians, and into the classical liberalism of John Stuart Mill.[1] It is written in the twofold belief that the liberal concept of the family is a significant one in its own right, with important implications for the sexual politics of our own society, and that it is a strategic point of entry into the broader contours of the theoretical tradition within which it is embedded.

The analysis will proceed with this twofold belief in mind. The evolution of the liberal concept of the family will be traced with a view to exemplifying a fundamental tension within this tradition: the tension between an abstract philosophical commitment to formal equality of civil and political right, on the one hand, and continuing acceptance of concrete inequalities in the distribution of economic and social power, on the other. Broadly, my argument will be that the classical or mature liberal commitment to equality of citizenship for the abstract individual has been persistently undermined or defeated by a simultaneous acquiescence in, or affirmation of, parallel asymmetries of power of both class and sex—by class inequalities in the ownership and control of property *and* by sexual inequalities of power and authority within the family.

The argument will proceed roughly as follows. First, an effort will be made to define with more precision the nature of the problem—the problem of liberal equality. To begin, the voluntaristic presuppositions of liberal theory, with their egalitarian implications, will be brought out briefly by way of contrast with the naturalistic presup-

positions, and inegalitarian conclusions, of classical, medieval, and
early modern political theorists from Aristotle to Filmer. Next, the
internal incoherence of liberal theory, the failure of liberal theorists
to carry through the full egalitarian implications of their own individualistic premises, will be considered; the essay will at this point
invoke, schematically, certain conceptual categories most fully developed in the Marxian critique of classical liberalism. Then, the context having been set, the problematic of liberal equality will be explored specifically through an examination of the liberal concept of
the family. The tradition herein labeled patriarchal liberalism[2] will be
examined briefly in both the contractarian liberalism of Hobbes and
Locke and in the utilitarian liberalism of Bentham and James Mill.
Both sets of theorists, it will be claimed, exemplify the liberal bifurcation between a public sphere, in which formal civil and political rights
are distributed to abstract individuals in more or less perfectly egalitarian fashion, and a private sphere, where concrete structures of economic and social domination and dependence—here most specifically
patriarchal distributions of power within the family—survive intact.[3]
Finally, and most fundamentally, we shall consider the attempted
resolution of this root liberal dilemma in John Stuart Mill's *The Subjection of Women* (1869).[4] Here it will be argued, first, that Mill's
liberal feminism moves very far in the direction of a transcendence
of patriarchal liberalism, but that his continuing affirmation of a traditional division of labor within the family, which he shares with his
male liberal predecessors, would on the logic of his own analysis defeat the sexual equality to which he is committed. Second, it will be
suggested that the conceptual resources for the resolution of this residual contradiction within liberal theory can in part be found in the
more radical position taken by Mill's wife, Harriet Taylor, in an essay
on "The Enfranchisement of Women" (1851).[5] And, third, the undeveloped implications of her position in that essay will be explored.

2

At the heart of the liberal vision of the nature and purpose of political society there resides a set of philosophical assumptions that clash
fundamentally with the deepest presumptions of classical political philosophy. In classical political philosophy and its Christian scholastic
variants, political society is conceived as an ordered hierarchy or great

chain of being derived from the purposes of nature or will of God; its function is to perfect human nature according to this objective natural purpose or revealed divine will. In the classical vision, here most especially its Aristotelian variant, man is by nature a being who consummates or perfects his nature only in and through life in a political association, which alone among human institutions aims at the most sovereign or inclusive good. Politics, the architectonic art, exists not for the sake of "mere" life, but for the sake of the "good" life—defined as the victory of mind over body, reason over passion.[6]

The exalted purposes of the classical vision come, however, at a severe price. Individual human beings are in this vision neither naturally free nor naturally equal; the political association is neither the product of their consent, nor the instrument of their subjectively determined wants, needs, and purposes. Rather, individuals fulfill or complete their nature only as the subordinate instruments, each contributing according to his or her supposedly unequal natural capacities, of a transcendent moral and political purpose—namely, the cultivation of differential human reason and virtue.

The role of the family in the life of the *polis* is determined by this transcendent purpose. Genetically, the family is in the order of history prior to the *polis*. But teleologically, the *polis* is in the order of nature prior to the family. The family exists for the sake of the *polis*, not the *polis* for the sake of the family. It exists, that is to say, for the sake of economic production and sexual reproduction—to provide the material basis upon which the spiritual life of the *polis* rests. The *polis* is the realm of *freedom*, or transcendence, where men pursue the good life through public forms of speech and action. The family or household is the realm of *necessity*, or immanence, where women and slaves preserve "mere" life through private forms of productive and reproductive labor. Only those in full possession of the capacity for rational public deliberation—for Aristotle, leisured and propertied males—may be admitted to the status of free and equal citizenship. Those by nature lacking this capacity for full human rationality—for Aristotle, women and "natural" slaves—are banished to the private realm of the patriarchal household, there to be ruled by the husbands and masters whose leisure their labor secures. In sum, while the polis of classical political philosophy cultivates the intellectual and moral perfection of its citizens, it does so only by permitting them to stand on the bodies of their disenfranchised subjects.[7]

It is often alleged that at the heart of the liberal rejection of the classical tradition is a decisive lowering of the ends or purposes of political society—the replacement of an obligation imposed from above, deriving from the purposes of nature or the will of God, by a right springing from below, deriving from the purpose and will of naturally free and equal individuals. In classical political philosophy, the state is an ethical association for the attainment of virtue. In liberal political philosophy, it becomes a purely instrumental association for the protection of life, liberty, and property. No longer the public agent of an objective moral purpose—the good life—the political association exists now only to protect its private atomic components in their separate and subjective pursuit of "mere" life.[8]

But if classical political philosophy purchased its objectives only at a heavy price, so conversely does liberal political philosophy have the virtue of its vices. In choosing the "low but solid ground," it has chosen a good that, although lower in light of the classical imperative, is by virtue of that fact more equally accessible to all. As the creation of the purpose and will of abstract, free, and equal individuals, as the product of their consent, the liberal polity must permit them to pursue comfortable self-preservation in equal freedom. Those categories of persons, such as women and "natural" slaves, previously consigned to the status of necessary conditions of the *polis*, literally the bodily instruments of its "integral parts," should by the voluntaristic logic of liberal consent theory now be accorded the status of equal civil and political citizenship. Given the liberal claim that authority within both polity and society is the contractual product of individual will and consent, individuals are no longer the subordinate instruments of a transcendent moral purpose ordaining perfection through public freedom for some, slavery to private necessity for others. Rather, the liberal polity can exist by natural right only as the subordinate instrument of the immanent wants, needs, and purposes of its separate component parts. If it no longer positively promotes the intellectual and moral perfection of a chosen few, it would at least appear to have the virtue of getting this minority off the back of the hitherto subject majority.

3

Thus runs the liberal indictment of classical political philosophy, what might be called the brief for liberal equality. However, it may in turn fairly be asked whether liberalism has itself delivered upon its own egalitarian professions. Are the abstract philosophical premises of liberal theory in fact realized in the concrete political and socioeconomic institutions and practices advocated by actual liberal theorists?[9] Clearly, they are not; and a powerful analysis of the reasons why can be found in the Marxian critique of classical liberalism.

Liberalism is, from a Marxian perspective, a doubly defective vision. It is, first of all, based upon an intrinsically impoverished vision of human mind and society—e.g., an egoistic moral psychology, an atomistic methodological individualism in sociology, an instrumentalist conception of human action or agency in political and productive activity.[10] But it is also an *internally incoherent* vision—i.e., one committed to institutions and practices that would have the consequence of subverting its *own* core values, of undermining *liberal* equality and *liberal* freedom.[11] I wish here to concentrate upon this second mode of attack, selectively appropriating conceptual categories deployed by Marxian critics of liberalism in order to focus upon the theoretical incoherence of that tradition with respect to sexual inequalities of power and authority within the family.

In the classical liberal vision, according to Marx, society is conceived as an atomistic collection of egoistic monads, each pursuing its separate private purposes under the protective aegis of the sovereign public state. Each of these abstract individuals is the bearer of formally equal rights of man and citizen, formal equality of civil and political citizenship.[12] But the civil society of bourgeois liberalism, from a Marxian perspective, is not merely an atomistic "heap" of abstract individuals; it is also a political economy of power, with those same individuals arrayed into concrete structures of *class* and *sex* domination and dependence. Thus, it is claimed, the formally equal civil and political rights proclaimed by liberal theory as its crowning glory stand exposed as ideological illusions—severely undermined if not entirely obviated by the persistence of class and sex inequality in bourgeois property and family relations. Liberalism is to this degree theoretically incoherent, its own central values undermined or negated by the institutions and practices of bourgeois society itself.

This tension between the abstract values of liberal theory and the actual practices of bourgeois society is most familiar, from a Marxian angle of vision, with regard to the class inequalities of power flowing from private ownership or control of productive resources. What is less widely appreciated, but of greater relevance to this essay, is the conceptual power of the Marxian critique when extended from class to sex, from private property to patriarchal family—an analogy first fully developed not by Marx but by Engels, in his *Origins of the Family, Private Property, and the State*.[13]

According to this view, here presented in freely adapted form, the subordinate position of women within the patriarchal family can be understood by analogy to the exploited position of hitherto subordinate classes—though not, of course, simply reduced to a class category, since there remain obvious and important differences.[14] In classical and feudal society, both the economic subordination of male slaves or serfs and the domestic subordination of women is transparent—and openly sanctified by the dominant political and religious ideologies as flowing from the a priori purposes of nature or will of God. In fully developed capitalist society, by contrast, both class and sex domination is concealed or denied by the liberal philosophy of uncoerced transactions between abstract individuals endowed with equal civil and political rights. But these theoretical imperatives become, in practice, a form of mystification, an ideology. Thus, for example, the civil rights of economic life, the freedom to own property and form voluntary contracts, are effectively undermined by a severely asymmetrical distribution of bargaining power between classes: the class that owns or controls the means of production will use this monopoly of access to set the terms of what formally had been "voluntary" bilateral exchange. Members of the subordinate class are free only to choose between work in these terms, however alienating or exploitative, and unemployment and poverty.

Analogously, women in liberal society, with its voluntarist ideology of contract and consent, may be formally free to determine their fate with respect to marriage in a way that their predecessors, the domestic counterparts of male slaves and serfs, were not. But removed by the development of industry from control over productive resources, lacking economic autonomy and educational opportunity, women in liberal society are in fact forced to choose between marriage on the patriarchal terms set by the dominant sex, with its compensating advantages, and a spinster's life of even more complete domestic dependence and servitude.[15] They are, at best, free to enter or not to enter any particular marriage contract; but they are not effectively free, or not fully so, not to enter the market in marriage at all.[16] Hence they are to that extent coerced by conditions of severely asymmetrical bargaining power into marriage on the unequal terms set by men. In this sense there is, for worker and woman alike, only Hobson's choice.

This asymmetry of power between the sexes would, moreover, survive the full legal enfranchisement of women. As with class, so again with sex—in both instances the presumption of formal equality before the law or formal equality of political right, without further change, would be rendered largely meaningless in practice by the persistence of vast inequalities in the distribution of economic and social power. Civil and political disenfranchisement, in short, is less a cause than a consequence of more deeply rooted structures of class and sex domination and dependence.[17]

Now for Engels, at least, the elimination of patriarchal domination will require both economic and social revolution. The root and branch elimination of patriarchy requires, first, that *all* women—married and unmarried alike—be endowed with the equality of material power that flows from fully coequal participation in the "social productive activity." Second, this full integration of women into the productive life of society will require in turn that the nuclear family be supplemented or supplanted as an organizing unit of economic and social life—with private housekeeping and, more important, child-rearing functions being simply absorbed by the larger society:

. . . to emancipate woman and make her the equal of the man is and remains an impossibility so long as the woman is shut out from social productive labor and restricted to private domestic labor. The emancipation of woman will only be possible when woman can take part in production on a large, social scale, and domestic work no longer claims anything but an insignificant amount of her time.

. . . With the transfer of the means of production into common ownership, the single family ceases to be the economic unit of society. Private housekeeping is transformed into a social industry. The care and education of the children becomes a public affair; society looks after all children alike, whether they are legitimate or not.[18]

It would take us too far afield to speculate in any detail here upon the adequacy of Engels's proffered solution, but it may be worth remarking parenthetically at least that it seems to pose its own internal coherence problems for any humane Marxian vision. If the integration of women into productive life is to do anything more than universalize the envy and egoism that from a Marxian perspective is the defining characteristic of bourgeois civil society, or reproduce the class inequalities of capitalism (now on a sex-blind basis), a

socialist transformation of economic life is presupposed. But if socialism in turn is to be anything more than an alteration of distributive
relations, crude communism, a qualitative transformation of human
consciousness—in the direction of simultaneously enhanced individual creativity and communal solidarity—is presupposed. And
whether this transformation of consciousness is compatible with the
cavalier attitude toward children evinced by Engels is problematic at
the very least. The abstract collectivism that permits him to resolve
this issue with a sweep of the pen ("society looks after all children
alike . . .") is, ironically, no less formal and ideological than the abstract individualism of liberal theory. Concretely, in order to emancipate women from the ghetto of the home, Engels would relegate
children to ghettos of the state (or its postrevolutionary equivalent).
But it is by no means clear that the values of individual autonomy
and self-consciousness prized in the more reflective versions of the
Marxian ideal would flourish in this context. To the contrary, a per-
suasive argument can be made that the preservation of autonomous
spheres of private thought and action, including "intimate, stable,
nurturant units that promote ties across generations while they prepare children for the linked responsibilities of citizenship, work, and
child-rearing as adults"[19]—families or their functional equivalents—
would be essential to prevent the subordination of these values to
one overarching collective imperative.

   This commitment to the preservation of some irreducible sphere of
private life, some public/private distinction, is absolutely central to
the liberal vision. But this then returns us immediately to the root
liberal dilemma under discussion here, viz., the incoherent form in
which this abstract commitment has manifested itself in the writings
of actual liberal theorists. Again, for the precise reasons specified in
the Marxian critique, the egalitarian logic of liberal individualism is
itself undermined by the persistence of class and sex inequality in the
private sphere of property and family relations. In the case of the
latter, more particularly, the voluntarist principles of individual contract and consent are subverted by the anachronistic survival of
patriarchal family formations that, no longer sanctified by the purposes of nature or the will of God, stand bereft of all justification
before the bar of liberal principles.

   We may now turn, more specifically, to the history of this legitimation crisis in liberal theory prior to John Stuart Mill.

4

Recent scholarship in the history of English liberalism has stressed the extent to which its seventeenth-century progenitors, Hobbes and Locke, founded their theories upon a self-conscious rejection of the patriarchal paradigm in political thought.[20] It is unnecessary to summarize the results of that research here. Instead, I would like to carry forward the implications of the above analysis by focusing specifically upon the survival of the patriarchal concept of the family within the heart of liberal theory, despite liberalism's rejection of patriarchy as a principle for the legitimation of political or social authority.

The tension between relations based on consent and those that are seen as more "natural" pervades the political thought of Hobbes and Locke. On the one hand, both insist upon the consent of naturally free and equal individuals as the sole legitimate basis for political or social authority. On the other hand, neither is willing, or fully willing, to pursue the principles of consent theory through to their final logical destination. The nature of this anomaly was accurately exposed by Filmer: "If but one man be excluded, the same reason that excludes one man, may exclude many hundreds, and many thousands, yea, and the major part itself; if it be admitted, that the people are or ever were free by nature, and not to be governed, but by their own consent, it is most unjust to exclude any one man from his right in government." Thus, for example, "women . . . who by birth have as much natural freedom as any other . . . ought not to lose their liberty without their consent."[21] Consent theory, Filmer argues, is not a cab that can be dismounted at will; and by riding to the end of the line, he seeks to demonstrate its patent absurdity. The response of Hobbes and Locke to this kind of reductio ad absurdum strategy is at best ambivalent, their pursuit of the principles of consent confused and inconsistent.

This is clearly evident, first of all, with respect to the rights of citizenship in the realm of politics. For Hobbes, most obviously, government by consent is not incompatible with, in fact it ideally requires, absolute monarchy: all save one are disenfranchised equally. For Locke, too, the principles of consent do not entail thoroughly democratic conclusions; they may be compatible with aristocracy or constitutional monarchy. Even in those spheres (such as taxation), where responsible or representative government is most required, the people offering express consent could, and almost certainly would, be limited to the "rational and industrious" class of property-owning males. The overwhelming majority of mature adults for both Hobbes and Locke expressly or tacitly consent only to be ruled on a day-to-day basis without their active or ongoing consent.[22]

Of more immediate relevance to our concerns, however, is the ambivalent extension by Hobbes and Locke of the principles of consent to the politics of the family. Traditional defenders of absolute monarchy in seventeenth-century England, notably Filmer, had pointed to the inevitable and irrevocable hierarchical structure of a patriarchal family which rested not upon individual will or consent, but upon natural or scriptural authority, as the paradigm of properly constituted civil government. Hobbes and Locke, wishing to found political authority instead upon contract and consent, were challenged by the patriarchalists and Royalists to extend the logic of those same principles to the structure of authority in the family. Both did so, but not without considerable equivocation.

Each, for different reasons, begins by rejecting natural hierarchy or scripture as a basis for the patriarchal authority of husbands over wives or parents over children.[23] Both insist that women, no less than men, are by nature free and equal individuals.[24] And both, albeit in different ways, insist that within "conjugal" society the terms of the marriage contract, based upon the consent of the contracting parties, need not be irrevocable (with Locke at least asserting the justifiability of separation and possibly even divorce)[25] or inevitably patriarchal.[26] Yet both, having pursued the logic of consent theory against the patriarchal assumptions of their time, insensibly backslide into more conventional practical conclusions. Hobbes insists that the family, like a miniature or microcosmic leviathan-state, must locate absolute authority in the hands of either husband or wife;[27] and Locke, though reserving a greater sphere to the respective parties for autonomous private decision and personal rights, likewise insists that in matters of common concern, final or ultimate authority must be placed in the hands of one of the two adult parties.[28] And here, despite lip service to the contrary, both finally capitulate to patriarchal assumptions: the great chain of being is smuggled in through the back door. For Hobbes, commonwealths having been "erected by the fathers, not by the mothers of families," it is normally the case that "the father or the master is the sovereign."[29] Patriarchal domination is, after all, part of the order of nature: "The Father of the

Family by the law of Nature was absolute Lord of his Wife and children."[30] For Locke, too, "there is . . . a Foundation in Nature" for this patriarchal domination: sovereignty within the family "naturally falls to the Man's share as the abler and stronger."[31]

Something can be learned of the material foundations of this patriarchal domination from the discussion of the authority of parents over children. Both Hobbes and Locke reject the bare fact of generation as a sufficient basis for parental authority, insisting instead that the rights of parental authority flow from the provision of nurture and education to the child.[32] Hobbes, pushing the concept to the breaking point, insists that the authority of parents rests upon the consent, "either express, or by other sufficient arguments declared," of the (infant?) child; Locke, similarly, insists that once children have attained rational maturity, further parental authority is exercised only by their tacit or express consent.[33] Now both Hobbes and Locke originally insist that mothers, who provide nurture and early childhood education no less than fathers (indeed usually more so), have an equal or even greater potential claim to parental authority both in the state of nature and in civil society.[34] Yet, for both, when children do sooner or later consent to parental authority, it is almost invariably to the power of the father alone—a move that is nicely captured by Locke's tacit linguistic slide from "parental" back into purely "paternal" authority.[35] But why, if both parents provide nurture and education, is the father alone enshrined as patriarchal monarch over their *joint* progeny? And what induces wives to consent to the autocratic power of husbands? Part of the reason, beyond the father's putative natural superiority as "being of the more excellent sex,"[36] may be found in a passage from Locke that provides insight into the operational meaning of "abler and stronger." Children, beyond owing both parents the duty of gratitude and respect, have an additional specific incentive to submit to paternal authority: "This is the Power Men generally have to *bestow their Estates* on those, who please them best." The economic power of the property-owning patriarch, Locke writes, is "no small Tye"[37] on the obedience of children to fathers— or, we might add, of wives to husbands.

Both Hobbes and Locke, therefore, manage in the end to reconcile the egalitarian logic of individual consent with the persistence of hierarchical authority in both civil and conjugal government, implicitly substituting the patriarchal family for the abstract individual as the central unit of political and social analysis. In so doing, they purchase greater sociological realism in the face of the historical actualities stressed by proponents of the patriarchal paradigm, but only at the price of violence to the logic of their own principles. We may now pursue the persistence of this inconsistency within liberal theory into the utilitarian predecessors of John Stuart Mill—his father James Mill and Jeremy Bentham.

The confusions of patriarchal liberalism come fully to a head in the transparent contradictions of James Mill's *Essay on Government*. Mill's argument can most fruitfully be read as an intended, but ultimately unsuccessful, immanent critique of an earlier inconsistency in Hobbes. Mill might have said that he found Hobbes standing on his head and turned him right side up, for his essay is largely an effort to enlist the premises of an egoistic, Hobbesian moral psychology in the service of democratic rather than monarchical political conclusions. From the moral premise that the human good resides in the maximization of aggregate pleasure and minimization of aggregate pain, and the psychological premise of a universal will to power as the "grand governing law of human nature," Mill deduces both the need for government, in order to restrain the natural rapacity of the ruled, and restraints upon government, in order to restrain the natural rapacity of rulers.

This second set of restraints, upon which Mill's argument focuses, can in turn be supplied only by securing an artificial identity of interests between rulers and ruled through the mechanisms of representative government; and "unless the Representative Body are chosen by a portion of the community the interests of which cannot be made to differ from that of the community, the interest of the community will unfallibly be sacrificed to the interests of the rulers."[38] Universal adult (i.e., male *and* female) suffrage would seem to be the inescapable implication of Mill's argument—an implication that is reinforced by Mill's insistence elsewhere upon alteration in the status of women as a convenient bench mark of historical progress:

As society refines upon its enjoyments, and advances into that state of civilization, in which various corporeal qualities become equal or superior in value to corporeal strength, and in which the qualities of mind are ranked above the qualities of body, the condition of the weaker sex is gradually improved, till they associate on equal terms with the men, and occupy the place of voluntary and useful coadjutors.[39]

When it comes to the extension of equal political rights to women, however, Mill demurs. Considering whether something short of universal suffrage would be compatible with the dictates of utility, Mill writes:

One thing is pretty clear, that all those individuals whose interests are indisputably included in those of other individuals may be struck off without inconvenience. In this light may be viewed all children, up to a certain age, whose interests are involved in those of their parents. In this light, also, women may be regarded, the interest of almost all of whom is involved either in that of their fathers or in that of their husbands.[40]

Now, clearly, Mill's argument is consistent only on the basis of some exceedingly dubious empirical generalizations about "natural" identities of interest between sexes and across generations. This point was seized upon by Macaulay in his critiques of Mill, where he argued that the interests of women were naturally "included" in those of husbands and fathers "exactly as much and no more as the interests of subjects are included in that of kings."[41] (In the defense of Mill published in the *Westminster Review*, it was at one point remarked—ironically in *support* of women's suffrage—that "whenever the camel is driven through the eye of the needle, it would be simply folly and debility that would leave a hoof behind."[42] To which Macaulay, with a Filmerian instinct for inconsistency, agreeingly responded "that when we join to drive the camel through the needle, he shall go through hoof and all. We at present desire to be excused from driving the camel. It is Mr. Mill who leaves the hoof behind.")[43]

Mill's *Essay on Government* was on this point a source of controversy in philosophic radical circles. In fairness to Mill it should be noted, as he explained to his son, that the disenfranchisement of women, along with adult males under the age of forty, was on his view not *required* but rather merely *permitted* by the logic of his argument.[44] But even this weaker claim is still vulnerable to Macaulay's criticisms and was decisively repudiated by John Stuart Mill and the other philosophic radicals—including, as J. S. Mill notes, Jeremy Bentham.[45]

The history of Bentham's views on female suffrage (and women's rights generally) is itself a complex subject which cannot be traced in detail here.[46] It is sufficient for our purposes simply to note that Bentham came to be explicitly critical of James Mill's position. He finally believed that the logic of liberal argument does not merely permit but in fact positively requires the extension of the franchise to all sane adults, not merely men over forty.[47] In a sense, therefore, the Benthamite or philosophical radical critique of James Mill's patriarchal democracy can be said to complete the agenda of liberal equality at the level of formal rights of political citizenship.

But political emancipation is not by itself full human emancipation from alienating or exploitative forms of class and sex domination/dependence. Once again, therefore, we must pursue the argument into the deep structures of economic and social power in the private realm of property and family relations.[48] And here again we find, in the latter instance, the persistence of patriarchal power and authority within the liberal concept of the family. Thus, for example, in his earlier *Principles of Morals and Legislation*, Bentham at one point provides a penetrating critique of the circular nature of Aristotelian justifications of the political and social wardship of women and "natural" slaves:

In certain nations, women, whether married or not, have been placed in a state of perpetual wardship: this has been evidently founded on the notion of a decided inferiority in point of intellects on the part of the female sex, analogous to that which is the result of infancy or insanity on the part of the male. This is not the only instance in which tyranny has taken advantage of its own wrong, alleging as a reason for the domination it exercises, an imbecility, which, as far as it has been real, has been produced by the abuse of that very power which it is brought to justify. Aristotle, fascinated by the prejudice of the times, divides mankind into two distinct species, that of freemen, and that of slaves. Certain men were born to be slaves, and ought to be slaves.—Why? Because, they are so.[49]

Yet despite this insight into the spuriousness of patriarchal presumptions and the advocacy of more nearly equal civil and political rights for women that flows from this recognition, Bentham quickly falls victim to inconsistencies in his discussion of power and authority in the family. Like Hobbes and Locke, he too insists that there is in the marriage relationship a sphere of common decision in which one of the two parties must exercise final or ultimate sovereignty. Who then, he asks, shall decide? Bentham's legislator, less than ten pages prior to unmasking the ideology of patriarchal domination, "finds almost everywhere the male the stronger of the two; and therefore possessing already, by purely physical means, that power which he is thinking of bestowing on one of them by means of law. How then can he do so well as by placing the legal power in the same hands which are beyond comparison in possession of the physical?" The legislator will simply stamp as de jure the de facto power already exercised by the male, not as the mentally "abler" but rather simply as the materially "stronger" of the two parties. The stunning implications of this survival of the law of brute force into the heart of liberal society go almost entirely unremarked. Since on the principle of utility "the interests of both alike ought to be consulted," Bentham can only retreat lamely into the hope that the interests of the wife will somehow be naturally "included" in those of her "master and guardian."[50]

With the expression of this pious hope, discussion of the tensions and contradictions of patriarchal liberalism prior to John Stuart Mill may be concluded. We may now turn to the attempted resolution of these inconsistencies in the liberal feminism of John Stuart Mill.

5

The Subjection of Women rests upon a deeply Tocquevillian vision of history as the progressive triumph of democratic equality in politics and society. For Mill, the subordinate position of women in modern society is the sole surviving vestige of a law of inequality based upon ascribed status doomed to extinction by the egalitarian tendencies of "the modern movement in politics and morals," that is, the movement from status to contract enshrined in the principle that "merit, and not birth, is the only rightful claim to power and authority."[51] Mill's treatise thus is offered as an attempt to resolve what is self-consciously seen as a massive anomaly within liberal ideology and society.

For Mill, justice and expediency alike require that this anomaly be transcended: "The principle which regulates the existing social relations between the two sexes—the legal subordination of one sex to the other—is wrong in itself, and now one of the chief hindrances to human improvement; and . . . ought to be replaced by a principle of perfect equality, admitting no power or privilege on the one side, nor disability on the other."[52] But what, more exactly, does this entail? Or to put it more precisely: is the emancipation of women from "legal subordination," while clearly a necessary step, sufficient in itself to secure Mill's objective?

The emancipation of women requires at a minimum, for Mill, a fully egalitarian extension of the formal rights of political and civil citizenship; i.e., female voter enfranchisement on an identical basis with men, and exact equality of civil rights.[53] And what this political and civil enfranchisement means for women, above all, is equality of opportunity to enter the "public" world of action and work—full individual citizenship in the broadest sense, and careers open to talent in political and economic life.

But Mill is acutely aware that the extension of formal equality of political and civil rights, while a necessary condition of the emancipation of women, is not in itself sufficient, not yet full "human" emancipation. As long as vestiges of patriarchal despotism survive in marriage and the family, he argues, so also will the subjection of women continue. The patriarchal family is seen by Mill as the last remaining bastion of despotism and the law of force surviving fully intact into the heart of modern liberal society, and he is eloquent in his strictures against it.

Far from sealing marriage and the family off in an autonomous or private sphere wholly beyond the scope of legitimate state or societal control, Mill's liberalism thus recognizes that, as realms of power and authority, these are intrinsically *political* institutions.[54] And qua political institutions, he advocates their reconstitution on a more democratic basis. In contrast to the patriarchal liberalism of his predecessors, Mill denies that the need for final or ultimate decision in the common affairs of the family requires the investment of sovereign authority exclusively in the hands of the husband/father. Instead, he argues that in the marriage partnership—as in a business partnership—there is no inherent necessity for a univocally hierarchical, much less specifically patriarchal, distribution of authority.[55]

Mill advocates this democratization of power and authority within the family both as a good in itself and as a precondition of meaningful civil and political equality outside the home. His arguments parallel his case for citizen participation in politics and social life more generally. Equality of power within the marriage relationship is necessary, first of all, to protect the material interests of the hitherto subordinate sex. But this equal participation is also necessary to promote the autonomy and self-development of women as moral and rational agents.[56] More generally, the family, more than any other private institution, is in Mill's view a crucial agency of moral and political *education* for parents and children alike. The victory of justice and humanity in society at large, he argues, requires full equality between adult partners in the marriage relationship, which alone can render daily life "in any high sense, a school of moral education." And this moral education, moreover, has a specifically political component: popular sovereignty for Mill requires fully nonsexist social training for democracy in the home. "The superstructure of free government," he writes, "cannot be based upon a legal basis of despotism on one side and subjection on the other."[57]

6

The central objectives of Mill's social and political thought can thus be seen to depend crucially upon his commitment to the full transcendence of patriarchal liberalism. But we must now inquire more directly whether Mill's liberal feminism is equal to the radical task he has set for himself, or whether Mill remains committed to institutions and practices that would, on the logic of his own analysis, defeat his own commitment. Does Mill, in other words, resolve the contradictions of patriarchal liberalism, or does he too remain wedded to certain key assumptions that would undermine his own egalitarian intent?

Now, again, Mill understood clearly that formal equality of civil and political right is a necessary but not sufficient condition of full female emancipation—that meaningful equality for women requires, in addition, the destruction of patriarchal domination in the family. Nevertheless, he sometimes writes as if this latter task can in turn be accomplished by purely legal means—as if all that is required for the triumph of equality in the family is reform in the law of marriage. To abolish the "almost despotic power of husbands over wives," he writes at one point, "nothing more is needed for the complete removal of the evil than that wives should have the same rights, and should receive the protection of law in the same manner, as all other persons."[58] Similarly, to secure equality for women generally, Mill sometimes suggests that nothing more is required than the simple repeal of legal discrimination: "nobody asks for protective duties and bounties in favor of women; it is only asked that the present duties and bounties in favor of men should be recalled."[59]

It is passages such as these that leave Mill vulnerable to the charge, pressed by critics on both the right and the left, that his liberal feminism is based upon a shallow and unrealistic refusal to confront the deeper currents of inequality—be they natural or cultural in origin— that flow through the sexual politics of marriage and the family. Thus from the right, for example, James Fitzjames Stephen charged in his

Liberty, Equality, and Fraternity that if marriage is regarded as a contract between equals, as Mill advocates, "it is impossible to avoid the inference that marriage, like other partnerships, may be dissolved at pleasure." But this, according to Stephen's utilitarian logic, "would involve cruel injustice in the sense of extreme general inexpediency" to women—leaving them vulnerable to momentary gusts of male mid-life passion and, lacking all autonomous economic capacity, abandoned without any means of support. The law of marriage, he goes on, must take cognizance of natural inequalities of physical and mental power between men and women, adjusting its distribution of duties and privileges accordingly. In return for legally sanctioned obedience to their male superiors, women as the naturally weaker and more dependent parties may then be granted, with paternalistic solicitude, the security of indissoluble monogamous marriage. On Mill's logic, which willfully ignores these differences, all that is solid melts in the air: women would be stripped of this essential "protective duty" and callously thrown back upon their own pitifully inadequate resources.[60]

Mill chose not to pursue the question of divorce in *The Subjection of Women*.[61] However in a much earlier essay on the subject (1832), Mill had in fact anticipated Stephen's objections directly—arguing there, on much the same grounds later urged by his critic, that under past and present conditions of inequality between the sexes "indissolubility of marriage acted powerfully to elevate the position of women."[62] The difference is that Mill, unlike Stephen, refuses to reify this inequality: he goes on to find the roots of the dependent status of women not in nature but in culture, and to advocate its elimination by conscious human agency. We must, Mill argues, consider not merely the specific question of marriage and divorce under the actual circumstances of an imperfect past and present, but the general question of woman under the possible circumstances of a more ideal future: "The question is not what marriage ought to be, but a far wider question, what woman ought to be. Settle that first, and the other will settle itself. Determine whether marriage is to be a relation between two equal beings, or between a superior and an inferior, between a protector and a dependent; and all other doubts will easily be resolved."[63]

For Mill, the root of the evil is that, under past and present circumstances, women have been radically dependent for material security and social status upon "the fact of [their] being married or not married."[64] Consigned to a life of even more severe dependence and servitude outside the marriage relationship, women have only "Hobson's choice, 'that or none' "[65]—marriage on the patriarchal terms set by the dominant sex, or worse still. And this radical asymmetry of power between the sexes operates entirely independently of any legally discriminatory features of the marriage contract: "It is not law, but education and custom which make the difference. Women are so brought up, as not to be able to subsist in the mere physical sense, without a man to keep them."[66] Clearly, legal reform alone will not melt down this ideologically frozen relationship of domination and dependence. More radical change is necessary.

What is required, above all else, is the attainment of economic and educational equality by women: "perfect independence of each other in all save affection, cannot be, if there be dependence of primary circumstances; a dependence which in the immense majority of cases must exist, if the women be not capable, as well as the man, of gaining her own subsistence." And meaningful equality of opportunity, careers open to talent in political and economic life, in turn requires genuinely equal education for women: "The first and indispensable step, therefore, towards the enfranchisement of women, is that she be so educated, as not to be dependent on her father or her husband for subsistence: a position which in nine cases out of ten, makes her either the plaything or the slave of the man who feeds her; and in the tenth case only his humble friend."[67]

Mill's argument rests upon a clear sense of the way in which women are coerced not merely by law and custom but also, as society moves from status to contract, by the impersonal operation of market forces. Women are free, at best, to enter or not to enter any particular marriage contract; they are not effectively free, or not fully so, not to marry at all. Hence they are to that degree coerced by their situation into marrying on unequal terms. Only when, by virtue of their independent economic and educational status, women are effectively free to abstain from marriage altogether will the contract be a genuinely voluntary exchange. Only when they are free to preserve their autonomy as discrete individuals will women be liberated from patriarchy in the family, empowered as they then would be to refuse marriage except on terms of equality.

The equality of power within the marriage partnership to which Mill is committed thus requires, beyond equality of rights before the law, that women be fully capable of surviving independently outside the family. But we must then ask whether this capacity alone, as potentiality alone, would be sufficient to preserve equality over time once *inside* the family? Or would still further change be required? Since Mill favored a more androgynous character type in his ideal of human personality,[68] one might here expect from him a frontal attack upon traditional sex role differentiation in the family. Instead Mill's argument begins to waver, his nerve begins to fail. In his early essay, quoted above, he writes "It does not follow that a woman should *actually* support herself because she should be *capable* of doing so: in the natural course of events she will *not*."[69] And he returns to this theme in *The Subjection of Women*: "In an otherwise desirable state of things, it is not . . . a desirable custom, that the wife should contribute by her labor to the income of the family. . . . The actual exercise in a habitual or systematic manner, of outdoor occupations or such as cannot be carried on at home, would by this principle be practically interdicted to the greater number of women."[70] Mill in the end capitulates to the traditional sexual division of labor within the family. Man is the public being, woman is the private being. The responsibility of the married man is action and work outside the home. The responsibility of the married woman is household superintendence and, more important, the care and education of children. In homes where the means to hire domestic help is lacking, "it is good and will naturally take place" that "the mistress of a family shall herself do the work of servants." In more affluent households, above and beyond the supervision of domestic help,

The great occupation of woman should be to *beautify* life: to cultivate, for her own sake and of those who surround her, all her faculties of mind, soul, and body; all her powers of enjoyment, and powers of giving enjoyment; and to diffuse beauty, elegance, and grace, everywhere. If in addition to this the activity of her nature demands more energetic and definite employment, there is never any lack of it in the world: If she loves, her natural impulse will be to associate her existence with him she loves, and to share *his* occupations; in which, if he loves her (with that affection of *equality* which alone deserves to be called love) she will naturally take as strong an interest, and be as thoroughly conversant, as the most perfect confidence on his side can make her.[71]

Mill does not believe that his continuing endorsement of a traditional division of labor within the family would threaten the ideal of marriage to which he is committed. But it seems clear, on Mill's own logic, that these separate spheres would remain inherently unequal.

As he himself writes, "There will naturally be more potential voice on the side, whichever it is, that brings the means of support." Mill was not unaware of this tension within his own argument. He conceded that under less than ideal circumstances, an independent income might be a source of power for a legally subordinate wife. But he maintained that under ideal circumstances—with marriage an equal contract, separation (not divorce) available to wives morally entitled to it, and careers open to talent for women outside the marriage relationship—the *power* to earn a living, without its actual exercise, would be sufficient to preserve equality within the marriage relationship.[72] The option of exit would preserve the reality of voice.[73]

Clearly, however, there remain serious problems with Mill's response to the dilemma posed by his own analysis. And on precisely these points, it is possible to locate the basis for a penetrating critique of Mill's liberal feminism in the more thoroughly radical posture of Harriet Taylor's fragmentary writings on the subject. It is to these writings, her contribution to the transcendence of patriarchal liberalism, that we may now turn.

7

The precise nature and extent of Harriet Taylor's influence upon John Stuart Mill is a large and vexing question that I do not consider here.[74] My remarks will focus exclusively upon those aspects of her writings on marriage and the family that expose the residual patriarchal dimensions of her husband's liberal feminism. After briefly mentioning an early fragment on marriage and divorce (1832), I shall focus upon "The Enfranchisement of Women."[75]

In her early fragment on divorce and marriage, Harriet Taylor takes an uncompromising—and, it must be added, morally disturbing—view of the matter, advocating "divorce which could be attained by any *without any reason assigned....*" In fact, she then goes on to argue, the true solution would reside in the immediate abolition of the law of marriage as such: "At this present time, in this state of civilization, what evil could be caused by, first placing women on the most entire equality with men as to all rights and privileges, civil and political, and then doing away with all laws whatever relating to marriage."[76]

Mill's views, to his credit, are more measured and complex ones.

His early essay is written defensively, as if in response to the militancy of his future wife. Mill stresses, as we have seen, the senses in which the indissolubility of marriage has in the imperfect circumstances of the past and present worked to protect the wife as the weaker party. In a more ideal future, where this underlying debility has been replaced by equality between the sexes, Mill advocates a liberalization in the law of divorce; but even here his argument is a circumspect one, stressing the need for *some* legal and moral restraint upon the momentary whim and caprice of the contracting parties.[77] And while Mill's later views on the subject are tentative and evolving, the emphasis upon caution predominates throughout.[78] The family—and here Mill agrees with Hegel and the early Marx[79]—constitutes an arena of *ethical* life—involving as it does concrete moral obligations to particular others (especially children). A contract that transcends the point of view of contract, the marriage relationship must be insulated against both the ice of egoistic calculation and the fire of romantic self-assertion.[80]

But however reasonable in itself, Mill's commitment to the preservation of some moral and legal restraints upon the facility of divorce[81] compounds the confusion created by his insistence upon preserving a traditional sexual division of labor within the marriage relationship. For to the extent that traditional roles diminish the option of exit, to that extent is the wife left disenfranchised before the potential for greater "voice," noted by Mill himself, flowing from the husband's position as the provider of support. This point is pressed relentlessly in "The Enfranchisement of Women," and in a way that flatly contradicts both Mill's earlier essay and his later *The Subjection of Women.* Even if, by increasing the labor force, the employment of married women were to reduce wages severely (the objection urged in Mill's earlier essay), nevertheless

. . . the woman would be raised from the position of a servant to that of a partner. Even if every woman, as matters now stand, had a claim on some man for support, how infinitely preferable is it that part of the income should be of the woman's earning, even if the aggregate sum were but little increased by it, rather than that she should be compelled to stand aside in order that men may be the sole earners, and the sole dispensers of what is earned. Even under the present laws respecting the property of women, a woman who contributes materially to the support of the family, cannot be treated in the same contemptuously tyrannical manner as one who, however she may toil as a domestic drudge, is a dependent on the man for subsistence.[82]

Only with the full employment of married women outside the home in political and economic life, Taylor maintains, will it be possible to abolish patriarchy within the home.

If women are to participate as co-equal partners in the political and economic life of society, they must be educated to that vocation. Mill had in his earlier essay advocated equal education for women, but had simultaneously insisted that the role of married women, as domestic creatures, is not "doing" but "being"—to "adorn and beautify" life as educated companions to their husbands.[83] The reader is thus left to wonder what incentive the majority of women, destined for the vocation of marriage, would have to endure the rigors of years of preparation for public and active life, knowing as they would in advance that these capacities could only then languish, and thus atrophy, in a doll's house of enforced domesticity. As if in direct response to this confusion, "The Enfranchisement of Women" castigates "moderate reformers of the education of women" who say that women should be "not slaves, nor servants, but companions; and educated for that office (they do not say that men should be educated to be the companions of women)."[84]

In sum, the root of the question, which is only partially resolved by John Stuart Mill's brand of liberal feminism, is:

. . . whether it is right and expedient that one-half of the human race should pass through life in a state of forced subordination to the other half. If the best state of human society is that of being divided into two parts, one consisting of persons with a will and a substantive existence, the other of humble companions to these persons, attached, each of them to one, for the purpose of bringing up *his* children, and making *his* home pleasant to him.

Without more radical change than Mill is willing to entertain, married women will of necessity remain in the status of "a mere appendage to a man"[85]—a perhaps not inaccurate description of Harriet Taylor Mill's own relationship, whatever the magnitude of her private influence, to her husband's life and thought.

8

We are now prepared to complete the argument. At the center of the liberal vision, I have claimed, there resides a deep tension between an individualist and egalitarian set of philosophic premises and concrete political and socioeconomic institutions and practices that would undermine or negate full actualization of these abstract liberal aspirations. John Stuart Mill's efforts, along with those of Harriet Taylor, to move once and for all beyond the confines of patriarchal liberalism can be understood as one specific moment in an overall movement to resolve this tension.

Mill's best efforts are, however, only partially successful ones. His commitment to the destruction of patriarchy partially founders upon his inadequate penetration, against the logic of his own analysis, into the hierarchical implications of the traditional division of labor between the sexes within the family. Mill, anticipating the Marxian critique, understood the ways in which women, not unlike wage-laborers, were coerced by a background of severely asymmetrical material and cultural power to enter upon highly unfavorable terms into a formally free and voluntary exchange; but he failed to note fully the ways in which the preservation of the traditional division of labor *within* the marriage relationship would, by undercutting his commitment to the elimination of these background conditions, work to reinforce patriarchy within the family. Here Harriet Taylor's insight, flowing no doubt in part from her own life experience, is clearer: only when married women are employed outside the home, fully integrated into the political and economic life of society, will patriarchy within the family finally be fully transcended.

But the far-reaching implications of this commitment remain undeveloped in "The Enfranchisement of Women." If, for example, bourgeois civil society in its extant form is presupposed as the given framework for the integration of women into political and economic life—the essay is silent on this issue—then one may legitimately wonder whether Taylor's brand of feminism, although perhaps more tough-minded and consistent than her husband's, in fact succeeds any better than his in disarming the full force of the Marxian critique of classical liberalism. Is the economic "emancipation" of women thus conceived, any more than a narrowly conceived "political" emancipation, the path to a fully humane society for men and women alike? Would not this arguably narrow, meritocratic formula for the emancipation of women, taken by itself, simply universalize the competitive and acquisitive ethos, the unbridled envy and egoism, of bourgeois civil society? And, would not the extension of full formal equality of economic opportunity to women, without further change, simply universalize the class inequalities of the capitalist economy, offering women (in return for the possibility of increased power within the home) only the freedom to dominate or be dominated, according to their class position, in a (now sex-blind) system of "free" wage-labor? Or, further, even as the grosser excesses of patriarchal despotism might thus be relieved, would not the inevitable persistence under these circumstances of alienation and exploitation in politics and work life substantially undermine the possibility of a fully humane organization of the family, continuing to poison its climate with the anxieties and frustrations induced in these otherwise unreformed spheres?[86]

Harriet Taylor's commitment to the full employment of married women outside the home would, moreover, affect the inner constitution of the family in an even more direct and immediate way, requiring its radical reconstitution in directions that equally remain unexplored in "The Enfranchisement of Women." Who will do the housework? And again, more important, What about the children? Here, too, the essay is silent. Tacitly, of course, the argument almost certainly resolves these issues by simply presupposing a readily available panoply of domestic servants. But what then is its relevance, if any, outside this radically class- and culture-bound context? It is unclear, for example, whether or not Taylor would have endorsed Engels's apparent advocacy of the wholesale absorption of child-rearing functions by the state (or its postrevolutionary equivalent). Those dimensions of her thought and personality that seem to define emancipation as the unlimited assertion of an imperial self—her fragment on divorce, for example—suggest that she might have. So, too, does her off-handed assertion, in a letter to Mill, that in a reformed social order the "cleverer" persons could make children "perfect" in ten years.[87] At a minimum, we may conclude from her scattered statements on the subject that she had not thought carefully about the issue.

Mill's views on this subject are, by contrast, more readily ascertainable. His strong opposition to a monolithic system of state-enforced public education would surely apply, a fortiori and with redoubled emphasis, to any scheme for the full collectivization of child-rearing functions.[88] Behind his insistence upon anchoring the mother qua nurturant presence within the home lies his emphasis, in contrast to cruder variants of the liberal vision, upon the development and self-development of persons as rational and moral agents and upon the (reformed) family, through its education of the young, as one essential vehicle for the promotion of this humanistic objective. Again, it is bedrock to liberalism as such, and to Mill's in particular, that the values of cognitive and moral autonomy and self-development, as well as individual creativity of thought and action—values common to purified liberal and humane Marxian aspirations—require for their cultivation in children and adults alike a sustained, intimate, nonpublic sphere. The preservation of such pluralistic loci of private thought and action, including families (or functionally equivalent forms of affective community), is at the heart of Mill's liberal vision.

It is crucial to note, however, that no iron laws decreeing the inexorability of hierarchical domination within these centers of private life follow necessarily from this core liberal commitment per se. To the contrary, it has been my claim, advanced through the medium of Marxian categories, that the logic of liberal equality itself, when properly unpacked, does not merely permit but in fact requires the emancipation of individual citizens from concrete structures of class and sex domination in property and family relations. Mill enhanced our understanding of this point, and in the process the cause of a purified liberal vision. His commitment to the preservation of a nonpublic sphere of thought and action is not incompatible with the simultaneous recognition that the "private," being shot through with power, rule, and authority, is at the same time in some basic sense irreducibly "political." His reconstructed liberalism, very much like Tocqueville's, rests upon the recognition that popular government requires "democratic institutions in detail"[89] in the associational life of society: that a "participatory society," to borrow the currently fashionable phrase, is both a necessary condition for a fully democratic polity and a desirable goal in its own right.[90] And Mill, far more resolutely than Tocqueville, pursued the implications of this insight into the political sociology of everyday life, advocating an attack upon despotic power in *all* private structures of authority.

This commitment, which Mill shared with Harriet Taylor, permits us to consider more fully the questions left unresolved by "The Enfranchisement of Women." It is important to note, first, that in the realm of property relations, Mill was led, under Harriet Taylor's influence, to embrace socialist aspirations.[91] As a political economist, he advocated the long-run elimination of private ownership of productive property by a restricted class, with its hierarchical division of labor, in favor of common ownership by workers of democratically con-

trolled cooperative enterprises.[92] This self-proclaimed socialist vision
was understood by Mill and Taylor, not simply or even primarily as
a program for distributive justice, but more fundamentally as a far-
reaching program for the democratization of power and authority
relations in the basic structure of work-life. It formed part of a much
broader strategy for the moral and rational development of citizens
through common democratic participation in both the political *and*
the economic life of society.

The Mill-Taylor program for the emancipation of women must be
seen against the backdrop of this commitment. It is *not*, or at least
need not be, a narrowly meritocratic program for the—partial or
full—integration of women into the unreformed structures of a class-
divided social formation. It does not, or need not, focus upon the
"political" or economic emancipation of women to the exclusion of
the broader "human" emancipation of men and women alike. Rather,
the abolition of both sex *and* class domination in both family *and*
property relations can be understood as converging to form an integrated vision of a more fully free and equal, communal and participatory society. Their liberal feminism is, implicitly, socialist feminism
as well. And, indeed, Mill explicitly saw these commitments as entirely of a piece: he identified the emancipation of women and cooperative production as the twin forces that would "regenerate" society.[93]

In contrast to capitalist private property, Mill viewed the family in
some form as "essential for humanity." He argued that his nonpatriarchal ideal of marriage, his vision of a *reformed* family life, "had
not yet had a fair trial."[94] He himself, to be sure, in this instance remained wedded to traditional assumptions about the sexual division
of labor within the family that would have the consequence of subverting his own unimpeachably egalitarian intent. Yet here, too, it
might be argued that the inner *logic* of Mill's commitment, as amended
by Harriet Taylor, points in the proper direction: that his *own* ideal
of a reformed family life, based upon a fully nonpatriarchal marriage
bond, can on the logic of his *own* analysis be said not merely to permit but positively to require a rejection of the traditional division of
labor between the sexes, as put forth by Taylor. And while Mill's firm
commitment to the preservation of the family, or a functional equivalent thereof, rules out some solutions to the problems posed by his
wife's bolder position—rules out, above all, the full collectivation of
child rearing by the state—other aspects of his theory suggest alterna-

tive possibilities. His Tocquevillian commitment to participatory forms of voluntary association, for example, is entirely compatible with the possible development of extensive networks of communal support, such as parent-controlled day care for children, *outside* the family. Similarly, his own androgynous ideal of human personality enjoins a far more exhaustive reexamination of traditional assumptions about sex-role differentiation *within* the family than Mill himself was willing to undertake. The freedom of women to cultivate previously foreclosed "public" dimensions of human personality ought ideally to be complemented by a corollary emphasis upon the freedom and obligation of men to cultivate previously foreclosed "private," nurturant and affective, dimensions of self. A reconstituted division of labor within the family, with men and women sharing "public" and "private" roles equally and in turn over time, would advance this—Mill's own—objective.

9

One final word about philosophy giving instruction to the world. No social or political theorist can ever fully "overleap his own age, jump over Rhodes."[95] The liberal vision was articulated by men who were themselves implicated in the structures of class and sex domination that the logic of their own theory, when unpacked, opposes. They were thus torn between the upward pull of abstract logical consistency, and the downward pull of concrete sociohistorical circumstance. Incoherence was virtually inevitable.[96]

What is truly remarkable in the thought of John Stuart Mill is the boldness of vision with which, against intense hostility, he worked to complete the liberal agenda by excising its patriarchal vestiges. He was, as Freud noted, "the man of the century most capable of freeing himself from the domination of the usual prejudices."[97] Today, more than a century later, it remains the task of those committed, like Mill, *both* to the preservation of the family as an essential locus of privacy, intimacy, and affective individualism—a haven in a heartless universe—*and* to true mutual sympathy and solidarity between equally autonomous men and women, to combine these commitments in practice.[98]

Oedipus as Hero: Family
and Family Metaphors in Nietzsche

🌞 *Tracy B. Strong*

> *The past is a nightmare from which*
> *I am trying to awake.—James Joyce*, Ulysses
>
> *If one does not have a good father,*
> *one must provide oneself with one.*—Human-all-too-Human

It is only a slight exaggeration to characterize political and social thought since Hegel as a series of attempts to come to terms with the manner in which the past impressed itself on the present. The past was a nightmare: it restricted autonomy, relativized moral choice, blinded the will. For most liberal thought, the hope of progress required that one live only in the present and future, never in the past. Marx hoped that praxis would sift historical reality and determine what would remain actual and what would be confined to the ash heap. For John Stuart Mill, freedom of choice itself encouraged the development of man "as a progressive social being" and made it possible to escape the threats to authenticity by which the modern world bound humans to the historical. Burckhardt held up the ahistorical vision of a historical period; the civilizations of the Renaissance and of Greece were at least dreams that things did not have to be as they were.

Clearly this list can go on; redemption from time past, whether in denial or acquiescence, was a central concern of those who thought seriously about the world. Clearly, also, different writers tried in different ways to avoid being time's fool. In this paper I am concerned only with that understanding of the past made in metaphors drawn from the family. Although a number of writers share this view, I shall be concerned here with an exegesis of Nietzsche's writings on the subject. For Nietzsche, human beings appear, so to speak, inevitably and forever as the children of their parents; their past lives on in them without dynamics that might enable them to escape from it. In this understanding human beings, indeed societies also, are the embodiment, a making-flesh, of that which has not died but continues to live on and grow as who they are. All that still was, now is: the adverbial paradox points at the implicit despair in the possibility of overcoming time. From this perspective, no matter what shape our lives may take, individually or collectively, we are still caught in and partake of who we were, of our genealogy.[1]

For Nietzsche, we are caught in a great and given historical family. The genealogy of slave morality informs us that a particular way of structuring existence has come to dominate in the West over the last 2,500 years, to the extent that there is now simply no other alternative. As he remarks in the end of *On the Genealogy of Morals*, the "ascetic ideal," itself the last stage of slave morality, has triumphed "out of lack of opposition."[2] As is known, Nietzsche contends that there is something radically and inalterably wrong with our genealogy and that that error will not permit, in and of itself, a deep alteration of existence. In this he differs from Marx: it is not in the nature of flies to find the way out of the fly bottle.

2

Eighteen eighty-eight marks the last year of Nietzsche's sanity. The year's conclusion accomplishes the last of the six-year cycles that Nietzsche sees making important changes in his life.[3] He has now, he indicates, completed the preliminaries necessary for his philosophy; with the ground sufficiently cleared, he will proceed to those writings that will "revolutionize the world." Accordingly, at the beginning of 1888, he writes to many friends that he is finally ready to begin his major work. By the end of the year, he sends a postcard to Peter Gast proclaiming good news: "The world is transfigured: sing me a new song."[4] The theme of most of the letters from this last year is a final break with his past: now he is himself and has accomplished his own person. Thus, to Paul Deussen, on January 3, 1889, he writes: "Basically, as concerns me, all is now epochmaking; my entire past (*Bisher*) crumbles away from me and when I add up what I have done in the last two years it appears to me now as always one and the same piece of work: to isolate myself from my past, to cut the umbilical cord between me and it." The theme is a new birth or a rebirth, separation from his parents, a theme repeated in a letter to the Danish critic Brandes on February 19, where Nietzsche indicates that he has "survived himself." All this is further linked to the repeated claim, such as the one he had made a week earlier to von Seydlitz, that he was the "first philosopher of this era" and stood "ominously between two millennia."[5] That which he was is dead; that which he is lives on.

Yet this claim is clearly a problem.[6] To Nietzsche it does not appear that one should be able to get rid of one's past, to be self-engendered. For, if one *is* because of one's past,[7] then everything one does to break the chains of that past must itself be subject to that past and must thus merely reinforce it in increasingly subtle and powerful ways. Kant establishes in the *Critique of Pure Reason* that no matter what one thinks, being human, one always thinks in the same structure. For Kant, there is no choice but to accept the limitations of reason as the sign of the value of one's humanity, rather than of humanity's failings. But because for Nietzsche humanity itself is profoundly flawed in its universal slave morality, there is no solace to be gained from the mere acknowledgment of one's past. How then can Nietzsche claim to have broken the hold of his past? How can he claim to inaugurate a new philosophical era? This is, one might say, a question about the possibility of revolutionary politics; what would it mean to be made new?

Nietzsche's judgment of a philosophy is also always a judgment of the philosopher. Any form of thought that excludes itself from its own critique is automatically suspect. To such thinkers, Nietzsche's first question is what might be called therapeutic: Why is it that the philosopher in question seeks to protect himself in an uncriticized redoubt? Hence we find Nietzsche's well-known attacks on Socrates' physiognomy, the accusation that Kant was morally deficient, and the attacks on Descartes's cowardice. Nietzsche will even profess a preference for thinkers with "small ears" rather than large ones.[8] All of this should seem strange, but it is not. If one cannot separate the doer from the deed, as Nietzsche argues in the *Genealogy of Morals*, then the judgment about one is the judgment about the other. No acts are immaculate.

I should note here that Nietzsche's position is not a kind of ideological reductionism: Nietzsche is not saying that it all comes *down* to a matter of physiology. He is saying rather something that we have known well at least since Freud. The deep meaning of the Socratic imperative to self-knowledge is that what a person says and does has something to do with who a person is. This is not immediately a judgment on the value of the act or person, but any such judgment will be a judgment about both.

With this in mind, it is only natural to turn the focus of Nietzsche's understanding of the past on Nietzsche himself, and to investigate Nietzsche's thought by investigating Nietzsche. Nietzsche himself does this. I am here in part merely explicating his own self-critique, for his self-critiques are an integral part of his thought. In these terms, who Nietzsche *is* becomes important, for it has something to do with what Nietzsche *says*. And it is all the more important in that the central investigatory concepts in Nietzsche are clearly those that relate to the general problem of identity, self, and family.

Consider for a moment "genealogy," the most basic conceptual tool of his general investigations into morality and Western culture. The approach is derived from Kantian premises, especially the use of the transcendental deduction. Like Kant, Nietzsche is trying to figure out how a given act or configuration of acts is (historically) possible. His claim is that Western morality forms a coherent structure that, through a set of comprehensible transformations, has assumed various forms (*ressentiment*, bad conscience, and so on). As with Freud's understanding of neurosis, the idea is that various facets of a person's behavior can be understood in terms of a common structure, itself implanted at an early age.

I have discussed the notion of genealogy in more detail elsewhere.[9] Such an understanding necessarily implies that radical change will not, in and of itself, come from willful human action, at least not as long as that action is *itself* a manifestation of the structure that had previously governed.[10] Nietzsche speaks, for instance, of "the strange family resemblance of all Indian, German and Greek philosophizing" and attributes this to the "unconscious domination by and orientation to similar grammatical functions."[11] We are caught, one might say, in a family portrait: to do anything, we must do something that we can do, yet everything we can do is structured by who we are and what we have been. Our actions will then reflect and make manifest that structure of ourselves.

Put it another way: one is always the child of one's parents. In *The Gay Science*, Nietzsche is involved in a discussion of attitudes and approaches to knowledge. He speaks of the sons of registrars and clerks. Should they turn to scholarship, they would be philosophers "who in the end are only systematizing minds—in them the form of the fathers' work has become content. One is not without retribution (*ungestraft*) the child of one's parents."[12] Nietzsche goes on to speak of other sons: "One recognizes the sons of Protestant ministers and teachers by their naive assurance; as scholars, they already take their subject matter as proven, if only it is given from the heart and with warmth: at bottom, they are thereby convinced that they are believed." In other words, insofar as Nietzsche is a scholar (*ein Gelehrter*), he remains the child of his parents. We know that he was a scholar and that he wished to leave that life. The scholar in fact "always has something of the old maid," in that (s)he is "conversant with neither of the two most valuable functions" of a human being, "to procreate and to give birth." As Nietzsche develops this section of *Beyond Good and Evil*, we find that scholarship, even philosophy that is "scholarly," will be only a "mirror," at most a great act of criticism. Nietzsche sees the creative alternative as a form of political change, "a compulsion to great politics."[13] Nietzsche is clear that not *any* politics will do; but some sort of political change will be required to overcome the naivete that he inherits as his father's son. The first thing that Zarathustra comes to realize on his return from the mountains is that speaking from the heart, even to a willing audience, will not be effective.[14]

"One is not without retribution the child of one's parents." We know that Nietzsche was the son of a Protestant minister and that his father died during his fourth year. We know also that Nietzsche spent much of his life proclaiming the futility of thinking that one might escape from one's genealogy. *Zarathustra* is filled with passages that praise those who would "go under," that is, who accept their genealogy for what it is, understand it to be flawed and thereby wish only to perish. As early as 1862, in an essay on "Freedom of the Will and Fate," Nietzsche writes that "the doings of a person (*Tätigkeit des Menschen*) . . . do not start with birth, but already in the embryo—who can know here—already in parents and ancestors."[15] In *Beyond Good and Evil* he describes as "the problem of race" that "one cannot wipe away from the soul of a man that which his ancestors liked most to do and did constantly. . . . It is simply not possible that a man would *not* have the qualities and preferences of his parents and ancestors in his body."[16] We know finally that at the end of his life, in haste, Nietzsche wrote as his last work an autobiography, which he entitled with the shout by which Pilate had presented Christ to the crowd, *Ecce Homo*. Family metaphors and concern with how his own family affects his self in his vocation run throughout Nietzsche's work. By an examination of these metaphors and their use, it is possible to cast light on what Nietzsche thought of the power and strength and effect of the family structure. Unpacking these metaphors will illuminate how Nietzsche thinks that he himself has at least partially escaped family and, in becoming who he is, has finally become his own person, able to be a *true* philosopher for the modern world.

In 1888 Nietzsche publishes six books. This output is much greater than that of the previous years, itself already impressive. Furthermore, Nietzsche projects a number of major works, which he says will in two years revolutionize the world. He writes to Georg Brandes, as well as to some others, that he is making arrangements to have his new works translated into six languages with a first edition of "c/ one million copies." Nietzsche, of course, did not accomplish this task; in Turin, in early January 1889, he became insane: nothing that is recorded of what he said in the last ten years of his life, either under treatment or under the supervision of his sister, appears to have more than clinical interest.[17] The works of 1888 look in two directions. Some of them look to the past: they come to terms with Wagner, the man he claims most to have loved, or with his own past and influences on him, especially in *The Twilight of the Idols*. Others look to the future: the *Antichrist* is subtitled the "First book of the Revaluation of all values" and through its "destruction" of Christianity is held to prepare the way for a philosophy of the future. Last, looking to the present in this year of summing up and anticipation, he writes *Ecce Homo*, an autobiography subtitled "How one becomes who one is." This remains unpublished until 1905. It is to the autobiography that I first turn to investigate Nietzsche's understanding of the family and of his family in relation to his work.

Ecce Homo represents for Nietzsche an account of what one might call his life project until that point. It is an explicit claim to have accomplished the task he had set out for himself some twenty-six years earlier. He wrote then: "If we wish to contemplate Christian teaching and church history with a free and impartial glance, then we must completely articulate many positions contrary to usual ideas. However, as we are restricted from our youngest days by the yoke of conventionality and prejudice and constrained by the impression our childhood makes on the natural development of our self (*Geistes*), we believe it almost to be an indecency (*Vergehen*) to have to consider if we have chosen a freer position, so as then to be able to pronounce an impartial and appropriate judgment on religion and Christianity. Such a task is not the work of a few weeks, but of a life."[18] This is, even though in youthful formulation here, the task to which he set himself. Already at eighteen, he had a complex understanding of his vocation. The endeavor that is his life turns out perhaps to be more complicated than he understood then; but *Ecce Homo* must be read as the *comte rendu* of what he sees himself as having accomplished, not "just" in terms of his writing, but also in terms of his self. He is ready to move beyond the scholar and the critic, "to become who he is," to be the person who he calls "the first philosopher of the modern age."

I propose then that one should read *Ecce Homo* precisely as what Nietzsche says it to be—an autobiography. As always, as I hope to show, if one takes Nietzsche on his own terms, one sees him both more clearly and with more interest.

The discussion in the preface to *Ecce Homo* focuses around two themes: the achievement of who one is and the loss of what we might call the parental or authority image. The self achieved is to stand immediately in the present; it is sufficient unto itself, not shaped by its ancestors. To achieve this involves, Nietzsche continues on, selectivity from what one has done. The formal epigraph to *Ecce Homo* is an exceptionally beautiful formulation: "On this perfected day, when everything ripens and not only the grape turns brown, a look of the sun just fell on my life: I looked backwards, I looked forwards, I never saw so many and so good things at once. It was not in vain that I buried my forty-fourth year today: I had the right to bury it—what was life in it is saved, is immortal." Nietzsche then lists three books, "presents of this last quarter" of 1888 and concludes the epigraph: "How could I not be thankful to my entire life? And so I tell myself my life." He is, now, immortal; his life is in recurrence, like a story told again for the first time. What follows then, one might say, must be the account of a sort of rebirth: whatever is "himself" is preserved and made eternal, reborn, as are gods; the rest has perished. The obvious question is how this extraordinary process has happened; it is precisely to that consideration that Nietzsche turns in the opening section of the book.

The good fortune of my existence [*Daseins*], perhaps its uniqueness, lies in its frailty: to express it in the form of a riddle, as my father I have already died, as my mother I still live and become old. This double descent, at once from the highest and the lowest rung on the ladder of life, at the same time *decadent* and beginning—this, if anything at all, explains the neutrality, that freedom from partiality in relation to the general problem [*Gesammtproblem*] of life, that characterizes me. For signs of rise and decline I have perhaps a better scent than any one has had until now; for this I am the teacher *par excellence*—I know both, I am both.

The passage proceeds immediately to a discussion of the death of his father.

The section is perhaps purposively dark with mystery, but one should not lose sense of its conventionality. This is, after all, his autobiography, in which he should tell us who he is. The usual way of beginning an autobiography would be with a description of one's birth and of one's parents. In fact, this is precisely what Nietzsche does and proceeds from there to a discussion of his childhood, the death of his father, and on to most of the events that mark the generality of any life.

There is, of course, more. In this opening section he also claims to know and be both his (dead) father and (living) mother. He links decadence and death to the father and beginning and growth to the mother. The whole passage in fact seems to be self-consciously written to call Oedipus to mind. Oedipus, too, had a most ambiguous relation to his father; indeed, it is the fact that he was *not* his father that stood as the source of all his problems. The question of identity by which Nietzsche introduces himself here is posed as a riddle, in the manner of the Sphinx to Oedipus. Although we cannot help thinking of Oedipus here, there is an important difference. The Sphinx had by its riddle queried Oedipus only about the truth of man's relation to nature and not about man's relation to himself. In *Ecce Homo* Nietzsche plays Sphinx to himself,[19] no longer confronting the differentiation of man from nature, but of himself from men. This paragraph then can be seen as representing the step that Nietzsche takes "beyond" the Greeks, responding here to his oft-expressed imperative to surpass even them.

Nietzsche associates himself with the classic birth of the hero.[20] Heroes are generally without parents, or at least without normal parents. Furthermore, they must die, in order to be reborn. Thus, in his autobiography, Nietzsche sees himself, like a hero, as already dead.

He is reborn autochthonically without parentage, or as his own parent. Such a person could truly be the beginning of a world, because he would share nothing with the past.

In a preliminary way, let us notice here that the hero is then a person who is not subject to the classical Oedipal situation as described by Freud. The hero has no known father, and generally no mother, or at least none of the usual sort. Thus he simply never has to do what the child with parents, with a past, must do to achieve a resolution of the psychological situation in which he finds himself. The hero constitutes an annihilation of the entire Oedipal situation; somehow, if he were subject to it, he would not be able to accomplish his task. At the writing of *Ecce Homo*, Nietzsche thinks himself the person who can accomplish his (own) task. But he has already gone the hero one better. He is not simply in the position of not having a father, as is the hero, but he is already dead *as* his father. Like Tiresias he has had both sexes.

Thus the deeper significance of the epigraph cited above is that by this day, his forty-fourth birthday, he marks the achievement of a self that is purely his and is no longer part of his family. He claims to have annihilated his genealogy. It is worth noting that the "decree against Christianity," which he appends to the *Druckmanuscript* of *Der Antichrist*, is dated to mark the inauguration of a new era; it is "promulgated on the day of salvation, on the first day of year One."[21] Furthermore, in one of the last pieces of work—a poem appended to *Nietzsche Contra Wagner* on January 2, 1889, we find:

Who is father and mother to me?
Is not Prince Abundance father
To me and quiet laughter mother?[22]

Here and in both *Antichrist* and *Ecce Homo* Nietzsche refers to himself as born posthumously. He has died to his self and is reborn as himself.

One is wrongly tempted here to begin by making an appeal to mythology and metaphor. It is more important to see precisely that Nietzsche is discussing relations to parents and why it was so important that he deal with them in the manner that he claims to have. Only then will we be able to arrive at an explanation of precisely what it means to escape one's genealogy, of how it was possible and why it was necessary to get rid of and annihilate one's family. Why is the family, or the family situation, such a problem for Nietzsche?

Why does it provide the metaphor for that which he sought to escape
and from which he hoped to help others escape?

3

If there is validity to Freud's claim about the universality of the
Oedipal situation, it comes preliminarily not in the fact that every son
wishes his father dead and his mother his, but in the fact that the
male child—and in fact all children—generally spends most of his
early years in a given sociopsychological structure. There is (almost)
always the trio father-mother-child. Inevitably, we are all children of
our parents. Who we are, therefore, is formed in relation to the particular *structure* that we call the family. Freud's claim about the
Oedipal situation was that the male child is put into an impossible
position: he must both get rid of the father and be the father. Yet, if
it was important to get rid of the father, then becoming the father
must in itself be threatening. The vocabulary was not available to
Freud, but we might call this now a schizophrenigenic situation: the
child is called by his sociopsychological environment to act in two incompatible yet equally necessary ways. The central recognition of
Freud's late work, such as *Civilization and its Discontents* and the
essay "Analysis Terminable and Interminable,"[23] is that the neurotic
resolution of the above situation appears as the only alternative to
schizophrenia. Better unhappiness than madness, one might say.[24]

The *Genealogy of Morals* is Nietzsche's account of this situation.[25]
Nietzsche argues that slave morality requires that one produce a
source of suffering in order to make possible a conclusion as to who
one is. Thus, though one tries to account for and escape from suffering, since the structure of one's self is dependent on that suffering,
one finally arrives at a situation where one generates one's own suffering. In Freudian terms, while remaining the son, one takes on the
father too: at this point, the dynamic is both self-sustaining and self-
destructive. Such, according to Nietzsche and to Freud, is the moving
logic of civilization, which appears universally necessary to Freud and
historically inevitable to Nietzsche.

I am here pointing to a structural similarity between the diagnoses
in the *Genealogy of Morals* and the Oedipal situation. What does it,
in fact, mean to resolve the Oedipal situation? The son, confronted
with his mother and father is faced with an apparently irresolvable

situation. If, on the one hand, he achieves the object of his desire—cathexis on the mother—he must kill the father. Yet, this must result in a death of the self, or at least a strong threat to self, since to obtain the mother he must be like the father.[26] Yet, if the (male) child were to "win" the Oedipal conflict, he would be maintained in a permanent stage of childhood and schizophrenia. Thus, for Freud, the price for avoiding schizophrenia was neurosis—civilization *must* have its discontents. Freud implies, though never explicitly argues, that we *should* pay the price for avoiding schizophrenia. Faced with irreconcilable objects of desire, individuals cannot resolve the situation directly; therefore they postpone and repress their desires, and the energy that was originally directed toward the parents surfaces in other areas. Eventually, as these individuals have children, the whole process starts again in relation to those children. The alternative of neurosis and schizophrenia is again proposed and again resolved in favor of the former.[27]

I do not want to be taken here to be giving a Freudian analysis of Nietzsche's childhood. I am arguing that the categories by which Freud analyzed the Oedipal situation are useful clarifications of the dynamics of genealogy. They cast light on the riddle that opens Nietzsche's autobiography. Nietzsche does intend to call our attention to Oedipus and the figure of the hero that is in a man who began his public career by trying to figure out the true identity of the hero in Greek tragedy. If we now turn to a reading of the *Oedipus Tyrannus*, additional clarifications may be found. In the *Tyrannus*, when Oedipus has his first suspicions that it may have been Laius whom he killed at the crossroads, he worries aloud to Jocasta, still, of course, without the suspicion that Laius was his father. Jocasta hastens to assure him and perhaps herself that even if the one guard who escaped changes his story from "many bandits" to "one bandit":

He cannot make the death of Laius
Accord with the saying of the oracle.
For Loxias expressedly said that Laius
Was doomed to die by my child; that child
However shed no blood, *since he first perished himself.*[28]

What she is telling Oedipus is that he is already dead. Tiresias, in his first appearance, has already told Oedipus that this day he would be born and die. But if Oedipus is dramatically and ironically dead, who is he? Or more precisely, *who will he be?* The central fact about

Oedipus' story is that it puts together the problem of self (Who am I?) with the problem of parents (Whose son am I?), and permits only *one* answer to those two questions.[29] And the answer is terrifying and clear. If Oedipus is to be *anyone* at all, he must be his own father (and therefore also his own patricide).

Being one's own father is recognized by the chorus as a terrible fate and productive only of unhappiness and suffering. The *Tyrannus* and the *Colonnus* study how men come to deal with unhappiness. At the end of the *Tyrannus*, "no man can be counted happy"—presumably no man who is what Oedipus is; but at the end of the *Colonnus* "all is ordered for the best" and the chorus glorifies the *polis*. We may take the ending of the *Colonnus* to be the claim that the *polis* is the solution to the problems of family.

Central here are the relations between self and polity. Over the developments of Sophocles' writing, there is a noticeable shift from the paternal tyranny of the beginning of the *Tyrannus* to the full *polis* of Athens in the *Colonnus*. Hannah Arendt has argued brilliantly that these plays show us that the only escape from the suffering of existence is in paying the price for politics, for the life with others as reciprocating individuals.[30] For this to be possible, Oedipus has to give up both his paternity of himself and his paternalistic rule of Thebes. The sufferers from the plague came to Oedipus explicitly as children. Politics, we might then say (as did Aristotle some years later), depends on being released from the family.

The problem, to put it crudely and enigmatically, is to avoid becoming your own father. If you become the father, you remain caught in the family tree. This may not be too bad if you have a good genealogy, but even then it will remain a vicious circle and merely a supportable compulsive repetition of the past. Oedipus shows us the curse and the suffering of genealogy; he is redeemed in the transformation of the world from the tyranny of Thebes to the *polis* of Athens. Indeed we might remember also that Theseus too killed his own father. With this we return to Nietzsche. He argues in the *Birth of Tragedy* that it is precisely in the drama that the Greeks understand what it means to renew oneself as oneself and not as a mere repetition of the past. Tragedy, with its focus on the hero ensured by the chorus, is a natural subject for Nietzsche from his earliest writing. The *Birth of Tragedy* is, he writes in *Ecce Homo*, an "exceedingly strange" beginning. "I had *discovered* the only metaphor and equivalent for my experience which history had. . . ."[31] Nietzsche's concern in the *Birth* is a concrete formulation of the experience that he knows himself to be going—or to have gone—through. It is thus central that he turns to Greece rather than to Christianity, for in the latter one dies for the father in order to be reborn *in* the father, but not as oneself.

4

Look then at Nietzsche's family and his understanding of it. He is born in 1844, on October 15. He is the first child of a Lutheran pastor; both his parents are themselves children of pastors. In 1846 a sister is born, and in 1848, a brother; in 1849 his father dies. In 1850 his brother dies suddenly, and the family moves from the small Saxon village of Röcken to the town of Naumburg. At twelve he suffers from headaches and eyestrain; two years later, he obtains a scholarship to a first-rate boarding school at Pforta.

We see in Nietzsche's life the occurrence of a situation not unlike the claim he makes at the beginning of his autobiography—that he is dead as his father and lives on and grows as his mother. Certainly, his father died no later than the first beginnings of the Oedipal period, during that time when the identification with the father figure may not yet have resulted in any conflict that required resolution. It is also clear that Nietzsche was raised by women; an aunt joined his mother after the move to Naumberg. This, however, has somewhat different significance for him than one might think. He makes a particular identification with his father in the first part of *Ecce Homo:* His father "dies at 36," the age that Nietzsche identifies as his own lowest point. It is at this age that Nietzsche writes "The Wanderer and his Shadow," the first part of the second volume of *Human-all-too-Human.* He refers to himself there as but a shadow; he has given up his Basel professorship, feels abandoned by the Wagners (and is), and writes to Malwida von Meyensburg that he "thirsts after the end" (January 14, 1880) and to Overbeck that he contemplates "the solution of a pistol."

Presumably, this is a death for Nietzsche: he does not expect to survive. At the lowest point in 1880 he begins anew: *Dawn of Day* is his next book. As his father, he sees himself as having died at the end of the decade; the years following are a slow, often painful, rebirth. Here his comments on father's character are important revelations of the sort of relationship that Nietzsche felt he had to resolve. His father was "delicate, kind, and morbid, as a being destined to merely pass by—more a gracious memory of life than life itself." Later on in the original section 3 of *Ecce Homo* (which I discuss below) he claims that he holds it "a great privilege to have had such a father; the farmers before whom he preached . . . said that an angel must have looked as he did." In sum, the general picture that Nietzsche gives us of his father is of a perfect being, not really of this earth, and destined to move rapidly away from it. At twelve, Nietzsche remembers his father as living a Christian life, "quietly, simply, but happily, . . . loved and respected" by all who knew him.[32] There is nowhere in his youthful writings (which date from twelve on) anything that presents his father as other than wonderful and perfect, nor his home then as other than quiet, interesting, and pleasant.

According to Nietzsche, his father becomes melancholic or mentally unwell (*gemütskrank*) in September 1848; this is diagnosed by a "famous physician" (Opolcer) as a "weakening of the brain."[33] His father suffers greatly, goes blind and eventually dies ten months later on July 27, 1849. In his description of his burial, Nietzsche pays much attention to the music, the bells, and the sound of the organ. The death of his father is the subject of several descriptions in Nietzsche's early writings. Again and again, he returns to his *Lebenslauf*, as if to get clear the nature of his earliest days. By 1861 (he is seventeen) he is comparing his father's disease to that which afflicted the king.[34] He repeats again that year his claim that his father took suddenly sick and adds that there were no known causes.

Nietzsche gives two extended versions of the importance of his father's death. Associated with both of these accounts of that death is a dream which Nietzsche characterizes as "extraordinary." In the months following the death of his father, Nietzsche's younger brother takes sick—his mother claims from "pains in the teeth"—and dies suddenly. Shortly before, Nietzsche has a dream of which he gives later two extended versions, once at fourteen and again at seventeen. In each account, he claims the dream to have been a premonition of the death of his brother. The dream, however, is clearly connected with the death of his father and may serve to illuminate what Nietzsche makes of his relation to that death. The first version:

When one carries away the top of a tree, it becomes withered and bare and the birds leave the branches. Our family was bereft of its head, all joy flowed out of our hearts and deep sadness reigned in us. The wound was barely slightly healed, however, when new pain tore at us once more. At this time, I dreamed that I heard organ music in the church as if for a funeral. As I looked to see what the reason for it was, suddenly a grave stone lifted itself up and my father clad in burial dress stepped out of it. He hurried in to the church and soon returned with a small child in his arms. The tumulus opened, he stepped in and the top sank once more down on to the opening. Immediately, the organ sound ceased and I awoke.

The day after that night young Joseph suddenly took sick with cramps and died in a few hours. Our pain was immense. My dream was entirely realized. The little body was lain in the arms of my father.[35]

Three years later Nietzsche takes up the dream again. In the interim he has several times picked up the theme of the loss of the top of the tree, and clearly associates the transfiguration of home, joy, and peace into sorrow and pain with the death of his father. Though he confounds the two events, he also associates the loss of home with the loss of his father. (They did not in fact move to Naumburg until 1850, about a year after the death of his father.) Along these lines, Nietzsche's youthful poems are filled with references to the loss of *Heimat* (home).[36] From this time forth, he thinks of himself as *"ohne Heimat."*

In the second version of the dream, the details become more precise; they concern especially those of activity and those of music. The change in focus is significant. I am concerned here, as is Pierre Klossowski,[37] not with the actual occurrence of this dream at age six, nor with its reality as a premonition. Rather, the elaborations of the dream over the two versions give an indication of the dream-work involved. We can learn what the dream was to Nietzsche's psyche. In the second version, Nietzsche repeats in a paragraph those characteristics of his father now familiar to us. He then proceeds to a couplet:

Ah, they have buried a good man
And he was more than that to me.

Some months after, a second unhappiness hit me of which I had a premonition in a dream. It seemed to me that I heard muffled organ sounds from the nearby church. Surprised, *I opened the window* which gave onto the church and the cemetery. The grave of my father opened, a white form climbed out and disappeared into the church. The dismal and disquieting sounds continued to ring out; the white shape reappeared, carrying something under the arm which I did not clearly recognize. The cover raised itself, the form sank into it, the organ was quiet—I awoke. The next morning my younger brother, a vivacious and gifted child, was overtaken with cramps and died in half an hour. He was buried directly *beside* the grave of my father.[38]

A number of things appear noteworthy. First, the second version seems clearly to benefit from details that Nietzsche must have gathered from his mother. The half-hour death time and the giftedness of the child are not likely to be part of the dream or the knowledge of a six-year-old. Second, the emphasis on the child is downplayed in the second version, and more emphasis is on Nietzsche himself. Though other details are less distinct, the music is much more important in the second. (Here it is worth remembering that Nietzsche associated the sound of organ most centrally with the death of his father.) In both, the child is not in the house but in the church. Last, the catalyst for the whole dream in both versions is the sound of the organ. It seems possible to conclude that the dream is more about Nietzsche than it is about a premonition of the death of his younger brother. Given that in the second version there is a parallel between the opening of the window and the opening of the grave, one suspects two things: first, that Nietzsche is trying to see his dead father; second, that because he is trying to see his father, his father carries him off. One should not seek to see one's father; if one does, one dies with him.

The death of the father is associated with music which in turn leads one to join the father. Thus Nietzsche is already dead in his father, but he has also joined his father and has in a certain sense become one with his father. *Therefore he does not need to replace his father with his mother*, which would be the standard resolution of the Oedipal situation. Instead, he becomes, as it were, his mother beside the father: it is thus, as both mother and himself, that he lives on and needs no parents other than himself to become who he is.[39]

This is the claim: the standard resolution of the Oedipal situation consists in adopting the paternal principle for oneself. This necessarily entraps one in a neurotic dilemma that Nietzsche, much as Freud, sees at the source of the discontents of civilization. One cannot be rid of what one has been. For Nietzsche, this discontent is somewhat more dangerous and less endurable than it is for Freud. The escape from the ascetic ideal which has no adversaries requires that one become one's own parents and that one die to one's own father and mother and engender oneself. That this is prompted by music gives us some insight into the initial attraction of the young scholar Nietzsche to his work *Birth of Tragedy from the Spirit of Music.*

The dynamic that Nietzsche poses as a riddle at the beginning of his autobiography thus finds itself biographically explicated in the account that Nietzsche gives of his childhood dream. One way of expressing the significance of this dream is to say that it points to a radical rejection on Nietzsche's part of the psychological structures that characterize the most prevalent experience of the formation of the self. The self that Nietzsche becomes has escaped from the tyranny of the Oedipalized past.[40] Jacques Derrida, in his recent book on Nietzsche, argues that the originality of Nietzsche's philosophy lies precisely in the fact that Nietzsche's work is beholden to no source of meaning. "There is . . . no truth in itself, but only a surfeit of truth; even for me, about me *(pour moi, de moi)* truth is plural."[41] For Derrida, the fact that Nietzsche can write like this makes his the voice to which modernity can respond. It is because Nietzsche has overcome the parentage of two sexes, because he is both male and female, writer and written, that he is able to be the voice for a time that can no longer acknowledge God, nature, or reason. Derrida shows us, I think, that to have escaped from the past implies that Nietzsche and his writings have no (one) meaning, or rather that they have more meanings than readers.[42]

An important question remains, however, which with the publication of a new edition of Nietzsche's works, we are for the first time able to answer. If the dynamics of the family situation are in fact what I claim them to be above, what are we to make of Nietzsche's mother and sister? As mentioned above, Nietzsche was brought up by his mother and by an aunt; but his was not a happy childhood. At twelve he begins to suffer from a set of headaches that plague him intermittently through the rest of his life. He is afflicted by the loss of home in the leaving of Röcken. He writes a poem upon his departure for Pforta that portrays his first sight of that place almost as a paradisical city.[43] Friendships—often more to him than to the other person involved—occupy a central and almost desperately important place in his life from a very early age.[44] Further, we know of the struggle that surrounded his relations with his sister, whom he repeatedly and in increasingly clear terms rejects because of her vision of him, for her presumptions to greatness, for her anti-Semitic husband, and for the nature of her encouragements to him. In fact, one suspects that if Nietzsche has taken his mother's place next to his father and has become his own mother, then his own mother and mothering relations would pose precisely the most important threat to his sense of self. They constitute a reminder that he may not be who he is, since his mother is there to prove it.

In early September 1882, Nietzsche writes to Overbeck that during an argument with his mother about Lou Salomé she "said something so rash that I had my trunks packed and left Leipzig early the next morning." In another letter to Overbeck, Nietzsche indicates his mother has accused him of defiling the tomb of his father by his writing; given the above dynamics, that would be the most psychologically threatening thing that she could say.[45] In fact, Nietzsche's letters from an early age are full of comments about the difficulty of the relation with his mother and sister. At times it becomes quite violent, as is evident in the draft of a letter dated Autumn 1882 during the height of the "Lou Crisis": "I have known for a long time that beings such as my mother and sister must be my natural enemies—The air for me is spoiled, to have to remain with such people."[46]

In the fall of 1888, Nietzsche prepares the manuscript of *Ecce Homo* and sends it to the publishers. At that time he receives a letter from his sister, then in Paraguay, which Nietzsche quotes indirectly to Overbeck in a letter dated Christmas 1888: she says that she supposes that he now "wants to be famous too" and makes disparaging remarks about the Jewish Danish critic Georg Brandes who had recently, to Nietzsche's great pride and delight, been giving lectures on Nietzsche in Copenhagen. Nietzsche is clearly furious—"seven years it has been going on," he exclaims, as he had earlier in the year to other correspondents after similar provocations. Upon receiving his sister's letter, he sends to a printer a new version of section 3 of the first chapter of *Ecce Homo*. *Ecce Homo* remains unprinted until 1905 and then comes out with an art-nouveau frontispiece by a printer who had not published Nietzsche before. Mazzino Montinari has detailed well the adventures of this new insert and of its surreptitious rescue by Peter Gast from the destructive intentions of Nietzsche's sister.[47] In his new critical edition of Nietzsche, it is now published in its rightful place for the first time. I give it here in its entirety, partly because, to my knowledge, it has not been rendered into English before, and partly because it reveals a lot about the relation of Nietzsche to the dangerous figure of his mother.

I hold it to be a great privilege, to have had such a father. The farmers before whom he preached—for he was, after he had lived several years at the Altenburger Court, for the last years a preacher—said that an angel would have looked the way he did.

And with this I touch upon the question of race. I am a Polish nobleman, *pur sang*, in whom there is not mixed a drop of bad blood, least of all of German. Were I to look for the deepest contradiction to me, I would always find my mother and my sister—to believe myself related to such *canaille* would be a blasphemy on my godliness. The treatment that I have experienced from the side of my mother and sister, up until this moment, infuses me with an unspeakable horror: here is at work a perfect infernal machine, with an unfailing certainty as to the moment at when I can be bloodily wounded—in my highest instances, . . . for then one lacks all strength to protect oneself against the poisonous worm. . . . The physiological contiguity makes possible such a *disharmonia praestabilita*. . . . But I recognize that the deepest objections to the "eternal return," my own most abysmal thought, are always mother and sister.

But as a Pole, I am also a monstrous atavism. One would have to go back centuries to find this race, the most noble there is on earth, as generally pure as I am. Against all that is today called *noblesse*, I have a superior feeling, one of distinction—I would not do the young Kaiser the honor to act as my coachman. There is only one particular case where I recognize my equal—and I do so with deepest gratitude. Frau Cosima Wagner is easily the noblest nature; and so that I do not say with this one word too much, I say that Richard Wagner is for me easily the noblest man . . . the rest is silence. . . . All ruling concepts about affinities are physiological nonsense, which cannot be outdone. The pope himself had commerce today with this nonsense. One is least related to one's parents: it would be the surest sign of commonness, to be related to one's parents. Higher natures have their origin much further back: it is with them that the most has been accumulated, saved, and increased. The greatest individuals are the oldest: I don't understand it, but Julius Caesar could have been my father—or Alexander, this embodied Dionysos. . . . In this moment, at which I write, the mail brings me a Dionysos head.[48]

This is a strange and difficult passage, perhaps touched by the onset of insanity. (In his last letter to Burckhardt, Nietzsche will identify himself in a schizophrenic fashion as "all names in history.") But the letter is not out of control. He shows care in his relation to the Wagners: in an earlier draft he had written that their (Cosima and Richard's) relation was adulterous, probably in relation to himself (i.e., that Cosima should have been—was—his wife); now this is "a word too much." Even the Dionysos head that he receives in the mail is conceivably a photograph of such a head, which he might have gotten from one Rosalie Nielsen.[49]

Most central here is that Nietzsche denies the importance of the biological family; he first claims to be a throwback to an ancient race of noble Poles, then finds a father in Caesar or Alexander. What is important is not that he is claiming paternity from some unknown or impossible source, but that he thinks that his relationship with his biological father to be now so attenuated that he (Nietzsche) now exists as a person, *as if* Caesar had been his father. The very next section in *Ecce Homo* starts with a discussion of another character trait he owes to his "incomparable father." Clearly this passage does not constitute a rejection of the father, but a rejection of taking his father's place, especially in relation to the mother.

The mother and sister, on the other hand, are the most single threats to his selfhood: indeed, they constitute the "deepest possible objection to the doctrine of eternal return." It is not possible to fully explicate in this essay what might be meant by that. I have elsewhere elaborated my understanding of eternal return,[50] and will simply assert here the conclusion of that argument: eternal return for Nietzsche stands as an understanding of the world that if practiced—a praxis, we might now say—will permit a change in *who* an individual is. To change who one is, however, means to change what one's past has been. Eternal return is thus a way of dealing with the past such that a particular past (still alive in one's present) is eliminated and replaced by another past. Thus "we plant a new form, a life, a new instinct, a second nature which withers the first."[51] With this we can now understand still better Nietzsche's epigraph to *Ecce Homo*. We also see why his mother and sister are such threats: they are embodiments of the genealogy that he is annihilating and serve as reminders of at least the difficulty if not the impossibility of escaping from a particular form of life.[52] They are one of the reasons he writes *Ecce Homo*—so that he be not mistaken. It is probably correct to see the book as Nietzsche's attempt to avoid precisely what happened to him after his insanity and death, namely, that his mother and sister become the official (and dangerously incorrect) interpreters of his writings. For Nietzsche, to be his own mother and to live on and grow as himself, he must necessarily eliminate his parental mother and her minion Elizabeth. Thus only then will it be true that "one is least of all related to one's parents": to the degree that one is so related, one has not become who one is.[53]

Nietzsche appears then as someone who has broken the hold of Oedipus, at least of the paternal Oedipus of the *Tyrannus*. He has broken the neurotic repetition—the *circulus vitiosus* as he calls it elsewhere—which would have kept him in bondage to the past, and he can now stand free before the world. He announces that he will in two months confront the world as it never before has been. Karl Jaspers thinks that Nietzsche was jealous of Christ and there is a grain of truth there. But Nietzsche also thinks now that he has overcome Christ: he has not joined his father in heaven, but has become his own progenitor on earth.

In the discussion of Nietzsche's dream above, I noted that his dream was a spectacle in which he was himself cast as the tragic hero: he dies and is reborn; music is at the origin of the whole vision. With the above discussion in mind, we have an understanding of precisely what attracted Nietzsche to the topic of the *Birth of Tragedy* and can now gain a better understanding of his interpretation of Greek sacred drama.

In the *Birth of Tragedy*, Nietzsche gives a portrait of Greek tragedy in what one might call its sociopolitical function. The great tragedians are able, as he hopes Wagner will later be able, to make "art seem natural," namely, to give to the *polis* a secure and unquestioned foundation inside which individual greatness becomes possible. The artistic foundation of the state is necessary because, Nietzsche argues, there is no natural basis to any culture. This is what "the Dionysian" means: a profound insight and understanding into the basic unjustifiability of any given configuration of events. Two moves compose the tragic process; these moves find their happy conjoining in the creative act of tragedy, which requires both the Dionysian insight and the Apollonian form-giving. Their union is the creation of tragedy and the foundation of the state. "We will have gained much for aesthetic science," writes Nietzsche, "when we have arrived not by logical insights, but by unmediated certainty, at the understanding that the development of further art is bound up with the quality (*Duplicitaet*) of the apollonian and the dionysian—much as procreation from the doubleness (*Zweiheit*) of the sexes depends on incessant quarrels and only periodic reconciliations." The aim of the book therefore is to produce the immediacy of insight, an insight that cannot be questioned and is not traceable to its origins.[54] The coming together of these two different drives produces a new birth, which is Attic tragedy.

Attic tragedy produces a certainty of what is, and of who we— here as audience—citizens are.[55] The great achievement for Greece is thereby a "self" that is authentically its own and not dependent on what comes before or on the empires that surround Greece. In Nietzsche's reading, tragedy forms the social and political means for a constant renewal of that which is properly Greek and in Greek. The Dionysian hero, Oedipus for instance, is for Nietzsche the key addition to the earliest Greek drama. It is when the illusion of the figure of Dionysus is added to the *"Ur-drama"* that tragedy can accomplish a vision in which the world is once again brought back to completion.

Here one is tempted to ask, *what* is complete? To answer this it is necessary to investigate the nature of the God that appears to make the tragedy whole and operative. Nietzsche indicates that the name Dionysos is a name given almost at random to the general drive or artistic principle that he is discussing; Prometheus, Orestes, and Oedipus serve as exemplars of this figure. In the *Birth of Tragedy,* Nietzsche takes over much from an earlier, privately printed essay on "Socrates and Greek tragedy."[56] Among the longer passages that remain unchanged we find a discussion of Oedipus as a tragic hero. Nietzsche argues that the image of Oedipus that the dramatist gives us is but a *"Lichtbild,"* a photographic slide seen only when projected. One can go even deeper into the myth. Here Nietzsche is claiming an understanding of the Oedipus myth even more profound than is the image immediately apparent in the plays.

Oedipus, the murderer of his father, the husband of his mother, the riddle solver of the Sphinx! What does this mysterious triad of these fateful deeds tell us? There is an age long *(uralt)* folk belief, especially Persian, that a wise magician can only be born from incest. Looking back on the mother-marrying and riddle-solving Oedipus, we immediately interpret this to ourselves to mean that where the spell of present future . . . has been broken by prophetic and magical powers, a monstrous unnaturalness—as there, incest—must have already occurred as cause. How else might one constrain nature to give up her secrets, if not through a triumphant resistance, that is, by means of something unnatural? This insight, I find expressed in the horrid triad of Oedipus' destiny: the same man who solves the riddle of nature—the Sphinx of double nature—must also as murderer of his father and husband of his mother break the most sacred natural orders. Indeed the myth seems to wish to whisper to us, that wisdom and particularly *Dionysian wisdom is an unnatural abomination*, such that he who by means of his knowledge plunges nature into the abyss of annihilation, *must also experience in himself* the dissolution of nature.[57]

Here Nietzsche describes the Dionysian magician in terms very close to those that he uses to describe himself in his autobiography. The unnatural birth of this figure is the precondition of its ability to resolve the tragedy. The tragedy can only perform its sociopolitical functions when it is resolved by the appearance of the figure of Dionysos. Therefore, for Nietzsche to perform for Europe the role that the spectacle of Oedipus performed for Athens, he, too, will have to die to his old identity to be reborn as his self. Only in this way can the "Dionysian phenomenon" be achieved for Europe. Of Nietzsche's last seven letters, three are signed "The Crucified" and three "Dionysos," each a figure who died and was reborn. The seventh one, his final letter to Burckhardt,[58] is signed first *"Astu"* (Greek: home city), then "Nietzsche," and contains the claim that he is "all names in history." These letters constitute the sign that Nietzsche has lost himself as he was and has now found himself newly at home. As befits a god or a hero, he is chthonically reborn, this time of himself only. The family he was in is no more. It is only properly Pirandellian to note that after visiting Nietzsche in the asylum in 1890, Peter Gast subsequently wrote to Fuchs that at times "Nietzsche almost seemed as if he were faking madness, as if he were happy to have ended in this manner."[59]

I do not want to say what we should conclude from all this. Nietzsche is claiming that there is a mode of existence radically different from that in which human beings have been living for the last 2,500 years. Nietzsche clearly identifies his ability to ground this new personality structure—one that is not human-all-too-human but *übermenschlich*—in his own heroic ability to overcome the lure and temptations of the neurotic slavish moral stance of the ascetic ideal.[60] He claims that, freed from entrapment in what has been, he will no longer be driven by his own past. But *we* do not know what to say. The discovery of his new self, nonfamilial in character, coincides with the advent of his insanity. Certainly nothing in his loss of self, nor even more in his preliminary concern at that point to "rule the world" (letter to Carl Fuchs, December 18, 1888) and have his own new identity publicly fixed once and for all, "for eternity" (to Fuchs again, December 27, 1888), necessarily leads us to the conviction that the new self is preferable to the old. The price of the family may be the *Unbehagen* that Freud saw and the neuroses that define it. To live without *Heimat*, as Nietzsche knew himself to be doing, is to live in the end in a dangerous and world historical gamble. Nietzsche's wager is that one can go through the abyss of selflessness in order to build a transfigured world from the destruction of the old. The "polar night of icy darkness" lay ahead for Nietzsche much as it did for Max Weber. We admire Nietzsche that he dared to go into it with a full sense of what lay behind. We do not say if the possible outcomes are endurable. If not, however, then we will have to revise the wisdom of Marsyas: it will be a far better thing not to have been born, than to have been born of oneself.

The Working-Class Family:
A Marxist Perspective

🌣 *Jane Humphries*

The meaning of the working-class family as an element in a society dominated by the capitalist mode of production has not been adequately explored in Marxist analyses. Although Marx's and Engels's writings contain important insights, their theoretical perspective inhibits comprehension of the material basis of the working-class family—in fact explicitly denies the existence of such a foundation—and therefore predicts the dissolution of working-class family life.

The urgent need to understand the relationship between capitalism and women's oppression has led to renewed interest in this topic with the contemporary emphasis being on the family as the site of domestic labor and the reproduction of labor-power. The effect has been to view the family in terms of the functional prerequisites of capitalism, and to locate its reproduction in the reproduction of capital. This is a distortion, for to look only from the perspective of capital is to ignore family life, which presents the most important single set of social relations that people experience. In this way Marxists have, until recently, neglected the entire area of psychic and sexual existence, with unfortunate effects on their understanding of crucial issues, such as the formation of consciousness, working-class culture, and so on.

Many of the essays in this volume are intended to redress just such a neglect. This paper is specifically concerned with the relationship between the institutionalized social relations of the family and struggle between the classes. The argument is that in certain periods of capitalist development the working class was motivated to defend the family, at least in part, by its role in the determination of the standard of living, the development of class cohesion, and the waging of class struggle. The discussion has political implications with regard to attitudes, not only toward the family itself, but also toward women's struggles against their specific oppression.

This paper will first present a brief and critical review of the recent literature, and follow with an alternative interpretation of the meaning of the family as the basic economic unit of society. The material basis of the proletarian family is then conceptualized in terms of three categories: (1) its role in the provision of a popular support system for nonlaboring members of the working class; (2) its role in the limitation of the supply of workers and thus in the determination of the value of labor-power; and (3) its role in the development of class consciousness and struggle. The arguments are developed with reference to nineteenth-century British capitalism; their applicability in other instances is not contested. The conclusion explores the political implications of the paper.

Contemporary Marxist Theory of the Working-Class Family

Recent Marxist analyses have attempted to rectify the failure by both Marx and Engels to explore systematically the meaning of the working-class family in capitalism. Contemporary writers have correctly avoided the traditional Marxist definition of the family in terms of its proprietary functions as unhelpful in a working-class context. Yet these writers follow Marx in their premature pronouncement of the destruction of family life under capitalism. The family survives only as the basic economic unit of society, and is now defined in terms of its role in the provision of domestic labor and the reproduction cycle of labor-power through which it relates to the functional prerequisites of capitalism. It is in terms of these categories that the debate has been pursued.[1]

The difficulty in comparing labor-time used in domestic production with that spent in capitalist production complicates generalization of the labor theory of value. Consequently there is disagreement about the precise theoretical reformulation required to accommodate the existence of domestic labor and explicate the relationship between the proletarian household and capitalism. Nevertheless, there is consensus on one fundamental point. All the participants see domestic labor as *functional* to capitalism because of its role in the reproduction of labor-power, the only "commodity" that has the capacity to create more value than it possesses itself.[2]

Politically this is very important. That domestic labor be demonstrably *essential* to capitalism is crucial to any attempt to construct a theory that ties women's specific oppression to capitalism and that therefore unites the feminist struggle with the historic struggle of the working class. Hence the emphasis on a generalization of value theory that demonstrates clearly the connection between domestic labor and capitalism. It does not appear necessary to argue that women produce surplus value, or value for that matter, to forge these links. All that is needed is that domestic labor be seen as necessary to the functioning of the capitalist system. The fervor with which this position is defended relates of course to its optimistic implications for unity in the struggle between the working class and the women's movement. Unfortunately, what is convenient may not always be what is real. In the long run it may be more sensible to confront the tensions between the women's movement and the working class, and to work to understand these strains, for only then will it be possible to unite in a truly viable struggle.

All variants of the position described above suffer from the reductionism involved in analyzing the family as the basic economic unit of society—a complex phenomenon—in terms of domestic labor, which is one aspect of that phenomenon. The identification of women's specific oppression under capitalism with domestic labor is also problematic. Most important of all, the functionalist approach that collapses what is rational for capital into what is real, denigrates the importance in any concrete instance of the struggle between capital and labor. For example, although the descriptions of the relationship between domestic labor and capitalism imply the possibility that the former can facilitate a higher working-class standard of living, this potentiality is never explored. Yet the ability or inability of capital to capture the fruits of household production surely depends on the state of the class struggle.

An understanding of the working-class family and the reasons for its persistence during two centuries of capitalism requires an enlarged perspective encompassing a materialist analysis based on a nonindividualistic theory of human needs. It is not that the working-class family is an essential component of the conditions of existence of the capitalist mode of production, but that in the context of developing capitalism the alternatives have always been resisted by the working class, which recognized in the erosion of traditional family structures a threat to its standard of living and ability to engage in class struggle. This hypothesis is explored below.

The Meaning of the Working-Class Family under Capitalism

If the focus on the functions of the working-class family, labor, and the reproduction of labor-power, leads to an unbalanced view, how can this distortion be corrected? It is necessary to begin from a different interpretation of the family as the basic unit of society.

Marx's writings contain a recurring vision of humanity as in need of a social existence. For Marx, man is only individualized through the process of history. He originally appears as a "generic being, a tribal being, a herd animal."[3] This definition of human existence implies that labor must relate to the maintenance and reproduction of the individual in certain definite relationships to his community. This, in turn, requires the existence of some surplus labor over and above necessary labor, as traditionally defined, *in all societies*, because the conditions of reproduction of the individual laborer are not equivalent to the conditions of his reproduction in certain definite relationships to his community.[4] Thus surplus labor does not exist only to provide for a *class* of nonworkers, which may or may not exist. Nonworking *individuals*, including children, the old, the sick, and those who perform unproductive but socially necessary functions, are ubiquitous and social formations in which there is no allowance for these individuals are unlikely to be resilient, progressive, or just. So in most historical instances the appropriation of surplus labor necessary to secure the reproduction of the economy and its conditions of existence in the totality of social relations has to include an allowance for these nonlaboring individuals.

The question then becomes, How is such surplus labor appropriated? Within primitive communism the collective means of appropriation, reflected in the communal property, is achieved by denying any necessary correspondence between labor spent and the share of the product received. Instead the product is distributed among the producers *and others* according to established social relations.

For redistribution to ensure the reproduction of the conditions of existence of the society, it must involve a network of individuals extending beyond those engaged in the immediate labor. By the simple extension of shares in the community's product to those who have little to contribute in terms of their own labor, surplus is appropriated and the nonlaboring individuals supported. Redistribution requires a communal network defining precise relationships between all pairs of individuals. These relationships then map out mutual responsibilities that, when mobilized by ideological conviction, translate into flows of labor-time socially demanded from each individual and each individual's relative share in the social product. So simultaneously the community possesses and allocates the surplus. The historical basis for such a network of defined relationships is kinship. Family ties provide a basic element in this mode of appropriation: the social significance of these ties constitutes the basis of the redistribution through which the surplus is appropriated.

These observations may appear unremarkable when directed to primitive communism. Their extension to other modes of production is more controversial. The argument is that family ties, vitalized by ideology and emotions, bind together laboring and nonlaboring individuals and secure for the latter a share in the product of the former, not only in primitive communism, but also in more developed modes of production. This interpretation provides an alternative vision of the family as the basic unit of society.

In precapitalist societies all the members of the family helped to produce the family subsistence, which included the support of the nonlaboring members and those whose *individual* productivity was insufficient to ensure their survival. The surplus labor involved in this support was appropriated by the family members themselves in the process of family production. The analogy with primitive communism is obvious.

Under capitalistic relations of production this role of the family became obscured as the direct producer was now separated from the means of production and appropriation was in the form of surplus value. Proletarianization of some family members became a prerequisite for survival. In capitalism, the family's product consists of commodities purchased with the family's wages and use-values produced by the family's domestic labor. But the extension of shares in this product to those family members who are unable to secure their own subsistence still ensures their survival. Both wage workers and domestic workers participate in this "mutual exchange of activities."

Even within the primitively communal family, division of labor is likely to engender hierarchy. Relations of dominance and subordination are intensified under capitalism. Nevertheless the family remains a union of laboring and nonlaboring individuals, which secures the survival of the latter. Capitalism makes this communal core harder to discern, and also unleashes forces antipathetic to such community. But capitalism, simultaneously, creates conditions that ensure that the working class struggle to retain family ties and affection, not only because within the latter they find a warmth that makes their lives more bearable, but also because such ties and affection help them in their historic struggle against oppression.

Family and community vs. bureaucratic and charitable support for nonlaboring members of the working class. In contrast to the view that the family survives only because it facilitates shifting responsibility for the reproduction of labor-power from capital to labor, this section builds on the notion that the family provides support for nonlaboring members of the working class. If such assistance is not forthcoming from labor via the primitive communism of the family, then it must come from capital in the form of state-supplied services or individualistic charitable impulses. The nature and implications of these alternative modes of support are usefully compared.

It is easy to document working-class resistance to any concerted attempt by the capitalist state, or individuals representative of the capitalist class, to usurp the traditional supportive functions of the family, and reduce the nonlaboring family members to a more direct and transparent dependence on capital. Instead, labor fought for a sufficient element of surplus in wages to support the nonlaboring family members, that is for a "family wage." Working-class strategy reflects the realization that the traditional arrangements can be of assistance in the struggle over the standard of living, and in the development of class consciousness and cohesion.

Initial support for such a perspective is provided by existing historical evidence. The official position in the early nineteenth century promoted family integrity and autonomy in the care of the young, the old, and the destitute. Legally families were still governed by the '43 Elizabeth, which exhorted them to provide for their dependents.[5] But in an era of wage dependence, cyclical and structural unemployment, increased longevity, and rising labor mobility, the traditional responsibilities could not be enforced. Industrialization and associated changes made the need for state-provided safety nets acute. Initially the Old Poor Law was expanded accommodatingly, but in 1834 new institutions were created. Capital's bureaucratic provision for the nonlaboring members of the working class was certainly not generous; but it did exist.

There is considerable evidence that the working class regarded the Old Poor Law as their ancient right, part of the social contract between classes. Certainly this was the position of nineteenth-century working-class radicals. Witness Bronterre O'Brien's denunciation of the New Poor Law:

Here is an Act to rob (we might almost say murder) some three or four millions of the most desolate of mankind. The right of these poor people to parish relief is of more than two centuries standing. It was given to them in exchange for their share of the church property, of which the reformation had despoiled them. It was their "vested interest" in the most enlarged sense of those words for it was not only guaranteed by the law of the land, but also by those of Justice, Humanity, and sound religion. Yet of this sacred of all sacred properties have the poor been despoiled by capitalists.[6]

The problem was that although nineteenth-century economic conditions necessitated the provision of bureaucratic safety nets, the governing class was constrained in its provision of relief by the need to secure an adequate supply of labor at low wages for the burgeoning industries and for agriculture. Modes of assistance that allowed the working class dignity and elemental security were not compatible with the maximal appropriation of labor-power from the body of living laborers. The obsession of the governing class with this problem is reflected in its concern over the corrupting influences of outdoor relief and the corresponding necessity for the principal of "less eligibility."[7]

It was not that the capitalist class was unable or unwilling to support the nonlaboring members of the working class but that it could only do so on certain terms, conditions derived from the requirement of the capitalist mode of production, that the mass of laborers have no means of production of their own, *and no means of livelihood other than through the sale of their labor-power.* The mere presence of an impoverished and propertlyless mass is not sufficient to ensure the sale of labor-power without additional coercion. "The bourgeoisie wants and uses the power of the state to 'regulate wages'; i.e., to force them within the limits suitable for surplus-value making, to lengthen the working day, *and to keep the labourer himself in the normal degree of dependence.*"[8]

The relationship between this process and the New Poor Law is amply demonstrated in the following quotation from the working-class newspaper *Northern Star*, June 7, 1845.

The abolition of the *legal* relief for the unemployed; the denial of all relief except on terms that would deter everyone but the soul destroyed starving slave from accepting it; the institution of the "Workhouse *test*" with its workhouse dress—its *brand* of poverty—its classification—its separation of man and wife and mother and child—its scientific dietaries . . . its dysentry hurrying off its inmates as if stricken with the plague; all this was well calculated to make the labourer offer his services for almost any amount of wage, sooner than subject himself to the cruelties that awaited him if he applied for aid in his necessity to those facetiously called his "guardians." And thus "philosophy" accomplished its aim. *It got at the wages of labour.* The poor law screw was well adapted to twine the labourer down to less and still less comfort. The less the "share" of his productions kept for himself, the more there was for those who lived on his labour.[9]

The New Poor Law was presented as an economy measure. Its authors were, however, profoundly affected by the belief that rural insurrection in 1830 had been more acute in those areas where the Allowance System prevailed most completely, fostering an independent and belligerent spirit. They were also obsessively preoccupied with the "corrupting effects" of outdoor relief. These concerns indicate the true nature of the New Poor Law. It was part of an institutional framework ensuring the dependence of the working class upon capital. It is not surprising then that the reports from the district commissioners on the progress of the new system are less concerned with the economies facilitated than with the willingness and docility of the working class in the context of "less eligibility."[10]

It could be argued that the justification of "the workhouse test" was relevant only to able-bodied paupers, which would exclude a large proportion of the nonlaboring members of the working class, who would, presumably, merit other treatment. This distinction was recognized in theory by the authorities. The Webbs emphasized how the original proposals involved the recognition of different categories of paupers and recommended differential treatment; but these recommendations were buried by the administrative difficulties involved in their enactment and the extra expense entailed in heterogeneous treatment. A parsimonious and primitive capitalism could not accommodate such niceties.

There were arguments for making the workhouse uncomfortable even for the aged, such discomfort providing "an inducement to the young and healthy to provide for their latter years."[11] Pauper children similarly had to live more miserable lives than the children of the self-sufficient poor lest some incentive be given to the abandonment of children to the Guardians' tender mercies. It is clear that the authorities were not concerned with the rights of individuals or piecemeal justice. The New Poor Law represented a *class* position and provided a confrontation with labor. Of course, coercive use of relief provision was nothing new in 1834 and even within the generally repressive framework of the New Poor Law additional oppression was possible. For example, poor relief was withheld during lockouts,[12] and denied to those who subscribed to the Chartist fund.[13]

Given the coercive use of bureaucratic methods of support, it is not surprising that they were hated and resented, and that the "rationalization" of relief provisions in the interests of capital in 1834 was strenuously resisted. The Second Annual Report of the Poor Law Commissioners noted that "partial riots have occurred in different counties, but by the aid of small parties of the metropolitan police . . . occasionally aided by the support of a military force, these disturbances have been put down without any considerable injury to property."[14]

The introduction of the New Poor Law into the industrial regions produced an even more violent reaction.[15] In these areas, control of the administration of Poor Law funds had long been regarded as an important political issue: witness the battle fought for such jurisdictions by the Oldham radicals early in the century.[16] The pauper press, as suggested above, denounced the 1834 law as a robbery of working people. The issue was taken up by the Chartists. John Fielden continued to campaign for more generous treatment until the end of his career.[17] That the hatred of the system ran very deep among the laboring class is illustrated in the few surviving nineteenth-century autobiographies,[18] and the commentaries on working-class life by the contemporary social investigators.[19] It was a refuge of last resort only.

It matters little that the cruelties of the system were sometimes exaggerated and often against the letter of the law.[20] They were certainly consonant with the spirit of the law. Moreover, the belief of the working class in the more outrageous stories—for example, that the Guardians intended to murder the babies of the poor, or that the bread given as relief was poisoned—merely illustrates the traumatic effect of the law on working people and the depth of the associated hostility.[21]

Much of the hatred of the workhouse stemmed not from the atrocities publicized and occasionally embroidered by opponents of the act, but rather from the harsh coldness of the provisions, from what today would be described as psychological deprivation. Most resented of all was the separation of families, a deliberate element in the new policy. Defended by the proponents of the act on the grounds that it was necessary for administrative efficiency or that such treatment actually benefitted the poor, the wrenching apart of families inflamed the working class. Frequently violence was precipitated, as in the case of the Chesham incident, when a crowd that gathered around the Chesham Workhouse to prevent the removal of some old male paupers to Amersham Workhouse eventually had to be dispersed by the police.[22] Very frequently the breaking up of families provided a crucial element in the dramatic, publicized examples of cruelty.

The other possible bourgeois source of support for nonlaboring members of the working class was charity. It is not surprising that the benevolence of the wealthy possessed many of the same drawbacks as formalized relief in the nineteenth century and that it was similarly despised and resented by the working class. For one thing, it too was manipulated to repressive ends. Employers, for example, "were suspected of the manipulation of charitable activity as yet another weapon in their disciplinary armour."[23] Joseph Arch's autobiography contains a vivid description of how charity was used to ensure conformity by the petty-minded parson's wife in the rural village of his childhood. Here charity was withheld not only as a punishment for dissidence (Arch's father had refused to sign for "a small loaf and a dear one" and so was denied not only charity but work), but also in retaliation for religious nonconformity. It could even be denied for unacceptable manners, and here Arch's mother would have been a victim had they ever needed to ask for help from the vicarage, as she could not provide "the smooth face and . . . smooth tongue . . . that their benefactors required of them."[24]

The repressive effects of working-class dependence upon charity are clearly illustrated in William Allen's defense of philanthropy written in 1812.

[C]harity operates as a real principle of virtue, as a motive to good conduct in the poor. It is the reward of merit. Throughout his whole life, the poor man, looking forward to the calamities to which his state is incident, must in this case be in the habit of asking himself, is my conduct such as to procure me friends in the house of need, to recommend me to the county of those who know me, in a period of sickness and want?[25]

To summarize: bureaucratic and benevolent methods of support for nonlaboring members of the working class are usually demoralizing and degrading and were chronically so in the nineteenth century. Simply from a materialistic viewpoint it may be that the welfare of the nonlaboring members of the working class was better secured by the traditional familial methods. Moreover, the organized benevolence of the state or the informal charity of the wealthy automatically involved pressures to conform with ruling-class ideology and to passively acquiesce in, if not collaborate with, class oppression, which clearly undermined the class consciousness and integrity of working people. These remarks illustrate the vital importance of alternative, traditional working-class support systems which must now be discussed.

The 1834 Poor Law was an attempt to discourage recourse to official channels and to make the poor "self-sufficient." What was promoted was class sufficiency via mutually reciprocal kinship ties.

For the working-class family in nineteenth-century British capitalism, kinship ties provided a major source of nonbureaucratic support in conditions of chronic uncertainty. The timeless rhythms of the agricultural cycle were now overshadowed by the cyclical fluctuations in industrial employment. Wage dependence increased insecurity and aggravated the problems implicit in "critical life situations," that is, events with which the individual was unlikely to be able to cope alone—such as sickness, death, disaster, old age, marriage, and childbirth.

Recent discoveries about the preindustrial family have cast doubt on the view that industrialization disrupts preexisting wider kinship ties. A comparison of the preindustrial situation with modern working-class communities, characterized by well-developed kin networks, as described by Willmott and Young, suggests, superficially at least, than in Britain "modernization" did not decrease kinship cohesion.[26] The same conclusion is reached in Michael Anderson's investigation of the family during the industrial revolution which documents the retention, indeed strengthening, of certain kinship connections. The vision is of a world where despite "migration, residential mobility, industrial employment and high mortality rates most people managed to maintain relationships with their family, both the current nuclear family and the family as a web of wider kinship ties."[27]

Working-class history in the nineteenth century clearly illustrates the material basis of such relationships in the importance of the family to nonlaboring members of the working class. The help given to orphans, widows and widowers, and to those temporarily unable to secure their own living as a result of one or another of life's critical situations is amply documented in Anderson. Rowntree's investigation of conditions in York at the end of the century documents the same mechanisms at work. For example, in the fifty-one annotated cases of abysmal poverty, households in a poor position to assist others, there are several examples of the extension of the family to nonlaboring relatives other than dependent children, for example, invalid siblings or aged parents.[28] This phenomenon should be distinguished from the "huddling" practiced by working-class families to economize on rent and housekeeping expenses. The latter involves sharing accommodation and expenses with other self-supporting families or relatives. Here concern is with the extension of the household to a dependent relative.

The same fifty-one cases also include several examples of families who received help from relatives not included in the household itself. For example the notes on case Number 40 state: "*Gilder.* Married, four rooms. One child. Out of work, ill. Man was in Sick Club, but benefit has run out. Wife Chars, is hardworking, clean and respectable. *Relations help them.* Rent 3s 9d."[29] It is also worth noting that despite the miserable poverty of this group only twenty-one of the fifty-one cases were in receipt of official relief. Frequent and vehement denunciations of such assistance were recorded.

Anderson emphasizes what he calls the "instrumentalist" attitude to family ties, that is that most of the kinship ties maintained were mutually advantageous within a rather short period of time. This is exactly what would be expected in the context of primary poverty where the family could not always bear the responsibilities involved in mutual support. Kinship ties were rationalized in the light of working-class realities. At times of crisis these support systems would be put under a severe strain, and family members were put on relief even under conditions of less eligibility, as reflected in the rise of the numbers of old and infirm on relief in the bad years 1839–1846, as families who had shouldered their responsibilities bravely enough in better times found that they could no longer cope.

The exertion involved in meeting family responsibilities, the repugnance of the workhouse and the material basis of the family ties that were desperately retained are all illustrated in the story of one of Mayhew's wretched "slop workers." Although starving and forced to prostitution to keep herself and her child, this woman took her mother out of the workhouse "because she was so wretched." Some semblance of mutual aid in the relationship is preserved as the slop worker notes her mother "thought she could mind the child" and thus contribute to the family's sustenance. The story continues in stark simplicity. "In this condition we were all starving together. No-one would come near us who knew my disgrace, and so I resolved I would not be my mother's death, and I left her. She went to her friend's but she was so excited at going that it caused her death, and she died an hour after she got into her friend's house. An inquest was held upon her, and the jury returned a verdict that she died through a horror of going into the workhouse."[30]

Migrants represented another group of temporarily nonlaboring members of the working class who sought to turn kinship ties with established residents to their own particular advantage. The underlying material base and the rationalization of the relationship in line with this base is documented by another of Mayhew's needlewomen who describes how, even though she and her daughter were in desperate financial straits, "a niece of mine came to me from Sheffield about this time and set to work with us. The three of us could earn 10s or 11s a week between us by sitting up three nights a week. Coal, candle, and twist had to be found out of our earnings. My niece left us dissatisfied with her lot."[31]

That kinship provided a structure for reciprocal relationships among the early industrial working class, just as it did in primitive society, is reflected in the way it was molded to meet particular circumstances. The extension of the household to encompass individuals who were not relatives, but who were able to contribute within the family configuration, was a frequent occurrence among the nineteenth-century poor. Mayhew's sketches provide many such cases. His shoebinder describes her situation as follows:

I have no home sir. . . . My work wouldn't allow me to pay rent—no, that it wouldn't at the price we have now. I live with this good woman and her husband. The rent is half a crown a week, and they allow me to live with them rent free. We all live in this one room together—there are five of us, four sleep in one bed; that is the man and the wife and the two children, and I lie on the floor. If it wasn't for them I must go to the workhouse . . . I give them and the little ones what I earn . . . and we all starve together as contentedly as we can.[32]

The woman with whom the shoebinder lived continued the description of their straitened circumstances, concluding with a report on her attempt to be confined within the workhouse: ". . . but when I asked what can I do with my husband and children, they must come in too was the answer; and so we must break up even the poor little home we have; but then you know, sir, it *is* a home, and once broken up we should never be able to get it together again. . . ."[33] As is evident from the above, individuals were sometimes taken into their adopted families as quasi-kin.[34] In this way mutual responsibilities usually associated with ties of blood or marriage were extended outward into the community.

Thus, although ties of blood or marriage create the basis for *possible* kinship links, true links have to be produced and maintained by practices relating to a specific material base, which so decisively influences the nature and extent of the kinship system that endures. During the nineteenth century, working-class kinship persisted because it provided the only framework that was both sufficiently defined as to guarantee help and controlled by the working class. According to this perspective, the endurance of the family reflects both a rejection of the co-operation threatened by official relief provision, and a struggle for popular methods of meeting the needs of nonlaboring comrades within a capitalist environment.

Such a struggle promoted social obligation, that is, concern among workers for nonkin. The mutual aid of the family becomes generalized to the community and the class. The importance of friends and neighbors in the mitigation of life's tribulations is one of the best documented characteristics of nineteenth-century working-class life.[35] Almost every case history recorded registers amazing generosity among members of the same class. The underlying rationale of this generosity, as well as a hint of its significance in the development of class consciousness, is revealed by the anonymous Navy, whose life story is included in Burnett's collection of working-class autobiographies. "It's not our way, don't you see, to ask anyone to help us, unless it's one of our own sort. We don't mind taking a few shillings from people like ourselves, so as we can do the same for them another time; but we never begs of anybody else. It's against our rules."[36]

So the desires of ordinary people for personalized nonmarket methods of distribution and social interaction have shaped the institution of the family. To ignore the role that these aspirations played in guiding human conduct and in shaping the class struggle is to fail to understand the nature of the family as the basic unit of society or the reasons for its persistence within the working class.

The value of labor-power and the family labor supply. The definition of the family as a collection of laboring and nonlaboring individuals with the latter supported by the wages and domestic production of the former, suggests another motive for a working-class defense of traditional family life. The argument is that the family provided one of the few available means for the working class to exercise some control over the supply of laborers and thereby over the value of labor-power.

Although traditional value theory abstracts from the complications created by workers' existence in families, Marx clearly recognized that the employment structure of the working-class family was critical in the determination of the value of any *individual* worker's labor-power.[37] Marx believed that the standard of living was tied to the reproduction cost of the proletarian family, which was the maximum that a family with the average number of wage earners could *continuously* obtain. The level of wages was therefore governed by the employment structure of the *typical* family and households that had a lower than average proportion of wage earners to dependents were condemned to chronic poverty. Thus the proletarianization of incremental family members could not in the long run raise the *total* family wage above the historically given subsistence level; instead, the intensified competition in the labor market and the lowering of rates of wages would simply spread that family wage over more workers. In this way the degree of exploitation would be increased.

Marx concluded that mass proletarianization of women and children, facilitated as it was by the increasing use of machinery in production, would be a characteristic of nineteenth-century capitalism linked to the immiseration of the working class. His analysis is, however, rich enough to accommodate the existence of countervailing forces, including other aspects of the complex conditions of existence of the capitalist mode of production, and also the resistance of the working class.

Most explanations of the failure of mass proletarianization to materialize during the 1800s concern the first type of countervailing force. Attention has been drawn to the changing needs of expansionary capitalism in terms of the quality and quantity of labor, lack of substitutes for use-values produced in the home, and the association between the maintenance of family structures and political stability. In short, emphasis has been on explanations that suggest a restraint in the attack on the family rationalized by the latter's usefulness to capital. The alternative perspective presented here is that the family was defended by the working class in part because of recognition that the family acted as an obstacle to the cheapening of the value of labor-power.

It is important to emphasize that it is invalid to compare one working-class family with a single breadwinner with another family with multiple wage earners. In a situation where most families contain several wage workers, competition would have driven down the price of labor-power and each worker would receive only a fraction of family subsistence. With labor-power so cheapened a family with only one wage earner would be in an unfortunate position indeed. Poverty would force other family members into wage work, the value of labor-power would sink even lower, and the vicious circle would be complete.

The relevant comparison is of two social settings, each characterized by a particular family employment structure and associated wage level. This approach reveals the material aspect of working-class determination to maintain family structures because it seems at least possible that a retreat of certain family members from the labor force, in conjunction with an organized attempt to secure a "family wage," could raise their standard of living.

There is considerable evidence that the proletarianization of the wives and children of male workers did lead to a cheapening of the value-power in certain trades. In Mayhew's interviews for the *Morning Chronicle* this is repeatedly suggested as an explanation for overstocked labor markets and falling real wages. An outdoor worker in the garment industry described the situation as follows:

I originally belonged to the honourable part of the trade. When working at the honourable trade my earnings were about £1, including vacation. Now I don't get half that amount. It is six or seven years ago since I worked out the west end shop. My wife did no work then. I could maintain her in comfort by the produce of my labour. Now she slaves night and day as I do: and very often she has less rest than myself, for she has to stope up after I have gone to bed to attend her domestic duties. The two of us working these long hours and the Sundays as well, can only earn 15s. . . . I attribute the decline in the wages of the operative tailor to the introduction of cheap Irish, foreign and female labour. Before then we could live and keep our families by our own exertions; now our wives and children must work as well as ourselves to get less money than we alone could earn a few years back.[38]

Mayhew's own description of the family employment system emphasizes its role in the cheapening of the value of labor-power as well as the compulsion exercised by those who practiced it on other members of their class.

The family system of working is one of the means by which the cheap system is maintained. The party pursuing it, though forced to resort to it for the maintenance of his wife and children, whom his own unaided labour is incapable of supporting, is enabled to produce the goods at so cheap a rate that it is impossible for a single handed artisan to do the work at the same price and live.[39]

In his book on class struggle and the industrial revolution John Foster compares conditions in the Northampton footwear industry at various stages in its development. The available evidence suggests that the proletarianization of the women and children, their employment in centralized and supervised conditions, which occurred after 1820, coincided with a deterioration in the real incomes of shoe-making families. In Foster's judgment, the fall in shoemaker's wages resulting from competition in the labor market was not offset by the incremental earnings of other family members.[40]

Working-class recognition that the proletarianization of incremental family members raised the degree of exploitation, and that this trend could be fought through a campaign for wages sufficient to maintain a family is reflected in the following extract from the *Trades Newspaper*, October 16, 1825.

Wages can never sink below the sum necessary to rear up the number of labourers the capitalists want. The weaver, his wife, and children, all labour to obtain this sum; the blacksmith and the carpenter obtain it by their single exertions. . . .

The labouring men of this country should return to the good old plan of subsisting their wives and children on the wages of their own labour and they should demand wages high enough for this purpose . . . by doing this the capitalist will be obligated to give the same wages to men alone which they now give to men, women, and children. . . . I recommend my fellow labourers, in preference to every other means of limiting the number of those who work for wages to prevent their wives and children from competing with them in the labour market and beating down the price of labour.[41]

This perspective provides a better understanding of the antagonism between male trade unionists and female workers in the nineteenth century.' That competition from cheap female workers undercut existing wage rates was not simply allegation. It was reality. The value of female labor-power was less than the value of male labor-power because of differences in the minimal diets needed and in the material inputs required by traditional leisure pursuits. In addition it was easier for women to sell their labor-power for less than its value because even when engaged in commodity production they were not expected to completely cover their subsistence. It remained appropriate that partial assistance be forthcoming from the family fund. The Fabian investigator, Clementina Black, received an education on this point during an interview with a "well-respected" employer.

He presently took us into a department where very young and very poor looking girls were employed; and one of our party shyly asked what were their wages. "Four shillings a week" was the answer. The first speaker said depreciatingly "But—surely—they can't live on that?" "On no!" returned their employer cheerfully. "They live at home with their parents." And I, new, then to the facts of commercial life, stood staring silent at this well fed gentlemen, with sons and daughters of his own, who frankly confessed that poor daughters had to be supported by their parents in order that he might have their work for less than it cost.[42]

The relentless competition among capitalists then ensured that the cheaper female labor was substituted wherever possible for the more expensive male labor. Of course some male occupations and positions were protected by the physical requirements of the job or entrenched practices, and there women were no threat. But in an era of rapidly changing technology, when skill and even strength requirements were being removed from more and more trades, the arena of effective female competition seemed to be widening.

Barbara Drake, in her historical study of women in trade unions, is well aware of the problems of dismissing male trade unionists as chauvinists. She admits that some men resented women's working because they felt it threatened their patriarchal position within the home: but she also points out that a husband may resent his wife's "exploitation by his own oppressor, and her competition with himself driving him from employment by her willingness to accept about one half his rate of wages."[43]

Women were frequently used as blacklegs and strikebreakers.[44] Moreover not all trade unions behaved in the same fashion. The Journeymen Bookbinders, for example, championed the women's cause along with their own during the famous dispute in the thirties and forties between the union and the Bible Societies.[45] The cigar makers met the challenge of women workers by amalgamating with the women's union and the Lancashire felt-hatters by prohibiting the women from some departments and organizing those in other departments.[46]

Drake also emphasized that in those situations where women received the same rates of pay as men the male trade unions were not exclusive, and that, in fact, the wage differentials constituted the root of the difficulties between men and women workers. Nineteenth-century women trade unionists were fully aware of this and urgently sought to persuade the men to help organize women, rather than try to exclude women from certain jobs by legal or trade-union fiat. Drake is careful to note the employers' part in fanning the flames of antagonism between men and women workers and their consequential alienation from the Women's Provident and Protective League in the 1880s when it secured an "entente" with the male trade unions.[47]

In Drake's summary the interpretation of male trade unionists as selfish is qualified by reference to the complexity of the problem and the material foundation of the antagonism between the unions and women workers.

Men trade unionists are accused of a policy of sex privilege and prejudice, especially by middle class women. The charge unfortunately has a basis of truth. A belief in the divine right of every man to his job is not peculiar to kings or capitalists, and democracy is hard to practice at home. . . . A more respectable motive, but one not less keenly resented by women, is the anxiety sometimes expressed by men to protect women folk from harm, and to confine them, if not to the home, at least to "womanly" occupations. Men's claim so to dictate to women their manner of employment has at no time been admitted by women trade unionists. . . . As a matter of fact, women's claim to earn their own living in their own way is not at present seriously disputed by men trade unionists who realize that a policy of sex-privilege and prejudice can only lead to the damage of their own cause, and obscure the real issue. The true cause of trade union restrictions on female labour are economic. From a long and bitter experience, trade unionists have learned that the introduction of women into men's trades is inevi-

tably followed by a fall of wages from the men's to the women's levels, so
that men are finally driven from employment. Like Chinamen or coolies
women are condemned as blacklegs. . . . Men's refusal to recognize
women, meanwhile, has the disastrous effect of delaying organization, so
that women develop a "non-union" instead of a "union" tradition, and employers a vested interest in "cheap and docile" female labour. For the men
on the other hand, to withdraw their restrictions without adequate safe-
guards against a fall of wages, would only be to precipitate a disaster. . . .
the problem is by no means a simple one.[48]

The campaign for a family wage was not the only example of the
use of this type of strategy by the working class. Notions of endangered family integrity, the "unsexing" of working-class men and
women and the adverse effects likely to become apparent in future
generations of workers, were also used in the battle for factory legislation concerning conditions and hours; in the latter case to such an
extent that Hutchins and Harrison, the historians of factory legislation, conclude "the battle for the limitation of the hours of adults in
general was fought from behind the women's petticoats."[49]

How can this working-class use of sexist ideology be judged in
retrospect? Undoubtedly the regulation of hours and occupations
caused acute misery in individual cases when women lost jobs that
were vital to their survival. More important, the use of sexist ideology
by labor to promote their own purposes must have reinforced sexism
among workers and employers, in the long run making the attainment
of economic equality more difficult. But to condemn this strategy out
of context is to be insensitive to the social realities of nineteenth-
century labor.

One of the few sources of working-class control over the supply
of labor lay in the levers that could be brought to bear on the labor
supplied by married women. This manipulation was also one of the
few tactics that could be accompanied by supportive mobilization of
bourgeois ideology. The tragedy is that action could not be controlled
on a class basis but had to be regulated *systematically* on the basis of
female labor, so reinforcing sex-based relations of dominance and
subordination.

Nevertheless, the strategy was not entirely disadvantageous to
working women. To think so is once again to misunderstand working-
class experience. First, the argument that male workers gained from
regulation at the expense of "protected" (female) workers is not easily
substantiated. Hutchins and Harrison argue that as men were earning

higher wages and working shorter hours they had little to gain from "supplanting" women. Gains were mainly at the lower end of the labor hierarchy where women themselves were concentrated. There does not seem to have been a trend to replace protected workers by unprotected workers.

Second, women workers as well as being female are also members of the working class. Class action that tries to raise the price of labor usually has beneficial effects—if not directly on women's wages, then indirectly through increased *family* wages. This exposes the fallacy in the argument that women workers might be subject to disabilities in the guise of protective legislation. Such calumny results from conflating the social and customary disabilities encountered by women in the professions with the constraints placed by law on women's work in industry. The two are very different. Their confusion illustrates the inability of protagonists of such views to understand the material conditions of the working class, especially as they are manifested in the industrial labor process.

The working-class family and class consciousness. In the modern literature the family is frequently seen as promoting false consciousness, furthering capitalist ideology, destroying class cohesion and endangering the class struggle. In short, it stands charged with being a bourgeois institution in collaboration with capital against the real interests of the working class. But these charges are seldom substantiated with anything more than the kind of anecdotes that can also be marshaled in defense of the family. Moreover, many of the scenarios depicted in this literature seem colored by stereotypic ideas of working-class family life. This section presents an alternative view of the role of the family in the development of class consciousness and struggle.

Links have been established between the existence of family ties and the growth of community and social obligation, important steps in the development of class consciousness. The existence of fictive kin, for example, involved an extension of family ties outward into the community. Frequently the family was itself the focal point of class struggle, that is, the working class organized around family related issues. The resistance to the New Poor Law was a struggle against capital's presumption in breaking up destitute families so that the individuals could be made more miserable and supervised more cheaply. The battle for a family wage was another demonstration of working-class insistence on the integrity of their own kinship structures in the face of the tendency within capitalism to universalize market relations.

The family provided a structure within the working class that could facilitate organization as demonstrated by the progress of trade unionism in the cotton industry. By 1900 the proportions of workers paying union dues were 80 percent in the cardroom and 70 percent in weaving. These returns were all the more impressive because the majority of the members were women and the degree of organization was not much less among the women than among the men.

How this degree of organization was achieved was not recorded but the standard work on British Trade Union history attributes a crucial role to the organizers' mobilization of the family.

> Given that they had some strength, the unions could acquire more through family influence. The men who took the lead in the affairs of the weavers' associations, or as overlookers, or as strippers and grinders in the cardroom associations, could recruit their wives, sisters and daughters. Lancashire cotton towns may not have been quite such cohesive communities as mining villages, but social pressure could be a powerful influence all the same. Once the unions had established their place in the community the head of the household, even the lordly spinner who would not accept women into his own organizations, might be ashamed to admit to a non-unionist in the family. This social pressure could be further exploited by the door to door collection of union dues practiced by all the cotton unions. The non-unionist could not hope to conceal his defection either from his family or from his neighbors.[50]

Family loyalties undoubtedly sustained many individuals through the turbulent period of industrialization, and engendered feelings of comradeship in oppression. This is important and often goes unrecognized. Class solidarity does not materialize from sudden recognition by isolated individuals of their common situation, their individual weakness, but rather from a realization of their collective power. It develops slowly over time as a result of real life experiences. Rather than promoting individualism, the mutual dependence of the family could well stimulate the social dimension of human development and, in turn, community and class ties.

Related to this point and in contrast to the idea of family socialization into acceptance of the dominant values stands the possibility that the family can, and sometimes does, promote alternative ideas and behavior. Evidence supporting this position is easy to find; witness the maternal but political objective of the first all-female offshoot of the Union Societies, which listed among its aims the desire "to install into the minds of our children a deep and rooted hatred of our corrupt and tyranical rulers."[51]

Such unconventional idealism could be nurtured within the family and transmitted to friends and relatives. Thus despite his background of yeoman farming and cotton manufacturing, John Fielden's radicalism did not isolate him from his family. All his brothers were also ardent radicals and, although their father regarded them as "arrant Jacobins," his sympathies must not have been entirely alienated, because John and the other brothers became partners in the business long before their father died.[52] A radical tradition could be preserved within the family during times of oppression and perpetuated intergenerationally. Such a mechanism is apparent in Joseph Arch's description of the importance of his own childhood in a nonconforming family to the formation of his principles and commitments. "The scenes I witnessed then made an indelible impression on my mind. I have often told the Tories, you made the iron enter into my soul very young and you will never draw it out. It will remain there till I die."[53]

The protection afforded by the family to radical doctrine is also illustrated in John Foster's analysis of Oldham's working-class leadership which emerges as bound together by ties of blood and marriage. The two Cleggs whom Foster lists were cousins; John Earnshaw, active in the 1816–1819 period was the uncle of John Lees, who was killed at Peterloo. Foster's conclusion supports the argument: "Though there were always tactical disagreements and a constant stream of new recruits, what strikes one most from the descriptive evidence is the degree to which members saw themselves as part of a continuing tradition. Radical allegiances tended to be inherited within families and associated with particular neighbourhoods. The Swires, Earnshaws and Warwicks were all families that produced at least two generations of radicals."[54]

Similarly, family responsibilities do not always operate to discipline workers but may sometimes promote their radicalization. John Barton, the working-class hero of Mrs. Gaskell's *Mary Barton*, undergoes just such an experience. Thrown out of work when his employer Mr. Hunter fails, his family slowly starves. One day he is standing outside a grocer's when Mrs. Hunter comes out: "She crossed to her carriage, followed by the shopman loaded with purchases for a party.

The door was quickly slammed to, and she drove away; and Barton returned home with a bitter spirit or wrath in his heart, to see his only boy a corpse!"[55]

Of course John Barton is a fictional character but this incident was undoubtedly inspired by numerous true stories that Gaskell heard in the bitter decade of protest Chartism. As Richard Marsdon, a Chartist delegate and handloom weaver from Preston, described: "There is something in the effects of hunger and of the sight of your family suffering from it which none can judge of but those who have felt it. The equilibrium of temper and judgment is deranged as your child looks up with piteous face and tearful eyes, asking with suppressed voice for the bread it knows you have not."[56]

Richard Pillings, another Chartist, told at his trial in 1843 a story that bore a close resemblance to the incident described by Gaskell. He told how the sufferings of his family and his desire to keep them from the workhouse provoked his action.

After working in the factory seven years, a reduction began to creep in one way or the other . . . it was then a hard case for me to support myself and family. My eldest son but one had fallen into a consumption last Easter and left his work. We were then reduced to 9 ¾ d a cut, which brought our earnings down to something like sixteen shillings a week. That is all I had to live on, with nine in my family, three shillings a week going out of that for rent, and a sick son lying helpless before me. If I have gone home and seen that son—(here Pillings was moved to tears, and unable to proceed for some time)—I have seen that son lying on a sick bed and dying pillow, and having nothing to eat but potatoes and salt . . . with neither medical aid, nor any of the common necessities of life. Yea, I recollect someone going to a gentleman's house in Ashton, to ask for a bottle of wine for him; and it was said, "Oh, he is a Chartist, he must have none." (Great sensation in court). . . . Suppose, gentlemen of the jury, you were obliged to subsist on the paltry pittance given to us in the shape of wages, and had a wife and six helpless children, five of them under thirteen years of age to support, how would you feel? . . . I have a nervous wife—a good wife—a dear wife—a wife that I love and cherish, and I have done everything that I could in the way of resisting the reductions in wages, that I might keep her and my children from the workhouse, for I detest parish relief. It is wages I want. . . . And now gentlemen of the jury, you have the case before you; the masters conspired to kill me and I combined to keep myself alive.[57]

Nor did all wives, daughters, or sisters, conscious of their material dependence, exercise conservative influences over their husbands, fathers, or brothers. Mrs. Arch is a good example of a supportive and resourceful wife and mother. George Julian Harney's wife, who afforded so much mirth to Marx and Engels, was described as "a Mauchline beauty of the Amazon type, whose heroism was notable . . . in times of danger she would say to her husband 'Do what you think to be your duty, and never mind me.' "[58]

Finally, working-class women played a part within the struggle that was specifically female and family based. The standard of living depends not only on the level of wages, the traditional trade-union concern, but also on the cost of living, which is the primary concern of the administrator of the wage—the housewife. Attacks on the working-class situation through price increases have historically produced concerted action. E. P. Thompson states that in the early 1800s the price of bread was the most sensitive indicator of popular discontent, and that consumer consciousness anticipated the development of class consciousness. The bread riot as an expression of workers' community of interest antedates the strike, and has remained, in various more modern guises, an important weapon in labor's arsenal down to the present day. The prominence of working-class women in these class struggles of the market place derives precisely from their familial roles as executors of the wage.[59]

Although women undoubtedly felt divided loyalties when class action incidentally imposed deprivation on their families, their concern for their family could also precipitate a class response. Recent historical research has documented working women's early and widespread involvement in the class struggle.[60] The charge that the nineteenth-century working-class woman was apathetic about, if not set against, class action must be revised in the light of new evidence. Similarly, the case against the working-class family remains in doubt.

The immediate conclusion to be drawn from this study is that the survival of working-class kinship structures under capitalism is not adequately accounted for by the family's role in the maintenance and reproduction of labor-power. It is possible to envision alternative private or state child-rearing agencies that, benefiting from economics of scale, would certainly give capital greater control over the administration of resources and facilitate streamlining and rationalization in the interests of capitalist production.

Capitalism has a history of market relations inexorably replacing social relations as capitalist expansion leads to the ascendancy of production for profit. The working-class family has escaped the drill of the market only because it has resisted that disciplinary power. A comprehensive explanation of labor's opposition to a total universalization of markets requires a theoretical framework based on a non-material as well as a material theory of human needs. The purpose of this paper was more modest; it was to demonstrate that in a capitalist environment the working class has certain well-defined reasons for defending the family that have been ignored in the literature. The preservation of nonmarket relations within the family emerges as neither an obsolete remnant of a less-developed mode of production, nor a sociological anomaly, but as a result of labor's struggle and way of life. The working-class family has not been idealized. There has been recognition that patterns of dominance relating to age, sex, and division of labor existed long before capitalism and remain characteristic of the family today. But the existence of these negative aspects of family life must not be considered in isolation: indeed, they are only comprehensible within the context of capitalist oppression. For the family does not merely *respond* to capitalism, or worse still, *reflect* capitalism; it also shelters working people from capitalist oppression and—most neglected function of all—plays a crucial role in their struggle against capitalism and toward a better life.

The Family in Contemporary
Feminist Thought: A Critical Review

✿ *Jane Flax*

It is extremely difficult to analyze the family. In no other area of our existence are ideology, feeling, fantasy, wishes, and reality so complexly intermingled. In fact, *the* family does not exist. A series of social relations crystallize into apparently concrete social structures; the reification of these structures creates an abstract entity which is then called "the family." In order to understand the family, this reification must be overcome and the family dissolved into the social relations by and through which it is constituted.

The family is constituted by three types of social relations: production, reproduction, and psychodynamics. In turn, the family itself is a part of other similarly constituted social structures. Each structure interacts with all the others in complex ways. The social relations out of which the family and all other social structures are constituted arise from and must meet material necessities that typify humans as a species. These necessities are (1) the need to construct environments in order to survive (production), which requires social relations of production; (2) the production of new persons and the transformation of the relatively unformed neonate into a well-behaved member of society, which gives rise to relations of reproduction. The stability of this behavior over time must also be insured by various cultural and ideological agencies, e.g., the state, religion; (3) the internal world of each individual must be structured, channeled, and regulated (psychodynamics). This internal world is quite complex and includes innate temperament, the interaction of psyche and soma (including sexuality), and internalized relations with other persons.

The interaction of gender[1] and class and the reverberations of unconscious experience in everyday life can be seen clearly and are felt intensely in the family. This fact and the importance of the family in producing persons who will, partly unconsciously, reproduce contemporary society including its gender-, race- and class-based relations of domination, make an investigation of the social relations of the family an especially important project for feminists. In addition, the family is of special importance to feminists because it is a primary beneficiary and focus of women's labor. The family is also the source of women's most fundamental identity to both themselves and others—that of mother.

Feminist writings on the family have rarely done justice to this complex series of interrelationships. Feminist analysis of the family is incomplete, fragmentary, and marked by a wide divergence of positions, approaches, and conceptual frameworks. These writings are remarkable not only for their lack of agreement but also for the avoidance of and/or failure to grapple with family-related issues: sexuality, child rearing, needs associated with kinship, and alternatives to existing practices. These failures arise not only from the sheer mass of material and the complexity of subject matter relevant to the study of the family[2] but also from the difficulties of sorting through what is inherently oppressive in an institution or experience and what is patriarchally constructed or controlled and hence oppressive, although not inherently so.[3] Further compounding the difficulties in creating a feminist analysis of the family are women's own ambivalencies about sexuality, child rearing, needs for intimacy, and the forms in which these needs can be best satisfied.[4] With the rise of the New Right these issues have become even more politicized. The importance of addressing them has increased for feminists, but at the same time there seems to be no neutral space in which family-related issues can be worked through with all the conflicts and mistakes that that process requires. This paper is intended to be a contribution to that process. I critically review some of the contemporary (1963–1979) feminist literature on the family, focusing on a few of the more influential writers of this period: Friedan, Millett, Firestone, Rubin, Mitchell, Dinnerstein, and Chodorow. Each writer tends to focus on one of the three aspects of the family but I evaluate each not only in terms of her contribution to an analysis of a particular aspect of the family but to the totality as well.

Reproduction: Mystique or Patriarchy?
Friedan, Firestone, and Millett

Betty Friedan, Kate Millett, and Shulamith Firestone agree that to define women exclusively in terms of their sexual roles, that is, as wives and mothers, is oppressive. However, they disagree on the source of this definition, the ultimate cause of women's oppression, and the means to overcome it. Despite these major areas of disagreement, it is surprising that these writers share certain fundamental presuppositions, especially in regard to the nature of motherhood and the meaning of individualism. They also share a blindness to important differences among women, especially those of class and race.

According to Friedan, women are suffering from a problem of identity. Women have accepted an ideology, the feminine mystique, which claims that their true vocation and only real fulfillment lie in the roles of wife and mother. A woman caught in this mystique "has no independent self to hide even in guilt; she exists only for and through her husband."[5]

Friedan's account of the origins and basis of power of this mystique is somewhat confusing. The feminine mystique allegedly derived its power from Freudian thought which "twist[ed] the memory of the feminists [the women's rights movement of the early twentieth century] into the man-eating phantom of the feminine mystique, shriveling the very wish to be more than just a wife and mother." The mystique was disseminated by mass media, social science, and schools. It appears to be deeply rooted in the society as a whole. "Our culture does not permit women to accept or gratify their basic need to grow and fulfill their potentialities as human beings, a need which is not solely defined by their sexual role."[6]

Friedan attributes the acceptance of the mystique to the traumas caused by the Depression, World War II, and the atomic bomb. There was a "pent-up hunger for marriage, home and children," a "hunger which, in the prosperity of postwar America, everyone could suddenly satisfy." The loneliness that women had felt while their men were absent or vulnerable during the war was "the necessary price they had to pay for a career, for any interest outside the home."[7] The choice appeared to be love or other goals and women "chose" love.

Despite this location of the feminine mystique within a certain culture and time, it also seems to float about, owing its existence only to women's mistaken ideas. According to Friedan, "all the legal, political, economic, and educational barriers that once kept woman from being man's equal" have been removed. Therefore, "the chains that bind her in her trap are chains in her own mind and spirit. They are chains made up of mistaken ideas and mistaken facts, of incomplete truths and unreal choices."[8] Clearly Friedan's assumption throughout her analysis is that to be "just" a wife and mother is a "trap" and that true fulfillment lies outside the home.

Kate Millett, along with other radical feminists,[9] would argue that the "mystique" that Friedan identified was the contemporary expression of "patriarchy," a systematic series of power relationships whereby men as a group control women as a group and possess more social wealth, power, and esteem as well as control over these resources than women.[10] Millett chooses the word "politics"[11] to define the relationship between the sexes "because such a word is eminently useful in outlining the real nature of their relative status historically and at the present." Patriarchy is a relationship of dominance and subordination governed by two principles: "male shall dominate female, elder male shall dominate younger" and "patriarchal government is the institution whereby that half of the populace which is female is controlled by that half which is male."[12]

According to Millett, the family is the primary territory of sexual politics. It is both reflective of patriarchy and necessary to its maintenance. What is presented ideologically as a private relationship of love is really a social relationship of power. Within the family, persons are "conditioned" to either a masculine or a feminine personality in early childhood. "The chief contribution of the family in patriarchy is the socialization of the young (largely through example and admonition of their parents) into patriarchal ideology's prescribed attitudes toward the categories of role, temperament and status."[13]

The family is also the "citadel of property and traditional interests." "Marriages are financial alliances" in which men control the resources, including women and children. All women belong to the same caste; class differences are likely to be more a matter of the variations in the male's attitude to and treatment of women rather than a result of real differences in women's situation.[14]

The entire culture supports and reinforces the patriarchal structure of the family. "The concept of romantic love affords a means of emotional manipulation which the male is free to exploit, since love is the only circumstance in which the female is (ideologically) pardoned for sexual activity." Love "obscures the realities of female status and the burden of economic dependency."[15] Economic dependency in turn reinforces the power of men, as does education, which reinforces the differences in temperament learned in the patriarchal family. Patriarchy is also maintained by force, including rape and other forms of violence against women. The male constructed and dominated legal system legitimates men's control of women's bodies as well as inequalities in marital rights and duties. Thus in Millett's analysis, the problem Friedan identifies extends beyond the definition of women exclusively as wives and mothers. The very structure of marriage itself within patriarchy is necessarily oppressive to women.

Firestone agrees with much of Millett's analysis of patriarchy and the family. However, she extends the notion of patriarchy into a more dynamic process, the "dialectics of sex." According to Firestone, the biological family (mother/child/father) is the root not only of women's identity and oppression but of all other forms of oppression and of a "power psychology" which threatens to destroy human beings and nature: "The heart of woman's oppression is her childbearing and childrearing roles. Children, in turn, are defined in relation to this role and are psychologically formed by it; what they become as adults and the sort of relationships they are able to form determine the society they will ultimately build."[16]

Women's oppression is basically caused by biology. "Sex class sprang directly from a biological reality: men and women were created different and not equally privileged." Before the advent of birth control, women "were at the continual mercy of their biology," which made them dependent on males for physical survival. Children cannot survive without adults at least for a short time, and child care has always been done by women. "A basic mother/child interdependency has existed in some form in every society, past or present, and thus has shaped the psychology of every mature female and every infant." The "natural reproductive difference" between the sexes "led directly to the first division of labor at the origins of class, as well as furnishing the paradigm case of discrimination based on biological characteristics."[17]

The "biological family is an inherently unequal power distribution"[18] in which a "need for power" arises from the psychosexual formation of each individual. This in turn leads to the development of class and caste. The ideological construction of childhood and romantic notions of love are both the reinforcement for and mystification of this basic power relationship.

The weaknesses of these three approaches to the family can be seen in the solutions they offer to women's oppression. The analyses made by all three writers and the solutions they propose are inadequate because one aspect of the family is mistaken for the whole. In other words, the interaction between the psychodynamic and productive aspects with the reproductive aspects of the family are not taken into account. According to Friedan, the answer to the feminine mystique is a "personal commitment to the future," to break out of the "housewife trap and truly find fulfillment as wives and mothers—by fulfilling their own unique possibilities as separate human beings."[19] The way out of the trap is better education, so that ultimately women practice professional occupations in addition to working as housewives.

Millett's solution is a "cultural revolution, which, while it must necessarily involve the political and economic reorganization traditionally implied by the term revolution must go far beyond this as well." Revolution is "basically a matter of altered consciousness, the exposure and elimination of social and psychological realities underlining political and cultural structures."[20]

According to Firestone, the only solution to the oppression of women and children is to destroy the biological family and negate female biology. Children should be produced technologically and cared for in households created by contract among adults for a specified length of time. Children would be allocated among households and would be free to leave them at any point (unlike adults who are bound for seven years to one household). Women would be "freed" from the "tyranny" of their biology, and childbearing and rearing would be diffused among men, women, and older children. Every person would be economically independent and self-determining, "totally self-governing as soon as he was physically able."[21] Women and children would be completely integrated into society. There would be no need for an incest taboo and all forms of relationships, including adult/child ones, would have a physical/sexual aspect, although genital sexuality would no longer be the central focus or source of pleasure in any relationship.

Friedan, Millett, and Firestone all fail to pay adequate attention to the importance of the social relations of production (or class structure) in women's lives. In their work, the full complexity of the determinants of women's identity are ignored, and falsely universalized claims about women's experience and needs are made. For example, black and working-class women tend through experience to have a better sense than any of these writers of the many, still-existing, economic and structural barriers to equality[22] and of the small number of professional or good jobs available. For some black and working-class women, families can serve as extended networks of support and sheer survival while middle-class white suburban families are often perceived as the locus of oppression.[23] The radical feminist attack on the family can be seen as a denigration of a source of pride among many black women—their ability to keep their families together despite adverse circumstances—and even as a racist attempt to destroy a "culture of resistance" to racial oppression. The cost to black women of this resistance needs to be sensitively thought through with careful attention to their dual status and loyalties.

Further, given the paucity and expense of decent day care, who will take care of the housework and children while women prepare for work? Many women, especially black and poor ones, as well as those who are single, unmarried or widowed, already work outside the home. Thus it is not correct to identify them solely as wives and mothers. Since husbands of working women rarely share housework, paid work is often a low-waged second job for married women. The labor market is highly sex-stratified. Women are concentrated in clerical, service, and certain professional jobs (especially elementary school teaching and nursing). In 1971, one-fourth of all women in the labor force worked in five occupations: secretary, household worker, bookkeeper, elementary school teacher, and waitress. One-half of all women working held jobs where 70 percent or more of the workers were female. In 1970, only 7 percent of all American women earned more than $10,000 a year, as contrasted to 40 percent of American men. In 1974, the median income for white females was $7,021 and for black females, $6,371, although it was $12,434 for white males and $8,705 for black males. In 1974, 37 percent of all black women worked in low-paying service and household jobs, and 94.2 percent of all clerical workers were female. One-third of all married working women in 1974 were clerical workers and one-fifth were service workers.[24] While gender clearly plays a role in the social relations of production, it does not follow that all women are members of the same caste or class, or that gender is the sole determinant of women's status.

Despite their dismissal of the importance of class and racial differences among women, the concept of patriarchy developed by Millett and Firestone is quite useful to feminist analysis. It points to the pervasiveness of male dominance throughout history and especially to the existence of power relations within apparently private ones. However, their works, although suggesting that patriarchy has a history, do not provide such a history. A number of important questions are left unresolved. What is the origin of patriarchy? Are all women's experiences fundamentally the same? Why have women not been successful in resisting and/or overthrowing patriarchy? What is the practice that follows from the theory—should all men be killed or all women become lesbians? What should women with male children do? How has patriarchy changed over time? How does patriarchy (if it does) interact with race and class? Can all dimensions of experience within the family be reduced to "sexual politics"? Are the gratifications and pleasure, however fragmentary, that women receive from child rearing and heterosexuality merely the products of false consciousness?

Problems also arise in Friedan's, Millett's, and Firestone's work from a failure to explore the psychodynamic aspect of the family. Friedan's concept of "identity," for example, is highly abstract. She does not explain what it means to be a person or why women are so vulnerable to the threat of loss of love. She cannot explain how ideas such as the feminine mystique keep women from becoming persons. As will become evident in the work of Dinnerstein and Chodorow, ideas cannot keep one from becoming a person unless the ideas are the expression of powerful social forces and/or reverberate with certain deeply felt wishes. Millett also has a very abstract notion of consciousness; she does not explain how it develops or in what it is anchored.

Firestone and Friedan also seem to accept uncritically liberal premises about selfhood. In Friedan, one achieves fulfillment by oneself, outside of relations with others. In Firestone, this assumption is carried even further. She assumes that dependence inevitably means a relation of domination and submission, that people act rationally out of their own individual self-interest, that this will lead to social harmony, and that "self-determination" is equivalent to the freedom to choose one's own life style, as long as it does not bother anyone else.

Although Firestone does not simply condemn Freud's ideas as Millett and Friedan do, she does provide a highly problematic and simplistic reading of him. Despite Firestone's criticism of Freud's determinism, she is actually far more determinist than he. She fails to take the character of the unconscious seriously. As a result, her treatment of biology and children are faulty. The unconscious has to be understood as a process or aspect of the mind in which psyche and soma interact and mutually determine each other. Yet in Firestone, biology, literally understood, becomes destiny. As later feminists will argue, biology is not a brute determinative fact; it is mediated by and through social relations. Women's experience of their bodies is always overdetermined; for example, "pain" in childbirth can be lessened or intensified by the environment in which it occurs, the character of interactions among attendants and the preparation and feelings of the mother. Reproduction has a social history. The availability of birth control, for example, depends not on the process of technology in some abstract sense, but on the social relations that permit or repress its development and use.[25]

Firestone at least tries to include children within her work, unlike many other feminist writers. However, her discussion of children suffers because she fails to take unconscious and psychosexual development seriously. Children appear not to have any special needs of their own, apart from a short period of physical dependence. They seem to be fully rational, theorizing adults, able to carry out a sophisticated political analysis of their parents' relationship by age three.[26] Firestone lacks any concept of the maturation process, of the normal human dependence on others for the formation of the self, and of the psychic consequences of this dependence, apart from the particular forms these may take under patriarchy.[27]

These three writers make several contributions to a feminist theory of the family. They open up to social and political analysis relationships within the family that had been considered private and ahistorical. The concept of patriarchy and a "dialectic of sex" points to the importance of understanding the historical content and dynamic of male dominance and the role of the family in maintaining and replicating those relations of domination. Firestone's location of the development of gender identity within psychosexual processes and patterns of child rearing provides an important clue to what maintains patriarchy. Firestone's clue will be developed much more adequately by subsequent writers like Chodorow and Dinnerstein.

Despite their contributions, the extent to which these writers replicate patriarchal values is striking. Firestone seems to have accepted a view of female biology more typically shared by men—as a source of endless "complaints and disorders." In Friedan's work housework is trivial, child care a necessary but oppressive prelude to "real" work. She offers no alternative means of caring for children and maintaining a household. None of these writers considers the gratifying and humane elements of women's traditional work and how these could be preserved or even turned into part of the attack on patriarchy, given that the oppressive social relations within which such work occurs must be destroyed. These failures cause feminism to be perceived by some women not as an attack on women's oppression but as an attack on themselves and/or a denial of their own experience.

The Relations of Production: Is the Family the Servant of Capital?

Firestone, Millett, and other radical feminists argue that the dialectics of sex is the moving force of history. All other conflicts, contradictions, or forms of oppression are derived from or are ultimately rooted in patriarchy. According to this approach, class conflict (in capitalism, the ongoing struggle between workers and capitalists) should be understood as either a struggle among men after they had subordinated women and/or as one particular form of patriarchal domination.

Orthodox Marxists, on the contrary, argue that history is best understood in terms of materialism[28] and class struggle. According to Marx, an examination of productive activity—that is, the relations of owners to producers on the one hand and the "forces" of production (types of machinery, accumulation of capital, and techniques used in production) on the other—will reveal both the determinants of the character of all human activity and the appropriate means to transform oppressive forms of social organization.[29] In this approach, the oppression of women would be considered a derivative of class relations and would disappear after a socialist revolution along with the exploitation of one class by another. The family and women's role within it could be comprehended by analyzing their functions within a particular mode of production and its corresponding class relations.

Marxism's claim to be a comprehensive, materialist theory of history that was tied directly to a definite revolutionary political practice appealed to many feminists of the contemporary period. Some had been active in left wing or socialist politics before they became feminists and sought to integrate their feminist experience within socialist categories. Others had become dissatisfied with the radical feminist analysis of patriarchy and thought that Marxism could correct the absence of a historical account of the causal explanation for the persistence of patriarchy within radical feminist writings. Still other feminists sought to analyze the ways in which class relations structured women's experience.[30]

Feminists turned to Marxism for an understanding of the family's relation to production, the origins and replication of women's oppression, and for guidance in developing a strategy to transform women's status. While Marxism enabled feminists to understand certain features of the family's productive aspect and the importance of class structure in women's lives, the utility of Marxism for feminist theory is problematic and frequently contested. Women's experience as women, the functions of patriarchy both for men and for capitalism, and the psychodynamic aspects of the family tend to be obscured or denied, at least by the orthodox Marxist approach. Many of these problems are evident in the classic Marxist text on women and the family, Engels's *The Origin of the Family, Private Property and the State*.[31] Engels argues that in "primitive" societies sexual relationships were promiscuous and descent could only be traced through the mother; hence these societies were matriarchal and communistic. All property was shared by the kinship group. The sexual division of labor already existed (women did the housework) but this division did not lead to inequality; instead the relations between men and women were equal and free. However, men did own cattle and slaves, and these in turn produced increasing amounts of wealth, whereas women's labor did not. As wealth increased, men wanted to be certain that their *own* children inherited it, therefore they overthrew the then traditional matrilineal order of inheritance by a "simple decree."[32] Simultaneously, monogamy replaced polygamous relationships, with women's consent and encouragement, and private property replaced communal property. Thus, women's inferior status was the consequence of the introduction of private property and the resulting emergence of the first class-stratified society, and not the consequence of male domination. Women will only be liberated when they enter the paid labor force and join a socialist movement committed to the overthrow of class society.

Engels's account raised more questions than it answered. He took a sexual division of labor for granted and assumed (rather than explained why) women have always done household labor. Engels argued that wealth was owned by the kinship group (gens) and that the gens was matriarchal, but he simultaneously argued that men owned cattle and slaves because they were the "heads" of households and that they were permitted to accumulate the wealth these produced rather than turn it over to the gens. He cannot explain *why* inheritance became an issue, or why men came to care who inherits their property as long as all persons share the property of their, or their wife's, gens. It also seems inconceivable that a "simple decree" that overthrew "mother-right" would be accepted passively by women or that legalistic methods would be employed or have much effect in a "primitive" culture in which custom, and not law, dictated social behavior. Finally, shifts in property would not bring about the total supremacy of men unless ownership of property was already the ultimate basis of power in the society. The institution of private property cannot be used to explain *male* supremacy, because the argument is circular.[33]

Once class society is introduced in history (and in Engels's account), the problems of gender and of the status of women seem to disappear, as does the problem of family. History becomes an account of the changes in the mode of production. No further history of the mode of reproduction was given by Engels, nor did he trace the interaction of production and reproduction. Further, the strategy that he proposes for women's liberation is not supported by subsequent historical evidence. The experience of women in and after socialist revolution is not encouraging. Women in China, the USSR, and Eastern Europe now have two full-time jobs—housework and paid labor—with at least the passive acquiescence of the state. They are not equal participants in the political process, and they earn substantially less than men.[34]

Given the problems within Engels's analysis and the paucity of Marxist writings on the status of women and the family, Marxist-feminist debate came to center on the best ways to appropriate and/or extend Marxist theory so that it could adequately account for the phenomena uncovered by feminists. Three primary tendencies emerged: Marxist-structuralism, the theories of "personal life," and the extension of the concept of "surplus value" to housework. These theories share certain basic assumptions: that the relations of production ultimately determine the character of the family and women's status, and that psychodynamic processes do not play a very significant role in history. The theories disagree on the extent to which the family experiences autonomy from the relations of production and on the role, if any, patriarchy plays in the constitution of the family and women's status. All agree, however, that the solution to women's oppression lies within a socialist revolution.

Juliet Mitchell is one of the most influential advocates of a Marxist-structuralist approach to feminist theory.[35] She argues that the family in general is a complex totality in which "each independent sector has its own autonomous reality though each is ultimately, but only ultimately, determined by the economic factor." The family has both an ideological and psychological aspect:

The germ of the family is the source of the psychic creation of individuals; this "germ" has certain universal characteristics—heterosexual parents and offspring. The dominant ideology of the family gives its very various forms and functions an atemporality and a permanence (the ideology creates a continuity by its backward-lookingness whereby the present family encapsulates values that were the ideals of previous systems). The economic function of the family gives it its specific highly temporal form: that this function is ensured success by the role played by ideology within the family—the inculcated obedience of the children, subservience of the wife, etc.—should not be confused with the ideological concept of the family as such.[36]

Within capitalism, the family has three interrelated aspects: the reproduction of children, sexuality, and socialization. Although interrelated, these structures are not identical, and each has its own "laws" and character. If any one structure changes, the whole character of the family will change. Changes in one sector may (but will not necessarily) lead to changes in another sector. Yet, ultimately the character of the family as a totality is determined by something outside it— the economic base. The family thus is a part of the superstructure. Women are *oppressed* because of their roles within the family, but they are *exploited* as workers. The family seems to be governed by and is an expression of an ideological *concept:* "individualism, freedom and equality (at home you're 'yourself')," which is in contradiction with the organization of capitalist production. Despite the ideological premise that the family is a unit, it is really composed of individuals, each of whom works for a different boss. Capitalism also stresses the importance of the individual; individualism contradicts the notion of family unity. "The woman's task is to hold on to the family while its separate atoms explode in different directions."[37]

Contrary to Mitchell, Zaretsky seems to argue that the family is not determined in "the last" instance by the relations of production alone.[38] According to Zaretsky, the crucial factor in the history of the modern family is its transformation from the primary locus of production to a unit of consumption and socialization. The family appears to be private because production is no longer carried out in households. More of the burden of family life falls on women because their traditional roles—child rearing and the maintenance of daily life— remain household tasks. Women are devalued because they are excluded from the world of production. This devaluation reinforces the preexisting relations of patriarchy.[39]

Despite the fact that the modern family is given its unique character by its place within capitalism, Zaretsky argues that the family, however imperfectly, retains an element of autonomy from capitalist social relations. Whatever genuine relations of love and reciprocity people share occur within the family. The family can serve as a source of resistance as well as an agent of socialization.[40] However, Zaretsky appears to argue ultimately that the ability to have a personal life, even within the family, is threatened by capitalist relations of production. It seems that in the "last instance" capitalist relations of production are the determining factors in the character of the family for Zaretsky, despite the relative autonomy he attributes to it. The clear implication in his work is that the real enemy of women is not patriarchy, but capitalism, and that women should join with men to form a united socialist movement.

A central focus of debate among Marxists, Marxist-feminists, and other feminists is the issue of the relative importance of capitalism and patriarchy in shaping the character of the family and women's status within it. In an attempt to resolve this debate within preexisting Marxist categories, the argument among Marxists and Marxist-feminists turned to whether housework produced surplus value. The fundamental issue underlying this debate is how to conceptualize women's activity within the family. Here the question is redefined within traditional Marxist concepts. In Marxist theory, labor is defined by its relation to capital and the production of commodities for the market. Those who control the means of production are owners (bourgeoisie) and those who must sell their labor power are workers (proletariat). Profit is derived from the exploitation of workers. Surplus value = value produced by the worker in a fixed amount of time—the cost of reproducing the labor power of the worker. According to Marx, only labor that creates surplus value is productive labor.

If housework produced surplus value, it would follow that women worked for capital, not for men; thus, capitalism and not patriarchy should be feminists' primary concern.[41] However, since women are not directly paid for their labor, and women's labor in the home usually creates services immediately consumed by family members and not commodities, it is not clear how and if Marx's theory applies to women's work in the home. Rather than conclude that Marxist categories are not adequate to the problem of women's labor within the home, the participants in this debate proposed a variety of reconstructions and extensions of Marx's theory; for example, women produce and reproduce the people whose labor power then produces surplus value; or, women increase profits for the capitalist by performing services that otherwise would have to be performed by waged workers, which would increase the cost of labor to the bourgeoisie.[42]

The participants in this debate came to no resolution among themselves on how to conceptualize women's labor within the home. While the debate was not fruitful in this regard, it did reveal problems in the Marxist approach to the family, as did the work of Mitchell and Zaretsky. In all three cases, the family became a dependent variable determined primarily by the relations of production. The effect family structure has had on production remains hidden.[43]

Further, the Marxist approach conceals the "sexual politics" of the family. While Marxist theory stresses the importance of the division of labor and class conflict in shaping the character of any society, Marxist writing on the family tends to ignore the sexual division of labor within the family. Marxist theory cannot explain why women do housework and men do not. In Zaretsky's work, for example, the avoidance of the sexual politics of the family leads to an incorrect notion of the family as the locus of "personal life." This notion obscures the asymmetries present within the family. The family is not personal for women in the same way it is for men, since it is also women's workplace. Men, women, and children benefit differently from women's work.[44] In Zaretsky's analysis, as in other Marxist writing, the specific experience of women and the patriarchal character of the family tend to be lost.

In Marxist writings, there is an abstract character to the account given of life as lived in the family. Children become potential workers, the potential commodity labor power, and are not seen as full concrete beings with their own problems and needs. The psychosexual development of persons within the family tends to be ignored or, in Zaretsky's case, not adequately differentiated by gender. In Mitchell's work, the family is conceptualized as ideological and atemporal and the economic base is historical and specific. Individual psychic structure is also atemporal and resistant to change. Given these premises it is difficult to understand how any interaction between these structures is possible, since they operate on such different "laws."

Marxism provides certain clues to understanding the family. Its concepts of materialism, division of labor, relations of production and class are especially useful. However, it cannot be simply applied but must be extended and even reconstituted by feminists. It is unfortunate that Marxist-feminist writing—especially the housework debate—seems often to be a rather arid and defensive way of justifying women's work and feminism itself to Marxists. Marxist-feminists tend to assume that Marxist categories are appropriate to analyze women's experience both within the family and the labor force, and that the problem is to somehow synthesize Marxism and feminism. Marxist-feminists have rarely considered the possibility that Marxist categories themselves should be subjected to a feminist critique, that such categories grew out of and reflect patriarchal as well as class relations, and hence Marxism as a theory is distorted in some fundamental ways by its failure to take patriarchal relations into account.

Important questions about the relations of the production aspect of the family remain: How do the relations of production interact with other aspects of the family, and how do these interactions change over time? How does the family as a totality as the mode of production interact? How does this interaction change over time, and what causes these changes? What would an adequate materialist theory of the family be? How should the class status of women be conceptualized—independently, in relationship to a man, within a family? Is "class" as Marx conceived it even adequate to account for women's socioeconomic status because it is so entangled both with women's relation to production and with their family constellation and race? Is there a Marxist explanation for the division of labor within the family—why it occurs, how it is maintained, who benefits, and what its consequences are both within the family and within other social structures?

Marxist approaches to the study of the family and women's oppression challenge the ahistoric and non-class-specific character of racial feminist analysis, but Marxist-feminist writings suggest more questions than they answer. Perhaps, contrary to Juliet Mitchell's suggestion, what feminist theory requires is not Marxist answers to feminist questions,[45] but the reverse.

The Psychodynamics of the Family: The Reproduction of Gender, Heterosexuality, and Patriarchy

According to Millett and Firestone, the family plays a crucial role in the creation of gender identity and in the replication of gender-specific behavior. Yet, neither writer could adequately explain how gender is created or the origins of men's wish to dominate women. Marxist feminists stressed the importance of the sexual division of labor within the family and class relations outside the family in determining women's status. Although Marxist-feminists offer some interesting ideas about the relationships between the sexual division of labor within the family, within the economy and class relations, they are unable to account for the origin of the sexual division of labor within or outside the family, or the dynamics by which such divisions were replicated.

Only when contemporary feminists began to reconsider their initial hostility to psychoanalysis[46] did it become apparent that the sexual division of labor within the family had fundamental and startling consequences for virtually every aspect of human existence. The work of Juliet Mitchell, Gayle Rubin, Dorothy Dinnerstein, and Nancy Chodorow was especially important in the development of a feminist analysis of the psychodynamics of the family.[47] Each of these writers agrees upon certain basic premises: the centrality of the unconscious in human life, the difference between biological sexuality and the organization of gender, and the importance of child-rearing arrangements, and hence the family, to the construction of gender identity. Child-rearing arrangements and the construction of gender identity are seen as central elements in the origin and replication of patriarchy.

Despite these areas of agreement, the four writers differ on the influence psychodynamic processes have on social structures such as the economy, and on the extent to which these structures influence the psychodynamic processes. These writers also differ in the type of psychoanalytic theory they adopt, in their conception of the unconscious, and in the political practice that would follow from their ideas. Each writer's work suffers in varying degrees from the same problem: the psychodynamic aspect of the family is not shown in relation to the

other two aspects of the family (relations of production and reproduction). Consequently, it is often difficult to conceptualize how interaction among the different aspects of the family occurs. At times the
psychodynamic processes seem somewhat abstract and ahistoric, affected by neither class nor race relations.

Juliet Mitchell was among the first feminists to argue for the importance of Freud's ideas to the development of feminist theory. While
her work provided a cogent defense of a particular form of psychoanalysis and was influential among feminists, ultimately it did not
point the way toward a successful appropriation of psychoanalysis
within feminist theory. Mitchell argues that Freud's theory must be
understood as an account of how each individual comes to acquire
"patriarchal law" and how this acquisition determines psychic structure. According to Mitchell, Freud's analysis of the psychology of
women must not be read as prescription—that is, as a justification of
women's suffering and "place" under patriarchy—but rather as a description of the inevitable consequences for psychic development of
patriarchal social relations. Female masochism, penis envy, and wom-
en's weak superego must be understood as results of the imposition
of patriarchal law upon women. For Mitchell, Freud's theory is revolutionary in content because it reveals more deeply and completely than
any other psychological theory the misery women will suffer as long
as they live under the "law of the father."[48]

The contention that Freud's theory should be read as an account
of psychological development that has its roots in patriarchal relations
rather than in biology is Mitchell's most important contribution to a
feminist analysis of psychodynamics. On the other hand, her work is
marred by a rigid insistence on the most orthodox and uncritical acceptance of every major Freudian concept.[49] She does not acknowledge the ongoing discourse among psychoanalysts concerning the adequacy of Freud's theory and the post-Freudian developments *within*
psychoanalysis.[50] The individual unconscious seems to exist for
Mitchell as a disembodied structure outside both history and social
relations. Despite her emphasis on the importance of sexuality and
fantasy within psychoanalytic theory, Mitchell reduces the unconscious to a series of structures, signs, and symbols. She rationalizes
the unconscious, the very aspect of the psyche that is constituted by
preconscious, preverbal, and prerational experience and in which body
and social, inner and outer are not yet distinguished. The unconscious
is *not* a linguistic structure. It can be interpreted through language,

but it is most powerfully revealed within the transference relation (the relationship of patient and analyst), much of which is nonverbal, and in dreams.

In Mitchell's analysis of the family, the complexity of sexual politics and of its interplay with other forms of politics is reduced to "the acquisitions of patriarchal law" by each individual and the contradictions between this law and the "social organization of work."[51] The intensity of the wishes and fantasies present in the unconscious, and the manner in which they affect and are affected by social relations are lost. This symbolic, structuralist interpretation of unconscious processes makes the power of both the pre-Oedipal period and the mother and their impact on women's and men's psychological development even more opaque. Further, in Mitchell's theory sexual and other forms of politics become parallel, not interacting structures; this makes it quite difficult to grasp the interrelationships between the structures and the dynamics of the whole.

Gayle Rubin was influenced both by Mitchell's work and by structuralism. She, however, introduced an important new concept into feminist theory, the notion of a "sex/gender system." The sex/gender system is "the set of arrangements by which a society transforms biological sexuality into products of human activity, and in which these transformed sexual needs are satisfied." Rubin argues that, "sex as we know it—gender identity, sexual desire and fantasies, concepts of childhood—is itself a social product." It is important to distinguish between "the human capacity and necessity to create a sexual world, and the empirically oppressive ways in which sexual worlds have been organized." The problem, Rubin continues, is not biology or the existence of the family, but particular *forms* of the social organization of biology, kinship, and child rearing. Kinship systems are, among other things, "made up of, and reproduce, concrete forms of socially organized sexuality. Kinship systems are observable and empirical forms of sex/gender systems."[52]

Any feminist theory of the family, then, would need to analyze kinship systems in order to understand how sexuality is organized and how gender is produced. Following Claude Levi-Strauss, the French structuralist anthropologist, Rubin argues that the essence of kinship is an exchange of women among men. The incest taboo is a means of regulating this trade. The exchange cements relations among groups and provides men with power. Those with "gifts" to exchange can enter the system of obligation and debt and accumulate power and loyalty. "The subordination of women can be seen as a product of the relationships by which sex and gender are organized and produced. The economic oppression of women is derivative and secondary. But there is an "economics" of sex and gender, and what we need is a political economy of sexual systems."[53]

A crucial factor in the political economy of sex is the division of labor according to sex. This division functions as a taboo that "exacerbates the biological differences between the sexes and thereby creates gender."[54] It also assures that men and women will desire each other and require each other's services, thus ensuring heterosexual relationships. The gender system is not the natural outgrowth of biological difference; rather, sex differences are created and accentuated by repressing similarities between the sexes. Part of being engendered or initiated into the sex/gender system is the channeling of sexual desire exclusively toward members of the opposite gender. The constraint of female sexuality is necessary so that men can allocate women among men. Female homosexuality would disrupt patterns of kinship and exchange by permitting close ties among women.

Like Mitchell, Rubin contends that psychoanalysis is central to feminist theory because it "describes the residue left within individuals by their confrontation with the rules and regulations of sexuality of the societies to which they are born."[55] Psychoanalysis enables us to understand how polymorphous, ambisexual children are transformed through social relations into specific gender identities and heterosexuality. Psychoanalysis also reveals the pain such transformation inevitably entails.

Rubin argues that the attainment of female identity is a process of repression and restraint, "based largely on pain and humiliation."[56] The culmination of this process is the "domestication of women"; women learn to live with their oppression. The family is the source of women's oppression, because under patriarchal domination, it is the agency in and through which women and men are engendered—replicating men who dominate, women who submit.

The concept of the sex/gender system is a crucial element of a feminist theory of the family. The concept counters the biological determinism of radical feminism, such as that found in Firestone's work, and is a useful tool for the analysis of changing forms of the family. Yet, even as Rubin argues that sex/gender systems are a product of human activity and always exist within a social-political context, she is not able to trace out the relations between sex/gender systems and other forms of exchange such as the economy. In part this gap in her theory is due to the use of structuralism, which contributes to similar problems in Mitchell's work. The sex/gender system appears to run "parallel" to, not in dialectical interaction with, other forms of human activity.[57]

Rubin argues that "a next step on the agenda is a Marxian analysis of sex/gender systems," and that "sexual systems cannot, in the final analysis, be understood in complete isolation. A full bodied analysis of women in a single society, or throughout history, must take *everything* into account: the evolution of commodity forms in women, systems of land tenure, political arrangements, subsistence technology, etc. Equally important, economic and political analyses are incomplete if they do not consider women, marriage and sexuality."[58]

Her contentions leave unanswered a crucial question: What is the relation between the "laws" of the sex/gender system and those of economic development? Sex oppression is rooted in the sex/gender system and is not a "reflex" of economic forces. Since Rubin says that the working-class (Marxist) movement and the women's movement address "different sources of human discontent,"[59] economic forces are presumably not a reflex of the sex/gender system. On the theoretical level there is no common ground for explaining the mutual interaction of the exchange of women and the exchange of commodities. In terms of practice, the relation between the transformation of the sex/gender system and the transformation of the class system is also not specified. This lack of specificity seems to imply a split similar to that in Mitchell's work: between women's oppression which arises from the family and *exploitation* which arises from the organization of production. In Rubin's work, however, the dynamics of oppression are analyzed in more detail, and she does not insist on economic factors being determinate in "the last instance."

The work of Dorothy Dinnerstein and Nancy Chodorow provides a concreteness that is lacking in Mitchell's and Rubin's analysis. The unconscious, its power and its centrality in human life, especially in the family, are fully explored. Dinnerstein attempts to explain the origin of the sexual division of labor, the ways in which it is replicated, and its influence not only on the relations of women to men but also on humans' relation to nature and the character of history itself. According to Dinnerstein, the current social arrangements of child rearing, in which women alone are responsible for infants, are the source of our current malaise and of the behavior that threatens to destroy

all forms of life. Thus the current organization of the family is far
from neutral, or simply private; familial organization not only oppresses women and children but it threatens the very survival of the
human species and its habitat. To a great extent, Nancy Chodorow
agrees with Dinnerstein's premises, but Chodorow attempts to locate
the dynamics Dinnerstein often discusses in an ahistoric manner
within the specific relationships of mother to daughter or mother to
son. Chodorow's work is also more limited in scope and less philo-
sophically daring. She explicitly limits herself to an analysis of one
aspect of Western capitalist social relations: the "reproduction of
mothering."

Dinnerstein locates the origin of the sexual division of labor within
biology. Because of the large brains of humans, children are born
earlier in terms of maturity and capabilities then any other species
and are dependent longer. For much of human history, women spent
"most" of their "vigorous adult life pregnant or lactating."[60] "Given
these handicaps to wideranging mobility, she has been the logical
keeper of the hearth and doer of domestic tasks."[61] Despite women's
shared ability with men to "make history," these prior conditions tie
women to child rearing.

According to Dinnerstein, humans are faced with a fundamental
dilemma: we have the power and necessity to create environments for
ourselves. To some extent we can master and dominate nature and
other persons, yet the ability to control our environment is never
total, and we alone bear the responsibility for our fate. The tension
between responsibility and lack of control leads to a desire to avoid
full knowledge of this fundamental dilemma and to either find a scapegoat for it or a superhuman way out of it.

Historically, women have served as this scapegoat. This role is possible because only women take care of infants and because of the
peculiar character of human infancy. The infant's mental and emotional development occurs much more rapidly than the development
of its physical capacities. The infant has needs before she/he is able
to fulfill them for her/himself. The mother is the first crucial link to
the world of life. She is the mediator between the sensitive infant,
the infant's own natural urges, and the outside world. With all its
pleasures and frustrations, the relationship between mother and infant
is our first major social encounter and our first experience of love.
The experience of dependence and of powerful desires not within the
infant's power to fulfill, occurs before humans are able to speak but

not before we are aware of such experiences. These experiences remain alive in our unconscious in the form of fantasy, feeling states, and desire. They especially affect our sexuality, impelling us to seek others who can gratify our wishes and with whom we can recapture something of that blissful infantile state. Yet this same state is terror-filled because it is permeated by the memory of our helplessness and by an intensity that threatens the adult ego. Hence, we seek sexual experience and intimate relations and also seek to make them safe by limiting their intensity and attempting to dominate and/or devalue the loved one.

Memory extends back to earliest infantile experience. The later rational and articulated processes are suffused with these earliest experiences. Within the infant/mother relation the general human dilemma, the desire for mastery and creativity versus the fear of responsibility, is first encountered. It is experienced in a relationship with a woman and *only* a woman (or women). Since only women take care of infants, the memory of this experience, our infantile powerlessness and fear of the mother are repressed. Humans therefore come to blame women for their malaise and do not face the more general existential dilemma, our fate as a species.

Repressed infantile experience continues to exert a powerful, although unacknowledged, influence over our conscious thoughts and behavior. Men must deny infantile experience and claim a dominating form of rationality to make history. Historically, men tend to be estranged from their own feelings and bodies and to have distanced themselves from nature in order to dominate it. Men must exclude women from history to maintain a "natural" sanctuary to which they can return after their history-making and often nature-destroying exploits. Women are our main contact with humanity and nature. They insist upon and remain anchored in early forms of relatedness and refuse to participate in, and have contempt for, history making. These unconscious activities distort the history men make, and the psychological development of men and women, and result in an unhealthy form of dependent heterosexuality.

Chodorow contends that men's denial of relatedness and need to make history, and women's identification as mothers, are not the products of biology or avoidance of human fate. They are instead the consequence of certain forms of family relations that exist within a specific social context. This social context reinforces and is reinforced by relations within the family. Humans are formed in and through social relations, but the social relations of the family cannot be understood apart from other forms of social relations, especially class.[62]

Chodorow is particularly interested in the "reproduction of mothering"—how and why only women "mother" (by which she means nurturing and caring for small children), how this pattern is replicated, and how it affects the psychological development of women. Chodorow, like Rubin, sees the family as a central element in the sex/gender system. She contends that

the sexual and familial division of labor in which women mother and are more involved in interpersonal, affective relationships than men produces in daughters and sons a division of psychological capacities which leads them to reproduce this sexual and familial division of labor, . . . Women as mothers, produce daughters with mothering capacities and the desire to mother. These capacities and needs are built into and grow out of the mother/daughter relationship itself. By contrast, women as mothers (and men as not-mothers) produce sons whose nurturant capacities and needs have been systematically curtailed and repressed. This prepares men for their less affective later family role, and for primary participation in the interpersonal extra-familial world of work and public life.[63]

Women's primary location is in the home, since "mothering" occurs there. Indeed, the sexual division of labor provides a basis for differentiating "public" and "domestic." However, these spheres are not equal, and since "the public sphere dominates the domestic, . . . men dominate women."[64]

Chodorow stresses the importance of infantile experience both for psychological development and the creation of gender. The infant develops a self by the internalization of its relations with its primary caretaker, usually the mother. Infants first form a symbiotic bond with the mother, which in turn enables the infant to separate from the mother and to develop into an individual. This intense process of separation-individuation, through which the infant becomes a person, takes place in relation to persons of only one gender—females. By the time the father appears as a significant person in the child's life, the child's core identity has already been established. Hence, relations with the father are less affectively charged.

"Mothering" has important but differing consequences for girls and boys. Girls, because they are of the same gender as the mother, tend not to develop firm ego boundaries; they never completely separate from the mother. The mother often treats the daughter as an extension of herself and discourages the daughter from establishing a separate identity. Boys, on the other hand, experience themselves and are experienced by the mother as an "other." The mother pushes the son toward differentiation, and this encouragement is motivated and reinforced by gender differentiation. Because they never resolve the primary attachment to the mother, girls remain more preoccupied with relational issues. Boys seem to be occupied with issues of differentiation and action in the external world. Boys must reject the female aspects of themselves and the primary relatedness to the mother to be male; girls can and must reject neither.

Thus there is a deep psychological basis for later sex role differentiation; girls have a greater potential capacity for intimate relations but men have repressed these capacities and turn their interest outward. Girls must reject the mother as primary love object to become heterosexual, despite their unresolved emotional ties to her, but boys must shift their love from mother to another female. The shift is usually not absolute in the girl; she retains an internal emotional triangle of mother/father/self. "Men tend to remain emotionally secondary"[65] for women.

Women satisfy their relational needs by becoming mothers; the baby creates a new triangular situation: husband/wife/child. Men satisfy their need for nonrelational activities and avoid their fear of returning to the infantile state by participating in the nonfamilial world of work and by controlling women. Men need women, and heterosexual women need men, to fulfill a desire for emotional and physical union. This is in part, especially for men, a replication of the symbiotic union of early infancy, but is more safe and controlled. Yet, men find it difficult and threatening to satisfy women's emotional needs, because they had to repress their relational capacities to become male, so women turn to their children to satisfy *their* relational needs. Thus women and men have differing but equally strong unconscious motivations to replicate the family, gender personality, and mothering by women.

The only solution to this endless cycle according to both Chodorow and Dinnerstein is the active participation of men in infant care. Under these circumstances, Dinnerstein contends, we would have to mature both as a species and as individuals. For the two writers, shared child care would have the following benefits:

Masculinity would not become tied to denial of dependence and devaluation of women. Feminine personality would be less preoccupied with individuation, and children would not develop fears of *maternal* omnipotence and expectations of *women's* unique self-sacrificing qualities. This would reduce men's needs to guard their masculinity and their control of social and cultural spheres which treat and define women as secondary and power-less, and would help women to develop the autonomy which too much em-beddedness in relationship has often taken from them.[66]

The work of Dinnerstein and Chodorow shares many strengths and weaknesses, although the focus of each is somewhat different. Both stress the power of the unconscious, the residues of infancy in adult life and the consequent centrality of child-rearing arrangements to individual development and history as a whole. In Dinnerstein's work child-rearing arrangements have more power to determine history than Chodorow admits, although both agree that without a radical change in child-rearing arrangements women's status will not be fundamentally altered. Both Dinnerstein and Chodorow, unlike the thinkers who focus on sex roles or conditioning, enable us to under-stand how intertwined gender is with our core identity, and accord-ingly how difficult it is to change our core selves. Their account of the particular forms of gender identity created through female-dominated child rearing provides an explanation for the phenomenon the radical feminists identified—the male desire to dominate women—although it cannot explain the origin of the sexual division of labor. These two writers' concrete analysis of early childhood counters the abstractness of Firestone's and others' treatment of children and points to the inevitable influence of early experience on children and to the child's need for constant, reliable, and loving care, as well as to the child's innate sociability and malleability within definite limits. Their work also reminds us of two unyielding features of human ex-perience; the helplessness of the infant and the longing for irresponsi-ble infantile bliss will never disappear. Dinnerstein's and Chodorow's work also provides the basis for a critique of the Marxist interpreta-tion of the family as a purely dependent or ideological institution. The sex/gender system as psychodynamically internalized provides a mo-tive and reinforcement for all other forms of differentiation, including race, class, and the sex-stratified labor force. Chodorow's and Dinner-stein's more interactive approach to psychological development, without denying the power and unique character of the unconscious, provides a more adequate ground for integrating the concerns of Marxism, feminism, and psychoanalysis than does Rubin's and Mitchell's use of structuralism. We can begin to understand the sex/gender system as arising out of a series of interacting social relations, including those of the family, rather than as one structure, lying parallel to others.

There are also problems with Dinnerstein's and Chodorow's work, some which they share and some unique to each. Dinnerstein's work treats biology in a determinist manner and consequently suffers from some of the same problems as Firestone's work. She also assumes that there is some ahistoric, universal fate shared by all persons. The attachment that both men and women have to current social and family arrangements seems to be ultimately rooted in a universal, general psychological motive: the avoidance of the human dilemma. This claim lacks specificity; it does not enable us to understand how the general motive is translated into and expressed through particular concrete forms of social relations. Although it is true that we are all born helpless and dependent, grow up, and die, how we experience these processes is socially mediated. The dilemma of responsibility versus imperfect control may only emerge under certain social conditions and is not felt by all persons at all times.[67] The dilemma may arise from the breakdown of religion and community and could be the consequence of a certain form of isolated individualism. Women tend to be blamed for whatever a culture perceives as its dilemmas, and Dinnerstein helps us to understand why this is so, but the character of the dilemmas changes over time. The abstractness present in Dinnerstein's theory can only be overcome by integrating more specific political, economic, and psychological analysis into the dynamics suggested by her.

Although Chodorow's work is more historically specific, neither she nor Dinnerstein adequately places child bearing and rearing into a political, economic, and social context. While women universally have primary responsibility for child care, the content of child care and other aspects of women's work and the family have changed. The relationship between the division of labor within the family, and its effect on and relationship to other divisions of labor, for example, class, should be explored. Although Chodorow is careful to state that her analysis arises from and applies to Western capitalist countries, she does not discuss class and race differences in child rearing and what these imply for a general theory of mothering and social psychology.

In both writers a truly social psychology is suggested but not fully developed. The remarks on the relation of the family to other social structures are not adequately integrated into the account of personality development. The concept of social relations that would allow such an integration is underdeveloped. In both authors' work, the parents appear primarily as the *child's objects*. The fullness of the parents' experience and the influence on the children is not analyzed. Such an analysis would be one way to begin to investigate the interactions of social relations within the family with forms of social relations outside it.[68]

In both writers' analysis, motherhood appears to be primarily an expression of neurosis—of women's unresolved infantile wishes and fantasies. The other aspects of motherhood, both positive and negative, its very real gratifications and costs, are not discussed. The economic, political, and social restrictions upon and barriers to good parenting and changing patterns of parenting are not fully acknowledged and integrated into the account of psychodynamics. The impression remains that such problems reside solely within the family; although this is clearly not Chodorow's position, it may be Dinnerstein's.

What Is Left Undone?

There are certain conclusions about the nature of the family suggested by a review of feminist writings on that subject: (1) The sexual division of labor, especially women's exclusive responsibility for young children, which is a persistent feature of history, is a crucial factor in women's oppression and the analysis of it. (2) Understanding the family, its history, psychodynamics, and relation to other social structures is a central task of feminist theory.[69] (3) The family is a complex structure composed of many elements: the sex/gender system, the varying relations to production and to other social structures, ideology, and power relations. (4) The family (at least as historically constituted) is oppressive to women and is a primary source of the maintenance and replication of both gender and identity and the pain and suffering endemic to being female. (5) The family as it is currently constituted must be changed, if not eliminated. At minimum this requires the equal involvement of men and women in the care of young children. (6) Gender is created by social relations experienced first in the family; it is not determined solely by or limited to biology.[70] Heterosexuality is also socially, not biologically, constructed, through social relations in the family. (7) The different roles women and men play both inside and outside the family are not natural but grow out of and are the expression of a complex series of social relations: patriarchy, economic systems, legal and ideological structures, and early childhood experiences and their unconscious residues. All these relations are mutually interacting and reinforcing, although some may be more determinative than others and the more determinant factors may also vary over time. (8) Nothing human is unchanging or absolutely unchangeable. This includes the character of childhood, the family and human nature (although Dinnerstein would disagree on this point) and the variations of each of these by gender. Everything human has a social history and a social root. Even biology is mediated by, or can potentially be affected or transformed by, social relations; biology is not simply a brute fact, immediately and directly expressed in human life.

There are also many important questions left unanswered by feminist theories of the family, and the writers reviewed here disagree on the answers and on their relative significance. What healthy motives and needs draw people into families? How can these best be met? How do we decide what constitutes a "healthy" need, or even a "need"? How do different types of social relations interact, reinforce and conflict with each other, and how do they congeal into social structures? How does this process vary over time? How can we understand the family in this context? What are the essential elements of "the family"? How do families vary by class, race, and historical period? What consequences do these variations have for psychodynamics, gender, and the status of women? What economic and social barriers exist to good "family" relations and how can these barriers be overcome? Does feminism and the liberation of women require the elimination of gender or differentiation according to gender? Are there positive aspects to gender differentiation? What are the consequences of different answers to these questions for the organization of family life? Does "the family" as such oppress women, or does the patriarchal (or capitalist) family oppress women? What would nonoppressive family relations look like? What do children really need to mature into healthy adults? How can these needs best be met? Must there always be some form of sexual repression? If so, why and what forms are least oppressive? Can there be a beneficial form of sexual repression? Does biology impose any limits on social relations? How can we know what these might be and how they could be incorporated into a nonoppressive society? What sort of social and political theory do we need to analyze and do justice to family and "personal" experiences? Is either liberal individualism or Marxism adequate to this task? Should all distinctions between the public and the private spheres be eliminated? In what ways should "feminine" experience and qualities enter the public sphere and "masculine" qualities enter the private?

The conception of the family as constituted by three interacting spheres enables one to grasp the family's character at any particular moment, but it does not explain the dynamics that cause the family to change over time or that govern the interaction between the spheres. This approach also does not provide a normative theory of how each sphere should be constituted or how each should interact with the others. It merely suggests what must be considered in the construction of an adequate theory and offers a method of ordering vast amounts of historical, economic, anthropological, political, biological, and sociological material.

A normative theory of the family would have to be grounded in a more adequate account of each aspect of the family. Such an account in turn depends upon the development of theories that do justice to not only one aspect of the family but the interactions between the aspects as well.[71] Existing theories such as those offered by psychoanalysis, political economy, and sociology would have to be transformed. Psychoanalysis, for example, should become a truly social psychology in which psychodynamics are understood to include not only the internal organization and interaction of psyche and soma but the internalization of class and other social relations as well.

On the basis of a more developed understanding of the currently available social and material resources and the limitations inherent within each person and form of social relations, feminists could begin to conceptualize alternatives to current family arrangements that are both possible and desirable. The development of alternatives would require thinking through what kinds of child care are best for parents and children; what family structures are best for persons at various stages of the life cycle and with differing needs for care (for example, elderly or handicapped persons); how the state and political processes should affect families; and how work and the organization of production should be transformed to support whatever family forms are preferred. Questions such as who should have the final authority to make decisions in matters of marriage, divorce, birth control, abortion, the "best interest" of the child, and appropriate family arrangement for different constellations of people must also be addressed. The resolution of these problems requires not only more empirical knowledge but the clear articulation of political and ethical principles as well.[72]

The absence of a normative theory of the family is a central problem in feminist theory and practice. The feelings that arise from and cluster around debates over "the family" are extremely powerful and affect political action both overtly and covertly.[73] These feelings will not disappear and are replicated and maintained by everyday experience. The family *is* central to the oppression and liberation of women. Therefore, the family must be central to feminist theory as well.

Contemporary Critical Theory
and the Family: Private World
and Public Crisis

❀ *Theodore Mills Norton*

As inheritors of the Marxian theory of capitalist development, the critical theorists of the Frankfurt School and the Institute for Social Research played a leading role in extending the theory
to unexplored regions of the new social formation, in widening its
horizons to incorporate recent philosophical themes and social science
methods, and in adapting it to significant changes in capitalist social
structure.[1] With different emphases this work of unpacking and re-
constructing Marxism has been carried forward by Jürgen Habermas
and his associates.[2] Today, in its older and newer incarnations, the
critical theory of society exerts a growing influence on the direction
of American social theory and research.[3]

Neglected by earlier Marxism, the fate of the family in capitalist
society more than once attracted the attention of the Frankfurt School.
Max Horkheimer, the leader of the school and second director of
the institute, inaugurated a major research project on authority and
the family to which he supplied a general introduction.[4] Even after the
institute completed its work on this subject, Horkheimer kept returning to it.[5] Although not all institute members shared his concern with
the family as such, the study of its modern transformations helped
to integrate psychoanalytic theory into critical social theory, and this
was reflected in later publications by former affiliates.[6] Right down
to the present the Frankfurt argument on the family has been considered and subjected to critical review by students of this institution.[7]

What interested the Frankfurt School was the social psychology of
the family and its interconnection with authority, or legitimate domi-

nation. With shifting stress on one or another of these aspects, the forms of the modern family (derived from the bourgeois family) were seen to incorporate moments of submission to and resistance against domination. In line with much recent socialization theory, the school viewed the family as a mechanism for the internalization and reproduction of authority structures. At the same time, the psychic economy of the family contributed to the formation of a character structure capable of sustaining a reflective distance between itself and aggregates of social power.

Unfortunately, it appeared that the weakening of family life under late capitalism had disrupted this economy, resulting in the relatively unmediated integration of exposed psychic contents into the iron cages of the totally administered world. Historically the movement is one from the assimilation of society by a developing individual personality to the assimilation by society of this individual—who thereby ceases to exist. With advancing age the critical theorists looked around them and, in effect, declared "no individuals here!" But this meant also that the classical bourgeois family, the family of liberal capitalism, paternalistic repression, padded interiors, string quartets, and almond afternoons at country homes, had also passed from the scene. The statement of the young Erich Fromm that "the family is the medium through which the society or the social class stamps its specific structure on the child, and hence on the adult. *The family is the psychological agency of society*." This claim, which in effect launched the career of the critical theory of the family, could not be sustained with the same force in the age of the "television family" and the "split-level" suburban household.[8] Surveying the ruins, and in a quite conservative vein, the old Horkheimer wrote:

The less the distinctive character of the individual plays a role in shaping his life and the more the members of the upcoming generation become simply functions in an increasingly planned and managed society, the more fact-oriented, unimaginative, and conformist their thinking becomes. . . . Young people . . . are no more irrational than earlier generations; on the contrary, they are more level-headed, utilitarian, and without illusions. . . .

A bridge to the old civilization still exists but its piers are becoming steadily weaker. Disillusionment, crass realism, and the absence of any dreams of personal fulfillment are the sign of an interior coldness and find further manifestation in the tendency to give imaginative expression only in quite undifferentiated form to sexual and related impulses. Young people do not have morality in their bones.[9]

Although a once fruitful line of inquiry has been historically exhausted, there is, nonetheless, no reason to ignore it or to deny its continuing capacity to stimulate reflection on its object. However, the complex discussion of the Frankfurt School on authority and the family has been analyzed elsewhere and will not be reiterated here. Instead, I will begin with a retrospective on the family, viewed mainly through the lenses of classical Marxism, but in partial opposition to Marx; and I shall follow this by presenting some elements of a possible theory of the family and domination derived from the critical theory of society after Horkheimer.

1

Although it was initially restricted to a small region of the globe, the triumph of industrial capitalism registered a moment of world historical defeat for the institution of the family. If we abstract from the plurality of processes through which this result was achieved, the catastrophe of the traditional family can be assessed within the economically determined, shifting parameters of the public and the private.

The organizational principle of capitalist society is the capital-wage labor relation.[10] The universalization of this relation, even to the point where unskilled labor can no longer serve as a standard measure of average labor time,[11] is a precondition of the unleashed process of economic growth through capital accumulation. The latter transforms the mode of exploitation from the production and expropriation of use values, i.e., useful goods,[12] to the expropriation of surplus labor under the economic form of "value," i.e., surplus value. This value is only realized in exchange: capitalism, as a system for the production of commodities, means that this social formation must in some form or at some level conserve the institution of the market.[13]

The reorganization of social systems on the basis of the new principle has its own preconditions. Among these is a norm of economic life that is always imperfectly realized. The sale of labor power on the commodity market presupposes the liberation of the capacity to work from a limitation by a variety of institutional bonds. Apart from (frequent) periods of military mobilization, political command over the labor supply must be sufficiently relaxed so that the "free" laborer can exchange his or her productive capacity against an economic wage. So, too, the domination of living labor (variable capital) by dead labor (constant capital) requires the radical separation of the former from the latter. Precapitalist commodity production is undertaken by producers who possess, but do not own, means of production, e.g., surplus production by dependent agriculturists of goods for local markets. It can also take place under conditions where labor power is not freely exchangeable against wages, e.g., in urban craft guilds and types of medieval sharecropping.[14] Capitalism, however, requires (1) the elimination of unmediated access to the means of production; (2) the domination of the unfettered wage labor contract over all other forms of the mobilization of labor. The de facto possession of productive forces by precapitalist workers not only blocks the universalization of the labor exchange (which is nevertheless to be found operating on a restricted basis in many traditional societies). It also enables these workers to control within limits the total productive process.[15]

The capitalist system, therefore, can only reproduce itself on its own foundations if it secures extensive institutional change through political revolution, long-range revisionary processes, or a combination of both. To be sure, the modern state plays an important supplemental role in the domination of labor. But the juridically secured and forcibly sustained labor exchange cannot be politically abrogated if capitalism as such is to survive—hence the famed "depoliticization" of the labor relation, in both its centralized and decentralized forms.[16] With this, the fundamental demarcation between the public and private spheres of life in modern industrial states is established. Capitalist production is enduringly "privatized" and must remain so throughout all expansion of government regulation of the economy.

Yet the big institutional loser under capitalism is not the state but the family. No matter how politically controlled and exploited it was in precapitalist societies, and no matter to what exent it had already shifted its activities from production for immediate consumption to production of commodities, the family in its various forms remained intimately linked to the productive process. As Aristotle well portrayed it, the family *was* the *oikos;* and it was the separation of the family from production, far more than it was the restraints placed upon state economic activity, that engendered the economization of social relations in modern societies.[17] From this perspective, one can agree with Marx's observation that the family had disappeared among the proletariat. And, the importance of the dissociation of family from production can be illustrated by the endless debate between Marxists and Freudians over the relative primacy in human affairs of biocultural reproduction or economic production, and over which of these aspects ought to be subsumed under the other.[18] One doubts that this polemic would have made much sense to most inhabitants of precapitalist societies.

In retrospect one can see to what extent the family-economy division helped to secure the alienation of the labor force from unfettered access to means of production, the dissolution of noneconomic bonds among the producers themselves, and the market form of labor utilization—aspects which, taken together, are both conditions and consequences of the rise of capitalism. It also resulted in a "second privatization" that may turn out to be more consequential for social change than the first. Here G. W. F. Hegel, despite his location in a Germany that was by no means a paragon of industrial capitalism, saw matters clearly enough. Well acquainted with British political economy, he drew clear demarcations between the spheres of family and civil society, as well as between the latter and that of the state.[19] What is world historically new in modern societies is the blossoming of civil society with its system of needs; and Marxist theory takes off from the rediscovery that the morphology of this system, its anatomy, is modern political economy.

Within the thought of Marx and Engels this insight results in a major conceptual transformation in the structure of political thought. With Hegel, the tradition of European political philosophy is brought to a close; when the young Marx undertook a critique of Hegel's *Philosophy of Right*, it was to be the last time that a major European thinker placed political philosophy at the center of his concerns.[20] The project, however, was abrogated. By 1844, Marx had redirected his efforts to the critique of political economy. Political theory thereafter no longer occupied the strategic place it once held in shaping the reflexive performance of steering functions in traditional social systems.[21] Ironically, Marx's ability to enter this turn was conditioned by the fate of the family, an institution that in its posttraditional forms receives no systematic attention in his work.[22]

To resume, the demarcation within capitalist societies of family from civil society, reproduction from production, the realm of "love" from that of economic competition may prove to generate important conflict potentials.[23] Despite the fact that this division never has been absolute, it remains a durable feature of contemporary social organi-

zation and consciousness. Certainly, the family may be usefully analyzed *as* an economic (or state) institution.[24] But a critical theory that
adheres too closely to the speculative tradition of Hegelian-Marxism
may suppress dimensions of the contradictory unity of capitalist development that it, in fact, needs to unearth.[25] Accordingly, it is the
division that I will stress; and I will try to illustrate with a few examples the ambiguities that it produces within the modern conception
of the private sphere.

To begin with, let us consider an aspect of the posttraditional
notion of the individual. As both Hegel and later sociology have
affirmed, modernization involves individuation; liberal capitalism goes
hand-in-hand with the victory of the subjective principle in the economy, polity, and culture. In this world, however, individuals demand
and are secured in their individuality by others of their kind. The question is, On what terrain is this recognition primarily sought?

With Marx, it can be argued that the abstract, isolated bourgeois
individual first clearly appears on the marketplace, at one remove
from the productive apparatus hidden just beneath the surface of civil
society. Against Marx, it can be observed that this individual is simultaneously isolated *and* confirmed in its individuality by way of reciprocal recognition in exchange.[26] Even the market relation is to be
understood as a "moment of ethical life," a medium of moralization.
And, the generalization applies not only to relations among merchants, or among merchants and customers, but to the capital-wage
labor nexus. As long as the last retains the form of an equivalent exchange, the employee receives a dose of "personality" along with the
wage packet. If anything, the value of this recognition quotient of
employment increases with the transition to *Spätekapitalismus*. For
those brutalized sellers of raw labor power in the Manchesterian era,
recognition counted little when faced with the interesting alternative
of being worked or being starved to death. But as capital is increasingly centralized and concentrated, undermining the illusion that hard
work and savings on wages can allow the working class to enter the
master class, the normative component of the wage bargain comes to
the fore. The job is now sociologically glossed as a "career orientation" or "occupational role." Only against this background can we
appreciate the immense psychic costs of even controlled recessions
and unemployment.

The point of this example is that, as the sociologists say, *modern*
individuality is implicated with the progressive shift from ascribed to

achieved status.[27] Achievement however, cannot be gauged exclusively with reference to income. It is always also a matter of public recognition; yet this is rarely to be obtained within the formally designated public sphere of polity or state. On the one hand, even with the expanded role of the state in the economy, the new individual continues to be defined as a private person. On the other hand, the individual subsists on whatever recognition can be wrung from members of the public, *that is,* other private individuals in civil society.[28]

Even less can individuality be validated (in this society) within the eminently private domain of the family. To be sure, in the calcified mythology of the disintegrating nuclear household, women can be recognized as "homemakers," men as "good providers." The limits of such recognition can be discerned with reference to the importance for male self-definition of occupational role identities and, more strikingly, in the feminist critique of the family and women's struggles for entry into the professions.[29] If the same mythology defends the family as "a haven in a heartless world," one can only become a "real individual" by braving an entry into that world, i.e., the private-public domain of civil society.

The development of the modern state yields a second example. When at the time of the Watergate scandal President Richard M. Nixon asserted his proprietorship over the White House tapes, his action recalled an earlier era when not only state papers but public offices and entire realms were "private," i.e., familial, property. In the era of Absolutism princely diplomacy and warfare were still mediated by the modalities and claims of kinship. The subsequent demarcation of the public from the private realm accordingly involved the uncoupling of the former from the economy but from the family as well. For this reason, the privacy of the nuclear family is as much a matter of its political privatization as its separation from production. As family status is progressively stripped of its claims to political power, the gulf is also widened between the bourgeois and the citoyen; the concept of the latter included that of the former, not least with reference to residential qualifications. Granted that we are talking about *formal* political status, whether of domination or subordination, its connection with family membership is severed. Certainly, outside the domain of the great bourgeoisie, families are subjected to intensifying administrative pressures.[30] But if the state cannot let the family alone, neither can it simply absorb it—to do so would undermine the legitimation structure of late capitalist democracy.

Still, it is perhaps with regard to their standing before the late capitalist state that the two arenas of private life can be most clearly distinguished. If anything reveals the integrally capitalist character of this state, it is the way it applies its preference rules in its dealings with the family and the economy, respectively. As the corporate monopoly and state sectors of the private economy become more broadly integrated with state administration and finance, the family is left to flounder in the interstices of administrative supervision. No doubt the continued existence of many small, low-status families comes to be predicated on the supply of state welfare and subsidized social commodities. It is precisely this supply that is endangered in times of economic crisis: it is the private economy and its proposed reindustrialization that hogs the lion's share of the public interest. To the family, the state offers traditionalist rhetoric, miniscule tax adjustments, and draconian measures designed to restore the dependency of women and unemployed youth upon an institution that can no longer sustain them. From the "heartless world" of civil society the family receives a familiar message. When push comes to shove it is the health of the private sector—the capitalist system of production, distribution, exchange, and capital accumulation—that must take priority over the intimate domain of private life, that is, families with their few remaining reproductive functions. Having long since transferred most of these to the state, economy, and other institutions of civil society, the family packs little clout with which to back up its demands. Cut off more than ever from the productive process, it can live free or die. Like those sturdy beggars that Elizabethan authorities tried to flog back to their dying villages, the family has no home to return to. Marx's notification of its demise may turn out to have been—merely—premature.

2

If we are not to conclude on this pessimistic note, we will have to change our perspective on the family. Initially, however, this will involve moving onto a level of abstraction on which families no longer appear.

So far I have mainly adopted classical Marxist approaches to the family and private world, even when subjecting them to critical reservations. I have also tended to view the family against the background of the European transition from traditional to capitalist society. This transition has now been completed in that region; and I would like to reconsider the family within contexts of systems and action theory.

As general theory, political theory today belongs to social theory. The chief analytic unit of the latter is the social system; that of political theory, the political system.[31] However, it may prove fruitful to set aside the conception of the political system as a subsystem of the social system that takes the latter as its environment. The system-subsystem construction is not entirely misleading. But it often leads systematic theorists of politics to identify the political subsystem with the state and its informal institutional outworks. With this, the value of the systems approach as an analytic of the universal constituents of social systems is lost.[32] For despite the continuing belief of some sociologists in the opacity, durability, and universality of institutions (including not least the state), ethnographers, historians, and "culturalist" psychologists have long since demonstrated the relativity, fragility, and indefinite plurality of such constellations. If, in an era when the world system is less a theoretical projection than a crisis-ridden reality, universalistic theories are to survive the dissolution of particular institutions speeded by the world market, they will have to move toward more abstract levels of generalization than ever.[33]

By the political system, then, I mean a universal dimension of the social system, a version of the social system to itself. Here the speculative heritage can assist a systems theory. At the same time, we must carefully demarcate the structural and functional *nonidentity* of the political with other moments of the social system. I distinguish at least two other such moments. First, social systems can be viewed as natural systems, second, as cultural systems. Each aspect has a definite structural location in the social system. To each is assigned a definite functional imperative it must strive to fulfill if it is to contribute to the continued existence of the whole. Each can be correlated with a feature of language.[34] Finally, each may be provisionally linked with a methodological norm.

1. As natural system, the social system is reproduced in what Marx called perpetual "metabolic interaction" with nonhuman systems in an open environment. In this perspective, the social system appears as a monitored feedback system of instrumental action. As such, it is constrained to secure at the very least its simple reproduction. Like a self-correcting device or an organism, it steers its way through an environment, the complexity of which it can never hope to reduce to

utter transparency. In this aspect the social system functions to sustain its continued existence—its biophysical survival—in a context to which it is never perfectly adapted. Nonexistence is the price of failure. Errors have consequences that can be retrodicted. This aspect can be linguistically correlated with the extension of natural languages by means of formal codes. With language acquisition, prelinguistic operations can be reformulated as technical rules. The latter may then be comprehended as instances of natural laws. As biophysical entity, the social system can be investigated with the methods of the empirical-analytic sciences.[35] The natural system is not a structural feature of the social system; rather, it is the condition of the system's having a structure. If the natural functioning of the system is suppressed, its structure collapses and it dies.

2. The cultural system secures to the social system that quality called "meaning." It is the social system "seen from the inside" by, and with reference to, its human individual and group components. Cultural systems offer identities and orientations to such components as actors and interactors. In the cultural system, structural change assumes a narrative and biographical dimension. The cultural system also serves to transform all by-products of system maintenance into meanings. On this model, secondary productions undertaken with regard to meaning rather than reproduction can proliferate. The cultural system functions to regulate the "supply of meaning," i.e., the amount and quality of interpretations, orientations, and identities required by the social system. The cultural dimension of the social system cannot be expunged or dismissed as ephemeral. Once the system of meaningful actions and objects is formed, its disintegration will throw the entire system into crisis, increasing the possibility of a natural system malfunction, even collapse. Cultural systems can be compared to the semantic component of natural languages. The system contains an open lexicon of meaningful actions and objectivations. Interpretations of both in everyday life are systematically extended through the methods of the hermeneutic or cultural sciences.[36] The cultural system can be conceived as a surface or super structure of the social system.

3. If the cultural system of the social system contains its lexicon, the political system comprises its system of syntactic rules. These include rules for the generation of social deep structures, as well as transformational rules by means of which deep are changed into surface structures.[37] The latter are not to be equated with the cultural superstructure; for the political system does not apply transformation

rules to the semantic contents but to the interaction structures—the institutions—of the social system.[38] In other words, it supplies the syntax of society. Were we in possession of a political linguistics that could reconstruct both sets of rules, we might be able to rationalize the process whereby the rules themselves are changed and, with them, the deep and surface structures of the social system.[39] The political system, then, contains finite rule sets that, even if they are not themselves changed to yield a new political language, can so operate as to generate an open set of surface interaction structures.[40] These syntactic rules cannot be adequately comprehended as cultural norms or technical rules—a social system that relied exclusively on the latter would cease to be social. More important, these rules are mediated through the interaction structures they generate. That is, those who occupy these structures must know how to apply the rules, and to be able to judge when they are being misapplied. The political system does not exist apart from the reflective judgments of the interacting individuals. The latter may be deemed politically competent. Institutions that lack members with the requisite level of competence will begin to decay. If the social system cannot reproduce them it will collapse.

Even if this crude model of a social system were to be adequately refined, it could not be directly applied to contemporary societies without mediating theories of socialization and the evolution of social formations. Granted that, I will conclude with some remarks on how it might orient a theory of the family today.

As already noted, no general social system level or function can be identified with a particular institutional complex. Functions are shared across institutions grounded in all three levels. Nevertheless, we can think of socially specific institutional roles that may be differentiated and then attached to particular structures in the course of social evolution. The assumption of these roles by interaction structures can simultaneously contribute to system maintenance and system crisis; or the respective contributions may be separated in time. The particular aspect of a function that gets integrated with a role, should it fail to be performed, may help to bring on a crisis or to push toward some resolution. If it should turn out that the contemporary family is in such a strategic position, it would be wise to place it at the center of our concerns.

The appearance of the family as a distinctive institution has attracted notice from most schools of sociology and human psychology.

By focusing on economic changes and the cultural ambiguities of modern interpretations of the private, I have wished to reemphasize its novelty. In a certain sense, there *was* no "family" prior to the separation of that institution from civil society and the state. What interested Marx and others of his era was the new institution of civil society. The state declined to secondary importance; the family nearly passed out of sight. With the Frankfurt School, the balance began to be redressed: the family and the state returned to play a role in the critical theory analysis of changing capitalism. Insofar as socialization became a major theme of the school, Habermas has more than made it his own.[41] We now want to ask if the family continues to merit this attention.

In the United States, scholars and the media are preoccupied with the matter of the family's decay. On the one hand, the image of "the family in crisis" is backed up by mounting statistical evidence on divorce, marriage, the brutalization of women and children, psychopathology, and more. The indicators do not paint a rosy picture. On the other hand, the family lives on, if only because the society has found no functional equivalent for it. Given this impasse, we can ask if the family's crisis might not prove fatal for the system.

Theory alone cannot answer this question. Again, it might offer some approaches to an answer. On our model, everything depends on which institutional roles the family has been playing.

By gradually separating the family from less differentiated complexes, these roles have been clarified: the famed loss of functions by the family, and their transfer to other institutions, has only contributed to this clarification. First, to the family has been assigned the task of the biological reproduction of the species. I am not claiming that the nuclear or other modern family forms are natural institutions, only that on the whole infants in *this* society are born into some type of family. And this is the family as it has been demarcated here. Matters could change: infants could be collectively raised in wings of factories or in state hatcheries: at one period, child labor came close to rendering the new family stillborn among the working class; and Ford might still produce a Bernard Marx in our future. All state control notwithstanding, this is not, on the whole, the way things have gone or the way we live now. As long as alternative arrangements are not universalized, this situation contains a terminal crisis potential: should the institution no longer sustain the biophysical reproduction of the system it will cease to exist. This outcome is most unlikely. But if the state attempts merely to shore up the family institution without forcing the economy to provide the support systems it requires under present conditions, the results may be mildly catastrophic.

Second, the family has become the seat of what the sociologists call "primary socialization." Even where the institution shares this role with others, it appears to play an important part in the process. The family provides the context in which elementary operations are mastered, language is acquired (as syntactic competence and lexical repository), interactive roles are internalized, and cultural norms are accepted or rejected. Socialization is a lifelong affair and not all its phases will be mediated primarily by the family. But if the latter should go out of business, the social order would have rapidly to supply an equivalent institution. That such a substitute could not be manufactured overnight goes without saying. Moreover, family socialization reacts back on biophysical reproduction. One need not be an orthodox Freudian to agree that psychosexual development integrates components of political—or interactive—competence and cultural attitudes.

Once again, it is unlikely that the family will not continue to play some socialization role for the growing child, and even the adolescent. If families, with or without both parents, are enabled to get enough calories, some kind of socialization will take place. As radiation spreads, garbage piles up, and parents go mad, the results may not be pleasing. Perhaps this would not be critical: the reindustrialized economy may prefer sociopathic runts, the hypermilitarized state may want creatures who have not developed beyond a punishment-obedience orientation.

All this, as they say, may go down. Yet it can be asked: Would such creatures be likely to mate? To raise children? Only, perhaps, if they were forced to "breed." Here, the modern institution reveals its fatal weakness, reaction its teeth, the future its hope. A condition of the possibility of the modern private family is that it takes sexually mature, reasonably hopeful, and faintly generous private individuals to found it and carry it off. Liberated from the imperatives of kinship, production, and the slave pen, the generation of new generations contains a moment of choice. Contemporary adults can choose to be married or single; regardless of marital status, to have or not have children; to care or not care for them if they have them. To use Erik H. Erikson's terminology, the postadolescent socialization process raises the problematic of generativity versus stagnation or self-indulgence.[42] If these terms or their author do not appeal to everyone, they still point to an abstract crisis potential that could be realized under appropriate conditions. Today those conditions are in place.

"What if . . . ?" What if a significant minority of an American generation were to turn aside, for whatever reasons, from the task of reproducing and socializing the next generation; or even from any significant part of that task? Then, indeed, the crisis might be upon us, even if it took some time to unfold. I will call this a "crisis of generativity"; and I will close with the suggestion that such a crisis is already well under way in our society.

As it deepens, a badly understood crisis of generativity will encounter some typical responses. First, without addressing the conditions that favored the decline of the family, repressive measures can be employed to preserve its integrity by force. Current attacks on homosexuals, free choice, birth control, all can be seen as groping attempts at regenerating the society, over the heads of those alone who can choose to renew it. It is to be doubted that these measures will do more than strengthen the tendencies they are designed to counteract. Second, the state can once again intervene in the economy to force it to restore some of the supports the family requires. But unless the economy is radically restructured, the benefits at best will be marginal. Nor is it clear that economic inputs by themselves will stimulate the desired response. Finally, from the convergence of many interests may arise renewed projects to supersede the family as the generative institution of the society. It cannot be said that they will fail to meet with partial success; however, we do not know within what limits surface structural changes can proceed without altering the structuring rules themselves.

One last possibility presents itself, even if its realization is unlikely. The pressure put on the system by an accumulation of crisis tendencies may force its rearticulation, a change in its organizational principle. As we are talking about more than mere institutional change, and, as in human systems, automatic self-correction is not possible, we must ask how the principle is to be superseded and by what agency. Instead of trying to answer these difficult questions directly, I will cast a final glance at the family. First, given its strategic location in this society, the family bears a peculiar relation to the political system. In light of the socialization aspect of its generative tasks, the family takes the initiative in orienting children toward nonfamilial institutional interaction roles. Little kids play—or used to—at house, at cops and firemen, at cowboys and Indians. Do they at the same time play at nuclear family, state economic sector, and imperialism? And could one design new games for them, e.g., communal family, collective ownership and democratic control of the means of production, and peaceful intercourse among peoples?

But it is unlikely that the family directly imprints highly specific role qualifications on children—this ignores the resocialization processes undergone by people as they are integrated into nonfamilial institutions. The firehouse, not the family, turns one into a fireman. To be more specific, given 'the modalities of the cultural system, it is unlikely that the family can create a forced consensus of role interpretations, *including* its own. In this connection we must speak of famil*ies*. The stereotypical role identities that reaction would like to force upon family members would dissolve with a democratization of the social formation. The variety and quality of interaction interpretations would be vastly augmented—it is quite possible that no one frozen *form* of reproduction would supersede the nuclear family.

So, it is along the line of interaction patterns rather than interpretations that the family might make a difference. This is to say that it can come to greater consciousness about its *political* content. What counts here is less children's games than games parents play. The family is not a ministate. It could become a kind of public sphere. Through the exercise of a political competence, the parents may help to develop new orientations among children.

Exactly at this point some of the qualifications I have raised are pertinent. Families cannot imprint participatory democratic institutional roles on children, especially when so few institutions exist. Political interpretations are likely to be reinterpreted by children, sometimes in opposition to their parents' views. An "open family discussion" is no doubt a good thing; it belongs to the "politics of the family" rather than the nation. In fact, if the former is to make a difference for the latter (and vice versa), then, without trying to politicize their families (in the sense of political institutions) parents must, as the social bearers of generative tasks, break into the public sphere, or reconstruct it if need be. It is when millions of families, representing the human interest in regeneration, confront civil society and the state with a bill of accounts that they can become factors in a positive resolution of the crisis. If so, the family would not become "a little commonwealth"; the great commonwealth once again would have to serve the family.

Kafka and Laing on the Trapped Consciousness: The Family as Political Life

❄ *James Glass*

Torment and the Family: The Injustice of Exchange

Both Kafka and Laing isolate similar phenomena: family systems whose dynamics work against the interests of individuals labeled weird, mad, crazy, or uncooperative. Both argue that the extent of psychological pain felt by an excluded self derives not from some mysterious, personal irresponsibility but from an insensitive set of interpersonal transactions blocked by misunderstood messages. The victims find themselves forced into disastrous psychological situations, existential fields that define their being as "weird" or sick and that allow them no escape, solace, or refuge. Everything for the victim becomes ominous and threatening. The family degenerates into a conspiracy, often unconscious, against the interests of the victim; we see nothing of a selfless, altruistic love acting without self-regard, demand, and power. The family pushes the victim toward extinction; and we witness a slow process of psychological death, the elimination of the self, and the destruction of any recognizable identity.

In Kafka's parable, "The Metamorphosis," and Laing's case studies, the family is demystified; the narrow, constrained, and often hypocritical structure of the family is described. It is the "son" (Kafka) or "daughter" (Laing) who, being the weakest "unit" in the system, experiences the contradictory messages, who finds it impossible to cope with double-bind commands, who ultimately slides toward madness.

Throughout their critiques, Kafka and Laing imply that authority performs less than adequately. The culture lacks a sufficiently developed notion of a nonrepressive authority, and authority, when it is forced to mediate and determine value, inevitably compounds injustice. Authority and its exercise reinforce those conflicts that bring disintegration. Rather than creating a sense of a center whose operation suggests supportive and compassionate qualities, authority alienates the self through hostility, fear, and denial. What we learn from authority is negative—primarily how to be afraid, confused, and mystified by demands that seem unjust, but that for the self seem vital to gain the attention of authority figures. For Kafka and Laing, authority—although it demands and claims love—refuses to express itself in terms that might open up or enlarge areas of communication and transaction. Inequality of meaning conditions the relationship between self and authority; it is the message system of the parent that remains dominant. Any misunderstandings that happen in the transmission of messages become the fault of the unequal self.

It is not at all exaggerating to suggest that Kafka and Laing's parents are "bad"—in the sense that what they do for the child brings disastrous consequences. It is a commentary on specific relationships generated within a single family as well as on patterns reinforcing perverse authority transactions in the culture, in its history, and in unconscious repression and anxiety. Families in these interpretations teach nothing of virtue, wisdom, or prejudice; what they do teach is sadism. Families serve as the initial school, our first playhouse in destructive instincts; it is a universe whose primary function lies in socializing the self into sado-masochistic patterns that remain with us throughout life.

Neither Kafka nor Laing offers comforting resolutions; they describe dismal events. Implicit in their arguments is the notion that social intelligence possesses feeble resources for finding solutions to contradictions in family transactions. Both have little faith in any technological or scientific reason rescuing the outcast consciousness. Laing resists the medical, psychiatric model that he finds deplorable in the treatment of schizophrenia. Kafka denies the possibility of political reason overturning any corruption inherent in bureaucracy, authority, or value. Both see authority and confusion as endemic problems in social and family life; neither offers any useful or pragmatic program for the political difficulties distorting the functions of the ego, and neither holds out any redemptive role for the family.

We met Gregor Samsa in "The Metamorphosis" as an already given fatality, a consciousness no longer attached to any recognizable or consensual externality.

As Gregor Samsa awoke one morning from uneasy dreams he found himself transformed in his bed into a gigantic insect. He was lying on his hard, as it were armor-plated, back and when he lifted his head a little he could see his dome-like belly divided into stiff arched segments on top of which the bed quilt could hardly keep in position and was about to slide off completely. His numerous legs, which were pitifully thin compared to the rest of his bulk, waved helplessly before his eyes.

What has happened to me? he thought. It was no dream.[1]

Gregor's madness, the terror following such a horrible transformation, structures Kafka's narrative. We see the Samsa family through Gregor's feelings, thoughts, and expressions. His condition does not suggest a fantasy, a wish, or a dream. The transformation is real; it has happened; Gregor believes himself to be a bug. His family similarly experience his change: all normal activity ceases and Gregor's buglike existence comes to dominate the exchanges within the Samsa family. Everything changes for Gregor—trapped in his internality, he discovers he cannot speak or, rather, that he "speaks" in a language of strange sounds that make absolutely no sense to others.

Gregor has experienced a radical, or what might be understood as a schizophrenic, break with reality. He experiences his being as different and the hallucinated condition of being a bug invades consciousness. He finds it nearly impossible to move in ways that hitherto had been easy. He maneuvers differently and discovers how to adapt to the new body. It is a terrifying situation. Psychically Gregor sees himself as separated from humanity; and that is how the reader sees the situation: a schizophrenic condition (radical separation or split between inner and outer) described from Gregor's point of view, from his delusional, inner world. What the audience receives is a picture of an ongoing delusional narrative, a self convinced that his images of reality are the true ones. Gregor's internality then is a complete and total repudiation of the consensual world; and he believes his parents perceive him as a bug. The story is a parable of Gregor's madness, his schizophrenia.

Gregor's adaptation to his inner reality takes on grotesque proportions. Frightened, without comfort, he lives in dread. The parable develops as a journey into this horror, into the consequences of an alienation so intense that no human identification remains. Gregor panics when he discovers that he no longer looks human. What he feels, no one, not even his family knows; it is an isolation so absolute that what remains is a knowledge defined only by the terms of the delusion. Gregor knows himself to be slimy, ugly, bad, and evil (he attributes to himself qualities that more appropriately belong to the family that drove him mad). He ceases to be socially functional, and quickly finds himself read out of the human community. His madness drives him out, but the madness also refracts the craziness and hostility of the family, if Gregor's parable be understood as a way of relating a peculiar form of internal truth.

Gregor's existence threatens the family's political system, particularly the rule of patriarchal authority because his madness removes his being from the father's domination. It also forces Gregor's withdrawal from the routinization and expectations implicit in the Samsas' sense of what is just or appropriate behavior. Gregor now becomes a problem just as any mad person who develops problematic behaviors disturbs the family. Gregor experiences the family (and in Kafka's view that experience is quite valid) as hating his "bug-being." Gregor prior to his metamorphosis (his schizophrenic break) had maintained the family's welfare, but he received nothing in return. The inference seems to be that the family saw Gregor only as a functional provider. We certainly receive no sense of any love or any real affection from the father toward the son. Gregor appears to have been a victim, either unaware of his own victimization or so cowed by his authority relationships—father/boss/firm—that, for purposes of self-preservation, he never made the necessary political connections.

Gregor is, and undoubtedly was, treated unjustly, but in the parable we see no evidence that Gregor ties together his madness and the political structure of the family. Kafka gives Gregor no political consciousness, no *concept* of his alienation, no theory to explain why he feels as he does. The only reality open to Gregor lies in his delusions, the knowledge that he has been transformed into a bug.

It is tragically true that only as a bug, as a mad person, a schizophrenic, can Gregor assert himself against the dominant authority figures with any kind of impact. Gregor removes himself completely from the family's economically determined system and values. It is an implicit rebellion, and he causes the consternation and provokes the anger of those who had victimized him. Because of his withdrawal and his removal from any known or established communication system, Gregor interrupts a whole set of economic operations that had persistently been oppressing him. As a metamorphosized being, Gregor brings embarrassment to the family, but by physically denying the family's reality, he refuses to recognize its system of values, its concept of organization, and, implicitly, its *politics*. If the story symbolizes madness, and if Gregor finds himself unavailable to the social and economic world because of his madness, he transforms into an economic liability. This accounts for his family's, and particularly his father's, hostility and neglect.

Gregor is emotionally and psychically disenfranchised because of the dysfunctional impact of his madness. The family's reaction only demonstrates the broader insensitivity and coldness of an authoritarian structure that is not only selfish and demanding, but apparently masterful at engaging Gregor in numerous double-binds. Gregor finally becomes so thoroughly overwhelmed that the only exit lies in withdrawal—in the psychic retreat of delusion and in the construction of an inner space that acts as the critical *existential* frame of reference.

Like all madness, Gregor's madness happens without hope, without any redemptive possibility. There is no joyful ending, no sensitive therapeutic intervention that rescues the lost, autistic self. Gregor "dies" in relation to all social communication, the victim of a family skillful in the political arts of depersonalization and appropriation. Premetamorphosis, Gregor had been effective as a quantifiable entity; his value as a person could be measured in terms of money. Now, however, Gregor ceases to be valued as human, because he has lost the ability or will (symbolized by his delusional identity) to provide. His being loses all of its social and economic personality; he forfeits any claims to rights or justice. This transformation reflects fundamental strains in the family itself, in its systemic operations, and in its values. It is Gregor's perception of himself, his family's treatment of him, and his withdrawal and autism, that is analogous to symptoms and etiology in schizophrenia. In Gregor's identification with a gigantic cockroach we see the dissociation of the ego from externality and the regression to primal or archaic representations within the self.

If we are to read Kafka's parable as more than a weird story about a person's becoming a bug, such an analogy may be instructive. Gregor's appearance is like that of the catatonic: totally silent on the outside (the bug cannot speak or communicate), and thoroughly frightened, terrorized on the inside. Gregor thinks, but it is the thinking of a thoroughly demoralized and terrorized being. His catatonia is a defense against the family; and inside of himself Gregor fights horrendous battles that are outwardly invisible. No one witnesses what is going on inside Gregor, and the family, unable to sustain or live with such madness, reduces him to an unhuman or antihuman representation. It is a mental operation by the Samsas consistent with general social attitudes toward madness: there is little concern for what madness means as questioning, complaint, or criticism, but a very real concern for removing that madness from any visible social field. Again, Gregor's significance as a symbolic representation makes sense as a reflection of madness whose only mode of survival lies in removing the self from contact with a hostile externality.

Gregor's regression forces him from the human or political world; he becomes like the schizophrenic whose false self system appears through the guise of being a bug; he is therefore useless and even dangerous to the predictable expectations of authority. It is so believable, the alienation so intense, that all associated with Gregor read his being as buglike (a set of reactions symbolizing, for example, how people regard the mad presence as something strange, animallike, and hostile). It is almost as if Gregor proclaims through his appearance to the family: "I am a being whose contact with you happens on the most primitive level of terror and disgust." It is, from Kafka's parabolic perspective, a translucent statement on depravity and insensitivity, on the power of "love" to drive the self into madness, and on those family systems whose operations act as thinly disguised exercises in appropriation and economic function. "The Metamorphosis" is a glimpse inside the catatonic self.

Laing gives us real world equivalents, not as bizarre as Kafka's, but the consequence of everyday events and of actions by everyday families. Both Kafka and Laing share a similar theme: families through impossible demands and situations force the dysfunctional self away from any viable externality and label that self as "vicious," "uncooperative," "sick," or "undesirable," what Hobbes might have called a "bile and scab" on the body politic. Families, in Laing's conception, conspire against their most vulnerable members; the offending person or self becomes the object of criticism, punishment, neglect, and denial. The family, when the disturbance increases, excludes the troublesome unit by discovering mental illness. Such exclusion serves to eliminate or at least to alleviate what the engineers call "noise" in systemic exchanges. In the family disruptive noise produces entropy and an entropic family system not only threatens the tacit arrangements making communication possible, but it also disrupts the rule-defining authority and endangers that authority's conception of political justice.

The Laingian "schizophrenics" act not so much illogically as defensively with attempts to protect themselves from a very real form of psychological violence. Message systems become so thoroughly confused that withdrawal often seems a sensible resolution to an intolerable situation. For example, in one case "each parent is simultaneously imputing and denying ambivalent feelings towards" their daughter, "denying they are imputing them, and imputing that the other is denying them." Mothers complain that the onset of an "illness" begins with the daughters' behavior changes—altering the parental expectation or the parental projection: "difference . . . seems to be the essence of the illness." In one instance, when the daughter "went from home to hospital she could hardly be expected to discriminate between the two social systems."[2] In each, she was treated as sick, as a patient. What the parents see as sick or "schizophrenic" becomes for Laing a logical attempt to defend the self—behavior that may make a good deal of sense in the daughter's movement to assert her autonomy. Such assertion is read by the parents as disobedience, and the praxis takes on the attribution of sickness.

From the perspective of the family, the patients resist socialization and learning patterns that for the parents seem to be right and effective. Schizophrenia implicitly repudiates the family's explicit and tacit rules. It is an implicit attack on authority. Frequently, Laing suggests, such rules disguise parents' fantasies about themselves, about what their children should be, about the world outside, and so on. The rules lack any objectivity in experience. They psychologically constrain movement within the family; and the sick find their status reduced to that of the incompetent and irresponsible. They cease to have any rights; their behavior pushes them beyond normality, a diagnosis that is usually confirmed by what the doctors judge and prescribe.

Families, Laing argues, see what they want to see. Ruth's breakdown "occurred suddenly and unaccountably," from the perspective of the family. "Until that moment Ruth had been a normal happy child and had never been a trouble." Yet, in fact, Ruth was having a "struggle to live." For the family, the "being" or "self" of Ruth becomes what the parents think that being should be. Laing calls this process "essentialism," the definition of self by parents who have not really looked at or understood the child's emotional reality. Such definition is often blind. When Ruth "is her 'real' self, that is, when she is 'well,' she is not to be seriously interested in writers or art, not to wear coloured stockings . . . not to stay out late." When Ruth associates with strange people, wears unusual clothing, refuses to come home on time, the mother sees an attack coming on. Such behavior indicates sickness, and the mother reacts: Ruth "is told she is being difficult, inconsiderate, disrespectful, thoughtless, when what Ruth is doing is asserting her autonomy and being," which in the political context of the family poses dangerous consequences. Ruth, because of the complex and on-going pressure of this process, is mystified. Placed in an intolerable situation, she becomes "excited and desperate, makes wild accusations that her parents do not want her to live, and runs out of the house in a disheveled state." With an interviewer, Ruth explicitly states her dilemma: "Interviewer: But do you feel you have to agree with what most of the people around you believe? Ruth: Well, if I don't I usually land up in the hospital."[3] Ruth, at twenty-eight, had spent most of the past eight years of her life as an in-patient, hospitalized on six occasions.

All the schizophrenics in Laing's analysis suffer blocked message systems in relation to parental authority. Everything is misunderstood, locked in the endless operations of attribution, projection, denial, and imperviousness. A mother might argue in one form or another "we are alike"; the daughter responds "we are not alike"; the mother might imply "you were always very affectionate"; and the daughter "you never gave me affection," and so it goes.[4] Communication ceases to have meaning; messages find themselves blocked, shorted-out, and trapped in closed, unyielding systems. The parent denies critical impulses in the daughter, and excludes her from equal and legitimate rights. What the daughter wants, the parents do not; thus the action or praxis of individuals desperately seeking autonomy, a refuge from the malfunctioning message system, ends up being defined as "mental illness." At times, Laing suggests, it is logical to withdraw feeling from a milieu where the pressure and demands close off the possibility for autonomy. It makes sense to reject the language and behavior the family regards as productive, useful, and necessary. The self experiences terror in the family situation; and such terror is repeated in the hospital. The only escape lies in blocking out the horror—thus, the odd and sometimes catatonic immobility of schizophrenia, Gregor's bug consciousness, a radical withdrawal.

Families in Laing's accounts subordinate "sickness" to the value orientations defined by power. The daughters lose their rights through behavior that apparently seems to be thoroughly unlike what the families expect; the aberrant response, the refusal to obey, subverts the authority of the parental messages. The consequence is exclusion of that unit creating disturbing noise in the system. No one, particularly not the parents, listens; each message is full of static, and if the daughter listens, the commands are so horrendous that they literally threaten her being. The messages appear so unreasonable that obedience becomes a form of torment and schizophrenia, a desperately forged escape. It is as if the family unconsciously, with the best intentions, moves to appropriate the being or autonomy of the daughter. The appropriation of self exercised by familial authority leaves the daughter without any freedom; she becomes trapped—by the parents, by the diagnoses, by the labels, and, ultimately, by the hospital.

These processes, happening to the disobedient self, indicate an operation deriving from what might be called "psychic capital," a constraint in the form of value as powerful in relation to behavior as the control of economic capital is in terms of labor and the nature of production.

Psychic capital, the manipulation of socially dependent message systems, lies with the family, in the case of Kafka, and in Laing, with the parents. Possessing psychic capital means that the family controls power and regulates the exchange of information and the value patterns determining how the members of the family perceive themselves. Psychic capital exercises a tremendous influence on the ego; it imposes meaning, structures, perceptual systems, and generally defines how the family acts, communicates, and behaves in distinct social and economic situations.

Psychic capital is stored up by the parents; and return on the capital appears in the family through such mechanisms as love, approval, praise, reward, and so on. Psychic capital punishes when it withholds, when through the agency of the parents the children find themselves tormented by the *lack* of love, approval, tangible reward, and, most important, autonomy. (Economically, such a situation might be equivalent to withholding or decreasing wages.) Gregor, for example, threatens the psychic capital of the Samsa family. His lack of communication, his repudiation of work through the disaster of being a dysfunctional bug, his refusal to cooperate, all represent a threat to power, to the defining prerogatives of the parents' control of psychic capital. Gregor's interruption of how that psychic capital operates, his implicit repudiation of its terms and constraints, is as serious and potentially damaging as the revolutionary proletariat's position in relation to economic capital: both, through praxis, repudiate the legitimacy of a dominant structure of power and a dominant pattern of product distribution.

The Erosion of the Ego and the Withdrawal
from Established Message Systems

Clinically, Gregor wakes up insane; the metamorphosis is total, irreversible, what psychiatrists might call "advanced" or hebephrenic." It is a descent into primitive fear, terror, an existential "no exit." Initially Kafka draws out some of Gregor's fantasies as evidence for his inference that the political relationships drove Gregor mad. These fantasies suggest repressed, rebellious impulses, aggressive intentions and wishes never brought to any conclusion. For example, Gregor muses that if it were not for his parents' debts, he long ago would have told his boss "exactly what I think of him." Survival, however, forces Gregor to accept his boss's authority, and to define his life in terms of the firm's expectations. Gregor chafes against authority, but the fantasies lack a public; he will knock his boss "endways from the desk"; he will escape from the trapped situation: "Well, there's still hope; once I've saved enough money to pay back my parents' debt to him [the boss] . . . I'll do it without fail. I'll cut myself completely loose then."[5] But it is too late and it never happens. Chained to the complex interweaving of malevolent authority figures and his own internal fear, Gregor's world disintegrates. The forces arrayed against his autonomy possess too much power; all sensation that Gregor receives from his family appears through torment and victimization.

Gregor adapts to his internality and learns how to live as an outcast, a pariah. Defined both by his desperation and the horror generated by the family, Gregor slowly moves toward death. The family acts as a kind of collective executioner. The Samsa family (again like Laing's families) refuses to see its own behavior as vicious; it is Gregor who exhibits the vicious qualities, who needs to be hidden, who is fed garbage. In breaking routine, in forcing the family to react to his situation, Gregor now becomes noticed (as opposed to his being tacitly accepted prior to the metamorphosis), *but noticed as an enemy*. Now the family accords him recognition, but it is an attention focused on a hostile Other: the weird, bizarre bug person is seen as an enemy to the financial expectations, social status, and political rules of the

Samsa family system. Gregor, having lost any rights to the human community, becomes expendable; and the family quickly decides to forget Gregor as a real, historical presence. The son is dead; what remains is the horrible reminder of *something*—but the family will not look at that something in terms of themselves. They reject responsibility by giving Gregor over to the animals; in their minds, not only is he a bug, but he deserves to be one. With their historical son dead, the Samsa family finds itself free to hate the substitute. Gregor, transformed into a bug, breaks with the tacit rules and arrangements that provided harmony and compliance within the Samsa family. From the standpoint of the family such a repudiation takes on criminal, evil, and radical qualities.

Laing argues that the family's tacit regulations (the laws of psychic capital) are ineffectual unless cooperation keeps the family actively involved in information exchange. Everything works as long as each unit receives a return—or thinks that it receives a return. Much can be tolerated, if it is believed that the transactions yield dividends. The entire process suggests a "transpersonal system of collusion whereby we comply with the others and they comply with us." Such collusion falters when the system breaks down because of entropy, when one of its units stops believing in reasonable yields and begins to relate to that information system in hostile and uncooperative forms (e.g., Gregor's appearance as a bug). Entropy, once it does intrude in the system, forces the family to reject the offending unit. The conscious terms of the investment—"I must collude with their denial and collusion, and they must collude with mine"[6]—disintegrate when one of the units suddenly becomes psychically sick.

Schizophrenic dissociation may follow a feeling on the part of the self that the message system's collusion represents such a horrendous fraud, that it becomes intolerable to live within that system. And the collusion falls apart when psychic capital ceases to regulate communication and feeling within the family. The affected member refuses to listen (and obey) and therefore functionally removes the self from an alliance with those operations that, hitherto, kept the family intact. Voluntary submission to the rules—implied and tacit consent—now transforms into behavioral aberrations that appear to lack any regard for the rules. Where before psychic capital fulfilled feelings of security, compliance, and need, now the dissociated self through its behavior and silence refuses to participate in the fraudulent exchange that made the family seem, at one time, a good, secure, and loving place.

Laing argues that "the 'deeper' social laws are implanted, the more 'hardprogrammed' or 'pickled' into us, the more like 'natural laws' they come to appear to us to be." Violating such programs, denying social necessity, moving beyond the control of the reality or performance principle, provokes a form of psychic terror—since the self is running from a demanding social Other that through its regulations and power seeks to constrain any movement toward autonomy. "Indeed if someone breaks such a 'deeply' implanted social law, we are inclined to say that he is 'unnatural.' "[7] For the family, then, the schizophrenic self, by breaking the rules, also commits an affront against the order of nature; such abnormality cannot be expected to assert any claim to rights. In a Laingian sense, Gregor had been "outlawed and excommunicated"; yet he still maintained an existence, but an existence whose relationship to sociality ceases and whose withdrawal into the archaic terror of a grotesque insect induces an endless terror.

Schizophrenia, the literature generally agrees, erodes social logic; the individual, through regressive movements, becomes increasingly lost to social forms of communication, to historically learned message systems. The self withdraws to a "primary process" universe filled with bizarre and unusual representations (phantasms, dreams, images, and hallucinations). Throughout the regression, the individual suffers a paralysis in interpersonal communication; with malfunctioning message systems, not very much flows between the schizophrenic self and the normal or habitual external world. Everything becomes difficult; what the normal ego might regard as trivial, for the schizophrenic presents innumerable obstacles. The sounds of the schizophrenic often are unintelligible to parents, doctors, friends, and work associates. What is observed seems incomprehensible, a shadow of the former self; the family expresses horror at what they see, at the state of the schizophrenic's condition (an example of this horror can be seen in the reaction of Gregor's parents when they discover his metamorphosis).

Like the withdrawn schizophrenic, Gregor performs no useful or interpersonal function; he has no social utility, no price and therefore no value. Discarded like the hebephrenic in the back wards of the asylum, Gregor's life lacks any significance, and his symptoms appear to correspond quite accurately with what normal families see in those siblings that have withdrawn and forsaken the family's political conception of rule. The callousness with which the family rejects Gregor mirrors a more extensive social pathology that willingly discards those individuals who because of psychological incapacity no longer perform socially useful skills or functions. We hide the schizophrenic self much in the same way the Samsa family hides Gregor. We refuse to acknowledge responsibility for communication failures that push individuals into schizophrenia; we disguise the recognition that the structures of normal communication may brutalize consciousness.

Gregor's death finally releases the family from the embarrassment of madness. Struck by an apple thrown by his father, Gregor rapidly loses strength and the will to live; invisible in his room, totally collapsed, Gregor dies. With Gregor's death, however, the family becomes joyful; the system is energized and everyone seems to prosper. With the absolute exclusion of the madness afflicting their family system, with its absence assured, the family celebrates. It suffers no remorse, shows no conscience and remains totally blind to its role in driving Gregor mad. The Samsas enter the world, resume their social function, and make economic connections. With the family's conception of political justice no longer threatened, their prospects look good. Gregor even ceases to be a memory. I should like here to quote at length, if only to show the grotesque way Kafka resolves the metamorphosis.

Leaning comfortably back in their seats they [the family] canvassed their prospects for the future, and it appeared on closer inspection that these were not at all bad, for the jobs they had got, which so far they had never really discussed with each other, were all three admirable and likely to lead to better things later on. The greatest immediate improvement in their condition would of course arise from moving to another house; they wanted to take a smaller and cheaper but also better situated and more easily run apartment than the one they had, which Gregor had selected. While they were thus conversing, it struck both Mr. and Mrs. Samsa, almost at the same moment, as they became aware of their daughter's increasing vivacity, that in spite of all the sorrow of recent times, which had made her cheeks pale, she had bloomed into a pretty girl with a good figure. They grew quieter and half unconsciously exchanged glances of complete agreement, having come to the conclusion that it would soon be time to find a good husband for her. And it was like a confirmation of their new dreams and excellent intentions that at the end of their journey their daughter sprang to her feet first and stretched her young body.[8]

Laing's parents do not seem so overtly cruel, but the structure of exclusion provokes similar consequences. Kafka has Gregor thrown into the garbage heap; Laing's schizophrenics suffer through neglect in mental institutions and hospitals. It is there that the offending self is eliminated psychically from the family process, from any presence in a social or political context, and from society's patterns of communication and reflection, which the schizophrenic self embarrasses. For Laing, the implications of such a system of exclusion, what he calls the *"normal social* lobotomy," point toward a depravity affecting everyone, the entire social system. In "The Metamorphosis," the parents refuse to dispose of Gregor's body and thus acknowledge their complicity. In real life parents delegate to doctors and other agencies of the state the responsibility for dealing with their sick child. In each instance, the schizophrenic self, because of its madness, becomes a being lying outside the human community.

The Politics of Love and the Hard Currency of Obedience

Political systems regulate the exchange of commodities; in an analogous fashion families regulate (1) the transfers of love, (2) the conditions governing the transfers, and (3) the approach to outcomes generated by the transfers. Love is hard cash; it is real. It initiates our first experiences of competition; it induces jealousy, rage, and fright. It is limited and precious, and it is rarely bountiful. To receive some of the cash requires immense struggle and often bitter disappointment. In the family we receive instruction in how to deal with this scarce commodity, how to evaluate it, measure its impact, and arrive at a judgment of its worth in terms of price. Love has the power to teach us blackmail, extortion, manipulation, and deceit. Love demands such operations; love, then, is not pure. It is surrounded by a cash nexus; it produces payoffs, and in its social form, particularly within families, it is not mystical. Love controls emotional profit; and the control of love means the control of power.

Love attains the status of a precious commodity; it makes us feel good, bad, beautiful, ugly, desired, rejected, envious, and complacent. Regulating this precious commodity takes on political significance in the family. Implicitly, certain behaviors are understood to be good and therefore deserving of love/cash. Parents through various means enunciate the terms under which love will be distributed; the entire family learns what cues in the form of obedience, conformity, the expectations of the Other, produce the desired payoff. A whole set of psychic operations are internalized, with the single aim of accruing to the self the limited capital of love/cash. Yet love demands conditions; investment capital is not freely given; and to gain love it is vital to give something back. For Laing this collusion is the trap; and its consequences for those who refuse the collusion may be disastrous.

In the family, those sources controlling the love/cash capital generally possess power; this may not always be true but the equation of love and power holds where the psychological goods are doled out according to how each unit conforms to what the familial authority decrees as appropriate (the paradigmatic behavior for Kafka and Laing). When a self feels as if that love is not coming, it begins to question its own values; and the withholding of love creates painful sensations, feelings, and thoughts. For the victim it means a lack of power (and notice) within the family, and a corresponding sense of desperation, brought about in large measure by the sanction of withholding the love/cash reward (the sign of approval).

The dialectic between love and power structures intrafamilial transactions. Whoever possesses the power (and thereby controls the love/cash capital) comes to be accepted as the authority, as the giver of laws and rules. An understanding of this system is generated in the ego as early as infancy. Love degenerates into a political event, into a competition for commodities, a claim for recognition that later becomes a claim for rights within the family. Its withdrawal is as punishing and devastating as the withdrawal of any precious commodity. The withdrawal of love, its implied threats, and the feelings induced in the victim, punish through fear. Experiencing that withdrawal means seeing the self as loose, feeling uncertainty, contingency, and terror. Love may not be withdrawn consciously; but the schizophrenic person understands when love becomes command, when it ceases to be a freely given activity of caring, when it degenerates into a demand for some kind of return impossible to give. The family, of course, sees schizophrenic behavior as illogical and entropic; it refuses to understand and still maintains that it loves the victim. What the schizophrenic perceives is something entirely different; the self feels the proffered love as hostile, as a trap, as a communication synapse, as any number of things. The self, then, builds elaborate defenses against the horrors of what such withdrawal signifies. The complex and often tormented internality of schizophrenia becomes a defense against the withdrawal of love.

For the person experiencing such a desolate hopelessness, the outcome can hardly be encouraging. Even though the parents may try to show or demonstrate love (by, for example, committing the person to a mental institution), the peculiar translucency of certain stages in the schizophrenic process sees through these illusions and falsifications. As with the Samsas, the parent figure becomes the tormentor, the love a horrible set of demands, and the conditions, intolerable to accept. It is impossible for the schizophrenic person to operate according to the laws and commands of psychic capital. The self finds it difficult to compete in the love/cash nexus, in the marketplace of the family. Schizophrenic dissociation constitutes a powerful critique of the extent to which psychic capital reinforces the love/cash transaction; and schizophrenia explodes all the expectations, all the laws of the marketplace. Its process has little to do with the rationality of exchange and the economics of psychic capital. Love for both Kafka and Laing initiates processes that ultimately deplete the psyche of its ability to organize, to communicate with others external to the self, and to maintain any relationship with an Other that is neither threatening nor false. Love, power, rules, and violence intertwine in these accounts; and the commodity of love induces horrendous transformations in character.

Conclusion: The Family and Its Political Environment

The act of withdrawal (schizophrenic dissociation) described by Kafka and Laing, is resented, misunderstood, and twisted by the family. The disintegration of the ego becomes a thoroughly incomprehensible event. It has no analogue in rational behavior; it brings no benefits, no dividends, credits, or approval. It seems to be completely irrational (e.g., "Why should my daughter act like this?"). Yet it is an action that sacrifices a great deal—joy, happiness, security, complacency, wealth, power, domination, and authority. The schizophrenic self unconsciously relinquishes those normal operations generally associated with the ego. It refuses any psychological contact with routine or habitual communication systems. It engages in an activity that severs communication with the parent society, thoroughly resists is rules and regulations, denies its socialization patterns, and withdraws from its economically determined functions. The schizophrenic psyche moves beyond the time of normality, lacks any social community or ideology, shows no interest in social or economic issues, and acts because of the cumulative impact of dissonant and frustrating experience on the ego.

It is clear that the schizophrenic is not equivalent to a political rebel; but the behavior of schizophrenia *implies* certain severances or dissociations that constitute a powerful *symbolic* statement about morbid psychological and cultural realities. The schizophrenic repudiates a given society, criticizes (through behavior) its values and communication patterns, and, most important, refuses to legitimize or accept laws governing the conditions of exchange and distribution— whether the commodity be concrete goods (like wages) or love. Schizophrenia is an autistic, tragic, and melancholy form of withdrawal. Yet in many ways it is an act of repudiation—unorganized and chaotic but nonetheless representing a denial, a refusal. In that sense, schizophrenia is more than just a sickness, or an illness. Gregor Samsa and Laing's case studies are more than just ill; they all seem to be conveying a message. It is society that refuses to listen.

Both Kafka and Laing find that we are plagued, defined, and oppressed by bad experience coming from intimidating or implosive others. In certain situations the ego finds itself defenseless in the sense that the Other exercises such an overwhelming hold on consciousness that it is impossible to escape. Its presence is always there; we are always confronting the bad. The self, struggling to survive, mirrors its existence in those situations conditioned by bad others and things. And ultimately with the defenses of the ego shattered, the bad invades the self, and the self comes to conceive of its being as bad and worthless. The process tormented Gregor Samsa and he found himself discarded by an insensitive family who refused to listen to the pleas of his madness. Kafka gives us a parable; such consequences, as Laing suggests, happen in real life and real politics.

Both the case studies and Gregor Samsa's delusional internality show family transactions that reflect skewed communication systems, frustration, anxiety, hatred, denial, and terror—a whole set of psychological operations characteristic of political life. Further, both argue that the patterns we learn in families derive from perverse relationships established with authority figures, from psychological maneuvers like complicity and collusion, from repressed or forgotten happenings that may have been instrumental in the formation of character.

It is in the family, both argue, that we initially learn a sense of what justice means or signifies. It is there that we learn political bad habits, discovering that politics is not about principle but about gain. Political exchange involves not questions of the common good but how the particular unit in the family might survive or further its own specific, local interests. We learn that the most effective politics is often that which employs techniques of coercion, blackmail, and psychological violence. The dismal state of political life begins in the family; bad politics does not just happen; it is not the consequence of a few misguided individuals nor a function of a small clique of the perverse whose cunning, skill, and graft propel them into positions of domination. Bad politics arises from a culture, from a history, from values, attitudes, and feelings generated at all levels of society. It capitalizes on a generalized fear of the Other, on mass social needs for identification with a powerful authority figure.

Surviving the early socializing experience of the family is an act of political survival. We learn how to be survivors in the family; we internalize the consciousness of how to manipulate the rules to our own advantage. We understand what it means to suffer victimization. We strategically master the techniques of avoidance (if we are lucky enough) and with that mastery develop the complex set of defenses that allows us to move into adulthood without serious regressive problems. We learn what not to do, how to predict the moves of the Other, and, depending on how well we have internalized these lessons, we construct barriers against the power intrusions of others and the persistent hostility in modern social life. Victims in this process emerge later on as statistics, cared for by a whole range of social agents and agencies: psychoanalysts, psychotherapists, medical technicians, pharmaceutical companies, mental institutions, asylums, hospitals, sanitaria, and so on. The business of mental illness and the structure of the family reinforce each other.

A family is a political mechanism for the control of energy, the distribution of a scarce commodity (love), and the socialization of instinct. The family is governed primarily through certain political judgments that affect everyone associated with its systemic operation and its patterns of commodity distribution. The given quantity of love, however, has limits; and it is distributed with a great deal of calculation. Love, then, within the family is limited and competition for it is intense. Families become caught up in this competition; and occasionally the governing authority finds itself so trapped by its perception of right and proper that it refuses to accept deviation as legitimate. Unusual behavior indicates dysfunction, a sickness, an unwillingness to accept the tacit and unconscious rules, socialized into the family consciousness and its values. Parental authority sees trouble and a whole set of reactions begins which in some instances may provoke the family to commit one of its members to a mental institution.

What a sick or dysfunctional unit shows through behavior may be so incomprehensible to the family that its only recourse lies in denying that unit any rights, any claim to autonomy. To see sickness means to deprive of rights; for the sick self becomes incapable of making rational or prudent decisions. Similarly in a political community, the violation of tacit assumptions, rules, and laws determining interpersonal transactions and accepted, historical values initiates a series of responses that may place the offending group or persons in an unfavorable position. It is the same in the family. Rebellion signifies sickness; therefore all spontaneous action takes on disruptive and unsettling attributes. The rules of the family, like those of a political system, feel danger and threat in unpredictable and nonroutinized behavior.

"Thank Heaven for Little Girls": The Dialectics of Development

✿ *Jean Bethke Elshtain*

The question is simply put: How is it that persons and their social contexts may be said to be related to one another? Unfortunately, it is not so simply answered. But there is an obvious place to begin such an inquiry, namely, with the self-evident proposition that we are all human beings. Surprisingly, many political scientists seem to forget that their subject matters are neither automata, nor particles of matter, nor faceless collections of medians and averages labeled "voters," "nonvoters," "apathetic masses," or "working-class authoritarians." To think of human subjects as particles or faceless aggregates is undoubtedly handy for a number of reasons. Indeed, this is part of the problem. The practitioners of a mechanistic or abstract political science can more easily avoid confronting the implications of their research if their assumptions and methods are abstracted from what it means to be human.[1]

A behaviorist starting point ill-equips the political scientist to ask—let alone answer—those questions that emerge from the complexities of a shared social existence, questions that make some necessary reference to human wants, needs, and purposes. For example: political scientists, for the most part, have not thought seriously about the relationship of women and children to politics. Children and women are presumed to inhabit the "private" sphere of the family. Politics, on the other hand, is one of several public spaces open to men. Men do participate in families, to be sure, but, unlike women, they are not defined by such participation.[2] At the risk of perching on the end of what may be an insubstantial limb, I will hazard a few additional hunches as to why children are largely invisible in political analyses.

Children serve as rather unpleasant reminders of our own mortality and they are living proof of male involvement with and dependence upon women—whom many men regard as necessary but somewhat inferior human beings. Children also speak to us of our own pasts and intimate that there may still be a "child" who lives in each of us. Finally, children can be quite irritating. They have a rather nasty habit of asking one what the *purpose* of something is: "Why are you *doing* this? What is it *for*? What does it *mean*?" These are questions the practitioners of behaviorism cannot answer except in terms that are transparently inadequate.

For many reasons, then, children have been the companions of women in the closet of political science. A few short years ago women began to set up such a clamor that a few were released from this closet. To the surprise (if not the indignation) of their male colleagues they have persisted in their noisy habits and give no sign of shutting up in the near future. Children remain, with few exceptions, both silent and invisible—relegated to a conceptual space (which is presumed to reflect social reality) that has been declared apolitical. The political study of childhood remains in its infancy.

My focus in this essay will be on children, with specific attention to female children. I shall not discuss in any explicit fashion the cognitive and psychosexual development of children following the theories of Piaget and Freud respectively. I assume that children are sexual beings and that their minds are the locus for complex, dynamic, interrelated conscious and unconscious processes of which cognition is one important dimension. I agree with Freud that childhood is, even in the "best" of families, a period characterized as much by Sturm und Drang as bliss and innocence.[3]

The term I will use to explore the experience of growing up female is "socialization."[4] It is not a term I find particularly compelling. It conjures up notions of "conformism" and "adjustment" (preferably uncritical adjustment for mainstream defenders of the status quo). But socialization—more specifically, "political socialization"—is the accepted verbal coin-of-the-realm, so I will stick with it. But I must note that I differentiate between "socialization," understood as "learning to conform to the ways of one's group or society" so that these ways become, as it were, "second nature," and the notion of "sociality."

The concept of human sociality holds that human beings are social creatures from birth.[5] In this century the most important theoretician of the social construction of human beings was Freud who, in his theoretical writings, set out to determine how people became the people they are; how the human mind is a social entity; and how the personal life histories of people inexorably intersect with, and are partially determined by, a particular cultural heritage.[6] I draw Freud into the discussion because I share his logic—a dialectical logic that refuses to capitulate to the demands of a logic of "either/or." I also reject that positivist epistemology, of which behaviorism is one variant, which celebrates "facts" even as it trivializes "values" to the level of "mere opinions," "feelings," or "tastes."

Unlike those behaviorists who turn their attention to the relationship between children and politics and limited as they are by the prior assumptions they bring to inquiry, pay persistent attention only to "externals," or to what they choose to call "behaviors." Freud, instead, apprises us that the innermost interstices of the human mind are formed through a dynamic, internal relationship with others with whom one shares a culture and a polity. The reciprocity between political and social movements and events and the activities of "everyday life" cannot be overemphasized. But a problem remains. We can agree that various spheres or areas of life cannot be bracketed off, or split rigidly from others. But unless we acquire a clearer, sharper picture of this relationship, we may be left with a dim awareness and an unanalyzable muddle because "everything is related to everything else."

In order to defend a dialectical inquiry I will, first, examine (in an admittedly schematic fashion) several alternative methods that have been deployed to explore my original question. The first of these is methodological individualism. A methodological individualist insists that society is "nothing but" the totality of individuals writ large. All explanations of complex phenomena that do not wind up, ultimately, as statements of facts about individuals are rejected as false. The position is best summarized by the words: "nothing but. . . ." Society is "nothing but" the totality of its isolated particulars. Civilization is "nothing but" a "new masculine behavioral mode, i.e., a sex-linked phenomenon. . . . History knows of no female civilizations."[7] All explanations of political life must and can be reduced to statements about individuals. (Those analysts indebted to physiological or ethological determinism go even further and discover the explanation of social life in hormones or primitive biograms.)

A second approach insists that "the system" as a reified, overweening presence is *all*. The imperatives of the system are ramified into all lesser institutions or units of the society. The nature of the system gives these subunits (and persons) their meaning. A systemic approach has the advantage of avoiding reductionism, but it replaces the methodological individualist's focus on particulars with an overweening determinism.

Finally, there is the functionalist approach. For functionalists all elements in a social system, including politics, are linked together in necessary harmony. The functionalist model features a system in equilibrium. All its units are tied together in a relationship of interdependence. The family, for example, is linked "functionally" to the total order in a hierarchical relationship. Both family structure and function are largely determined by the "needs" of the macroorder. American functionalism as an explanatory theory is associated with the name of Talcott Parsons whose rather dense works are the functionalist equivalent of *Das Kapital*.[8]

When functionalism is represented schematically it is usually portrayed as a number of boxes said to be in a "functional relationship" to one another. The smaller boxes, including the family, are "subsystems." Each box is connected to others by means of a line or an arrow. But the line stops at the outer perimeter of the box, that is, the boxes are linked externally. Moreover, the boxes are empty—without content. There is, after all, no need to supply content as this is *given* by the implicit teleology that underlies functionalist assumptions.

We are told, for example, that some institution performs a particular function in a given society. A connection between that institution and the society is assumed. But functionalism cannot tell us *why* some institutions exist rather than others. Why, for example, couldn't "banks" serve the function assigned to families, namely, "nurturant socialization"? There are many reasons, the reader must cavil. Indeed, there are, but we must go outside the conceptual boundaries of a strict functionalist model to discover them. A functionalist response to the question would be lodged in the presumption that the society in question, acting as an irresistible force, pulls the institution in question along without the rude incursion of politics, force, power, manipulation, or coercion. The formulation is a bit too neat—and empty—to serve us in an attempt to probe beneath the surface as we think about female children within families and societies. Indeed, if we followed Parsons on this issue we would rest content with the image of an entity rather grandiloquently termed the "Normal American Family" fixed before our eyes.[9] This ideal typical family features (necessarily) a male instrumental-adaptive father and a female nurturant-expressive mother, a rigid role division which stabilizes the family and "serves the ends" of the total system.

A dialectical approach provides neither easy answers nor neat diagrams, but it does help us to *understand* and to *interpret* the connections between people and politics. What does this mean in terms of my stated intent to explore briefly the dynamics of female socialization? It means, first, that we avoid the distortion that occurs if women, as adults or children, are abstracted from their social relationships and historic milieu so that they can be held up and examined under the bright glare of "scientific objectivity." As I pointed out in an earlier article that was addressed to the questions raised by the failure of the American suffrage movement: "They [the Suffragists] did not see through the fact that the ideal of 'woman' which they celebrated *included* the ideal of 'man' which they denigrated, that these concepts were necessarily connected. The controlling images of 'woman' and 'man,' in turn, were linked to a larger matrix, a social structure within which these relations made sense."[10]

Peter Winch, Stuart Hampshire, and Alasdair MacIntyre, among others, have pointed out that the idea we form of an object includes the idea of connections between it and other objects.[11] The relations between ideas are internal relations, just as social structures and arrangements, a political economy, a history, and a grammar of moral and political discourse are internally related. Meaning is tied to contrasts and to opposites within a language system. Change in any one of the associated ideas in a system of meaning necessarily ramifies into others. As I discuss female socialization, therefore, it is with the recognition that this process is inseparable from, and internally related to, the socialization of their male counterparts.

The human infant is a psychosexual being implicated in a dynamic interrelationship with his or her culture. Throughout infancy the child learns to speak and to apprehend the meaning of a language; indeed, language is "a set of social relationships in which my own intentions are continually understood and fulfilled by others and in which I encounter their corresponding intentions."[12] Erik H. Erikson's developmental model of the human life cycle helps to clarify some of the differences between male and female socialization—differences that feed upon one another.

Although Erikson himself rarely confronts the ways in which the dynamics of development diverge for the sexes, his work is suggestive because it delineates in a cogent manner what might be termed a paradigm of human development that males alone can fully share. Erikson's eight-stage life cycle progresses through old age. I will explore only the first five stages. A word of warning, however, first: Erikson's theory of development is sometimes rather misleadingly represented (by Erikson himself) as a grid pattern with vertical and horizontal lines that bisect one another to create a diagram within which one builds from the "lowest" stage to the "highest."[13] The schematic form distorts his insistence that each stage overlaps the others, that is, that development is a gradual process during which certain modalities tend to predominate at different points. Movement from stage to stage is not analogous to climbing a stairway one stair at a time and methodically destroying and removing each stair as one moves to the next. The relationship between stages is a dynamic one.

Precisely *because* children are social creatures who cannot isolate themselves from others and whose minds are shaped by the "outside" social world, the development of a child may either support the emergence of trust, autonomy, a sense of initiative, a conviction of inner integrity and worth and, ultimately, an identity perceived as worthy, or thrust a child instead into lingering mistrust, shame, doubt, guilt, inferiority, isolation, and, ultimately, stagnation and despair.

What, specifically, can be said about the dialectics of female development? Erikson's first stage of development, during which an infant moves toward the modalities of either ontological trust or mistrust, is bound up with the mother's attitude toward her child.[14] The subtle and delicate kinetics of child handling may reflect, in ways that are not immediately obvious, the differential value and respect accorded men and women in modern society. A mother's reactive attitudes toward her male and female infants will be touched in powerful ways by the social arrangements of a society characterized by sex inequality.

In the second stage of development (up to about age four), a child begins to evolve a sense of autonomy and self-certainty or, instead, becomes bogged down in patterns of shame, doubt, and embarrassed self-consciousness. The parents' own sense of autonomy or shame is obviously crucial to the child. It is more difficult for a child to achieve dignity in a milieu in which, as Erikson puts it, parents are frustrated in marriage, work, and citizenship.[15] An unjust social order reverberates through the walls of our private havens. The female child during this period increasingly "picks up cues" from parents, as praise and punishment are differentially accorded to male and female children.

Boys already have a wider sphere for action, and demands for decorous and proper behavior fall disproportionately on girls.

With the dynamics of the third and fourth stages, differential sex socialization is both easier to see and more explicitly linked with the imperatives of the social system. The child not only grows *up*, but grows *into* his or her sociohistoric milieu, into those institutions and traditions that either nourish developing capacities and delimit fears, or starve those capacities and engender anxiety. The third stage is one of emergent initiative and of role experimentation. The child pretends what kind of person he or she may become. Young boys have a wide range within which they can pretend. The social order provides what might rather inelegantly be termed a syntonic medium for his development. Little girls, however, experience discontinuities, conflicts, ambiguities, and ambivalence as they encounter sex-appropriate games, toys, and activities. Girls perceive, quite accurately, that boys have more fun because they are not only allowed but encouraged to move about more freely, to run, cavort, and shout.[16] "Ladylike" behavior, however, is the preferred social norm for young women. The social medium for girls, then, has sharp breaks, roads that turn back upon themselves, and deep valleys that girls crawl out of with increasing difficulty.

Erikson links the third development stage or moment to the "intrusive mode." Intrusion is implicated in the emergence of a sense of initiative as the child gains motor mastery via intrusion into space by running and bounding, into unknown situations by curiosity, into the ears of others by loud shouting, and into the bodies of others by physical attack.[17] The one exclusively female dimension of the intrusive mode is the thought of the phallus intruding the female body and this is linked not so much to initiative and mastery as to fear and, perhaps, guilt.

The emergence of a sense of industry (or inferiority) is the task of Erikson's fourth developmental stage. A disjuncture between the young girl's sense of herself as a female, and the manner in which this femaleness relegates her to an inferior status within the boundaries of a social system that reserves its highest rewards and accords its most effusive respect to male achievers, becomes increasingly clear. The discrepancy between being encouraged to do well in school, coupled with the insistence that she will grow up to be a wife and mother someday, pushes a girl into that confusion, doubt, and ambivalence that may become a permanent insistence on her own incompetence and lack of worth. When this occurs, it must not be seen solely as an idiosyncrasy peculiar to a particular child. Her confusion reflects as well an underlying cultural imperative—it is the result of structural sex inequality and the internalized force of those conflicting ideologies I will explore. The more vulnerable the individual child, the less likely that she will be able to live with a mounting ambivalence.

Erikson's fifth stage is that developmental space in which the teen-ager and young adult achieves a relatively clear sense of "who I am," an identity grounded in the assurance of inner continuity and integrity, or in which confusion, insecurity, and perception of worthlessness predominate and harden. Identity is not a thing possessed. The concept must not be rigidified. Rather, identity is that sense of self dependent upon, and emerging from, the psychosocial links between a person and his or her culture.[18] Futility, inhibition, self-doubt, and autistic isolation are symptomatic of identity confusion. But such confusion is never merely an individual phenomenon. The social world is implicated in the distress and misery and sense of hopelessness.

A female child enters Erikson's fifth stage having already been bombarded by contradictory imperatives. It is difficult for her to act meaningfully, for if she acts in the manner she perceives is true to herself she may find that her own idea of self is strikingly at odds with the expectations of others. She is confused and deterred by the contradiction between being female and her socially acquired needs to achieve and to excel. Female identity formation is prejudiced by what a woman *cannot* be or become; thus, for many young women, the transition to work experimentation, mastery of worthwhile tasks, and a grounded sense of self is never made. If she decides to be a female, to snuggle down into a ready-made ascriptive blanket and to practice the art of being pleasing, unstintingly devoted, down-to-earth, apolitical, disinterested in politics and power, incapable of abstractions, and warm—all those traits that are supposed to be natural—she learns that the very society that would censure her refusal to be "natural" will accord her no meaningful recognition when she is.[19] She must live in a psychosocial double-bind.

There are fewer more telling indictments of modern society than the lifelong suffering, anguish, incapacity to act in a manner free from shame, doubt, guilt, and destructive repetition of the past that it imposes upon a major portion of its members, male *and* female (though female bears the brunt of it) from the moment of birth. No ego is an island to itself.[20] Human strength, from one interconnected stage to the next, is dependent "upon a network of mutual influences. . . ."[21] A desperate longing for the less-troubled past, which usually takes the form of a nostalgic re-creation of girlhood, precludes meaningful action in the present.

The socialization of children, their entrance into the adult community, is not a semiautomatic process: a child is born and a child grows up. Children do indeed grow older and taller, but *human development*, as Erikson outlines it, cannot be taken for granted as a process that is "virtually inevitable barring any but the most traumatic insults to the individual's personality."[22] Human development is intertwined with its bio-social-historic matrix. What goes on within that human space, in all of its complex dimensions, can arrest, fix, foreclose, and retard irreversibly the cognitive and psychosocial growth of human beings.

What purposes are served by differential socialization, that socially constituted repetition of processes that seem to confuse (at best) young women? There is a point to it, certainly, but to say this is *not* to agree with the vague notion that men in toto are the agents designated to implement a vast sexist master plot that has the victimization of women as its raison d'être. There doesn't have to be a plot. All there has to be is a set of social structures and arrangements that disproportionately distribute burdens and benefits. Those who are most favored will always wish to protect the mechanisms that enabled them to achieve their superior status. But this is only a part of the story. Certain psychological needs (socially acquired and reinforced, not somehow innate!) to have power over another are at stake as well. There are many ways to have power over others. Power ranges widely over the entire spectrum of social relationships. Relationships of dominance and submission do not have to be explicit, or consciously intended, or tied to an official position of some kind. This makes it more difficult for persons who feel somehow violated, cheated, put-upon, short-changed, and not taken seriously, to determine what is going on, and where, and who is responsible for what.

The complexities of the question of power cannot be unraveled here.[23] But one set of social relationships—namely, the family—deserves particular scrutiny from the presumptions of a perspective at odds with the behaviorist and functionalist models that predominate in contemporary political science. If we focus on "the family" as a subsystem of a greater system, or as a congeries of related persons who can be abstracted out and studied by surveys, the dynamic interior texture of family life will remain opaque and inaccessible to us. Yet the family is the locus of our most intimate, intense, and meaningful human relationships, attitudes, and loyalties. It is the tumultuous social space within which the majority of little girls learn to adjust to their ascribed status as one aspect of their socialization, a status that comes into direct conflict with another dimension of socialization in America, namely, the induction of all children (to a greater or lesser extent) into our driven, competitive, individualistic culture. The family is a contradictory institution; it serves several masters.

Max Horkheimer observed that "force in its naked form is in no way sufficient to explain why a dominated class so long endures the yoke; it is especially insufficient in periods when the economic apparatus is ripe for a better system of production, the culture is in dissolution, and the property relations and existing forms of life in general overtly become a fetter to social forces." To understand this perplexing phenomenon, Horkheimer continued, we must try to understand the "psychic composition of men in various social groups."[24] The family is crucial for it is the most important "agent of education" concerned with the "reproduction of human character." Psychoanalytic theory has discovered, Horkheimer concludes, "the historical dynamics of society in the microcosm of the monad, as it were, in the mental conflicts of the individual."[25]

It isn't sufficient, therefore, to argue that the predominant forces ranged against sex equality are economic interests intent on profit maximization for whom women comprise a handy unskilled, low-paid reserve labor force; or to insist that some sort of male machismo leads men to fight the inclusion of women in politics; or any of a number of other simplistic answers to Why sex inequality? There are many forces implicated in the persistence of female inequality, and they are related to one another in complex ways. I will conclude this brief overview of a difficult question by exploring one such force, that of *ideology*, from a vantage point that seeks to avoid abstract idealism, on the one hand, and deterministic materialism on the other.

Ideology is a constituent feature of a way of life. Within the framework of social relations and history, ideology is a force that may act as a brake on movements for social change or serve as a catalyst to inspire such change. (It more often performs a conservative or reactionary role for reasons I will outline.) Ideology should not be conceptualized as an evanescent free-floating vapor that hovers above and occasionally descends to exert its influence on human life; nor should one collapse ideology totally into, say, the mode of production that may predominate in a given society. Ideology lies within each of us; it gets reproduced in our intimate social relations. Families and schools are implicated explicitly in the reproduction of inequalitarian social relations. This reproduction, of course, is inseparable from production but is not wholly determined by it.

One of the Wilhelm Reich's provocative additions to psychoanalytic theory, made early in his troubled career, was his insistence that the reproduction of social relations could best be described as "the manner and mode by which ideology is translated in the everyday life and behavior of the individual,"[26] and ideology thus understood had to be taken into account in the articulation of social and political theory and the development of strategies for change.

The internalization of what may be a repressive, even reactionary ideology occurs as the child grows up; in this manner, that ideology is psychically reproduced. We may then find individuals affirming a social order that systematically exploits, demeans, paternalizes, and oppresses them. Marx described in forceful detail the implications of a past that "weighs like a nightmare on the brain of the living."[27]

The family is instrumental in the reproduction of repression, but that is not all it is, for the family is not of a piece. It may (and usually does) contain several contradictory moments that coexist side by side. Thus families may serve as instruments of social authority, and prepare their children to capitulate before it (and their female children to capitulate to the needs, interests, and demands of men), but the family also resists that authority and provides some "protection . . . against social domination." Families partake "of the prevailing inhumanity" but embody as well "the possibility of something else and better" is preserved as well.[28]

To complicate the scenario further, it is necessary to point to the existence of not one but several ideologies reproduced through mediating institutions like families and schools. Erikson would insist that ideology is the social institution that guards, protects, and defends identity. Ideally, perhaps this might be true. But ideology more often twists, distorts, and bewilders the young, leaving them hurt, confused, cynical, and convinced of the irremediable corruption and hypocrisy of the adult world. For young women there is the additional recognition that an ideology of womanhood is expressly geared toward keeping them in their place.

Instead of the single ideology Erikson seems to find,[29] several ideologies are being reproduced in contemporary American society. They cohere and conflict with one another along a range of possibilities. The vagaries of female development—the ambivalence and mental conflicts of growing up female—reveal the historical dynamics of a society, as Horkheimer suggested. The development of the female is intertwined with the three moments of ideology I find within contemporary society. The first is the *ideology of womanhood*. Sex stereotypy and differential socialization are the mechanisms that translate this ideology, via mediating institutions, into the everyday lives of young women. The ideology of womanhood is suffused with constraints to female development, but it is frequently presented as the only path to fulfillment, to a sentimental femininity. The "nature-made woman," is seen as the perfect companion to the "self-made man" whose tough, pragmatic, no-nonsense code is "free choice," "no constraints," and "my life is my own." They are a perfect dialectical match—or, more properly, they *would* be a perfect match were it not for those irritants in the image sustained by the force of alternative ideologies.

The ideology of womanhood interrelates in conflicting and harmonious ways with the second and third ideological moments. The prevailing, explicit *political ideology* has both official and popular variants. The official ideology, for example, taught in civics classes and celebrated in textbooks, holds that America is the land of freedom, equality, justice, and unlimited opportunities for those who will work hard and take advantage of the opportunities that come their way. The rewards for the plucky, hard-working lads who make it are status, honor, and financial affluence. Political office sometimes follows. The socialization of females within America's public schools and within most American families incorporates this ideological moment. A young girl, too, is taught that rewards go to those with merit; that capable individuals can, through their own efforts, gain the prizes the society has to offer.

The official political ideology must not exempt women from this official American mythology for several reasons. First, women will be key figures in the future reproduction of that ideology as they socialize their own children. Second, in a society that sees itself as one in which no group is singled out and handicapped in the race for reward and status, the ideal must be preserved even though it is importantly false or misleading. (Believing in equality of opportunity, persons who fail will place the blame, not on social institutions, but on themselves for not having had what it takes; thus the official ideology buttresses the status quo.)

The official ideology of equal opportunity says nothing about whether individuals will take advantage of their ostensibly equal opportunities and it serves to obscure the constraints that prevent individuals and groups from either seizing opportunities or finding them.[30] The ideology of womanhood serves to "ease the pressure" on the official ideology because it pushes toward the reproduction of "women," those idealized and sentimentalized creatures who are softer, less competitive, and less political and who, therefore, rarely (until recent years) entered the race for high status jobs. Thus the ideology of womanhood masks the fact that women are systematically excluded from the system of rewards and benefits and, in this manner, it shores up the official political ideology at the same time.

Ideology has yet a third variant or moment that intersects with the ideology of womanhood and the official political ideology in complex ways. I term the third ideological moment the *popular ideology,* by which I mean those common-sense, often cynical truisms about politics and social life that help shape the realities of everyday life. The popular ideology, too, both undermines and buttresses the status quo. For example: popular ideology, as a set of "everybody knows," strengthens the forces arrayed against sex equality even as, in a somewhat inchoate fashion, it exposes the worm in the democratic apple; but it remains loyal to the system nonetheless.

The cynicisms of the popular ideology betray a deep sense of wounded pride and personal injury in the guise of surface toughness. "Everybody knows" that rewards are not handed out equitably—it depends on who you know or who you are, not on what you do or what you know. Or "everybody knows" that all politicians are crooks and bums. "Everybody knows" that "rich kids get the breaks" and have a head start in the race for success. Yet this recognition of social injustice rarely gets beyond cynicism and hopeless dismay. And the popular ideology buttresses the official political ideology through the insistence that "everybody knows America is the greatest country in the world," or "everybody knows that we may have our problems but Americans are still richer and better off than anybody," and so on.

The popular ideology denigrates politics and public life in a systematic and unrelenting fashion. Yet that same ideology would *refuse* women access to the public world—worthless though it may be. For "everybody knows," or did until recently, that women are too emotional to handle really important roles in politics. "Everybody knows" that women are too sentimental to make "tough" decisions. Invariably the image of a hysterical female, sobbing loudly, sniffling pitifully, with the prospect of war at hand (this desperate female is often pictured with her trembling finger on the "nuclear button") and she just "doesn't know what to do." These admittedly silly but often resonant stereotypes of women in their popular variants buttress the ideology of womanhood.

Ideology—in all its moments—is implicated in, and reproduced through, our lives from the first. It forms a necessary element in the maintenance of sex inequality. Through its internalization women unwittingly become perpetrators of their own second-class citizenship. The subordination of women emerges, through interiorization of the ideology of womanhood, as one possible dimension within the psyche of each growing female. It helps to shape her understanding of the world and it may act as a deterrent to public action.

One of the first steps women took, as a central feature of feminist awareness, was to break through moribund assumptions that decreed and applauded female frivolousness, pettiness, narrowness of outlook, and repetitive pointlessness of purpose. Although ideology in its womanly and popular moments forms a relatively cohesive whole, the disjuncture between these and the official ideology of democracy and egalitarianism creates those fissures or cracks through which critical consciousness may arise. Unless that consciousness is turned inward as well as outward, that is, unless women look at themselves with the same fervor and commitment they bring to bear in characterizing the policies and actions of others, the ultimate result will not be a restructured society but a reshuffling of personnel. If the "new woman" is not to be the "old man"—a distinct possibility given the ready-made ideology of "free choice" and stalwart independence at hand—they must see themselves as responsible human agents, not victims, and subject themselves to a self-scrutiny that reveals to them their own involvement in patterns of collusion, manipulation, feigned helplessness, all the corrosive effects of that "impersonal poison" Doris Lessing has called "the disease of women in our time." Feminist theory must push women away from "destructive and sentimental idealizations of their 'specialness' " and help them to "recognize that powerless persons are persons denied both responsibility and respect and that those thus deprived have been denied a precious human good which carries with it not simply rights and privileges but duties and obligations to self and others."[31] Women need, if they are to be a radical force, what Erikson has called a "cold self-appraisal in historical terms. . . ."[32] The beginning of that historical self-appraisal lies in our recognition of the hard but inescapable truth that suffering and inequality may sometimes ennoble the spirit—but they more often impoverish and distort it. The distortion begins early and goes deep. So must our analysis and our self-recognition.

Notes

Preface

1. See Talcott Parsons, "Age and Sex in the Social Structure of the United States," in *Selected Studies in Marriage and the Family*, ed. Robert F. Winch and Robert McGinnis, (New York: Henry Holt, 1953), pp. 330–45.
2. Seymour Martin Lipset, *Political Man: The Social Bases of Politics* (Garden City, N.Y.: Doubleday and Co., Anchor Books, 1963).
3. But see R. W. Connell and Murray Goot, "Science and Ideology in American 'Political Socialisation' Research," *Berkeley Journal of Sociology* 17 (1972–73): 165–93, for a discussion of socialization scholars as rather uncritical celebrants of the status quo.
4. Jonathan Yardley, "All in the Family," *Commonweal*, May 11, 1979, pp. 265–66.
5. Norman Jacobsen, *Pride and Solace: The Functions and Limits of Political Theory* (Berkeley: University of California Press, 1978), p. 10.

Introduction

1. Plato, *The Republic*, trans. Allan Bloom (New York: Basic Books, 1968), Book 5./460e-462d (p. 141).
2. Abigail Rosenthal, "Feminism Without Contradictions," *Monist* 57 (1973): 36.
3. Philip E. Slater, *The Glory of Hera* (Boston: Beacon Press, 1968), pp. 3–4, 6, 8. See the very similar views expressed in the feminist treatments by Nancy Chodorow, *The Reproduction of Mothering: Psychoanalysis and the Sociology of Gender* (Berkeley and Los Angeles: University of California Press, 1978), and Dorothy Dinnerstein, *The Mermaid and the Minotaur: Sexual Arrangements and Human Malaise* (New York: Harper and Row, 1976).
4. Robert Filmer, *Patriarcha and Other Political Works*, ed. Peter Laslett (Oxford: Basil Blackwell, 1949).
5. Thomas Hobbes, *Leviathan*, ed. Michael Oakeshott (New York: Collier Books, 1966).

6. Jean-Jacques Rousseau, *On the Social Contract with the Geneva Manuscript and Political Economy*, ed. Roger D. Masters (New York: St. Martin's Press, 1978); Jean-Jacques Rousseau, *The First and Second Discourses*, ed. Roger D. Masters (New York: St. Martin's Press, 1964).

7. Rousseau, *The Social Contract*, p. 47.

8. Ibid., pp. 48, 169.

9. Ibid., 170.

10. But see Rosenthal, "Feminism Without Contradictions," and Jean Bethke Elshtain, *Public Man, Private Woman: Women in Social and Political Thought* (Princeton: Princeton University Press, 1981), chap. 5.

11. Sigmund Freud, *The Complete Psychological Works of Sigmund Freud* (London: Hogarth, 1975), vol 21, *Civilization and Its Discontents*, pp. 57–145.

12. See Hannah Arendt, *The Human Condition* (Chicago: University of Chicago Press, 1973).

13. Dinnerstein, *Mermaid and Minotaur*, 275.

14. Jean Bethke Elshtain, "Feminists Against the Family," *The Nation*, Nov. 17, 1979, pp. 481, 497–500. See also the subsequent exchange between Elshtain and critics, "Exchange: Feminists and the Family," *The Nation*, April 5, 1980, pp. 386, 392–95.

Philosopher Queens and Private Wives: Plato on Women
and the Family   *Susan Moller Okin*

1. *The Republic of Plato*, trans. Allan Bloom (New York. Basic Books, 1968), 420b.

2. *Statesman*, trans. J. B. Skemp, *The Collected Dialogues of Plato*, ed. Edith Hamilton and Huntington Cairns (Princeton: Princeton University Press, 1961), 297b. Cf. *The Laws*, trans. R. G. Bury (Cambridge, Mass.: Harvard University Press, 1926), 630c, 644–645, 705d–706a, 707d; *Euthydemus*, trans. W. H. D. Rouse, *The Collected Dialogues*, 292b–c; and see also Sheldon Wolin, *Politics and Vision* (Boston: Little Brown, 1961), pp. 34–36.

3. *Laws*, 731e, 743d–e.

4. Glenn R. Morrow, *Plato's Cretan City* (Princeton: Princeton University Press, 1960), p. 101; cf. *Laws*, 736e.

5. *Republic*, 372e–373e, and 8.

6. *Ibid.*, 462a–e.

7. *Laws*, 739c–740a.

8. *Republic*, 416c–417b.

9. *Ibid.*, 416c–d, 417a–b.

10. *Ibid.*, 423e; *Laws*, 739c.

11. *Republic*, 423e.

12. *Ibid.*, 423e, 462, 464; *Laws*, 739c, 807b.

13. The Greeks' basically proprietary attitude toward women is well illustrated by the following statement from Demosthenes' account of the lawsuit, *Against Naera*: "For this is what living with a woman as one's wife means—

to have children by her and to introduce the sons to the members of the clan and of the deme, and to betroth the daughters to husbands as one's own. Mistresses we keep for the sake of pleasure, concubines for the daily care of our persons, but wives to bear us legitimate children and to be faithful guardians of our households" (Demosthenes, *Private Orations*, trans. A. T. Murray, Loeb edition [Cambridge, Mass.: Harvard University Press, 1939], 3: 122). For confirmation that this was a prevalent attitude, see Victor Ehrenberg, *Society and Civilization in Greece and Rome* (Cambridge, Mass.: Harvard University Press, 1964), p. 26.

14. See G. M. A. Grube, *Plato's Thought* (London, Hackett Publishers, 1935), p. 89.

15. *Republic*, 464c–d.

16. *Laws*, 805e.

17. *Republic*, 547b, 548a, 549c–e.

18. See Morrow, *Plato's Cretan City*, p. 102, n. 13, in which he notes that in Athens custom forbade the alienation of family land. The connection in classical Greek thought and practice between the wife and custody of the household property is amply confirmed in the descriptions of household management given by Xenophon and Aristotle.

19. See, for example, Thucydides, *The Peloponnesian War*, p. 46; Sophocles, *Ajax*, trans. F. Storr, Loeb edition (Cambridge, Mass.: Harvard University Press, 1913), pp. 291–93; Xenophon, *Oeconomicus*, in *Xenophon's Socratic Discourse*, trans. Carnes Lord, ed. Leo Strauss (Ithaca: Cornell University Press, 1970), p. 29 and cf. pp. 30–33; Aristotle, *The Politics*, 1. 13. 11; Victor Ehrenberg, *The People of Aristophanes*, 2d rev. ed. (Oxford: Porcupine Press, 1951), pp. 202, 295.

20. M. I. Finley, *The Ancient Greeks* (New York: Penguin, 1963), pp. 123—24; Ehrenberg, *Society and Civilization*, p. 59.

21. Finley, *The Ancient Greeks*, p. 124.

22. *Laws*, for example, 866 and 873e.

23. *Euthyphro*, 4a–b.

24. Grube, *Plato's Thought*, p. 270. Cf. A. E. Taylor, *Plato, The Man and His Work* (1926; 7th ed., London: Methuen, 1960), p. 278.

25. Leo Strauss, "On Plato's Republic," in *The City and Man* (Chicago: University of Chicago Press, 1964), p. 117.

26. Taylor, *Plato*, p. 278; see also Grube, *Plato's Thought*, p. 270, and Strauss, "On Plato's Republic," p. 117.

27. Jean Ithurriague, *Les idées de Platon sur la condition de la femme* (Paris, 1931), p. 53.

28. Grube, *Plato's Thought*, p. 270.

29. Stanley Diamond, "Plato and the Definition of the Primitive," in *Culture in History*, ed. Stanley Diamond (New York: Octagon Books, 1960), p. 126.

30. *Timaeus*, trans. Benjamin Jowett (Oxford, 1871), 18c–d.

31. *Republic*, 463c–e, 464d–e, 465a–b, 471c–d.

32. Gregory Vlastos, *Platonic Studies* (Princeton: Princeton University Press, 1973), p. 11.

33. Rousseau, *Emile*, Édition Pléiade (Paris: P. Pourrat, 1914), 4: 699–700 (my translation).
34. For examples of these three positions, respectively, see Christine Pierce, "Equality: *Republic* V," p. 6; Strauss, "On Plato's Republic," p. 116; A. E. Taylor, *Plato*, p. 278. The objections of William Jacobs ("Plato on Female Emancipation and the Traditional Family," forthcoming in *Apeiron*) have caused me to revise my original wording of this passage.
35. *Republic*, 370; this is graphically illustrated by the assertion at 406d–407a, that if one can no longer perform one's task, it is worthless to go on living.
36. *Republic*, 454b; cf. 454–56 in general for source of this paragraph.
37. Ibid., 460b, 540c.
38. Strauss, "On Plato's Republic," pp. 116–17; Allan Bloom, "Interpretive Essay," *The Republic of Plato*, pp. 382–83.
39. *Republic*, 451c, 453d.
40. *Laws*, 806a–c.
41. *Republic*, 417a–b.
42. It is illuminating that in Aristotles' response to the proposals of Book 5, once the issue of the family is settled, the role of women is not considered an independent one. It is clear that, since Aristotle considers himself to have refuted the proposal for the community of women and children, he does not deem it necessary to argue against Plato's wild ideas about women and their potential as individual persons. Given the family and the private household, women are private wives with domestic duties, and further discussion of the subject would be superfluous (*Politics*, 2. 1264b).
43. *Republic*, 592b; *Laws*, 739.
44. *Laws*, 805a–b.
45. Ibid., 794c–d; see also Morrow, *Plato's Cretan City*, p. 329.
46. *Laws*, 805c–d.
47. Ibid., 740a–c.
48. Morrow, *Plato's Cretan City*, pp. 118–19.
49. *Laws*, 866a, 868bc, 871b, 879c; cf. Morrow, *Plato's Cretan City*, pp. 120–21.
50. *Laws*, 772d–773e, 774e, 773c.
51. Ibid., 923e. I am grateful to William Jacobs for helping me clarify this point (private correspondence, 1977).
52. *Laws*, 928e–929a.
53. Morrow, *Plato's Cretan City*, p. 113, n. 55.
54. *Laws*, 784b, 929e, 930b, 882c; cf. Morrow, *Plato's Cretan City*, p. 121.
55. *Laws*, 784d–e, 937a–b.
56. *Republic*, 540c. The fact that Plato's rulers have always been referred to as philosopher kings suggests that the reminder was, and still is, necessary.
57. *Laws*, 741c, 759b, 764c–d, 800b, 813c, 828b, 784a–c, 790a, 794a–b, 795d, 930, 961, 765d–766b.
58. Ronald Levinson agrees with this conclusion—see *In Defense of Plato* (Cambridge, Mass.: Russell, 1953), p. 133–and Morrow notes that Plato gives no hint that women should perform the basic civil function of attending the assembly of the people (see *Plato's Cretan City*, pp. 157–58).
59. *Laws*, 785b.

60. *Laws,* 947b–d, 764e, 804e–805a, 806b, 794c–d, 833c–d, 834a, 834d.
61. *Laws,* 785b.
62. *Laws,* 808a, 808e.
63. *Laws,* 833d.
64. Compare *Laws,* 781c–d with *Republic,* 452a–b.

Aristotle, the Public-Private Split, and the Case of the Suffragists
Jean Bethke Elshtain

1. Abigail L. Rosenthal, "Feminism Without Contradictions," *Monist* 57, no. 1 (January 1973): 42. For a discussion by a historian that parallels my own in important ways see Ann Douglas, *The Feminization of American Culture* (New York: Avon Books, 1977).
2. Ernest Barker, ed., *The Politics of Aristotle* (New York: Oxford University Press, 1962), pp. 4, 5.
3. See Alasdair MacIntyre, *A Short History of Ethics* (New York: Macmillan, 1971), p. 63.
4. *Politics,* p. 3.
5. Ibid., p. 15, esp. nn. 1, 3.
6. Ibid., pp 34, 35–36.
7. Ibid., pp. 93, 95.
8. Ibid., pp. 108, 106.
9. Although the term was intended as an epithet for men who withdrew or were debarred from the administration of justice and the holding of public office, all women within Aristotle's system are appropriately termed "idiots" because they are exclusively private people.
10. I contrast "typologies" with a divergent mode of structuring reality which I label the "populational" approach. These categories—the typological and populational—go back at least as far as the logic and natural history of Aristotle and Plato's concept of plenitude. A typological thinker sees individuals, first, as members of a category—"women," "Jews," or "blacks." Each ideal type or class possesses its own set of traits. It follows that individuals within each type are defined by the characteristics of the collective category. "Woman," for Aristotle, is a typological category isolated from a political context. There is a separate goodness for women, slaves, and children; therefore, individuals from these categories or types can never possess the full qualities that individuals of another type, e.g., free males, participants in the *polis,* share.
11. See Thomas S. Kuhn, *The Structure of Scientific Revolutions* (Chicago: University of Chicago Press, 1973), p. 104. In his discussion of Newton's work, Kuhn points out that its impact on seventeenth-century science was abetted by the fact that scientists in the previous century "had at last succeeded in rejecting Aristotelian and scholastic explanations expressed in terms of the essences of material bodies. To say that a stone fell because its "nature" drove it toward the center of the universe had been made to look a mere

tautological world-play. . . ." Aristotle's concepts on the nature of women is a similar tautology.

12. See William E. Connolly, "Theoretical Self-Consciousness," *Polity* 6, no. 1 (Fall 1973), pp. 5–35, for a discussion of the manner in which "presumptions, concepts, theory, test procedures and normative conclusions" interconnect. If there was no more to Aristotle than a series of ideological justifications of a way of life, there would be little to commend him to contemporary thought; however, Aristotle's smugness about Athenian social arrangements is only part of the story. He also presents his image of the political realm as aiming at certain public, moral goods and citizenship as a form of action geared toward the good of the whole. That Aristotle himself excluded particular categories of persons from politics places no continuing claims on us. Political theorists of feminist sensibilities are free to turn Aristotle to their own purposes and to take up and insist upon a concept of "citizenship" as the basis of collective and individual public identity.

13. Although St. Augustine believed that earthly peace and security, the good at which society aimed, was a real good, he added that true justice and true peace were unobtainable in that society. Later medieval theorists were not unaware of politics as force and violence—they simply rejected this point of view as one degrading to man as a moral being. Medieval theorists did recognize justifications for overriding the higher law on grounds of necessity, but they labeled these emergency measures regrettable and (probably) sinful—never "normal" political behavior. The idea of emancipating politics from theology, or moral from political behavior, was anathema to the medieval world view.

14. Jean Bodin, *Six Books of the Commonwealth*, trans. M. A. Tooley (Oxford: Basil Blackwell, 1956). Bodin also urges that the power, authority, and command a husband has over his wife is "allowed by both divine and positive law to be honourable and right." The father, as the image of God on earth, has a "natural right to command." Cf. Alexander Passerin d'Entreves, *The Notion of the State* (Oxford: Clarendon Press, 1967), p. 6. Bodin's definition of the state comprises what d'Entreves calls the "state of legal theorizing," i.e., the presumption that politics is power as force qualified by law but not necessarily bound by it.

15. Niccolo Machiavelli, *The Prince and the Discourses* (New York: Modern Library, 1950). See also an article celebrating Machiavelli's "public morality" by Isaiah Berlin, "The Question of Machiavelli," *New York Review of Books*, Nov. 4, 1971, pp. 20–32.

16. For Machiavelli and Bodin this meant open justification of amoral politics. For others, including natural-law theorists in the Catholic tradition, it involved an unfortunate, occasional need to transgress the higher law for reasons of state.

17. These concepts are not archaic. In a major work on women in American history, Page Smith observes: "Women are 'private,' men are 'public.' A woman's life turns inward. Her 'internality,' her privateness, is symbolized by if not directly related to the fact that her sex organs and above all, her womb, are interior. Man's external organs symbolize his 'externality,' his outward-

ness, his 'publicness' . . ." (*Daughters of the Promised Land* [Boston: Little Brown, 1970], p. 317).

18. As J. G. A. Pocock points out in his essay, "Languages and their Implications: The Transformation of the Study of Political Thought," in *Politics, Language and Time* (New York: Atheneum, 1973), paradigms must be thought of as existing in many contexts and on many levels simultaneously (p. 18).

19. Elizabeth Cady Stanton, Susan B. Anthony, and Matilda Joslyn Gage, eds., *History of Woman Suffrage*, vol. 1 (Rochester, N.Y.: Charles Mann, 1881), p. 145.

20. Cited by Barbara Welter, "The Cult of True Womanhood, 1820–1860," in Ronald W. Hogeland, ed., *Women and Womanhood in America* (Lexington, Mass.: D. C. Heath, 1973), p. 111.

21. Alexis de Tocqueville also developed a separate but equal view of the sexes. He was pleased that Americans, unlike his European contemporaries "who would make man and woman into beings not only equal but alike" agreed with him that true sex equality lay in allowing each sex to fulfill its own innate capacities to the highest extent. American women, within their domestic sphere, were equal to, but never the same as, men. See *Democracy in America*, ed. Phillips Bradley, 2 vols. (New York: Vintage Books, 1945), 222–23, 225.

22. Susan B. Anthony and Ida Husted Harper, eds. *History of Woman Suffrage*, vol. 4 (Indianapolis, Ind.: Hollenbeck Press, 1902), pp. 95–96, 106–8. The first two sentences are drawn from an 1887 antisuffrage speech by Sen. George Vest; the remainder are taken from a similar speech by Sen. Joseph E. Brown.

23. Ann Battle-Sister, "Conjectures on the Female Culture Question," *Journal of Marriage and the Family* 33, no. 3 (August 1971), pp. 411–20).

24. Elizabeth Cady Stanton, Susan B. Anthony and Matilda Joslyn Gage, eds. *History of Woman Suffrage*, vol. 2 (Rochester, N.Y.: Charles Mann, 1882), pp. 351–52.

25. Ibid., 1:126.

26. Anthony and Harper, *History of Woman Suffrage*, 4:308–9.

27. Ida Husted Harper, ed. *History of Woman Suffrage*, vol. 5 (New York: J. J. Little and Ives, 1922), p. 125.

28. Stanton, Anthony, and Gage, *History of Woman Suffrage*, 2:785; 1:19–20.

29. Harper, *History of Woman Suffrage*, 5:126.

30. Emma Goldman, a feminist anarchist, rejected both universal suffrage as a political panacea and the notion of woman's unique nature. She claimed that universal suffrage had become a "modern fetich [sic]." Women had yet to realize "that suffrage is an evil, that it has not only helped to enslave people, that it has closed their eyes thatt they may not see how craftily they are made to submit." Not only was suffrage a hoax, but American women believed they could "purify politics." To Goldman, this was dangerous nonsense. By insisting on woman's purity, the suffragists magnified further the mystification surrounding woman, who is always regarded either as an angel or a devil, but never as merely human. See *The Traffic in Women and Other Essays in Feminism* (New York: Times Change Press, 1970).

31. Manicheans believed in the ulitmate principle of a dualism between good and evil, God and matter. According to their theory there were two ultimate principles in eternal conflict. See Frederick Copleston, S.J., *A History of Philosophy* (Garden City, N.Y.: Doubleday and Co., Image Book, 1962), vol. 2. Victorian Manicheanism revolved around the sexless immateriality of women and the flesh-bound materiality of men. The lower classes in toto were seen as creatures "of the flesh" and, as such, they were invidiously compared with the less matter-bound upper classes.

32. Aileen S. Kraditor, *The Ideas of the Woman Suffrage Movement* 1890–1920 (New York: Doubleday Anchor Book, 1971), pp. 38–39.

33. Elizabeth Cady Stanton, Susan B. Anthony, and Matilda Joslyn Gage, eds., *History of Woman Suffrage*, vol. 3 (Rochester, N.Y.: Charles Mann, 1886), p. 88.

34. Anthony and Harper, *History of Woman Suffrage*, 4:39, 84, xxxvi.

35. Harper, *History of Woman Suffrage*, 5:77.

36. Consider the ostensible silliness and naivete of the following: the mother of a political leader notorious for his villainy and chicanery parries a question concerning her son with the comment: "But he's a *good* boy." The statement makes perfect sense. He may indeed be a "good boy" according to the set of standards used by the privatized mother to judge him.

37. Rosemary Radford Ruether, "The Cult of True Womanhood," *Commonweal* 149, no. 6 (Nov. 9, 1973): 131.

38. Ibid.

39. Rosenthal, "Feminism Without Contradictions," p. 29. As Rosenthal points out, a victim is "supposed to have moral authority or purity because the exploitative terms in which her suppression is couched have been imposed on her by others. Her real voice has been silenced. . . ."

40. Stanton, Anthony, and Gage, *History of Woman Suffrage*, 3:67.

41. Anthony and Harper, *History of Woman Suffrage*, 4:116–17.

42. Stanton, Anthony, and Gage, *History of Woman Suffrage*, 2:17.

43. Peter Winch, *The Idea of a Social Science* (London: Routledge and Kegan Paul, 1958), p. 124.

44. See William E. Connolly, ed., *The Bias of Pluralism* (Chicago: Aldine; New York: Atherton, 1972), for a series of critiques of pluralist theory, especially the article by Peter Bachrach and Morton S. Baratz, "Two Faces of Power," pp. 51–66.

45. Cf. Stuart Hampshire, *Thought and Action* (New York: Viking Press, 1967), pp. 236–37.

Political and Marital Despotism: Montesquieu's *Persian Letters*
Mary Lyndon Shanley and Peter G. Stillman

1. Montesquieu, *The Persian Letters*, ed. and trans. J. Robert Loy (New York: Meridian Books, 1961); Montesquieu, *Lettres Persanes*, ed. Paul Vernière (Paris: Garnier, 1960). Citations from the *Persian Letters* are in parentheses

in the text; the letter number is cited, except for letters that Montesquieu excluded, which are noted as "Appendix" and cited by the page number of Loy's edition.

Montesquieu, *The Spirit of the Laws,* trans. Melvin Richter in *The Political Theory of Montesquieu* (Cambridge: Cambridge University Press, 1977) is also cited in parentheses in the text, as *SL,* followed by the book and chapter number.

2. Richter uses the wives' relationship to Usbek to illustrate the consent or complicity of the ruled, which he sees as part of every despotic regime (*Political Theory of Montesquieu,* pp. 45–50). Marshall Berman, *The Politics of Authenticity* (New York: Atheneum, 1972), pp. 15–32, attends carefully to the lack of authenticity in the human relationships of the harem, but primarily in order to speak of authenticity as a quality of human life, not to analyze the corruption of marital ties. Nannerl O. Keohane, *Philosophy and the State in France* (Princeton, N.J.: Princeton University Press, 1980), pp. 400–401, recognizes Roxane as "one of the first genuine feminist heroines in literature" who "shows herself a woman of true 'virtue' in the ancient sense: a courageous, brave, resourceful leader of a revolution against arbitrary mastery." But Keohane is more interested in the light the *Persian Letters* sheds on Montesquieu's analysis of political despotism than on his analysis of marriage itself. David Kettler, "Montesquieu on Love: Notes on the *Persian Letters,*" *American Political Science Review,* 58, no. 3 (September 1964): 658–61, and Mark Hulliung, *Montesquieu and the Old Regime* (Berkeley: University of California, 1976), are notable among recent critics for their attention to the interrelationships of larger social and political institutions and marriage. For treatments of other themes, Loy's translation contains an extensive bibliography which can be supplemented and brought up to date by the notes in Richter.

3. The plight of a "victim of amorous negotiation" was not unknown in France. Rica writes to a friend that "there is nobody with some post at court in Paris . . . who hasn't some woman through whose hands he dispenses all the favors and sometimes all the injustices of which he is capable" (108).

4. For Montesquieu, the members of the seraglio are like the subjects of despotism he describes in his *Greatness of the Romans and their Decline,* trans. David Lowenthal (Ithaca, N.Y.: Cornell University Press, 1968), p. 94: "in the concord of Asiatic despotism—that is, of all government that is not moderate—there is always real dissension. The worker, the soldier, the lawyer, the magistrate, the noble are joined only inasmuch as some oppress the others without resistance. And, if we see any union there, it is not citizens who are united by dead bodies buried next to the other." Machiavelli saw that tyrants had to act as Montesquieu described. For instance, a conquering prince cannot bestow honors on or encourage the growth of cities; rather, like the chief eunuch with the women, "it is to [the prince's] interest to keep the state divided so that each town and each district may recognize only him as ruler" (Machiavelli, *Discourses,* Book 2, chap. 2).

5. The results of despotic rule throughout a country are most vividly portrayed when Usbek describes Turkey; the catalog reads like a longer version of

Hobbe's depiction of the state of war (*Leviathan*, chap. 13). "From Tocat to Smyrna ['a journey of 35 days'] there is not a single city worth mentioning. . . . The fortresses are dismantled; the cities deserted. The countryside is desolate; cultivation of land is uncertain. . . . These barbarians have abandoned all the arts. . . . [They are] incapable of carrying on commerce . . ." (19).

6. One contemporary American institution that duplicates many of the features of despotism that Montesquieu describes is the prison, although the chain of command from the state government and the fear of the courts may temper the tyranny of a prison's warden.

7. Kettler, "Montesquieu on Love," pp. 658–59.

8. Richter, *Political Theory of Montesquieu*, p. 47.

9. Hulliung makes a similar point, asserting that "love is the illusion of the wives," who hide the truth of their subjection even from themselves. According to Hulliung, the eunuchs, because of "their singular freedom from illusion, are unique in comprehending the ways of despotism and in transforming their comprehension into self-conscious weapons" (*Montesquieu and the Old Regime*, pp. 123–24). But the eunuchs do not see that their manipulation of others helps to preserve a system in which they themselves are dehumanized and are themselves manipulated.

10. Kettler, "Montesquieu on Love," pp. 658–59.

11. These themes also pervade John Stuart Mill's *The Subjection of Women* (1869). See Mary Lyndon Shanley, "Marital Slavery and Friendship: John Stuart Mill's *The Subjection of Women*," *Political Theory*, forthcoming 1981.

12. Montesquieu wishes his reader to *feel* the awful horror because "there are certain truths that it is not enough to impress by rational conviction, that must be felt. Such are the verities of ethics" (11).

13. On this point see Keohane, *Philosophy and the State*, p. 401.

14. In drawing so clearly the contrast between Usbek's enlightened words and his destructive despotic practices, Montesquieu was criticizing in 1721 the chimerical ideal of enlightened despotism that was to be so popular later in the eighteenth century.

15. Hulliung, *Montesquieu and the Old Regime*, p. 135. Hulliung also advances the idea that the reason Rica can become an Enlightenment man and make a new life in Europe while Usbek reverts to a despotic use of force and returns to Persia is that Rica is a bachelor and has few personal ties to Persia, whereas Usbek "carries across Europe the memory of his wives." But even in Europe Usbek still rules his harem, and its effect upon him is more powerful than that simply of memory. Similarly Rica, never having ruled a harem, has not suffered the psychic and moral corruption that inevitably besets a despot.

16. At the same time that Usbek is giving his head eunuchs "unlimited power" to punish and wreak "vengeance" on his wives (148, Gemmadi I, 1718; 150, Shalval, 1718; 153, Shahban, 1719), he is writing letters expressing wise and enlightened opinions on a number of topics, including the problems of marriage and family in both Islamic and Christian nations (112–22, Shahban and Ramadan, 1718), the dangers of arbitrariness by princes (124, Shalval, 1718),

the need for wise legislators (129, Gemmadi II, 1719), and—after he has ordered vengeance—the need for princes to have integrity and give a good example to the people (146, Ramadan, 1720).

Marriage Contract and Social Contract in Seventeenth-Century
English Political Thought *Mary Lyndon Shanley*

1. Richard Baxter, *A Christian Directory* (London, 1673), p. 514.
2. Later discussions that draw on arguments suggested in the seventeenth-century debates are found, for example, in Mary Wollstonecraft, *A Vindication of the Rights of Women* (New York: Norton, 1967), and in Harriet Taylor Mill and John Stuart Mill, *Essays on Sex Equality*, ed. Alice Rossi (Chicago: University of Chicago Press, 1970).
3. J. W. Grough, *The Social Contract: A Critical Study of Its Development* (Oxford: The Clarendon Press, 1936), pp. 78, 79.
4. Henry Parker, *Observations upon Some of His Majesties Late Answers and Expresses* (London, 1642), pp. 18–19; John Spelman, *A View of the Printed Book* (Oxford, 1642), p. 9.
5. Sir Dudley Digges, *The Unlawfulness of Subjects Taking up Armes against their Soveraigne, in what Case Soever* . . . (n.p., 1643), pp. 3–4.
6. The debates over the nature of the original contract between king and people are too extensive to go into in this paper. See J. G. A. Pocock, *The Ancient Constitution and the Feudal Law: A Study of English Historical Thought in the 17th Century* (New York: Norton, 1967), for an excellent summary of the issues involved.
7. Henry Ferne, *Conscience Satisfied: That there is no warrant for the Armes now taken up by Subjects* . . . (Oxford, 1643), p. 12. In Ferne's eyes, indeed, the case against resistance was even stronger than that against divorce. While divorce was forbidden to Christians, it had been allowed under Mosaic law, but no similar biblical sanction was given for political resistance. (p. 70).
8. Digges, *The Unlawfulness*, pp. 112–13.
9. Ibid., p. 121.
10. Henry Ferne, *The Resolving of Conscience upon this Question, Whether* . . . *Subjects may take Armes and resist?* . . . (Cambridge, 1643), p. 19.
11. This and the following two paragraphs draw upon George Howard, *History of Matrimonial Institutions*, 3 vols. (Chicago: University of Chicago Press, 1904), 2:60–75; L. Chilton Powell, *English Domestic Relations, 1487–1653* (New York: Columbia University Press, 1917), pp. 1–100, esp. pp. 61–65; Ernest Sirluck, "Introduction," *Complete Prose Works of John Milton*, ed. Don M. Wolfe, 6 vols. (New Haven: Yale University Press, 1953–74), 2:144–57, 237.
12. Powell remarks that posting a bond against remarriage did not curb the abuse of remarriage after divorce *a mensa et thoro*. The bond functioned

more as a penalty than an insurmountable impediment; the party who re-married sacrificed the security he had posted (Powell, *English Domestic Relations*, p. 87, n. 1).

13. Ibid., p. 81.

14. William Whately, for example, in his book *A Bride-bush* (London, 1619), as quoted in Powell, *English Domestic Relations*, pp. 68–69, wrote that: "if it shall fall out, that either of the married persons shall forwardly and perversely withdraw themselves from this matrimoniall societie (which fault is termed desertion), the person thus offending, hath so farre violated the covenant of marriage, that . . . the bond of matrimony is dissolved, and the other party so truly and totally loosed from it, that (after an orderly proceeding with the Church and Magistrate in that behalf) it shall be no sinne for him or her to make a new contract with another person."

15. Ferne, *The Resolving of Conscience*, p. 21.

16. William Bridge, *The Wounded Conscience Cured* . . . (London, 1642), p. 44. An anonymous Parliamentarian had introduced the notion of tacit agreement and limitation about a year earlier with the argument that "when the *Militia* of an Army is committed to the Generall, it is not with any express condition, that he shall not turn the mouths of his Cannons against his own Souldiers, for that is so naturally and necessarily implyed, that its needlesse to be expressed . . ." (*A Question Answered: How Laws Are To Be Understood, and Obedience Yeelded*, quoted in Sirluck, "Introduction," *Complete Prose Works of John Milton*, 2:19).

17. Henry Parker, *Jus populi* (London, 1644), pp. 4–5.

18. Herbert Palmer, *Scripture and Reason Pleaded for Defensive Armes* (London, 1643), pp. 35–36, emphasis added.

19. Milton, *Complete Prose Works*, 2:229.

20. Powell, *English Domestic Relations*, p. 93, notes that the *Doctrine and Discipline* was considered "revolutionary." The Presbyterian clergy apparently attempted to get the work suspended (Sirluck, "Introduction," *Complete Prose Works of John Milton*, 2:140).

21. On Tyrrell's relationship to Locke see Peter Laslett, "Introduction," in John Locke, *Two Treatises of Government*, ed. Peter Laslett, rev. ed. (New York: Mentor Books, 1963), esp. pp. 69–74).

22. James Tyrrell, *Patriarcha non Monarcha* (London, 1681), p. 64.

23. Hugo Grotius, *De Juri Belli ac Pacis Libri Tres On the Law of War and Peace* (1625), trans. Francis W. Kelsey (Oxford: Clarendon Press, 1925), bk. 2, ch. 5, sec. 1, p. 231; bk. 5, ch. 8, p. 234.

24. Samuel Pufendorf, *De Jure Naturae et Gentium Libri Octo On the Law of Nature and Nations* (1673), trans. C. H. Oldfather and W. A. Oldfather (Oxford: The Clarendon Press, 1934), bk. 6, ch. 1, sec. 9, p. 853.

25. Tyrrell, *Patriarcha non Monarcha*, pp. 14–15.

26. Ibid., pp. 14, 110.

27. Ibid., p. 111.

28. John Locke, *Two Treatises*, 2. 55, p. 347; 2. 66, p. 354.

29. "The *Power*, then, *that Parents have* over their Children, arises from that Duty which is incumbent on them, to take care of their Off-spring, during

the imperfect state of Childhood" (ibid., 2. 58, p. 348). Also, "The first part
then of *Paternal* power, or rather Duty . . . is Education . . ." (ibid., 2. 69,
p. 356). Locke remarked in his notebook that "education not generation gives
the obligation and the affection of children to their parents (John Locke, *The
Educational Writings of John Locke*, ed. James L. Axtell [Cambridge: Cambridge University Press, 1968], p. 112, n. 4).

30. Locke, *Two Treatises*, 2. 56, p. 347; 2. 53, p. 346.
31. See, for example, ibid., 2. 105, 107, 110, 112, 118.
32. See, for example, ibid., 2. 69, 170, 173. See also Gordon Schochet, *Patriar-
    chalism in Political Thought* (New York: Basic Books, 1975), p. 249.
33. Locke, *Two Treatises*, 2. 52, p. 343; see also, 1. 55 and 61 and 2. 86.
34. Ibid., 2. 78, p. 362.
35. Ibid., 2. 83, p. 365. This passage makes it clear that an earlier passage in the
    Second Treatise that states that God may "by manifest Declaration of his
    Will set one [being] above another, and confer on him by an evident and
    clear appointment and undoubted Right to Dominion and Sovereignty," does
    not refer to the rule of men over women (ibid., 2. 4, p. 309).
36. Ibid., 2. 78, p. 362.
37. Ibid., 2. 83, p. 365; 2. 81, p. 364.
38. Ibid., 2. 82, p. 364. Locke, here, anticipates Jeremy Bentham who makes a
    similar argument in *The Principles of Morals and Legislation* (New York:
    Hofner Publishing Co., 1948).
39. Locke, *Two Treatises*, 2. 83, p. 365.
40. Locke does acknowledge that certain inequalities (such as one person being
    "abler" than another) may give "a just Precedency," but not a right to rule
    (ibid., 2. 54, p. 346). I am indebted to Dr. Nathan Tarcov of the University
    of Chicago for this observation.
41. Ibid., 2. 1, p. 308. My sense that Locke was considerably less happy than his
    fellow contractarians with the assumption of male dominance in marriage is
    reinforced by his attitude toward women in *Some Thoughts Concerning Edu-
    cation*. Locke thought that girls might well receive much the same education
    as boys.
42. The idea of "contract marriage," in which couples would themselves decide
    such matters as the goals of their relationship, what support and property
    divisions they desire both during the marriage and in the event of divorce,
    and when and under what conditions they will divorce is the latest manifes-
    tation of the continuing discussion of the extent of contract in marriage. See,
    among many others, L. Edmiston, "How to Write Your Own Marriage Con-
    tract," *Ms.* (Spring 1972), pp. 66–72; K. Fleishmann, "Marriage by Contract:
    Defining the Terms of the Relationship," *Family Law Quarterly* 8 (Spring
    1974): 27–49; N. Sherensky and M. Mannes, "A Radical Guide to Wedlock,"
    Saturday Review, July 29, 1972, p. 33; L. Weitzman, "Legal Regulation of
    Marriage: Tradition and Change," *California Law Review* 62 (July–September
    1974): 1249–78.
43. Locke, *Two Treatises*, 2. 2, p. 308.
44. The common law held that husband and wife were "one person" in the law.
    As a consequence, marriage resulted in the "civil death" of the women. A

wife could contract neither with her husband nor with third parties; a husband took control of his wife's property; a wife could not sue or be sued without her husband's joining her. The Married Women's Property Acts declared that women could buy, sell, and otherwise manage their own property. The acts were therefore an important attack on the common-law doctrine of spousal unity. See Leo Kanowitz, *Women and the Law: The Unfinished Revolution* (Albuquerque: University of New Mexico Press, 1969).

45. On the legal duties of husbands and wives, see Kanowitz, *Women and the Law*, pp. 35–99.

46. I find evidence of Locke's more tender sensibilities both in the *Two Treatises* and, particularly, in *Some Thoughts Concerning Education*. For example, with regard to the relationship between parent and child, Locke advises Clarke, "as your son approaches more to a Man, admit him nearer your familiarity: So shall you have him your obedient Subject (as is fit) whilst he is a Child, and your affectionate Friend, when he is a Man" (sec. 40, p. 145). Children should come to regard their parents as "their best, their only sure Friends; and as such love and reverence them" (sec. 41, p. 145). And Locke also recognizes that nurtured by the parents' efforts as much as by the child's: "Many Fathers, though they proportion to their Sons liberal Allowances, yet they keep the knowledge of their Estates, and Concerns, from them with as much reservedness, as if they were guarding a secret of State from a Spy, or an Enemy. . . . And I cannot but often wonder to see Fathers, who love their Sons very well, yet so order the matter by a constant Stiffness . . . as if they were never to Enjoy or have any comfort from those they love best in the World . . . (sec. 96, p. 202). This aspect of Locke's work lends a new perspective to the dominant contemporary view of Locke as the apologist for the acquisitive ethic and material inequality of modern society. That view owes much to C. B. Macpherson, *The Political Theory of Possessive Individualism: Hobbes to Locke* (Oxford: The Clarendon Press, 1962).

Julie and "La Maison Paternelle": Another Look at Rousseau's
La Nouvelle Héloïse   Tony Tanner

1. This and all subsequent passages quoted in English are taken from *La Nouvelle Héloïse. Julie; or, The New Eloise: Letters of Two Lovers, Inhabitants of a Small Town at the Foot of the Alps*, trans. and abridged Judith H. McDowell (University Park, Pa., 1968).

2. This is a vast subject with a great deal of well-known work written about it. For a felicitous and brief summary of just this one point I have tried to make here, see Michel Foucault "Le 'Non' du Père," *Critique*, March 1962.

3. I quote one sentence from Lacan asserting the ancient association between the name of the father and the figure of the law: "C'est dans le *nom du père* qu'il nous faut recommaître le support de la fonction symbolique qui, depuis l'orée des temps historique, identifie sa personne à la figure de la loi" (*Ecrits* 1:157–58).

4. Jacques Lacan, "Seminaire sur 'la Lettre volée," *Yale French Studies*, no. 48 (1972), p. 69.

5. I am taking these words as they are used by Freud (in *Jokes and Their Relation to the Unconscious*, where he writes that words can be taken according as they are "voll" or "leer") and, subsequently, Lacan (in "Fonction et champ de la parole et du langage," where he discusses the "parole vide et parole pleine").

Hegel's Conception of the Family
Joan B. Landes

1. For a discussion of the theme of family and society in these bodies of literature, see Gordon J. Schochet, *Patriarchalism in Political Thought: The Authoritarian Family and Political Speculation and Attitudes, Especially in Seventeenth-Century England* (New York: Basic Books, 1975); R. A. Chapman, "*Leviathan* Writ Small: Thomas Hobbes on the Family," *American Political Science Review*, 69 (March 1975); and Teresa Brennan and Carole Pateman, " 'Mere Auxiliaries to the Commonwealth': Women and Liberalism" (Paper presented at the Annual Meeting of the Australian Political Studies Association, Sydney, Australia, August 26–28, 1976).

2. The nineteenth-century romantic version of this argument, as well as its popular Victorian counterpart, corresponded to the separation of private life and public existence—the interior (the private home) from the exterior (the workplace and marketplace)—and of the private citizen from the burgher that accompanied the rise of industrial capitalism. See, for example, Walter Benjamin, "Paris—The Capital of the Nineteenth Century," in *Charles Baudelaire: A Lyric Poet in the Era of High Capitalism* (London: NLB, 1973). A recent statement of this viewpoint appears in Christopher Lasch, *Haven in a Heartless World: The Family Besieged* (New York: Basic Books, 1977).

3. G. W. F. Hegel, *Hegel's Philosophy of Right*, trans. T. M. Knox (London: Oxford University Press, 1952), para. 255. In subsequent citations to the *Philosophy of Right*, material from the main text of the paragraph is referred to by the paragraph number alone. Where the citation refers to the "remarks" Hegel added to the text, the paragraph number is followed by "R"; where it refers to the "additions" that later editors added to posthumous editions of the text by collating student lecture notes, the paragraph number is followed by "A."

4. See ibid., para. 157.

5. On Hegel's attitude to the classical *polis*, see Georg Lukacs, *The Young Hegel: Studies in the Relation Between Dialectics and Economics*, trans. Rodney Livingstone (London: Merlin Press, 1975), especially part 1; Judith Shklar, *Freedom and Independence: A Study of the Political Ideas of Hegel's Phenomenology of Mind* (Cambridge: Cambridge University Press, 1976); Charles Taylor, *Hegel* (Cambridge: Cambridge University Press, 1975), especially part 4; Shlomo Avineri, *Hegel's Theory of the Modern State* (Cam-

bridge: Cambridge University Press, 1972); and Raymond Plant, *Hegel* (Bloomington: Indiana University Press, 1973).

6. Immanuel Kant, *The Philosophy of Law: An Exposition of the Principles of Jurisprudence as the Science of Right*, trans. W. Hastie, B.D. (Edinburgh: T. and T. Clark, 1887), para. 22, p. 108.

7. See, for example, Thomas Hobbes, *Leviathan*, ed. C. B. MacPherson (Baltimore: Penguin, 1968), chaps. 13 and 14; and John Locke, *Two Treatises of Government*, ed. Peter Laslett (New York: New American Library, 1960), chap. 5.

8. Peter G. Stillman, "Hegel's Critique of Liberal Theories of Rights," *American Political Science Review* 68 (1974): 1087.

9. See, for example, the critique of Hegel's view of the family by Carol C. Gould, "The Woman Question: Philosophy of Liberation and the Liberation of Philosophy," *Philosophical Forum*, 5:33–38.

10. See *Philosophy of Right*, para. 200 and translator's note to para. 169. I am indebted to Peter G. Stillman for drawing this to my attention and for pointing out that the first use of the term *Kapital* in the text coincides with the discussion of classes (for Hegel, *Stände*).

11. This insight has profound importance for a theory of the family today when the form of family life originally associated with the bourgeois class has extended to broad sectors of the proletariat in advanced capitalist societies. See, on this point, Eli Zaretsky, *Capitalism, The Family and Personal Life* (New York: Harper and Row, 1976).

12. See Hegel, *Philosophy of Right*, para. 159A, para. 171, and para. 174 on the subject of children's rights.

13. Although Germany at this time was not yet a developed industrial capitalist society, Hegel was well aware of the characteristics of such a society, especially after undertaking a comprehensive study of English political enonomy. Indeed, his last published writing was an essay on the English Reform Bill, which is evidence of his continued interest in the political and economic consequences of industrial development. Thus, Hegel is not writing solely from a German standpoint, but rather from a broader modern European one. He recognizes that the further development of civil society in the less advanced areas will lead in the direction already observable in England during his lifetime. For a discussion of Hegel's use of political economy and concern with English political life, see Shlomo Avineri, *Hegel's Theory of the Modern State*, pp. 132–55 and 208–21.

14. See Herbert Marcuse's discussion of this point in "A Study of Authority," in *Studies in Critical Philosophy* (Boston: Beacon Press, 1972).

15. See Leonore Davidoff, Jean L'Esperance, and Howard Newby, "Landscape with Figures: Home and Community in English Society," in *The Rights and Wrongs of Women*, ed. Juliet Mitchell and Ann Oakley (Harmondsworth: Penguin Books Ltd., 1976), pp. 139–75; and Francoise Basch, *Relative Creatures: Victorian Women in Society and the Novel*, trans. A. Rudolf (New York: Schocken, 1974).

16. Hegel, *Philosophy of Right*, para. 238. Significantly, Hegel recognizes that although the discussion of family life *logically* precedes that of civil society

Notes 319

and the state, the existence of the modern family is predicated on the prior
emergence of both civil society and the state. On this point, Hegel breaks
with all those theorists of the family who conceive of an isomorphic family
form that exists almost unchanged throughout history, with possible adjustments resulting from new demands or the loss of older functions.

17. Johann J. Bachofen, *Das Mutterrecht* (Stuttgart, 1861); Lewis Henry Morgan,
*Ancient Society or Researches in the Lives of Human Progress from Savagery
through Barbarism to Civilization*, ed. Eleanor Burke Leacock (Cleveland:
The World Publishing Co., 1963); Frederick Engels, *The Origin of the Family,
Private Property and the State* (New York: International Publishers, 1972).
The very title of Engel's work and its tripartite conception is indebted to
Hegel's threefold division of ethical life into family, civil society, and state.

18. Hegel is aware of the contradictions that abound in family life insofar as
property, which in principle is held in common, must be transferred to individual heirs as private property. Thus, the right of each family member in
the common stock "may come into collision with the head of the family's
right of administration" (para. 171). Hegel abhors the arbitrary character of
final wills and testaments; yet he deplores any legislative restrictions on the
father's right to dispose of his property. Although he indicates a preference
for freedom of property and equality of inheritance, he never clarifies
whether by "children" he means to include daughters in an equal right to
inheritances.

19. This argument, of course, conceals a strong class bias in Hegel's presentation, for it omits entirely the social situation of working-class and peasant
women who participate directly in social production.

20. See the excellent discussion of *Antigone* in Judith Shklar, *Freedom and Independence* and the relevant passages in G. W. F. Hegel, *The Phenomenology
of Mind*, trans. J. B. Baillie (New York: Harper and Row, 1967), pp. 462–82.

21. Rudolf Siebert, "Hegel's Concept of Marriage and Family: The Origin of Subjective Freedom," in *Hegel's Social and Political Thought: The Philosophy of
Objective Spirit*, ed. Donald Phillip Verene (Atlantic Highlands, N.J.: Humanities Press, 1980), p. 180. Siebert provides a comprehensive and very helpful overview of Hegel's attitudes toward family matters in the body of his
writings. Although Hegel does not clarify the specific inheritance rights of
daughters, in one remark he attacks unequal inheritance measures including
those whereby daughters could be disinherited. He writes: "The instituiton
of heirs-at-law with a view to preserving the family and its *splendor* by
means of *fidei-commissa* and *substitutiones* (in order to favour sons by excluding daughters from inheriting, or to favour the eldest son by excluding
the other children) is an infringement of the principle of property, like the
admission of any other inequality in the treatment of heirs" (para. 180R).

22. Rudolf Siebert, "Hegel's Concept of Marriage and Family," p. 180.

23. Hegel, *The Phenomenology of Mind*, p. 474.

24. Hegel, *Philosophy of Right*, para. 167. In a much earlier work Hegel seems
to defend the equality of lovers. He states that: "True union, or love proper,
exists only between living beings who are alike in power and thus in one
another's eyes living beings from every point of view; in no respect is either

dead for the other . . . in love, life is present as a duplicate of itself and
as a single and unified self. . . . In love, the separate does still remain, but
as something united and no longer as something separate; life [in the sub-
ject] senses life [in the object]" (G. W. F. Hegel, "Love," in *Early Theological
Writings*, trans. T. M. Knox [Philadelphia: University of Pennsylvania Press,
1948], pp. 304–5).

25. On this point, see Christopher Hill, *Society and Puritanism* (New York:
Schocken, 1964); Michael Walzer, *The Revolution of the Saints: A Study in
the Origins of Radical Politics* (New York: Atheneum, 1965); and Eli Zaretsky, *Capitalism, the Family and Personal Life.*

26. Rudolf Siebert, "Hegel's Concept of Marriage and Family," p. 181.

27. Hegel's views on women cannot be attributed simply to the attitudes of his
age. Indeed, among Hegel's younger contemporaries, the early nineteenth-
century Utopian socialists Henri Saint-Simon, Charles Fourier, and Flora
Tristan, one encounters bold criticisms of women's position in family and
society. The Utopian vision was committed to a society in which women
would be equal to men. Family and personal life, even sexuality, were subject to criticism by theorists who sought a radical transformation of society.
In the eighteenth-century Enlightenment, Condorcet and Mary Wollstonecraft,
among others, promoted the view that male and female qualities were the
product of socialization rather than innate biological or natural characteristics. The earliest intellectual foundations for the nineteenth-century feminist movement were laid by the Enlightenment insistence on women's intellectual, social, and political equality. Hegel is perhaps closer to the romantic
belief that women and men possess separate natures. However, he takes
from this tradition the most conservative understanding of woman's nature,
turning upon her natural capacity for motherhood, whereas to some extent
the romantic appreciation of women's special qualities as lover and of her
humanity in an inhumane social world was consistent with more progressive
attitudes toward women. On these themes, see Richard J. Evans, *The Feminists: Women's Emancipation Movements in Europe, America and Australia
1840–1920* (New York: Barnes and Noble, 1977); Marilyn Boxer and Jean H.
Quataert, eds., *Socialist Women: European Socialist Feminism in the Nineteenth and Early Twentieth Centuries* (New York: Elsevier, 1978); Sheila
Rowbotham, *Women, Resistance and Revolution: A History of Women and
Revolution in the Modern World* (New York: Random House, 1972); Charles
Fourier, *The Utopian Vision of Charles Fourier*, ed. Mark Poster (Garden
City, N.Y.: Doubleday, 1971).

28. Jean Hyppolite, *Genesis and Structure of Hegel's Phenomenology of Spirit*,
trans. Samuel Cherniak and John Heckman (Evanston: Northwestern University Press, 1974), p. 344.

29. Karl Marx, *Economic and Philosophic Manuscripts of 1844*, ed. Dirk J. Struik,
trans. Martin Milligan (New York: International Publishers, 1964), p. 134.

30. As Max Horkheimer and Theodore Adorno remark: "As representative of
nature, woman in bourgeois society has become the enigmatic image of irre-
sistibility and powerlessness. In this way she reflects for domination the pure

lie that posits the subjection instead of the redemption of nature. Marriage is the middle way by which society comes to terms with itself. The woman remains the one without power, for power comes to her only by male mediation. . . . Renunciation is the prerequisite" (*Dialectic of Enlightenment*, trans. John Cumming [New York: The Seabury Press, 1972], pp. 71–72).

31. Max Horkheimer, *Eclipse of Reason* (New York: The Seabury Press, 1974), p. 93.

32. See Sigmund Freud, *Civilization and Its Discontents* (New York: W. W. Norton, 1971), pp. 51–52. For a recent attempt to compare Hegel and Freud on another dimension, see Jean Hyppolite, "Hegel's Phenomenology and Psychoanalysis," in *New Studies in Hegel's Philosophy*, ed. Warren E. Steinhaus (New York: Holt, Rinehart and Winston, 1971), pp. 57–70.

33. Russell Jacoby, *Social Amnesia: A Critique of Conformist Psychology from Adler to Laing* (Boston: Beacon Press, 1975), p. 80.

34. On these two kinds of arguments see Gordon J. Schochet, *Patriarchalism in Political Thought*.

35. For this view of the family, see Herbert Marcuse, "A Study in Authority" in *Studies in Critical Philosophy; Eros and Civilization: A Philosophical Inquiry into Freud* (Boston: Beacon Press, 1966); and *Reason and Revolution: Hegel and the Rise of Social Theory* (Boston: Beacon Press, 1960).

Patriarchal Liberalism and Beyond: From John Stuart Mill
to Harriet Taylor   *Richard W. Krouse*

1. For a fuller discussion of the liberal concept of the family in seventeenth-century English political thought, to which this essay is indebted, see Mary Lyndon Shanley, "Marriage Contract and Social Contract in Seventeenth-Century English Political Thought," above.

2. "Patriarchy" will be defined as rule by men over women, and by older men over younger men.

3. For a fuller discussion of the public/private theme, see Jean Bethke Elshtain, "Moral Woman and Immoral Man: A Consideration of the Public-Private Split and Its Political Ramifications," *Politics and Society* 4 (Fall 1974): 453–73, a revised version of which appears above.

4. Reprinted in John Stuart Mill and Harriet Taylor, *Essays on Sex Equality*, ed. Alice Rossi (Chicago: University of Chicago Press, 1970). All references are to this edition.

5. Reprinted in ibid.; all references are to this edition.

6. Aristotle, *Politics*, ed. Ernest Barker (London: Oxford University Press, 1968), Book 1.

7. On the Aristotelian conception of freedom through public action, and its dependence upon leisure secured by the labor of others, see Hannah Arendt, *The Human Condition* (Chicago: University of Chicago Press, 1958).

8. For a classic contemporary statement of this view, see Leo Strauss, *The Po-*

litical Philosophy of Hobbes: Its Basis and Genesis (Chicago: University of Chicago Press, 1963); and *Natural Right and History* (Chicago: University of Chicago Press, 1965).

9. For an insightful discussion focusing upon contemporary issues of the relationship between the egalitarian "constitutive political morality" of liberalism and the "derivative" institutions and practices advocated by any given liberal theorist, see Ronald Dworkin, "Liberalism," in *Public and Private Morality*, ed. Stuart Hampshire (Cambridge: Cambridge University Press, 1978), pp. 113–43.

10. For the most comprehensive recent statement of this position, see Roberto M. Unger, *Knowledge and Politics* (Glencoe, Ill.: The Free Press, 1975). See also the discussion of the implications of Mill's epistemology for his politics in Jean Bethke Elshtain, *Public Man, Private Woman: Women in Social and Political Thought* (Princeton: Princeton University Press, 1981).

11. For an apposite example of this kind of immanent critique, see Susan Moller Okin's argument that Plato's rehabilitation of the patriarchal family in *The Laws* would undermine or defeat the meritocratic ideal of equality of opportunity for women to which he himself professes commitment in both *The Republic* and in *The Laws* ("Philosopher Queens and Private Wives: Plato on Women and the Family," above).

12. For the *locus classicus* of this view, see Marx, "On the Jewish Question," in *Writings of the Young Marx on Philosophy and Society*, ed. and trans. Lloyd D. Easton and Kurt H. Guddat (Garden City, N.Y.: Anchor Books, 1967), pp. 216–41. In what follows, *civil* rights are defined as "liberty of the person, freedom of speech, thought, and faith, the right to own property and to conclude valid contracts, and the right to justice." A *political* right is defined as "the right to participate in the exercise of political power." My use of the concept of civil and political rights, or civil and political citizenship, follows both Marx, ibid., and T. H. Marshall, *Class, Citizenship and Social Development* (Garden City, N.Y.: Anchor Books, 1968), pp. 78–79, from whom the quotes are drawn.

13. Frederick Engels, *The Origins of the Family, Private Property, and the State* (New York: International Publishers, 1975).

14. Engels himself is often guilty of precisely this kind of crudely reductionistic slide from analogies to identities, which severely vitiates the power and plausibility of his analysis. In what follows, as well as generally throughout, I am indebted more heavily to C. B. Macpherson—whose conceptual categories are here extended to the analysis of sexual inequality and the family—than to Engels. See especially C. B. Macpherson, *Democratic Theory: Essays in Retrieval* (London: Oxford University Press, 1973).

15. See Eli Zaretsky, *Capitalism, the Family, and Personal Life* (New York: Harper and Row, 1973). It is important to emphasize that in preindustrial societies, or traditional sectors of industrial society, in which women retain some control over productive resources within the political economy of the household, formally patriarchal marriage arrangements often mask a more equal distribution of power *within* the family (though not in politics and society at large). See especially Joan Scott and Louise Tilly, "Women's Work

and the Family in Nineteenth-Century Europe," *Comparative Studies in Society and History* 17 (1978): 36–64.

16. I am here specifically borrowing, and adapting, the formulation of C. B. Macpherson in his devastating critique of Milton Friedman, "Elegant Tombstones: A Note on Friedman's Freedom," in *Democratic Theory*, pp. 145–47.

17. See Engels, *Origins of the Family*, p. 137.

18. Ibid., pp. 221, 139.

19. William Connolly, *The State and the Public Interest* (Washington, D.C.: The American Political Science Association), p. 37.

20. See especially Gordon Schocket, *Patriarchalism in Political Thought* (New York: Basic Books, 1975); W. H. Greenleaf, *Order, Empiricism, and Politics* (London: Oxford University Press, 1964); Peter Laslett, "Introduction," to *Patriarcha and Other Political Works of Sir Robert Filmer*, ed. Peter Laslett (Oxford: Basil Blackwell, 1949) and "Introduction" to *John Locke, Two Treatises of Government*, ed. Peter Laslett (Cambridge: Cambridge University Press, 1960), hereafter cited as *T.T.*; Shanley, "Marriage Contract and Social Contract in Seventeenth-Century English Political Thought," above; and Melissa A. Butler, "Early Liberal Roots of Feminism: John Locke and the Attack on Patriarchy," *American Political Science Review*, 72 (1978): 135–50.

21. Filmer, *Patriarcha and Other Political Works*, pp. 211, 287.

22. On the class boundedness of seventeenth-century English political theory from Hobbes to Locke, see especially C. B. Macpherson, *The Political Theory of Possessive Individualism: Hobbes to Locke* (London: Oxford University Press, 1962).

23. Locke in his *First Treatise* does seem to find in Genesis 3:16 a scriptural basis for the subjection of women to men; but he goes on to argue that God "only foretells what should be the woman's lot" and that this condition is not immutable (*T.T.*, 1, para. 47).

24. Hobbes, *Leviathan*, ed. W. G. Pogson Smith (London: Oxford University Press, 1965), p. 154, hereafter *Lev.*; *T.T.*, 2, para. 78.

25. *T.T.*, 2, paras. 81–82.

26. Both insist that the normally patriarchal pattern can be altered by contract: *Lev.*, p. 154; *T.T.*, 1, para. 47.

27. *Lev.*, pp. 156–57. On this point especially see Richard Allan Chapman, "*Leviathan* Writ Small: Thomas Hobbes on the Family," *American Political Science Review*, 69 (1975): 76–90.

28. *T.T.*, 2, para. 28.

29. *Lev.*, pp. 154, 157.

30. Thomas Hobbes, *A Dialogue Between a Philosopher and a Student of the Common Laws of England*, ed. Joseph Cropsey (Chicago: University of Chicago Press, 1971), p. 159. On the residually patriarchal character of Hobbes's political thought, see also R. W. K. Hinton, "Husbands, Fathers, and Conquerors," *Political Studies* 16 (1968): 55–59; and Keith Thomas, "Social Origins of Hobbes' Political Thought," in *Hobbes Studies*, ed. K. C. Brown (Oxford: Basil Blackwell, 1965), pp. 184–236.

31. *T.T.*, 1, para. 47; 2, para. 82.

32. *Lev.*, pp. 153–55; *T.T.*, 2, paras. 53–76, esp. 55, 58, 65.

33. *Lev.*, p. 153; *T.T.*, 2, paras. 74–76.

34. *Lev.*, pp. 154–55; *T.T.*, 2, paras. 64–65.
35. Cf. *T.T.*, 2, paras. 52–53 with 67–76.
36. *Lev.*, p. 154.
37. *T.T.*, 2, paras. 72, 73.
38. James Mill, *Government*, reprinted in *Utilitarian Logic and Politics*, ed. Jack Lively and J. C. Rees (London: Oxford University Press, 1978), p. 89.
39. James Mill, *History of British India*, 6 vols. (London: Baldwin, Craddock, and Jay, 1820), 1:385.
40. Mill, *Government*, p. 79.
41. Macaulay's major criticism on this point was lodged in "Mill's Essay on Government: Utilitarian Logic and Politics," *Edinburgh Review* 97 (March 1829), reprinted in Lively and Rees, *Utilitarian Logic and Politics*, pp. 116–18. John Stuart Mill, who was deeply influenced by these critiques, summarized the argument in his *Autobiography* (New York: Columbia University Press, 1960), p. 73.
42. "Greatest Happiness Principle," *Westminster Review* 21 (July 1829), reprinted in Lively and Rees, *Utilitarian Logic and Politics*, p. 147.
43. "Bentham's Defense of Mill: Utilitarian System of Philosophy," *Edinburgh Review* 98 (1829), reprinted in Lively and Rees, *Utilitarian Logic and Politics*, p. 168.
44. J. S. Mill, *Autobiography*, p. 73. On this point, see Joseph Hamburger, "James Mill on Universal Suffrage and the Middle Class," *Journal of Politics* 28 (1962): 174–75.
45. J. S. Mill, *Autobiography*, p. 73.
46. See Mariam Williford, "Bentham on the Rights of Women," *Journal of the History of Ideas* 36 (1975): 167–76.
47. See *The Works of Jeremy Bentham*, ed. John Bowring, 11 vols. (Edinburgh: William Tait, 1838–43), 10:450; "On James Mill," an unpublished fragment printed in *Bentham's Political Thought*, ed. Bhikhu Parekh (New York: Barnes and Noble, 1973), pp. 311–12.
48. In what follows, I focus upon sexual inequalities of power in the family. For a parallel discussion of class inequalities of economic power in utilitarian theory, see C. B. Macpherson, *The Life and Times of Liberal Democracy* (London: Oxford University Press, 1977), pp. 23–43.
49. J. H. Burns and H. L. A. Hart, eds., *An Introduction to the Principles of Morals and Legislation* (London: The Athlone Press, 1970), p. 245.
50. Ibid., pp. 238, 254–55.
51. J. S. Mill, *The Subjection of Women*, p. 220; also, pp. 143–44, 146–47, 173–75, and passim.
52. Ibid., p. 125.
53. On these points Mill never wavered. See ibid., and *Autobiography*, p. 173. On the extension of the rights of citizenship to women see esp. *The Subjection of Women*, chap. 3; and *The Collected Works of John Stuart Mill* (hereafter *C.W.*), vols. 18 and 19; *Essays on Politics and Society* (hereafter *E.P.S.*), ed. J. M. Robson (Toronto: University of Toronto Press, 1977), 19:479–81, "Considerations on Representative Government."
54. See *The Subjection of Women*, esp. pp. 162–63, where the analogy between

"legal despotism" and "despotism in the family" is developed explicitly. Mill, both here and elsewhere in his writings, forms a clear exception to the argument pressed, for example, by Carole Pateman that classical liberal theory is seriously deficient by virtue of its failure to recognize private institutions as intrinsically *political* arenas of power, rule, and authority ("A Contribution to the Theory of Organizational Democracy," *Administration and Society,* May 1975, pp. 6–25); thus, as I argue below, Mill's concept of the family is consistent with Pateman's treatment of him elsewhere as an early advocate of a fully "participatory society" (*Participation and Democratic Theory* [Cambridge: Cambridge University Press, 1970], pp. 27–35). Mill can be contrasted fruitfully on this point with Locke, who asserts a qualitative discontinuity between public and private, or civil and conjugal, authority; see Shanley, above.

55. *The Subjection of Women*, pp. 168–71.
56. On the protective and educative purposes of participation more generally, see E.P.S., 19:389–92, 399–412; and Dennis F. Thompson, *John Stuart Mill and Representative Government* (Princeton: Princeton University Press, 1976), pp. 13–53.
57. *The Subjection of Women*, pp. 173, 171.
58. E.P.S., 18:301 (*On Liberty*).
59. *The Subjection of Women*, p. 154.
60. James Fitzjames Stephen, *Liberty, Equality, and Fraternity* (Cambridge: Cambridge University Press, 1967), pp. 195–98.
61. *The Subjection of Women*, p. 161. See C.W., vols. 14–17, *The Later Letters of John Stuart Mill, 1849–1873*, ed. Francis S. Mineka and Dwight N. Lindley (1972), 17:1751, where Mill states that in *The Subjection of Women* he "carefully avoided giving any opinion as to the conditions under which marriage should be dissoluble, for the very good reason that I have not formed . . . a well-grounded opinion on the subject" (to Henry Kuylock Rusden, July 22, 1870).
62. "On Marriage and Divorce," in Mill and Taylor, *Essays on Sex Equality,* p. 70.
63. Ibid., p. 73.
64. Ibid., p. 72.
65. *The Subjection of Women*, p. 156.
66. "On Marriage and Divorce," p. 72.
67. Ibid., p. 74.
68. ". . . is there really any distinction between the highest masculine and the highest feminine character? . . . the women, of all I have known, who possessed the highest measure of what are considered feminine qualities, have combined with them more of the highest *masculine* qualities than I have ever seen in any but one or two men, and those one or two men were in many respects almost women. I suspect it is the second rate people in both sexes that are unlike—the first rate are alike in both . . ." (C.W., vols. 12–13, *The Earlier Letters of John Stuart Mill, 1812–1848*, ed. Francis C. Mineka [1963], 12:184 [to Thomas Carlyle, October 5, 1833]).
69. "On Marriage and Divorce," p. 74.
70. *The Subjection of Women*, p. 179. Mill does insist upon wide latitude of ex-

ception, and does envisage the employment of "widows and wives of forty or fifty" outside the home (pp. 240–41).

71. "On Marriage and Divorce," pp. 75, 76–77.

72. *The Subjection of Women*, pp. 170, 178–79.

73. I borrow the terminology here from Albert O. Hirschman, *Exit, Voice, and Loyalty* (Cambridge, Mass.: Harvard University Press, 1970).

74. For studies emphasizing the magnitude of her influence, see, e.g., Michael Packe, *The Life of John Stuart Mill* (London: Secker and Warburg, 1954); Ruth Barchard, *John Stuart Mill and Harriet Taylor* (London: Routledge and Kegan Paul, 1951); and, most recent and controversial, Gertrude Himmelfarb, *On Liberty and Liberalism: The Case of John Stuart Mill* (New York: Alfred A. Knopf, 1974). For dissenting views that downplay without denying her influence, see, e.g., H. O. Pappe, *John Stuart Mill and the Harriet Taylor Myth* (Cambridge: Cambridge University Press, 1960); and J. M. Robson, *The Improvement of Mankind: The Social and Political Thought of John Stuart Mill* (Toronto: University of Toronto Press, 1968).

75. The authorship of this essay has been the subject of continuing scholarly dispute, with some attributing sole responsibility to Harriet Taylor and others insisting upon the co-authorship of husband and wife. Nothing in my argument turns upon this dispute, however, and I make only the limited claim that responsibility for those aspects of the argument that clash most palpably with Mill's earlier and later writings on the same subject may reasonably be imputed to Harriet Taylor. Compare Rossi, "Sentiment and Intellect," in Mills and Taylor, *Essays on Sex Equality*, pp. 41–43, with Himmelfarb, *On Liberty and Liberalism*, pp. 183–86, both of whom review the evidence. For reasons indicated in note 82 below, I incline to Himmelfarb's view.

76. Mill and Taylor, *Essays on Sex Equality*, pp. 85, 86. This essay—with its emphasis upon the unlimited assertion of self as the criterion of human emancipation, and its corresponding lack of emphasis upon moral obligations to others—in some ways epitomizes the less attractive dimensions of her thought and personality emphasized by critics such as Himmelfarb. For a discussion of some of these same tendencies in contemporary feminist theory, see Jean Bethke Elshtain, "Liberal Heresies: Existentialism and Repressive Feminism" in *Liberalism and the Modern Polity*, ed. Michael C. Gargas McGrath (New York: Marcel Dekker, 1978), pp. 33–61.

77. "On Marriage and Divorce," pp. 78–83.

78. Compare, however, *Later Letters*, 14:500 (to an unidentified correspondent, November 9, 1855), which comes close to endorsing Taylor's earlier position, with the more characteristic circumspection of his letters to John Nichol, August 18, 1869 (17:1634); and to Henry Rusden, July 22, 1870 (17:1751). There is a more thorough discussion of the evolution of Mill's views in Himmelfarb, *On Liberty and Liberalism*, pp. 273–75.

79. Cf. Hegel, *The Philosophy of Right*, ed. T. M. Knox (London: Oxford University Press, 1952), pp. 105–22; and Marx, "On a Proposed Divorce Law," in *Writings of the Young Marx on Philosophy and Society*, pp. 136–42.

80. See especially Mill's criticisms of Wilhelm Von Humboldt's advocacy of complete liberty of divorce (*E.P.S.*, 18:300–301 [*On Liberty*]).

81. This also presumably applies to some degree to separation as well as divorce, since the logic of the argument applies here equally.
82. "The Enfranchisement of Women," p. 105.

    In the 1852 edition of his *Principles of Political Economy* (*C.W.*, vols. 2 and 3, ed. J. M. Robson [1965], hereafter *P.E.*), which coincides roughly with the publication of "The Enfranchisement of Women," Mill himself—in all likelihood under Harriet's prodding—introduced the following revision: "No argument can be hence derived for the exclusion of women from the liberty of competing in the labor market: since, even when no more is earned by the labor of a man and woman than would have been earned by the man alone, the advantage to the woman of not depending on a man for subsistence may be more than equivalent" (*P.E.*, 2:394 [2, xiv, 5]). However, in the 1865 edition—which contains revisions made after his wife's death—Mill reintroduced the following caveat: "It cannot, however, be considered desirable as a *permanent* element in the condition of a laboring class, that the mother of the family (the case of single women is totally different) should be under the necessity of working for a living, at least elsewhere than in their place of abode." The timing of these revisions inferentially strengthens the plausibility of the case for co-authorship of "The Enfranchisement of Women," because it suggests that Mill might have temporarily altered his earlier and later views under his wife's influence. Mill's more radical position on divorce in 1855 (n. 78, above) also appears to support this view.

83. "On Marriage and Divorce," p. 75.
84. "The Enfranchisement of Women," p. 111.
85. Ibid., p. 107.
86. For a helpful discussion of these themes in contemporary feminist theory, see Jean Bethke Elshtain, "The Feminist Movement and the Question of Equality," *Polity*, Summer 1975, pp. 452–57.
87. See *Later Letters*, 14:19 (to Harriet Taylor, March 21, 1849).
88. See *E.P.S.*, 17:301–4 (*On Liberty*); and *P.E.*, 3:947–50 (5, xi, 8).
89. *P.E.*, 3:944 (5, xi, 7).
90. See Pateman, *Participation and Democratic Theory;* and Peter Bachrach, *The Theory of Democratic Elitism: A Critique* (Boston: Little, Brown, 1967).
91. *Autobiography*, pp. 162–64.
92. *P.E.*, 3:785–96 (4, vii). Mill credited his wife with having inspired, and in part dictated, the content of this chapter (*Autobiography*, p. 174).
93. *Later Letters*, 17:1535 (to Parke Goodwin, January 1, 1869).
94. Ibid., 17:1638 (to Emile de Laveleye, September 9, 1869); and 17:1693 (to Lord Amberly, February 2, 1870).
95. Hegel, *The Philosophy of Right*, p. 11.
96. Cf. Neal Wood, "The Social History of Political Theory," *Political Theory* 6 (1978): 345–67.
97. Cited in Ernst Jones, *The Life and Work of Sigmund Freud*, 3 vols. (New York: Basic Books, 1953–57), 1:116.
98. I am especially indebted to Jean Bethke Elshtain, Michael McPherson, Rick Nuccio, Peter Ericson, and Patricia Leach for helpful comments on an earlier draft of this essay. I would also like to acknowledge the financial support of Williams College.

Oedipus as Hero: Family and Family Metaphors
in Nietzsche   *Tracy B. Strong*

1. The dynamic of rebellion against parental authority is at the center of Carl Schorske's important book, *Fin de Siècle Vienna: Politics and Culture* (New York: Knopf, 1980). See my review in *Worldview*, 1980.
2. *Genealogy of Morals*, 3:25–26. Citations from Nietzsche are my translations, which, however, have been constantly informed by those of Walter Kaufmann, when available.
3. He writes to Franz Overbeck, February 11, 1883, of his "eerie, deliberated secluded secret life, which takes a step every six years, and actually wants nothing but the taking of this step." Letters are cited from Friedrich Nietzsche, *Werke in drei Baenden* (Munich, 1955), vol. 3. An English translation may be found in *Selected Letters of Friedrich Nietzsche*, ed. and trans. Christopher Middleton (Chicago: University of Chicago Press, 1969). Any letters not found in these editions will receive specific citation.
4. See letter to Peter Gast, December 1889.
5. These last two citations are from Carl A. Bernouilli, *Franz Overbeck und Friedrich Nietzsche. Ein Freundschaft* (Iena, 1908), 3:221-22.
6. This is recognized in J. P. Stern, *A Study of Nietzsche* (Cambridge: Cambridge University Press, 1979). See my review in *Ethics*, 1980.
7. The best extensive coverage of this question is in Alexander Nehamas, "The Eternal Recurrence," *The Philosophical Review* (forthcoming).
8. See Werner Dannhauser's anguished discussion of this preference of Nietzsche's in his *Nietzsche's View of Socrates* (Ithaca, N.Y.: Cornell University Press, 1976).
9. See Strong, *Friedrich Nietzsche and the Politics of Transfiguration* (Berkeley and Los Angeles; University of California Press, 1975), pp. 29–49.
10. This theme is the basis of Hannah Arendt's important discussion of Nietzsche in *The Life of the Mind: Willing* (New York: Harcourt Brace Jovanovich, 1978), pp. 158–71. See also Strong, *Nietzsche and the Politics of Transfiguration*, chap. 8.
11. *Beyond Good and Evil*, #20.
12. *The Gay Science*, #348.
13. *Beyond Good and Evil*, #206, 208.
14. *Thus Spoke Zarathustra*, prologue. See the discussion in Strong, *Nietzsche and the Politics of Transfiguration*, p. 174.
15. Friedrich Nietzsche, *Jugendschriften* (Munich, 1923), p. 68.
16. *Beyond Good and Evil*, #264.
17. For accounts of this material, see E. F. Podach, *Nietzsches Werk der Zusammenbruch* (Heidelberg, 1961), as well as Schechta's account at the end of the third volume of his edition, and especially Curt Paul Janz, *Friedrich Nietzsche. Biographie* (Munich, 1979), 3:9–226.
18. *Jugendschriften*, p. 60.

19. This is what J. -P. Vernant would have us see in his "Ambiguité et renverse-ment," in *Mythe et tragédie en grèce ancienne* (Paris, 1972), pp. 114ff.

20. See Otto Rank, *The Myth of the Birth of the Hero* (New York: Random House, 1959).

21. For this see the edition of *Antichrist* in *Werke. Kritische Gesamtausgabe.* Hrg v. G. Colli und M. Montinari (Berlin: De Gruyter, 1967ff), 6. 3. 252. The passage is not in Kaufmann's edition, nor in Schlechta's. The edition is here-after cited as *WKG*.

22. *WKG, Nietzsche Contra Wagner*, p. 442.

23. Freud's essay may be found in *Collected Papers* (London: International Psychoanalytic Library, 1953), 5:316–57.

24. See here G. Deleuze et F. Guatarri, *L'anti-Oedipe. Capitalisme et schizo-phrénie* (Paris, 1972); M. Foucault, *Madness and Civilization* (New York: Random House, 1973); and Gerard Mendel, *Le révolte contre le père* (Payot, 1968).

25. It is worth pointing out that both the *Genealogy* and *Civilization and its Discontents* have approximately the same structure. They proceed from a rejection of religion, through an analysis of the palliatives, to the resulting unhappiness to the major problems, and conclude on a note of world histori-cal pessimism.

26. Anthropological evidence for, if not analysis of, this may be found in Sir James Frazer, *The Golden Bough*, as well as in Mendel, *Le révolte contre le père*.

27. See the end of *Civilization and its Discontents*.

28. Lines 851ff.

29. See André Green, *Un Oeil en trop. Le complexe d'Oedipe dans la tragédie* (Paris: 1969), esp. pp. 219–88.

30. Hannah Arendt, *On Revolution* (New York: Penguin, 1963). See George Kateb, "Freedom and Worldliness in the Thought of Hannah Arendt," *Politi-cal Theory* 5 (1977): 2. Much of my essay is a disguised discussion with Kateb and Arendt.

31. *Ecce Homo*, "The Birth of Tragedy 2."

32. All of this material is cited unless otherwise indicated from the third volume of Schlechta. I have also learned additional details from Janz, *Friedrich Nietzsche*, vol. 1.

33. See the discussion in Janz, *Friedrich Nietzsche*, 1:44.

34. Schlechta, 3:91. See Janz, *Friedrich Nietzsche*, 1:43.

35. Schlechta, 3:17.

36. See *Jugendschriften*, pp. 7, 10, 12 and passim.

37. I owe much in this essay to the strange and brilliant work by Pierre Klos-sowski, *Nietzsche et le cercle vicieux* (Paris, 1969).

38. Schlechta, 3:93.

39. See Klossowski, *Nietzsche et le cercle vicieux*, pp. 255–60.

40. Some contemporary writers such as Deleuze and Guattari argue that the price in neurosis that one pays for capitalist civilization is too great and that the schizophrenia and polymorphous sexuality corresponding to the nonresolution

of the Oedipal situation is a preferable alternative. See Dusan Makavejev's wonderfully knowing view of this position in *Sweet Movie*.

41. Jacques Derrida, *Spurs: Nietzsche's Styles* (Chicago: University of Chicago Press, 1979), p. 102.
42. Ibid., p. 138. See my review in *Ethics*, 1980.
43. *Jugendschriften*, p. 3.
44. See H. Roeschl, "Nietzsche et la solitude," *Bulletin de la société française des études nietzschéenes* (1958).
45. The second letter is February 1883. It is discussed in E. F. Podach, *The Madness of Nietzsche* (New York: Gordon Press, 1931), p. 85.
46. See the seminal article by M. Montinari, "Ein neuer Abschnitt in Nietzsches 'Ecce Homo,'" *Nietzsche Studien* (Berlin: De Gruyter, 1972), 1:382–418 (passage cited is p. 391). See also the letter to von Seydlitz, June 11, 1878 (p. 392).
47. See Montinari, "Ein neuer Abschnitt," and especially Bernouilli, *Franz Overbeck und Friedrich Nietzsche*, pp. 304ff. for a long and pained discussion of the politics of the Nachlass.
48. Punctuation is Nietzsche's original. The text is in *WKG*, 1. 3. 265–67.
49. So speculates Montinari, "Ein neuer Abschnitt," p. 382.
50. Strong, *Nietzsche and the Politics of Transfiguration*, chap. 9.
51. *The Use and Misuse of History for Life*, #3.
52. See Derrida, *Spurs/Eperons*, pp. 88–96.
53. Janz, *Friedrich Nietzsche*, 3:82, notes that one of the few traits Nietzsche displayed during his stay in the asylums was an occasional violent hostility to the presence of his mother.
54. *Birth of Tragedy*, #1 (first sentence).
55. See Strong, *Nietzsche and the Politics of Transfiguration*, pp. 161–68.
56. *WKG*, 3. 2. 95–132.
57. Ibid., p. 106; *Birth of Tragedy*, #9.
58. See the discussion in G. Deleuze, *Logique du sens* (Paris, 1968), p 75. See also Christopher Middleton's discussion of the significance of these syllables in his edition of *Selected Letters of Friedrich Nietzsche*, p. 316.
59. See the short discussion in R. J. Hollingdale, *Nietzsche. The Man and his Philosophy* (Baton Rouge, 1965), p. 291.
60. It is worth noting that Nietzsche uses the term *übermenschlich* from his early adolescence on. See Schlechta, 3:60.
Thanks to Helene Keyssar for a sensitive reading.

The Working-Class Family: A Marxist Perspective
Jane Humphries

1. See Margaret Benston, "The Political Economy of Women's Liberation," *Monthly Review* 21 (1969): 4; Mariarosa Dalla Costa, "Women and the Subversion of the Community," in *The Power of Women and the Subversion of the Community*, (Bristol, England: Falling Wall Press, 1972); Wally Seccombe,

"The Housewife and her Labour under Capitalism," *New Left Review*, no. 83 (1974); Jean Gardiner, "Women's Domestic Labour," *New Left Review*, no. 89 (1975); Wally Seccombe, "Domestic Labour—Reply to Critics," *New Left Review*, no. 94 (1975); Jean Gardiner, Susan Himmelweit, and Maureen Mackintosh, "Women's Domestic Labour," *Bulletin of the Conference of Socialist Economists* 4, no. 2 (1975). A useful survey of this literature is provided by Susan Himmelweit and Simon Mohun, "Domestic Labour and Capital," *Cambridge Journal of Economics* 1, no. 1 (1977).

2. For a more detailed discussion of this point of consensus see my article, "Class Struggle and the Persistence of the Working Class Family," *Cambridge Journal of Economics* 1, no. 3 (1977).

3. Karl Marx, *Precapitalist Economic Formations* (London: Lawrence and Wishart, 1964), p. 96.

4. For a careful statement of this position see Barry Hindess and Paul Q. Hirst, *Precapitalist Modes of Production* (London: Routledge and Kegan Paul, 1975), pp. 23ff.

5. S. G. Checkland and E. O. A. Checkland, eds., *The Poor Law Report of 1834* (Harmondsworth: Penguin Books, 1974).

6. Patricia Hollis, ed., *Class and Conflict in Nineteenth-Century England, 1815–1850* (London: Routledge and Kegan Paul, 1973).

7. This was a phrase used to describe the requirement that life in the workhouse be less pleasant than the life of the poorest independent worker. Only if this "principle" were maintained could the workhouse provide "a test" in the sense of deterring from entrance those who could possibly earn a bare living. See Sidney Webb and Beatrice Webb, *English Poor Law History: Part II: The Last Hundred Years* (Private Subscription Edition, 1929).

8. Karl Marx, *Capital* (New York: International Publishers, 1967), 1:737, my emphasis.

9. Hollis, *Class and Conflict*, p. 212.

10. *Parliamentary Papers*, vol. 35 (1935), vol. 29 (1836).

11. Report of the Poor Law Commissioners on the Continuance of The Poor Law Commission, 1840, quoted in Webb and Webb, *English Poor Law History*, p. 160.

12. R. V. Clements, "British Trade Unions and Popular Political Economy, 1850–1875," *Economic History Review* 14, no. 1 (1961), p. 102.

13. Hollis, *Class and Conflict*, p. 211.

14. *Parliamentary Papers*, vol. 29 (1836), pt. 1, p. 5.

15. J. D. Marshall, *The Old Poor Law, 1795–1834* (London: Macmillan, 1968).

16. J. L. Hammond and B. Hammond, *The Age of the Chartists, 1823–1854* (London: Longmans, 1930), p. 44; John Foster, *Class Struggle and the Industrial Revolution: Early Industrial Capitalism in Three English Towns* (London: Weidenfeld and Nicholson, 1968).

17. G. D. H. Cole, *Chartist Portraits* (London: Macmillan, 1941).

18. J. Burnett, ed., *Usefoil Toil: Autobiographies of Working People from the 1820's to the 1920's* (London: Allen Lane, 1974).

19. Henry Mayhew, *London Labour and the London Poor* (London: Griffin, 1862); Charles Booth, *Life and Labour of the People in London* (London: Macmillan,

1902); B. S. Rowntree, *Poverty, A Study of Town Life* (New York: Macmillan).

20. D. Roberts, "How Cruel was the Victorian Poor Law?" *Historical Journal 6* (1963).

21. *Parliamentary Papers*, vol. 25 (1835); Cole, *Chartist Portraits*, p. 18.

22. *Parliamentary Papers* (1835), p. 165.

23. J. Benson, "English Coal Miners' Trade Union Accident Funds, 1850–1900." *Economic History Review* 28, no. 3 (1975), p. 402.

24. Joseph Arch, *The Life of Joseph Arch by Himself* (London: Hutchinson, 1898), pp. 10–35.

25. Hollis, *Class and Conflict*, p. 323.

26. P. Willmott and M. Young, *Family and Kinship in East London* (London: Routledge and Kegan Paul, 1957); see also Peter Laslett, *The World We Have Lost* (New York: Charles Scribners' Sons, 1965).

27. Michael Anderson, *Family Structures in Nineteenth Century Lancashire* (Cambridge: Cambridge University Press, 1971).

28. Rowntree, *Poverty*, pp. 33 ff.

29. Ibid., p. 37 (my emphasis).

30. E. P. Thompson and E. Yeo, eds., *The Unknown Mayhew* (Harmondsworth: Penguin Books, 1973), p. 212.

31. Ibid., p. 211.

32. Ibid., p. 313–14.

33. Ibid., p. 314.

34. Anderson, *Family Structures*, p. 143.

35. Mayhew, *London Labour*; Booth, *Life and Labour*; Rowntree, *Poverty*; Clementina Black, *Sweated Industry and the Minimum Wage*, (London: Duckworth, 1907); Gareth Stedman Jones, *Outcast London: A Study in the Relationship between Classes in Victorian Society* (Harmondsworth: Penguin Books, 1971); Burnett, *Useful Toil*.

36. Burnett, *Useful Toil*, pp. 55ff.

37. Marx, *Capital*, pp. 395, 519.

38. Thompson and Yeo, *The Unknown Mayhew*, p. 251.

39. Ibid., p. 319.

40. Foster, *Class Struggle*, p. 87.

41. Hollis, *Class and Conflict*, pp. 193–94.

42. Black, *Sweated Industry*, p. 168.

43. Barbara Drake, *Women in Trade Unions*, Special Edition for the Labour Movement, Trade Union Series no. 6 (1921), p. 6.

44. Ibid., p. 4; H. A. Clegg, A. Fox, and A. F. Thompson, *A History of British Trade Unions since 1889*, vol. 1, *1889–1910* (Oxford: Clarendon, 1964), p. 170.

45. Drake, *Women in Trade Unions*, pp. 6ff.

46. Clegg, Fox, and Thompson, *A History of British Trade Unions*, p. 170.

47. Drake, *Women in Trade Unions*, p. 23.

48. Ibid., p. 221.

49. B. L. Hutchins and A. Harrison, *A History of Factory Legislation* (London: P. S. King and Son, 1903), p. 186.

50. Clegg, Fox, and Thompson, *A History of British Trade Unions*, p. 121.

51. Joyce Marlow, *The Peterloo Massacre* (London: Parthenon Books, 1971), p. 79.
52. Cole, *Chartist Portraits*, pp. 220–21.
53. Arch, *Life*, p. 10.
54. Foster, *Class Struggle*, p. 138.
55. Elizabeth Gaskell, *Mary Barton* (Harmondsworth: Penguin Books, 1970), p. 61.
56. Hollis, *Class and Conflict*, p. 227.
57 Ibid., pp. 293–98.
58. Cole, *Chartist Portraits*, p. 279.
59. E. P. Thompson, *The Making of the English Working Class* (New York: Vintage Books, 1963).
60. Sheila Rowbotham, *Women, Resistance and Revolution* (New York: Vintage Books, 1974).

The Family in Contemporary Feminist Thought: A Critical Review
Jane Flax

1. By gender I mean the social construction of biological sexuality, the meanings and character a society attributes to biological sexuality. When referring to biological sexuality I will use the word sex. For more discussion of the differences between sex and gender, see the discussion of Gayle Rubin's work in this paper.
2. There is a vast literature on the history, sociology, and ideology of the family, most of which is not feminist. Useful collections of historical and sociological material include: John Demos and Sarane Spence Boocock, eds., *Turning Points: Historical and Sociological Essays on the Family* (Chicago: University of Chicago Press, 1978); Michael Gordon, ed., *The American Family in Social-Historical Perspective* (New York: St. Martin's Press, 1978); Rose Laub Coser, ed., *The Family: Its Structures and Functions* (New York: St. Martin's Press, 1974); Alice S. Rossi, Jerome Kagan, and Tamara K. Hareven, eds., *The Family* (New York: W. W. Norton, 1978). For useful critiques of the theoretical assumptions underlying much of this material, see Christopher Lasch, *Haven in a Heartless World* (New York: Basic Books, 1977); Wini Breines, Margaret Cerullo, and Judith Stacey, "Social Biology, Family Studies and Anti-Feminist Backlash," *Feminist Studies* 4 (Spring 1979): 174–200. Critical theorists have developed the deepest, if flawed, political analysis of the family. See Max Horkheimer, "Authority and the Family," in *Critical Theory* (New York: Herder and Herder, 1972); Herbert Marcuse, "A Study on Authority," in *Studies in Critical Philosophy* (Boston: Beacon, 1972); the Frankfurt Institute for Social Research, "The Family," in *Aspects of Sociology* (Boston: Beacon, 1972). See also Mark Poster, *Critical Theory of the Family* (New York: Seabury Press, 1978). Any adequate analysis of the family would also have to incorporate material from biochemistry, psychology, anthropology, political economy, literature, law, theology, and political theory.

3. An important example of the process of distinguishing experience and the patriarchal construction and control of that experience is Adrienne Rich, *Of Woman Born: Motherhood as Experience and Institution* (New York: W. W. Norton and Company, 1976).

4. On these ambivalences, see the work of Dorothy Dinnerstein discussed in this paper and Jane Flax, "The Conflict Between Nurturance and Autonomy in Mother-Daughter Relations and Within Feminism," *Feminist Studies* 4 (June 1978): 171–89.

5. Betty Friedan, *The Feminine Mystique* (New York: Dell, 1963), p. 41.

6. Ibid., pp. 94, 69. For a different view of Freudian thought, see the discussion of Juliet Mitchell, Nancy Chodorow, Dorothy Dinnerstein and Gayle Rubin, below.

7. Ibid., pp. 174, 175.

8. Ibid., pp. 61, 26.

9. I define radical feminist as anyone who believes that the fundamental cause of women's oppression is patriarchy and that all other forms of oppression, e.g., race and class, are derived from patriarchy and are subordinate to it.

10. See also The Feminists, "Leaflet," and Beverly Jones, "The Dynamics of Marriage and Motherhood," in *Sisterhood is Powerful*, ed. Robin Morgan (New York: Vintage, 1970).

11. Kate Millett, *Sexual Politics* (Garden City, N.Y.: Doubleday, 1970). Millett defines politics in terms of asymmetric control (p. 22).

12. Ibid., pp. 24, 25.

13. Ibid., p. 35.

14. Ibid., pp. 36, 38.

15. Ibid., p. 37.

16. Shulamith Firestone, *The Dialectic of Sex: The Case for Feminist Revolution* (New York: Bantam, 1970), p. 72.

17. Ibid., pp. 8–9.

18. Ibid., p. 8.

19. Friedan, *Feminine Mystique*, p. 325.

20. Millett, *Sexual Politics*, p. 362.

21. Firestone, *Dialectic of Sex*, p. 239. For a similar but more humane vision of a feminist future see Marge Piercy, *Woman on the Edge of Time* (New York: Fawcett, 1976).

22. On the remaining economic and political barriers, see, for example, Diane K. Lewis, "A Response to Inequality: Black Women, Racism and Sexism," *Signs* 3 (Winter 1977): 339–61; Patricia Albjerg Graham, "Expansion and Exclusion: A History of Women in American Higher Education," *Signs* 3 (Summer 1978): 759–73; Francine D. Blau, "Women in the Labor Force," in *Women: A Feminist Perspective*, ed. Jo Freeman (Palo Alto, Calif.: Mayfield, 1975).

23. See Lillian Breslow Rubin, *Worlds of Pain: Life in the Working-Class Family* (New York: Basic Books, 1976), especially; Nancy Seifer, *Nobody Speaks for Me: Self-Portraits of American Working Class Women* (New York: Simon and Schuster, 1976); Diane K. Lewis, "A Response"; Michele Wallace, *Black Macho and the Myth of the Superwoman* (New York: Dial Press, 1978). For a more complete critique of Friedan, see Zillah R. Eisenstein, *The Radical*

Future of Liberal Feminism (New York: Longman, 1981), pp. 177–92. On the difficulties in analyzing the black family see Bonnie Thorton Dill, "The Dialectics of Black Womanhood, *Signs* 4 (Spring 1979): 543–55. On the blindness of feminist theory to racial differences among women see Margaret A. Simons, "Racism and Feminism: A Schism in the Sisterhood," *Feminist Studies* 5 (Summer 1979): 384–401.

24. Rubin cites studies to indicate "that, in the aggregate, husbands contribute the same amount of time to the family—about 1.6 hours a day—whether their wives work or not. Furthermore, husbands' family time remains independent of wives' employment when age, class and number of children are controlled for" (p. 228). Labor force and income statistics are taken from the U.S. Bureau of the Census, cited in D. Lewis, "A Response," pp. 351–52. On the sex segregation of the labor force, see Francine D. Blau, "Women in the Labor Force," pp. 220–23. But later feminists did correct some of the problems that an individualistic bias can create. See Caroline Bird, "The Case Against Marriage," in *The Future of the Family*, ed. Louise Kapp Howe (New York: Simon and Schuster, 1976); Elizabeth M. Havens, "Women, Work and Wedlock: A Note on Female Marital Patterns in the United States," in *Changing Women in a Changing Society*, ed. Joan Huber (Chicago: University of Chicago Press, 1973); Jessie Bernard, *The Future of Marriage* (New York: Bantam Books, 1973).

25. See Barbara Ehrenreich and Deirdre English, *Complaints and Disorders: The Sexual Politics of Sickness* (Old Westbury, N.Y.: The Feminist Press, 1973); Linda Gordon, *Woman's Body, Woman's Right: A Social History of Birth Control in America* (New York: Grossman, 1976), esp. pp. xi–46. On the relationship between technology and social relations see Herbert Marcuse, "Industrialization and Capitalism in the Work of Max Weber," in *Negations* (Boston: Beacon, 1968).

26. See Firestone's "political" reading of the Oedipus situation in *The Dialectic of Sex*, pp. 46–61.

27. For a very different account of children's development see D. W. Winnicott, *The Maturational Processes and the Facilitating Environment* (New York: International Universities Press, 1965), pp. 15–105.

28. Materialism is a theory usually associated with (although not necessarily limited to) Marx and subsequent Marxists. Engels's definition of the term is clear, widely accepted and cited: "According to the materialist conception, the determining factor in history is in the final instance the production and reproduction of immediate life. This, again, is of a twofold character. On the one side, the production of the means of existence, of food, clothing, and shelter and the tools necessary for that production; on the other side, the production of human beings themselves, the propagation of the species" (Frederick Engels, *The Origin of the Family, Private Property and the State*, ed. Eleanor Burke Leacock [New York: International Publishers, 1972], p. 71). See also Annette Kuhn and Ann Marie Wolpe, eds., *Feminism and Materialism* (London: Routledge and Kegan Paul, 1978), especially the first three essays.

29. On Marx's method see Karl Marx and Frederick Engels, *The German Ideology* (New York: International Publishers, 1970), especially part 1. For

an application and extension of his method, see Karl Marx, *Capital* (New York: International Publishers, 1967), vol. 1, esp. part 1.

30. On the struggle to integrate (or at least harmonize) Marxism and feminism, see Sheila Rowbotham, *Woman's Consciousness, Man's World* (Baltimore: Penguin Books, 1973), especially part 1; Rosalind Petchesky, "Dissolving the Hyphen: A Report on Marxist Feminist Groups 1–5," and Zillah Eisenstein, "Developing a Theory of Capitalist Patriarchy and Socialist Feminism," in *Capitalist Patriarchy and the Case for Socialist Feminism*, ed. Zillah Eisenstein (New York: Monthly Review Press, 1979). On the origins of American Marxist-feminism see Nancy Hartsock, "Fundamental Feminism: Process and Perspective," *Quest* 2 (Fall 1975): 67–80.

31. See esp. pp. 71–146 of Engels, *The Origin*.

32. Ibid., p. 120.

33. For a more complete explication and critique of Engels's theory, see Jane Flax, "Do Feminists Need Marxism?", *Quest* 3 (Summer 1976): 46–58.

34. For historical evidence that supports this judgment, see Sheila Rowbotham, *Women, Resistance and Revolution* (New York: Vintage, 1972); Hilda Scott, *Does Socialism Liberate Women: Experiences from Eastern Europe* (Boston: Beacon, 1974); Gail Warshofsky Lapidus, *Women in Soviet Society* (Berkeley: University of California, 1978).

35. On Marxist-structuralism see Louis Althusser, especially the essay, "Contradiction and Overdetermination," in *For Marx* (New York: Vintage, 1970).

36. Juliet Mitchell, *Woman's Estate* (New York: Pantheon, 1971), pp. 101, 171–72.

37. Ibid., pp. 160–62, 156, 158.

38. Eli Zaretsky, *Capitalism, the Family, and Personal Life* (New York: Harper, 1976). In many ways his theory is similar to that of Lasch, Horkheimer, and Marcuse (see n. 2).

39. Zaretsky, *Capitalism, the Family*, p. 31.

40. Some theorists argue, however, that this possibility declines as patriarchal authority declines, especially Horkheimer, "Authority and the Family," and Lasch, *Haven in a Heartless World*.

41. On this debate see Lisa Vogel, "The Earthly Family," *Radical America* 7 (July-October 1973): 9–50; Ira Gerstein, "Domestic Work and Capitalism," *Radical America* 7 (July–October 1973): 101–28; John Harrison, "Political Economy of Housework," *Bulletin of the Conference of Socialist Economists* 3 (1973); Wally Seccombe, "The Housewife and Her Labour under Capitalism," *New Left Review* 89 (January–February 1975): 47–58; Ian Gough and John Harrison, "Unproductive Labour and Housework Again," *Bulletin of the Conference of Socialist Economists* 4 (1975); Wally Seccombe, "Domestic Labour: Reply to Critics," *New Left Review* 94 (November–December 1975): 85–96; Terry Fee, "Domestic Labour: An Analysis of Housework and Its Relation to the Production Process," *Review of Radical Political Economics* 8 (Spring 1976): 1–8; Susan Himmelweit and Simon Mohun, "Domestic Labour and Capital," *Cambridge Journal of Economics* 1 (March 1977): 15–31. I owe this listing of citations to Heidi Hartmann. See her forthcoming essay "The Unhappy Marriage of Marxism and Feminism: Toward a More Progressive Union," in *Women and Revolution*, ed. Lydia Sargent (Boston: South End

Press, 1981). The original debate was stimulated by Mariarosa Dalla Costa, "Women and the Subversion of the Community," in *The Power of Women* (Bristol: Falling Wall Press, 1972). For a more detailed critique of the problems of orthodox Marxist theory on the "woman question" see: Hartmann, "Unhappy Marriage"; Jane Flax, "Do Feminists Need Marxism?"; Rosalyn Baxandall, Elizabeth Ewen, and Linda Gordon, "The Working Class Has Two Sexes," *Monthly Review Press* 28 (July–August 1976): 1–9; Zillah Eisenstein, "Developing a Theory of Capitalist Patriarchy and Socialist Feminism"; Nancy Hartsock, "Response to 'What Causes Gender Privilege and Class Privilege?' by Sandra Harding" (Paper presented at the annual convention of the American Philosophical Association, 1978).

42. This is Dalla Costa's argument in "Women and the Subversion of the Community," pp. 25–39.

43. See Heidi Hartmann, "Capitalism, Patriarchy, and Job Segregation by Sex," in *Capitalist Patriarchy*, pp. 206–47.

44. See esp. Marx and Engels, *The German Ideology*, part 1.

45. Mitchell, *Woman's Estate*, p. 99.

46. See Betty Friedan's comments discussed above; Millett, *Sexual Politics*, pp. 176–220; and Naomi Weisstein, "Kinde, Kuche and Kirche as Scientific Law: Psychology Constructs the Female," in *Sisterhood Is Powerful*.

47. Mitchell, *Psychoanalysis and Feminism* (New York: Pantheon, 1974) — Mitchell's interpretation of Freud is heavily influenced by the work of Jacques Lacan, a highly abstract, linguistic-structuralist French psychoanalyst; Rubin, "The Traffic in Women: Notes on the 'Political Economy' of Sex," in *Toward an Anthropology of Women*, ed. Rayna R. Reiter (New York: Monthly Review Press, 1975); Dinnerstein, *The Mermaid and the Minotaur: Sexual Arrangements and the Human Malaise* (New York: Harper and Row, 1976); and Nancy Chodorow, *The Reproduction of Mothering: Psychoanalysis and the Sociology of Gender* (Berkeley and Los Angeles: University of California Press, 1978).

48. Mitchell, *Psychoanalysis*, pp. 113–19, xv–xxiii.

49. Ibid., pp. 401–6.

50. See for example, Frieda Froman-Reichmann, *Principles of Intensive Psychotherapy* (Chicago: University of Chicago Press, 1950); Harry Guntrip, *Personality Structure and Human Interaction* (New York: International Universities Press, 1961); Gertrude Blanck and Rubin Blanck, *Ego Psychology: Theory and Practice* (New York: Columbia University Press, 1974). Especially problematic is Mitchell's positivistic conception of science that she applies to psychoanalysis. Mitchell calls psychoanalysis a "science concerned with human social laws as they are represented in the unconscious mind" (*Psychoanalysis*, p. 402). For different views, see Guntrip, *Personality Structure*; also the essays by Salmon, Glymour, Alexander, Mischel, and Wisdom in *Freud: A Collection of Critical Essays*, ed. Richard Wolheim (Garden City: Doubleday, Anchor, 1974).

51. Mitchell, *Psychoanalysis*, p. 413.

52. G. Rubin, "The Traffic," pp. 159, 166, 168, 169.

53. Ibid., p. 177.

54. Ibid., p. 178.

55. Ibid., p. 183.

56. Ibid., p. 197.

57. For a more complete critique of Rubin's work focusing on the problems with structuralism see Nancy Hartsock, "Is There a Specifically Feminist Materialism?", in *Discovering Reality: Feminist Perspectives on Epistemology, Metaphysics and Philosophy of Science*, ed. Sandra Harding and Merrill Hintikka (Dordrecht: The Netherlands: D. Reidel, 1981).

58. G. Rubin, "The Traffic," pp. 205, 209–10.

59. Ibid., p. 203.

60. Dinnerstein, *Mermaid and Minotaur*, p. 20. These assertions are contested by many feminists who point out that the availability of birth control varied, depending often on social and political factors. On birth control see Gordon, *Woman's Body*. Other feminists have documented the many and varied types of female labor. See, for example, Margaret Mead, "On Freud's View of Female Psychology," in *Women and Analysis*, ed. Jean Strouse (New York: Dell, 1974); Michelle Zimbalist Rosaldo, "Women, Culture and Society: A Theoretical Overview," in *Women, Culture and Society*, ed. Michelle Zimbalist Rosaldo and Louise Lamphere (Stanford: Stanford University Press, 1974). Dinnerstein's work is heavily dependent on the work of Sherwood Washburn. For a feminist reinterpretation of Washburn's theory see Nancy Tanner and Adrienne L. Zihlman, "Women in Evolution, Part I: Innovation and Selection in Human Origins," *Signs* 1 (Spring 1976): 585–608, and Adrienne L. Zihlman, "Women in Evolution, Part II: Subsistence and Social Organization Among Early Hominids," *Signs* 4 (Autumn 1978): 4–20.

61. Dinnerstein, *Mermaid and Minotaur*, p. 20.

62. Chodorow draws on "object-relations" psychoanalysis for her conception of human development. The best general introduction to object-relations psychology is Guntrip, *Personality Structure*. See also Winnicott, *The Maturational Processes*; Margaret Mahler, Fred Pine, and Anni Bergman, *The Psychological Birth of the Human Infant* (New York: Basic Books, 1975).

63. Chodorow, *Reproduction of Mothering*, p. 7.

64. Ibid., p. 10.

65. Ibid., pp. 169–170, 167.

66. Ibid., p. 218.

67. Herbert Marcuse, in "Sartre's Existentialism," in *Studies in Critical Philosophy*, suggests this idea.

68. L. B. Rubin, *Worlds of Pain*, is a good example of this approach. I owe many insights into the limitations of object-relations theory to Kristin Dahl.

69. Rapp, Ross, and Bridenthal emphasize this point in "Examining Family History."

70. On this point see John Money and Anke A. Ehrhardt, *Man and Woman and Boy and Girl* (Baltimore: Johns Hopkins University Press, 1972). See also Eleanor Emmons Maccoby and Carol Nagy Jacklin, *The Psychology of Sex Differences* (Stanford: Stanford University Press, 1974), vol. 1.

71. For more discussion of the epistemological problems posed by feminism see the essays in Harding and Hintikka, eds., *Discovering Reality*.

72. For a sophisticated and subtle political-ethical analysis of "reproductive rights" see Rosalind Pollack Petchesky, "Reproductive Freedom: Beyond 'A Woman's Right to Choose,'" *Signs* 5 (Summer 1980): 661–85.

73. Reich's arguments on this point remain cogent. See his "What Is Class Consciousness?" in Wilhelm Reich, *Sex-Pol: Essays, 1929–1934*, ed. Lee Baxandall (New York: Vintage, 1972). See also Jane Flax, "The Conflict Between Nurturance and Autonomy."

Contemporary Critical Theory and the Family: Private World and Public Crisis   *Theodore Mills Norton*

1. "Critical theory" was initially employed by Max Horkheimer as a substitute for "Marxism." It was subsequently used to distinguish the perspectives of Horkheimer and his co-thinkers from those of other Marxists; and, in a wider application, to encompass the entire range of Western Marxist thought. The Institute for Social Research was established in Frankfurt during the Weimar period. Horkheimer took over its directorship after 1930—just in time to lead it into exile, in Geneva, Paris, and New York. Several years after World War II, it was reestablished in Frankfurt. The "School" that bears the name of that city never flourished in its environs. If there ever was such a school, it existed only during the New York years. Critical commentary has revealed both continuities and discontinuities in the evolution of critical theory, as well as significant differences among its exponents. However, the views of at least three of these—Horkheimer, Theodor W. Adorno, and Herbert Marcuse—bear a striking family resemblance. Other important members of the institute included the young Erich Fromm, Leo Lowenthal, Otto Kirchheimer, Friedrich Neumann, and Friedrich Pollock. Walter Benjamin, the literary critic, maintained an ambivalent relationship to the school and institute. Useful overviews of the history and argument of critical theory include Martin Jay, *The Dialectical Imagination: A History of the Frankfurt School and the Institute of Social Research, 1923–1950* (Boston and Toronto: Little, Brown, 1973); David Held, *Introduction to Critical Theory: Horkheimer to Habermas* (Berkeley and Los Angeles: University of California Press, 1980); and Paul Connerton, *The Tragedy of Enlightenment: An Essay on the Frankfurt School* (Cambridge: Cambridge University Press, 1980). The postwar history of the refounded institute has yet to be written. The most widely recognized critical theorist is, of course, Herbert Marcuse. For a learned, if critical, treatment of his thought, see Morton Schoolman, *The Imaginary Witness: The Critical Theory of Herbert Marcuse* (New York: Free Press; London, Collier Macmillan, 1980).

2. Held, *Introduction*, includes a useful survey of Habermas' thought. The most comprehensive commentary is Thomas McCarthy, *The Critical Theory of Jürgen Habermas* (Cambridge, Mass. and London: MIT Press, 1978). See also Trent Schroyer, *The Critique of Domination: The Origins and Development of Critical Theory* (Boston: Beacon Press, 1973); Garbis Kortian, *Metacritique: The Philosophical Argument of Jürgen Habermas*, trans. John Raffan

(Cambridge: Cambridge University Press, 1980); and Fred R. Dallmayr, *Twilight of Subjectivity: Contributions to a Post-Individualist Theory of Politics* (Amherst: University of Massachusetts Press, 1981), chap. 4. The work of Habermas' associates is not yet well known in the United States. Among this group may be included Karl-Otto Apel, Albrecht Wellmer, Claus Offe, Oskar Negt, Ranier Döbert, Klaus Eder, and Ulrich Övermann.

3. Studies in history, the social sciences, and other fields that are clearly indebted to the Frankfurt School and Habermas are by now too numerous to cite. Trent Schroyer pioneered in introducing Habermas to an American readership. Russell Jacoby is still the most authentic younger representative of Frankfurt critical theory in this country; see his *Social Amnesia: A Critique of Conformist Psychology from Adler to Laing* (Boston: Beacon Press, 1975). For contributions to critical social theory, the reader is directed to the journals *Telos* and *New German Critique*. However, it would be erroneous to describe either of these journals as vehicles of critical theory. The thought of the Habermas group especially lacks an adequate American outlet.

4. See his "Authority and the Family," in *Critical Theory: Selected Essays*, trans. Matthew J. O'Connell et al. (New York: Herder and Herder, 1972). For both the studies on authority and the family and the associated integration of psychoanalytic theory, see Jay, *Dialectical Imagination*, chaps. 3–4; and Held, *Introduction*, chap. 4.

5. Horkheimer, "Authoritarianism and the Family Today," in *The Family: Its Function and Destiny*, ed. Ruth Nanda Ashen (New York: Harper, 1949); "The Family," in The Frankfurt Institute for Social Research, *Aspects of Sociology*, trans. John Viertel (Boston: Beacon Press, 1972); and "The Future of Marriage (1966)," in *Critique of Instrumental Reason*, trans. Matthew J. O'Connell et al. (New York: Seabury Press, 1974). The essay in *Aspects* originally appeared in 1956, in the postwar institute series *Frankfurter Beiträge zur Soziologie*. Although it cannot be attributed without further verification to Horkheimer, it clearly bears the stamp of his evolving views on the topic.

6. These are too numerous to cite. But see Herbert Marcuse, *Five Lectures*, trans. Jeremy J. Shapiro and Shierry M. Weber (Boston: Beacon Press, 1970); and Theodor W. Adorno, "Freudian Theory and the Pattern of Fascist Propaganda," in *The Essential Frankfurt School Reader*, ed. Andrew Arato and Eike Gebhardt (New York: Urizen Books, 1978). This volume contains useful editorial introductions to aspects of Frankfurt critical theory, as well as an introductory Bibliography of the Authors' Works in English.

7. See, for example, Jessica Benjamin, "The End of Internalization: Adorno's Social Psychology," *Telos*, no. 32 (Summer 1977), pp. 42–64, and her "Authority and the Family Revisited: Or, A World without Fathers?", *New German Critique*, no. 13 (Winter 1978), pp. 35–57; Christopher Lasch, *Haven in a Heartless World: The Family Besieged* (New York: Basic Books, 1977), pp. 85–96; and Mark Poster, *Critical Theory of the Family* (New York: Seabury Press, 1978), pp. 53–63. Despite his choice of a title, Poster concludes

that "the first generation of Frankfurt theorists set the stage for the inability of critical theory to conceptualize the family."

8. Fromm, "The Method and Function of an Analytic Social Psychology: Notes on Psychoanalysis and Historical Materialism [1932]," in Arato and Gebhardt, *Frankfurt Reader*, p. 483. Urie Bronfenbrenner, "The Split-Level American Family," in *Sociology Full Circle: Contemporary Readings on Society*, ed. William Feigelman (New York, Washington, and London: Praeger, 1972).

9. Horkheimer, *Critique of Instrumental Reason*, pp. 95–96. One recalls that these words were published in the aftermath of the student lunch-counter sit-ins; the Freedom Rides; the voter registration drive; the murders of Schwerner, Goodman, and Chaney, successive revolts of Berkeley students against McCarthyite inquisition, capital punishment, and technocratic administration; and the first teach-ins and mass mobilizations against the Southeast Asian war. But perhaps Horkheimer had stopped reading the American press.

10. The concept of the "organizational principle" of social formations has been developed by Jürgen Habermas as a more abstract alternative to Marx's concept of the "mode of production." The point is that a particular social formation can so combine different modes of production that it is difficult to determine its fundamental character on that level. Certainly societies rightly described as capitalist have combined the capital-wage labor relation with chattel slavery, sharecropping, and other forms of expropriation. But the conception of an "organizational principle" has yet to be sufficiently clarified. See Habermas, *Legitimation Crisis*, trans. Thomas McCarthy (Boston: Beacon Press, 1975), pt. 1; and *Communication and the Evolution of Society*, trans. Thomas McCarthy (Boston: Beacon Press, 1979).

11. On this, see Jürgen Habermas, *Toward a Rational Society: Student Protest, Science, and Politics*, trans. Jeremy J. Shapiro (Boston: Beacon Press, 1970), p. 104. Compare Habermas, *Theory and Practice*, trans. John Viertel (Boston: Beacon Press, 1973), pp. 222–35; and *Legitimation Crisis*, pp. 50–60. Habermas has in mind the indirect role of "science and technology" in the production of surplus value. However, one would have to assess the conditions under which the labor capacity of scientists and technicians is employed in industrialized research and development. Compare Thomas Ferguson, "The Political Economy of Knowledge and the Changing Politics of the Philosophy of Science," *Telos*, no. 15 (Spring 1973), pp. 124–37.

12. The semiologist Jean Baudrillard has extensively criticized the Marxist conception of "use value." See his *The Mirror of Production*, trans. Mark Poster (St. Louis: Telos Press, 1975). One should recall, however, Marx's observation on the nature of wants satisfied by useful objects: "whether . . . they spring from the stomach or from fancy makes no difference" (*Capital* [Moscow: Progress Publishers, 1965], 1:35). See also the quotation from Nicholas Barbon on the same page.

13. Important local, regional, and international markets have of course arisen in and among precapitalist societies; just as they continue to play a role in the

economic life of state socialist countries. What is difficult to conceive is the *absence* of the market mechanism in capitalism. Moreover, although domestic markets have been restructured by oligopolistic competition and the state, capitalist development today must also be grasped on the now primary level of the world market.

14. These points have been called to my attention by Vito Caiati, an economic and social historian of early modern Tuscany. Sharecropping in that region presented a *non*capitalist road away from feudal manorialism. There, the family as a productive *unit* entered into a contractually disguised wage relation to the patron—labor was no longer attached to the land. But this mode of production, as so many others, was eventually submerged by the advance of capitalism.

15. Wage labor, too, is found in precapitalist social formations. What counts is the sway of this form over the total productive process. What counts also is the content of this form—the separation of the producers from the means of production. The flip side of this is the radical increase in the geographic mobility of labor power. The latter is not only alienated from technologies but from attachment to the primary nonhuman "means of production," the land. It is frequently not seen that Marx was as interested in what may be called the "mode of settlement" as the "mode of production." An important effect of capitalist development is to shatter the organic connection between persons and places. The posttraditional family is also shaped by this loss.

16. Partisans of decentralization should recall the old slogan of the pro-Absolutist, preindustrial bourgeoisie: "Better one tyrant than a thousand!" Smoothly functioning feudal manorialism subsisted on the direct political-juridical domination of dependent producers by a radically decentralized nobility. Noxious Absolutist institutions like the *corvée* should not obliterate the fact that the Absolute Monarchy, initially called into existence to shore up the crumbling feudal order, also helped to undermine its basis of local control. Medieval serfs were not primarily exploited and oppressed by the central authorities of pope and emperor, but by local lords, bishops, and gentlemen. The depoliticization of production, which under liberal capitalism handed over the proletariat to the mercies of local captains of industry, was the ironic culmination of a long struggle against decentralized domination. To the extent that remote authority allows for effective appeal against the dictates of immediate oppressors, it helps to alleviate some of the worst features of such domination. Patriarchal despotism is also a form of decentralized oppression, a fact that has conditioned the struggle of women for political citizenship and legal recognition.

17. *Familia* was the Roman Latin term for a slave gang. Many preindustrial family-households include members who are not, or are not yet, or who never will be what from our perspective would count as blood relations of the heads of the household. In each case the exact socioeconomic content, as well as the political authority hierarchy, of a type of household requires detailed study. However, one can risk the generalization that the capitalist separation of family from civil society more or less rapidly defamilializes social relations within the latter sphere. Formulistically, we can say that civil

society relations are progressively economized, and that they are, negatively, depoliticized (with regard to the state) and defamilialized. In this way relations of production are stripped of their kinship *forms;* just as relations of exchange are freed from their community ties and restrictions. To be sure, right down to the age of the corporate family, capitalist management seeks residual legitimation from the dying ideology of the old household; but only at the cost of hypocrisy and sloganeering. Finally, whereas romantics mourn the loss of affective ties resulting from the eclipse of the household and community, while authentic liberals point to the liberatory aspects of both, Marxists tend to regard the transition from *Gemeinschaft* to *Gesellschaft* as from one form of slavery to another, accompanied by an advance in productive forces.

18. Compare Karl Marx and Frederick Engels, "The German Ideology [Part I]," in *Writings of the Young Marx on Philosophy and Society*, ed. Loyd D. Easton and Kurt H. Guddat (Garden City, N.Y.: Doubleday, 1967), esp. pp. 419–21; and Jürgen Habermas, *Knowledge and Human Interests*, trans. Jeremey J. Shapiro (Boston: Beacon Press, 1971), chap. 12, esp. pp. 282–83. If we interpret both Marx and Freud in the speculative tradition of Hegelian-Marxism, this antinomy can be resolved by treating modern society as a totality that can then be atlernatively reconceptualized from the standpoints of production and family "propagation" (Marx). If we emphasize moments of ontogenesis (socialization) and phylogenesis (social evolution) within the unfolding of this totality, the same approach may also prove useful: despite the material separation of family from civil society under capitalism, we can understand the ways in which both developmental aspects interpenetrate and reciprocally condition each other. Unfortunately, even for Hegelian-Marxists this strategy has never quite overcome the opposition between the standpoints; e.g., in the chapter cited, Habermas—who is already moving toward another conception—clearly comes down on the side of Freud.

19. Of course, in any Hegelian or Hegelian-Marxist treatment, such analytical demarcations must then be dialectically (critically) dissolved and reintegrated as moments of an unfolding speculative totality. Contrary to the self-understanding of some exponents of this method which, secretly or overtly, is supposed to guarantee the absolute identity of subject and object, it is preeminently speculative, not dialectical-critical. Among the Frankfurt School, T. W. Adorno saw this most clearly; and, without entirely rejecting the "standpoint of totality," attempted to secure the supremacy of "negative dialectics." See Adorno, *Negative Dialectics*, trans. E. B. Ashton (New York: Seabury Press, 1973); Susan Buck-Morss, *The Origin of Negative Dialectics: Theodore W. Adorno, Walter Benjamin, and the Frankfurt Institute* (New York: Free Press; London: Collier Macmillan, 1977); and Gillian Rose, *The Melancholy Science: An Introduction to the Thought of Theodor W. Adorno* (New York: Columbia University Press, 1978). Jürgen Habermas, in turn, has stressed the importance of the analytic. See, e.g., *Theory and Practice*, p. 169. Granted that no regression to a pure analytic approach is entertained, in this paper I am stressing the nonidentity of family and civil society, a nonidentity that is not only methodological but material.

20. Karl Marx, *Critique of Hegel's "Philosophy of Right,"* trans. Annette Jolin and Joseph O'Malley (Cambridge: Cambridge University Press, 1970). Certainly, important contributions to political theory were produced after Marx—J. S. Mill's political writings are an obvious example, even if one questions his status as "a major European thinker." But Mill was also a political economist and methodologist. In these capacities he is as much bound to the concerns of his age and the sociology of the future as he is to the old philosophical tradition. Concerning the latter: although it would be disastrous to dismiss it as merely sexist, it is clearly a male-dominated enterprise. Its breakup corresponds historically to the revolutionary and other struggles of women to enter the public sphere and reshape it. Political economy, sociology, and depth psychology are not exactly feminist undertakings. Yet it is arguable that they provide conceptual means for criticizing women's oppression that (for good reason) the political philosophers failed to develop. Nor, can the place of women in the unfolding of the psychoanalytic movement be ignored.

21. The displacement of political theory by political economy is not simply brought about by Marx's interest in the latter but by the place held by this subject in liberal capitalist societies characterized by the predominance of civil society. See also Habermas, *Legitimation Crisis,* pp. 20–31. However, the displacement of political theory was to survive the relative demotion of political economy. Ours is an age of psychology and political sociology, as the Frankfurt School recognized. See A. Arato's introduction to the first part of the *Frankfurt Reader.* Still, sociology lowers a veil that obscures the expanding role of the state in the late capitalist economy. Today Marxism returns as the theory of the late capitalist state, and, with it, political theory, as the critique of political sociology.

22. This is not the only hiatus in Marx's work. Although he gave signs of recognizing linguistic communication as the medium of social relations, he failed to elaborate this insight. "Orthodox" Marxists engage in evasive strategies when confronted by such gaps. Whereas some think it enough to supply random quotations to show that Marx had a theory of this or that aspect, others affirm that the correct application of Marx's method will supply all omissions. The methodological posture is most emphatically assumed by Hegelian-Marxist orthodoxy. But even if Marx's method could be reconstructed definitively from his few unpublished and fragmentary "methodological texts," or from his work as a whole, the claim remains invalid in the absence of specific investigations. Of course, such investigations are never methodologically neutral; and it would be useful to reconstruct Marx's half-hidden assumptions on language and the family. But what is left undone cannot be retrospectively redressed—to expect everything from a single individual is to receive nothing.

23. By stressing the factual and, for many purposes, practical nonidentity of institutions of family and civil society, we may be helped to explore the ways in which their interest structures could drive them into conflictual opposition. As I shall note, families and corporations may collide over the flow of direct and indirect administrative outputs. And this may happen not least

because of the prior impact of the economy on the formation of the mobile, two-generation family, as well as the remedial activity of the state (social welfare and commodities). If critical sociology can intervene in this crisis to shape the family's self-understanding of its generative interest, corporate domination could eventually confront a formidable opponent.

24. Recent Marxist and Marxist-feminist investigations on the role of the family in the total productive process have embraced this approach. For a discussion of this literature, and related approaches, see Joan B. Landes, "Women, Labor, and Family Life: A Theoretical Perspective," *Science and Society* 41 (Winter 1977–78): 386–409.

25. Speculative idealism, even when it denies the separate existence of the whole, must still insist on the mediation of all parts or aspects to each other through this whole. In other words, because equal weight cannot be assigned to the moments of identity and nonidentity within the speculative construction, it is tempting to embrace the speculation that the tendency of the whole to reshape the parts is realized in principle before it occurs. Thus, despite it reservations toward speculation, the Frankfurt School sometimes acted as if its negative ideal type of the totally administered society were an empirical fact. Habermas has escaped this problem, if only at the cost of the conceptual flexibility (in certain contexts) that the Hegelian-Marxist method affords. *Above all*, it is necessary to cast doubt on the notion that the "economization" of social relations in capitalist civil society is capable of engulfing every aspect of social existence with the same virulence. Certainly the family is *also* an "economic" institution with definite relations to the politicized economy that can be reconstructed. But if by "economic" we mean economically productive, the modern forms of the family may be less economic in content than any of their preindustrial predecessors.

26. To the extent that the market, however oligopolistically managed, has been gradually extended to take in as consumers the lower strata of advancing capitalist society, the relation between merchant and customer may be drained of its ethical content. See Horkheimer, "Feudal Lord, Customer, and Specialist," in *Critique of Instrumental Reason*. For many members of the same strata, the quasi-"professionalization" of their jobs (occupations) may provide compensatory forms of recognition.

27. In an ingenious monograph Claus Offe has argued that with the change under capitalism from task-continuous to task-discontinuous status organization of work, it proves increasingly difficult to measure achievement by objective standards, e.g., increasing mastery of techniques. With the expansion within the work role of normative over technical components, achievement is rendered evermore illusory as an indicator of modernity. Here indeed is an area where the family may become crucial to the economy—but as an agency of socialization rather than consumption. See Offe, *Industry and Inequality: The Achievement Principle in Work and Social Status*, trans. James Wickham (London: Edward Arnold, 1976).

28. In *Legitimation Crisis*, Habermas points to what he calls "syndromes" of "civic, familial, and vocational privatism" that he feels are essential for state regulated capitalist societies to preserve. Unfortunately, the spread of ad-

ministrative rationality into the cultural sphere (called into being by the need to compensate for dysfunctional side effects of irrational growth in the private sector) tends to dissolve these syndromes. One might extrapolate from his discussion the possibility that the state will then increase its interference on behalf of the private family, thus rendering its continued existence as such even more problematic. Civic privatism, which results in only a generalized orientation to administrative performances, is negatively motivational with regard to democratic participation. The more positive "familial-vocational privatism . . . consists in a family orientation with developed interests in consumption and leisure on the one hand, and in a career orientation suitable to status competition on the other. This privatism thus corresponds to the structures of educational and occupational systems that are regulated by competition through achievement" (pp. 75–76). While agreeing that there is an important connection between familial and vocational privatism and their orientations, I would like to bracket the hyphen that links them in Habermas long enough to see if they might not come into mutual conflict—especially when more is at stake in the family than "consumption and leisure."

29. I am not arguing that feminism exhausts its mission with schemes for family reorganization or the entry of middle-class women into the professions—as important as these may be. On the contrary, the women's movement, as a long-range historical phenomenon, has a definite political content, from the rise of women in the radical English Civil War sects down through the battle for suffrage. If we agree with the late Hannah Arendt (herself not evidently a feminist) that the dialectic of recognition only fully comes into play in the political realm—and that it exists only in a flawed form in civil society—then the feminist trajectory is incomplete until women break en masse into the public sphere. As J. B. Elshtain argues, anything less is a "displacement" of feminism from its enduringly political aims. However, today the fulfillment of these aims would require that women take a leading role in opening up a public sphere that has long since become truncated under late capitalism.

30. For the history of this, see Lasch, *Haven.*

31. The godfather, as it were, of contemporary social systems theory was of course the late Talcott Parsons. For a survey of political systems theories, see H. V. Wiseman, *Political Systems: Some Sociological Approaches* (New York and Washington: Frederick A. Praeger, 1966). David Easton is perhaps the preeminent American political systems theorist. See his *A Framework for Political Analysis* and *A Systems Analysis of Political Life,* both originally published in 1965, and now republished by the University of Chicago Press.

32. In the first part of *Legitimation Crisis,* Habermas simultaneously utilizes and criticizes systems perspectives developed by Parsons and by the German theorist Niklas Luhmann. In what follows, I draw on Habermas' work without sticking to his text. It is my impression that Habermas, too, equates abstract subsystems too closely with contemporary institutions.

33. My claim is not that general social theories can escape cultural determination through appeals to ontological primacy. It is rather that no analysis of his-

torically specific societies can proceed without at least implicit reference to universals. The latter should be made explicit so that they can be criticized.

34. I cannot here adequately develop the linguistic foundations of social and political theory. I am attempting an approach to this in a work with the working title, "The Syntax of Democracy." See also my dissertation, "Language, Communication, and Society: Jürgen Habermas, Karl-Otto Apel, and the Idea of a Universal Pragmatics" (New York University, 1981).

35. For discussion of the first two methodological categories mentioned here, see Brian Fay, *Social Theory and Political Practice* (London, Boston, and Sydney: George Allen and Unwin, 1975). If I am not mistaken, the core idea of the political system in Easton has affinities with the informal model of the natural system sketched here. Although this differs considerably from my idea of a political system (see below), it is certainly useful for the study of political institutions, e.g., the state. The latter cannot be completely comprehended from political culture or political-linguistic perspectives. Whether or not even the natural systems model is ultimately compatible with the methodology of the "hard" or biological sciences is a matter that requires further investigation.

36. See Habermas, *Knowledge and Human Interests*, chaps. 7–8. Of course, the analogy with linguistic semantics already shifts from a discussion of hermeneutics (Wilhelm Dilthey to H. -G. Gadamer) to a discussion of recent linguistics, which has been bedeviled by the problem of where to locate the semantic component.

37. The linguistic model I have in mind is that contained in Noam Chomsky, *Aspects of the Theory of Syntax* (Cambridge: MIT Press, 1965). Naturally, no rigorous application of this model is undertaken here.

38. I owe the initial insight that institutions have grammars, deep and surface structures to H. Mark Roelofs. But Roelofs has not developed this scheme with reference to the apparatus of linguistic theory. Of course, this is an old staple of French structuralism. But Chomskyan linguistics has yet to be explored by American political theorists for its relevance to their field.

39. A promising beginning has been made by Habermas. See his "What is Universal Pragmatics?" in *Communication and the Evolution of Society*.

40. This consideration bears on the conception of a social organization principle mentioned earlier. We need a more rigorous way of accounting for the wide variety of forms that a single social system may assume. For example, a general theory of capitalist society that does not come to terms with the ways in which the system may be remodeled without losing its identity falls considerably short of bridging the gap between theory and practice. In my view, a political linguistics could contribute to our understanding of intrasystemic variations, especially where explanations pitched at the level of the natural system or schemas drawn from textual hermeneutics prove inadequate.

41. For Habermas' views on socialization, see the essay "Moral Development and Ego Identity," in *Communication and the Evolution of Society*. See also McCarthy, *Critical Theory of Jürgen Habermas*, chap. 4, and Dallmayr, *Twilight of Subjectivity*, chap. 4.

42. Despite the extensive criticism to which he has been subjected, Erikson's

views on the life cycle seem still fruitful for a theory of family crisis. See his *Dimensions of a New Identity* (New York: W. W. Norton, 1974), esp. the last chapter.

Kafka and Laing on the Trapped Consciousness:
The Family as Political Life   *James Glass*

1. Franz Kafka, "The Metamorphosis," in *The Penal Colony: Stories and Short Pieces* (New York: Schocken Books, 1971), p. 67.
2. R. D. Laing and A. Esterson, *Sanity, Madness and the Family* (New York: Basic Books, 1971), pp. 211, 105, 204.
3. Ibid., pp. 155, 162.
4. See ibid., pp. 93–94.
5. Kafka, "The Metamorphosis," pp. 68–69.
6. R. D. Laing, *The Politics of the Family and Other Essays* (New York: Pantheon Books, 1971), p. 99.
7. Ibid., p. 90.
8. Kafka, "The Metamorphosis," p. 132.

"Thank Heaven for Little Girls": The Dialectics of Development
Jean Bethke Elshtain

1. A responsible scholar demands of self and others a public articulation, elaboration, and defense of all the elements that comprise his or her perspective. The insistence upon epistemological awareness and candor emerges from a recognition that the activities of political science have an influence upon the activities of politics.
2. See Jean Bethke Elshtain, "Moral Woman and Immoral Man: The Public/ Private Split and its Political Ramifications," *Politics and Society*, 4 (1974): 453–73 (revised version above). The world of bourgeois society is characterized by a bifurcation between a number of modalities: the public and the private, economics and politics, thought and emotion.
3. See Sigmund Freud, *Three Essays on the Theory of Sexuality* (New York: Avon Books, 1962), and Juliet Mitchell, *Psychoanalysis and Feminism* (New York: Pantheon Books, 1974).
4. The term "socialization" first came into use in political discourse in the 1950s. Most practitioners of political socialization labor in the positivistic vineyard. But there have been some thoughtful efforts: Fred Greenstein, *Children and Politics (New Haven:* Yale University Press, 1965), and R. W. Connell, *The Child's Construction of Politics* (Melbourne: Melbourne University Press, 1971), a particularly rich account, should be mentioned. Socialization experts tend to be rather unabashed celebrants of the status quo (see

R. W. Connell and Murray Goot, "Science and Ideology in American 'Political Socialization' Research," *Berkeley Journal of Sociology,* 17 [1972–73]: 165–93). In fact, the socialization process is seen (correctly!) to foster it, and this is deemed good. One rarely finds the questions: Is this particular status quo one children *ought* to be socialized into? or What if the status quo is a corrupt or inegalitarian one? For a sensitive, non-political-science look at "Children and Politics," see the three-part series by Robert Coles in *New York Review of Books,* Feb. 20, 1975, pp. 22–24; March 6, 1975, pp. 13–16; March 20, 1975, pp. 29–30. Coles *does* see the problematics of political socialization in a country characterized by race, sex, and class inequality and he makes the "startling" suggestion that *we listen to what children have to say* in a thoughtful, serious, respectful manner that does justice to the rich complexity and depth of their political analyses and attitudes. The inconsistencies and ambiguities of a child's thought on politics cannot be captured through the use of short-answer or open-ended questionnaires.

5. See Mitchell, *Psychoanalysis and Feminism;* Russell Jacoby, *Social Amnesia* (Boston: Beacon Press, 1975); and any of Freud's metapsychological essays. Freud has taken his lumps from feminists who seem, for the most part, never to have read him at all but to have relied instead on secondary sources or hostile and distorted accounts of his thought. One recent feminist writer, Barbara Deckard (*The Women's Movement* [New York: Harper and Row, 1975]), after what one hopes was a thorough and careful reading of one excerpt from a single paper, decides to dismiss a careful exploration of Freud from the entire feminist enterprise through vilification. In *four* pages (imagine treating the thought of Marx or Hegel in four pages and presuming one has "done the job") Deckard stomps her verbal foot and declares that she is "tempted to dismiss Freud and his theories as a sick joke" (p. 17).

6. Mitchell, *Psychoanalysis and Feminism,* and Jacoby, *Social Amnesia,* are both valuable sources on this. Also see Sheila Rowbotham, *Woman's Consciousness, Man's World* (Baltimore: Penguin Books, 1973).

7. Peter Zollinger, *The Political Creature* (New York: George Braziller, 1972), p. 22.

8. A functionalist view on the family, written by Parsons and several others, should be checked out on this question. See Talcott Parsons et al., *Socialization and Interaction Process* (Glencoe, Ill.: The Free Press, 1955).

9. Talcott Parsons, "Age and Sex in the Social Structure of the United States," in *Selected Studies in Marriage and the Family,* ed. Robert F. Winch and Robert McGinnis (New York: Henry Holt and Co., 1953), pp. 330–45. I repeat: for the functionalist the question of *why* some institution or set of social relationships exists need never be raised. If, however, the teleology imbedded within functionalist theory operated smoothly, there would be no need for politics at all and I wouldn't be writing this paper. Functionalism may come to us in the guise of "systematic theory" but once the outer garments are shed, the unmistakable costume (characterized by a series of splits) of liberal ideology may be seen. The remark is quite serious. For if we assume that we can say, as functionalists do say, what a thing (person

or institution) is in terms of its function or purpose we simultaneously set up standards of evaluation. Once we can state the function of any X we can say what a good X is, or we can say that X is good to the extent that it (he, she) performs its functions. The "modal-personality" school is infused with such functionalist presumptions reducible, in most instances, to the tautology that societies, without coercion or politics, may demand or "need" a certain personality type and primary institutions exist to form that personality.

10. Elshtain, "Moral Woman and Immoral Man," p. 470.
11. Peter Winch, *The Idea of a Social Science* (New York: Humanities Press, 1963); Alasdair MacIntyre, *Against the Self-Images of the Age* (New York: Schocken Books, 1971); Stuart Hampshire, *Thought and Action* (New York: Viking Press, 1959).
12. Hampshire, *Thought and Action*, p. 85.
13. Erik H. Erickson, *Identity: Youth and Crisis* (New York: W. W. Norton and Co., 1968), p. 94.
14. Ibid., pp. 96–107. Discussions appear in most of Erikson's works.
15. Erik H. Erikson, *Identity and the Life Cycle, Psychological Issues*, vol. 1 (New York: International Universities Press, 1970). See also Erikson, *Identity: Youth and Crisis*, pp. 113–14.
16. Erikson, *Identity: Youth and Crisis*, pp. 107–14.
17. Ibid., pp. 115–22.
18. Ibid., pp. 128–35. See also the discussion in Erik H. Erikson, *Insight and Responsibility* (New York: W. W. Norton and Co., 1974), pp. 81–107.
19. See Rowbotham, *Woman's Consciousness, Man's World*; Juliet Mitchell, *Woman's Estate* (New York: Vintage Books, 1973); Erik H. Erikson, *Life History and the Historical Moment* (New York: W. W. Norton and Co., Inc., 1975), pp. 225–47.
20. Erikson, *Life History*, p. 259.
21. Erikson, *Insight and Responsibility*, p. 165.
22. Kenneth Keniston, "Psychological Development and Historical Change," *Journal of Interdisciplinary History* 2 (Autumn 1974): 329–45, 336.
23. For a lucid discussion of the problem of power see William E. Connolly, *The Terms of Political Discourse* (Lexington, Mass.: D. C. Heath and Co., 1974), pp. 85–138.
24. Quoted in Jacoby, *Social Amnesia*, p. 87.
25. Ibid., p. 34.
26. Quoted in ibid., pp. 91–92.
27. Karl Marx and Frederick Engels, *Basic Writings on Politics and Philosophy*, ed. Lewis S. Feuer (Garden City, N.Y.: Doubleday and Co., Inc., 1959), p. 320.
28. Jacoby, *Social Amnesia*, p. 108. Cf. Rowbotham, *Woman's Consciousness, Man's World*, p. 68.
29. Erikson, *Identity: Youth and Crisis*, pp. 128–35; Erickson, *Insight and Responsibility*, 161–215 passim.
30. See Jean Bethke Elshtain, "The Feminist Movement and the Question of Equality," *Polity* 7 (Summer 1975): 452–77, for a discussion on equality as

an essentially contested political concept. The choice of one formulation of equality over another implicates the analyst in assenting to, or dissenting from, the social structures and arrangements of his or her own society.

31. Ibid., p. 477.
32. Erikson, *Life History*, p. 241.

Index